THE ULTIMATE DICTIONARY
of SPORTS QUOTATIONS

THE ULTIMATE DICTIONARY
of SPORTS QUOTATIONS

CARLO DE VITO

Checkmark Books®
An imprint of Facts On File, Inc.

Checkmark Books
An imprint of Facts On File, Inc.
11 Penn Plaza
New York, NY 10001

Library of Congress Cataloging-in-Publication Data

The ultimate dictionary of sports quotations / [compiled by] Carlo De Vito.
   p. cm.
  Includes index.
  ISBN 0-8160-3980-1 (hard)—ISBN 0-8160-3981-x (pbk.)
    1. Sports—Quotations, maxims, etc. 2. Sports personnel—Quotations.
  I. De Vito, Carlo.
GV707.U47 2001
796—dc21
                                               99-059375

Checkmark Books are available at special discounts when purchased in bulk quantities for businesses, associations, institutions or sales promotions. Please call our Special Sales Department in New York at (212) 967-8800 or (800) 322-8755.

You can find Facts On File on the World Wide Web at
http://www.factsonfile.com

Text design by Joan M. Toro
Cover design by Cathy Rincon

Printed in the United States of America

MP Hermitage 10 9 8 7 6 5 4 3 2 1
    (pbk) 10 9 8 7 6 5 4 3 2 1

This book is printed on acid-free paper.

Contents

TO DOMINIQUE—
my wife and the only real athlete in our household—
and to my parents, who instilled in me a love of athletics and competition.

Acknowledgments

First and foremost, I would like to thank my brother, Eugene T. Venanzi II, for his help and encouragement, whether it be a simple conversation during a game of catch or a meal, or a loan of some of his highly prized first editions; he was both critical and generous to a fault.

To the staff of the Monmouth County Library, Symmes Road, who suffered my many greedy borrowings with both amusement, humor, and horror.

To Buz Teacher, for his acquiesence, approval, and friendly advice.

And to a whole round of friends and family who offered suggestions and pointers, including Scott Liell, Gil King, Rob McMahon, Ken Samuelson, Chris Terry, and Rick Wolff.

Thank you.

Thanks to Bert Holtje, who found a home for this project, and was shepherd to it like no one else.

Special thanks to my kind, patient, and prodding editor, James Chambers. His persistence and demanding standards made this a better book than the author could have provided. Also, thanks to copy editor Jerry Kappes.

Introduction

Games lubricate the body and the mind.
—Benjamin Franklin

The term *sports* can be defined as any activity or experience that gives enjoyment or recreation. Sports are also referred to as pastimes or diversions. Many dictionaries follow exactly such a line. By defining our editorial content to "athletic sports" we keep a truer course to the spirit of the book, and what we naturally assume when we refer to the term *sports.* The word *athlete* is of Greek extraction and in classical times meant one who competed for prizes in the public games. The sports mentioned herein are restricted to those sports calling for some measurable degree of physical skill or prowess, and the quotations are confined to just that.

However, they are not without their human element. The following pages feature quotes from such notable sports figures as John Wooden, Arthur Ashe, and Vince Lombardi, as well as from gregarious individuals like Casey Stengel, Yogi Berra, and Charles Barkley. Their words are funny, inspirational, honest, stupid, truly thought-provoking, and incredibly hilarious. From U.S. presidents to outrageous fans, from Roman historians to taxi drivers, sports in all cultures have been held up for inspection as a metaphor for life.

Sports have been a popular form of recreation and entertainment since the Egyptians, Greeks, and Romans ruled the world. Sports such as footraces and swimming contests, wrestling and boxing, feats of strength and skill, have forever given to those who observed them the opportunity to comment and debate. Many games in the earliest times were in fact conditioning and training for combat and warfare or for hunting, trapping, or herding. Sometimes contests were held near religious shrines either in conjunction with funeral rites or as offerings to a particular god or group of gods. Despite such serious intent, most of the earliest organized games were almost always festive and purely recreational.

The Olympic Games are of course the most famous of all organized sporting events. In 776 B.C. the first champions of these games were recorded, and this tradition continued for 382 years, or until 394 B.C. The games were not revived for more than 2,000 years. In those times many smaller towns also held public games. The most popular sports featured footraces, broad jumping, spear throwing, discus, and chariot racing. In Rome public games were referred to as *ludi publici,* and included gymnastics and forms of mock combat. The first gladiatorial combats were not recorded until 264 B.C.

Horse racing, while not an Olympic sport, was incredibly popular from the fifth century A.D. onward in Western civilization. Many Asian countries had such events, largely predating the Christian era, and it was reported by Homer as a popular event among the Greeks during the Trojan War.

The Middle Ages saw a reduction in the role of sports in everyday life. In the Middle Ages self-denial and preparation for the afterlife were of paramount importance. Various forms of combat sports, racing, and throwing were practiced, though almost entirely military in nature. Jousting on horseback was the most popular of these events, which were greeted enthusiastically throughout Europe. These events spawned the word *tournament.* Favored by nobility, these contests were first recorded in the year of the Norman Conquest, 1066 A.D., and ended sometime around the 16th century. Archery enjoyed widespread popularity in the Middle Ages among both nobles and commoners, although also encouraged largely by the military, as were fencing and other types of swordplay.

From the Middle Ages to the Renaissance, sports were at the mercy of the fancies and whimsies of the nobility. For example, football was banned in England by Henry II (1154–1189) and by James I (1603–1625), who both considered it an excuse for public brawling. The Puritan era, especially in England, in the 17th century, saw the temporary end of sports.

But the 1700s and the 1800s saw a return to sports. By 1743 the London Prize Ring rules had been established by James Boughton. These were the rough-and-tumble days of the bare-knuckle fighters. Not until 1867 was the contest divided into rounds and contestants provided with gloves (however slight). These changes were termed the Marquis of Queensbury rules.

Rugby as we know it today was established at the Rugby School in England in 1823. Originally a form of soccer, the Rugby School provided that any player, not just the goalie, could pick up the ball and run with it. Football (soccer in the U.S.) aficionados began forming organizations around this time to keep out Rugby School type teams. Rowing, golf, lawn tennis, and track and field all enjoyed rejuvenation in the 1800s throughout Europe.

Sports were not so popular in America during the 1700s as they were in Europe. Americans were consumed with building a new country. The Dutch at New Amsterdam were most notable for their interest in bowling, skating, sleighing, and various forms of ball playing. Generally however, America was so lacking in athletics that even Charles Dickens and Anthony Trollope remarked on how serious Americans were. In fact, it was not until after the Civil War that spectator sports began to experience a rise in interest. With the reintroduction of the Olympic Games in 1876, track and field gained in popularity in America, as did rowing.

American football became one of the more popular sports. In 1875 Harvard played McGill, which played rugby. Harvard liked the game so much it prevailed on friendly schools such as Yale, Princeton, Columbia, and Rutgers to follow suit. Thus American football was born, a game in which a back would run up into the line.

Baseball was also extremely popular at this time. A version of rounders, this game was played from the time of the Civil War on. In fact, the 90-foot base paths date from 1845. By 1890 many colleges and universities had baseball teams. In addition, many professional teams and leagues were soon formed.

With baseball we see the real beginnings of professional sport. Famous boxers and jockeys were also more plentiful around this time, and so was born the professional athlete. The years after World War I produced an ever growing number of professionals as the popularity of other sports began to emerge. Tennis, golf, swimming, polo, hockey, and basketball gave rise to a whole culture. As more and more Americans wanted to see these events, more and more arenas were built, as were golf courses with larger gallery areas. These large gates provided more cash prizes, and the skill level of participants grew ever more boundlessly. Ever since sports have been a chance for many to advance themselves, not only as individuals but also for their race. While sports have provided opportunities since Roman times for the disadvantaged to improve their standing in society, never was it so evident or important as when Jesse Owens beat the athletes of Hitler's Germany, or as when Jackie Robinson broke the color barrier in America's preeminent sport of baseball in 1946. Standouts such as Wilma Rudolph not only made strides for African Americans but also for the physically disadvantaged when she won an Olympic gold medal. Such people help raise sports from games or entertainment to life lessons for the ages.

Even today, when sports may seem like a training ground for the broadcasters and actors of tomorrow, we must remember that those who strive for excellence, who pursue greatness of skill or effort personify the values we find worthwhile in celebrating sports. The effortless smoothness of Ted Williams or Willie Mays's swing, the artfulness of Michael Jordan's gliding drives to the basket, the careful pirouette of Lynn Swann or Del Shoffner catching a football in midair, the quick-wittedness of John McEnroe, the grace of Bill Tilden, the swiftness and balletic form of Peggy Fleming, the imposing presence of Alberto Tomba navigating a mountain, these are the qualities we watch in awe, understanding that we are capable of so much as human beings. To see others will themselves to do what seems effortless or impossible is to understand what the human body is capable of achieving and finally to see what a glorious thing being a human is. The artfulness of any one of the above-mentioned athletes or of so many in other sports is what we celebrate in these pages.

Sports teach about dedication, single-mindedness of purpose, knowledge, understanding, the importance of practice, and, most important, teamwork and a sense of fair play. These qualities are the classroom for life. The great coaches throughout time, the Vince Lombardis and the John Woodens, and the unsung coaches of the world teach the value of hard work, patience, practice, rules, skill, and understanding. These hard-learned lessons are what make sports invaluable to society and why sports are so celebrated.

While individuals are often singled out for their achievements or abilities, teamwork is probably one of the most important lessons that sports teach. The receiver in football cannot catch a pass if the lineman does not protect the passer; the left fielder must hit the cutoff man in baseball; the center in basketball cannot post-up if the guard does not set up the play and make the assist; the soccer player cannot score if no one passes. The list of cause and effect goes on and on. In short, it teaches that everyone's job is valuable. And more important, everyone must do his or her job if the team is to be successful. In the end, sports teaches about competition and fair play, about achievement and striving for excellence, and that we are all in the game together.

★ ★ ★

The quotes in this book not only celebrate sports, they are also a mirror of our world, and so I have included quotes ranging from the themes that celebrate our athlete culture to those that decry it. As we find in newspaper sports pages, I have also shown sport's foibles, whether it be ego, greed, sex, or drugs. Whatever are our darker sides, they appear here as well. Especially in the more prominent sports, i.e. baseball, football, basketball, soccer, each has had its share of heroes won and lost, as well as tales of sadness and disappointment in human faults.

At the risk of being morbid, I was most surprised at the section on death. Obviously, sports are meant to be fun; that's why we enjoy them so much. However, some sports are fun but dangerous, and it usually takes a tragedy to remind us that some sports, while not well covered by the media, can lead to a very mortal end. Mountain climbing is always perilous, but then so is sailing. Some of the most dramatic moments in sports come from scenes too horrible to imagine—and help us to remember the beauty of life.

Even truer is that this collection as a whole shows what all athletes have in common. There is not a section that doesn't reflect what unites all athletes in the same cause—drive, effort, pain, success, failure—all these are common experiences in each athlete's life. What also struck me as I emptied out my local library's shelves was that most of the athletes we celebrate are winners, or people we perceive as winners. But most athletes lose more than they win. Great athletes use losses to spur themselves on. Many athletes are remembered for a pinnacle, but there are also many losses on the path to victory. We often forget that. How many playoffs did Michael Jordan lose? How many tournaments ended in despair for Pelé? How many Super Bowls did John Elway lose? We usually consider winning as everything.

Vince Lombardi was the well-known coach of the Green Bay Packers, a championship dynasty. The quote he was most famous for is a reflection of what I was just talking about—"Winning isn't everything—it's the only thing."

People are still awed by the sheer power of that remark. *The only thing.* We have taken it to heart and forgotten what is best about sports—sportsmanship, the true teacher, why sports helps us to grow as human beings.

Vince Lombardi was a good man, and he believed in playing hard. He was one of the Seven Blocks of Granite as an underclassman at Fordham University. In the end it deeply offended him that people so misunderstood the quote. He was horrified that people turned it just slightly from what he meant to an ultimatum to win at all costs. He later said, "I wish to hell I'd never said the damn thing. I meant the effort . . . I meant having a goal. I sure as hell didn't mean for people to crush human values and morality."

Vince Lombardi celebrated what is best about the athlete, which is to say that the sportsmanlike athlete personifies the goals to which we should all aspire. To understand ourselves, what we are like under duress, what we are like *in the moment,* we should celebrate that understanding and the fun involved, no matter who wins or loses. Sports is the most enjoyable and best learning experience there is, and it's about our favorite subject—ourselves.

Notes on This Collection

I have tried to avoid separating out personalities as their own entries. I have saved this "honor" for those athletes whose feats or celebrity have both outgrown their particular field of endeavor as well as that of sport itself. Athletes who have transcended sport and whose names have become part of the everyday language have been broken out, i.e., Babe Ruth, Michael Jordan, Wayne Gretzky, Pelé, Ali, etc. These people have soared above the arenas and stadiums of the world to occupy a more iconic realm.

The idea is to keep quotes within their respective sport or fit them into a category more universal to the athlete. Whether athlete, coach, or fan, one can look up themes that stretch across all fields of endeavor, i.e., focus, training, effort, etc., and find it therefore a much more useful volume.

THE ULTIMATE DICTIONARY
of SPORTS QUOTATIONS

Aaron, Henry "Hank"

(b. Feb. 5, 1934) *Hall of Fame baseball player; holder of the all-time home run record of 755, all-time RBI record of 2,297, played in 24 All-Star Games*

Babe Ruth may have died twenty-five years ago but his ample ghost has been with us all summer and he seems to grow more insistently alive every time Henry Aaron hits a baseball over a fence.

> *Red Smith, sportswriter*

Trying to sneak a fastball past Hank Aaron is like trying to sneak sunrise past a rooster.

> *Curt Simmons, professional baseball player*

Abdul-Jabar, Kareem

(b. Lew Alcindor April 16, 1947) *Hall of Fame basketball player; won three NCAA basketball championships; won six NBA titles; league MVP six times*

He scored 40 points against me on Mother's Day . . . and my own mother called me to complain.

> *Darryl Dawkins, professional basketball player*

One of the smallest men I ever met.

> *Joe Falls, sportswriter, "Farewell, Alcindorella," after Jabar was rude to a group of sportswriters in Detroit*

Ability

He could only jump over the Thursday newspaper.

> *Darryl Dawkins, professional basketball player, about Wes Unseld, professional basketball player*

I've seen him make chicken salad out of chicken feathers many times.

> *John Brockington, professional football player, about Walter Payton*

Academics

I play football. I'm not trying to be a professor. The tests don't seem to make sense to me, measuring your brain on stuff I haven't been through in school.

> *Clemson University football recruit Ray Forsythe, ineligible because of academic requirements*

Son, looks to me like you're spending too much time on one subject.
Shelby Metcalf, basketball coach at Texas A&M, to a player who received four F's and one D

Achievement

Achievement is difficult. It requires enormous effort. Those who can work through the struggle are the ones who are going to be successful.
Jackie Joyner-Kersee, Olympic track and field gold medalist

In the NBA, you're a piece of meat. That's it, bottom line. Well, if I'm a piece of meat, I want to be the best piece. I don't want to be hamburger.
Doc Rivers, National Basketball Association player and coach

Back when I came up, baseball was about establishing yourself. You wanted to get into a position to break the records of the players you grew up watching.
Tony Gwynn, Major League Baseball player, perennial batting champion and All-Star

At eight I decided that I wanted to be the best tennis player in the world. From then on, it was always in the back of my mind.
Tracy Austin, tennis champion, from her autobiography, Beyond Center Court

Adversity

Adversity teaches a man about himself.
Alonzo Mourning, professional basketball player and All-Star

African Americans

Being a Black heavyweight champion in the second half of the twentieth century was now not unlike being Jack Johnson, Malcom X, and Frank Costello all in one.
Norman Mailer, Pulitzer Prize–winning writer from his essay "King of the Hill"

Proportionately, the black athlete has been more successful than any other group in any other endeavor in American life. And he and she did it despite legal and social discrimination that would have dampened the ardor of most participants.
Arthur Ashe, champion professional tennis player, writer

The path to fame and wealth for all but a few black athletes has been "A Hard Road to Glory."
Arthur Ashe, champion professional tennis player, writer

Agassi, Andre

(b. Apr. 29, 1970) *Tennis champion—won Wimbledon; U.S. Open; Australian Open; French Open*

If he was ranked two-hundred-and-fifty and he dressed like that, people would make fun of him.
Andrea Temesvari, professional tennis player

Age

Age is like a bulldozer. It's gonna push you out of the way once you stop moving.
Archie Moore, champion boxer

All the rookies call me Mr. Long and I can't recognize any of the music they listen to.
Howie Long, professional football player, Hall of Famer, and broadcaster

Back in the good old days, I was what you might call a "poor man's Bruce Jenner."
Bob Mathias, two-time gold medalist decathlon competitor, politician, and actor

Contrary to popular opinion, I have not worn that uniform before.
Jackie Slater, professional football player, one of the oldest players in the National Football League, commenting on a reproduction of a Rams uniform from the 1950s

He's twenty. In ten years he'll have a chance to be thirty.
Casey Stengel, Hall of Fame baseball player and manager

He thinks when I was born I was already sixty years old and had a wooden leg and came here to manage.
Casey Stengel, Hall of Fame baseball player and manager, referring to Mickey Mantle

He wanted to block, dodge, or pick off punches as used to be his custom, and strike with lightning speed and with savage finality, but he never quite could do it. He didn't have the coordination, that irreplaceable element so necessary to boxing which vanishes so rapidly as you grow old.
James P. Dawson, sportswriter, about Joe Louis's last fight

He won on points, but I proved my point.
George Foreman, champion boxer, who at 40 years of age, lasted fifteen rounds with Evander Holyfield, heavyweight boxing champion

I am not the pigtailed girl anymore, but I hold her dear to my heart.
Olga Korbut, Olympic gold medalist gymnast

I feel two hundred years old. All they got to do is lay me down and close the box.
Bill Russell, Hall of Fame basketball player referring to his last year in the National Basketball Association

If I get tired now, it's not because of my surgery. It's because I'm old.
Joe Torre, professional baseball player and manager

I just started to feel the fatigue, mentally and physically, that I've never felt before.
Wayne Gretzky, Hall of Fame hockey player

It's like suddenly they say, "Give me your skates, you're done."
Wayne Gretzky, Hall of Fame hockey player

I'll never make the mistake of being seventy again.
Casey Stengel, Hall of Fame baseball player and manager

I'm sort of like a late model car that rattles a lot. It's a lot of little things.
Tim Green, National Football League player & broadcaster

I'm still Reggie, but not as often.
Reggie Jackson, Hall of Fame baseball player

I swing just as hard, but I walk slower and get to my ball quicker.
Sam Snead, champion professional golfer, when asked if age had affected his golf game

It ain't what it was, but then what the hell is?
Dizzy Dean, Hall of Fame baseball player,
speaking about his arm and aging

I've lost a step, I can't leap like I used to, and the rim looks a little hazy from the three-point line. But I can still take you to the hole on one leg. And I may have to.
Rick Telander, sportswriter

I was raised, but I never did grow up.
Pete Rose, professional baseball player
and all-time hits leader

No, but I used to be.
Frank Shorter, champion marathoner, when asked
by a fan if he was Frank Shorter

No, Jackie, this isn't a coach-athlete thing. This is your husband telling you it's time for you to go.
Bob Kersee, track and field coach to Jackie
Joyner-Kersee, Olympic gold medalist track
and field competitor, asking her to retire

One of those guys who hangs on and on, telling himself that he can still be competitive when he knows good and well he can't.
Ambrose "Rowdy" Gaines IV, Olympic
champion swimmer, commentary
on his own retirement

Sometimes I wonder if the years that slip
   beyond recall
Are marked upon the Book of Time as
   weekends after all?
We hit the line with unchecked youth—
   and as a vision gleams
We find that we are gray and old along the
   road of dreams.
Grantland Rice, sportswriter

Sooner or later, God takes it away from all of them—all of them.
Bill Parcells, professional football coach

The older I get, the better I used to be.
Connie Hawkins, professional basketball player
and playground legend

The only thing old on me is this bald spot, and I'll have that fixed the next time we're in L.A.
John Lucas, professional basketball player
and coach, when he was still playing
as one of the oldest players in the
National Basketball Association

The sadness of the end of a career of an older athlete, with the betrayal of his body, is mirrored in the rest of us. Consciously or not, we know: There, soon, go I.
Ira Berkow, sportswriter

They got to lower the roof or raise the floor. 'Cause the Hawk don't soar no more.
Connie Hawkins, professional basketball
player and playground legend

We looked young.
Larry Brown, professional basketball coach,
after a lopsided losing effort

Who's this guy? He's too old for our games. Is he supposed to be good?
Joe Hammond, college basketball player, to a
teammate before a one-on-one with Herman
"The Helicopter" Knowings, street player
legend of Harlem

My mind's right there. Tells me just what to do. But my legs ain't with it. In their own world. I send the message and by the time they move, it's too late.

John Edgar Wideman, award-winning novelist, college basketball player, from Philadelphia Fire

They tell you things change at 40. But they don't tell you how much.

Johnny Unitas, Hall of Fame quarterback, who spent his last few years on the bench and unhappy

Agents

From drugs to prostitutes, to vacations, cars, and envelopes of cash, some agents will give whatever it takes. When the player's contract is ultimately signed, the agent of course deducts the cost of these predraft perks directly from the player's signing bonus. What appear to be lavish gifts of friendship turn out to be merely unsecured loans for vices and luxuries.

Tim Green, professional football player, broadcaster, and writer

He sees all the devious ways you can rip people off.

Unidentified baseball executive about sports agent Scott Boras

I swear those agents could sell swampland in Manhattan.

John Feinstein, writer, from Hard Courts

I want to be remembered for making rich people richer.

Hughes Norton, sports agent

Kids have agents now before they even make it into their teens.

Mary Lou Retton, Olympic gold medal gymnast

My opinion has always been that I would rather work for the star than work for the movie house. The star is always going to be pursued.

Scott Boras, sports agent

Sports agents have become a virus in sports.

Mike Lupica, sportswriter

We got sick and tired of being put in the position of constantly having to call people and make excuses for our clients, which, often as not, we knew weren't true and they knew weren't true.

Ivan Blumberg, sports agent

AIDS

I could name close to thirty people in skating who have died from AIDS. A lot of skaters aren't admitting that we've lost skaters to AIDS. Hell, it's a disease that people are dying from.

Randy Gardner, Olympic pairs skater

I know what it's like to learn that you are HIV-positive, to face your own mortality.

Greg Louganis, Olympic gold medal diver

We all say things we don't mean. We mean things we don't say. When a very close personal friend is afflicted, you begin to realize the depth of this whole thing, and you think, "Holy smokes, this is not a joke anymore."

Bill Toomey, Olympic track and field medalist about Dr. Tom Waddell, who was dying of AIDS

Alcohol

Football players go together with beer like wine goes with cheese.

Tim Green, professional football player,
broadcaster, and writer

I always assumed no one knew about my drinking because, in my mind, I was perfectly normal when I drank. In reality everyone knew. The girls on the tour would smell alcohol on my breath at eight in the morning, then roll their eyes and go about their business.

Laura Baugh, professional golfer,
and recovering alcoholic

The pitfalls are drink. And at his age, women—and then believing what other people tell him, other people than us. If he believes what we tell him, he'll go a long way—but if he believes people outside the game saying he's the best thing on earth, he'll come unstuck.

Brian Flynn, soccer manager, speaking of
Johnathan Cross, professional soccer player

Ali, Muhammad

(b. Cassius Clay, b. Jan. 17, 1942) *World Heavyweight Champion; won the title on three different occasions; Olympic gold medal boxer (1960)*

Astute, double-hearted, irresistible.

Toni Morrison, Pulitzer Prize–winning author

He worked apparently on the premise that there was something obscene about being hit.

Norman Mailer, Pulitzer Prize–winning author
about Ali's early career

The bluegrass bard from Louisville.

Red Smith, sportswriter

Alternative Lifestyles

From the very beginning the worlds of athletics and homosexuality have intersected more often than many people realize . . . The root word for gymnasium—*gymnos*—has nothing to do with athletics; it means nude.

Dan Woog, writer

Gay athletes and coaches are nowhere near as visible as say, gay actors, musicians, or even student government leaders. The reason has less to do with percentages than it does reality. The sports world does not exactly high-five them or grasp them with a winner's hug.

Dan Woog, author

I was welcomed as an openly gay athlete. It was a real thrill for me, and that experience made me realize how important it is for athletes to feel welcomed for who they are.

Greg Louganis, Olympic gold medalist diver

There was so much camaraderie. There was this whole crowd of guys just like me—people with real jobs, who didn't abuse their bodies. And to top it off, it was extremely competitive, too.

Gene Dermondy, wrestling coach,
about the Gay Games

What matters to me is setting an example so that other gay and lesbian athletes don't feel compelled to hide. I had hoped that my example would quickly change things . . . that hasn't been the case, and it's taught me a valuable lesson. Deciding to be openly gay or

lesbian is a very personal decision, and it's one I can't make for someone else.
Rudy Galindo, champion figure skater

Welcome to the Games. It's great to be out and proud!
Greg Louganis, Olympic gold medalist diver, at the opening of the Gay Games

Amateurs

Amateurism, after all, must be the backbone of all sport.
Richard S. Tufts, writer

In love as in sport, the amateur status must be strictly maintained.
Robert Graves, writer and poet

It has always been a source of pride for me that I competed in a sport that, by and large, was purely amateur.
Dan Jansen, Olympic gold medalist speed skater

It is a rare bird who can hustle a living in today's going and still have time to excel as an amateur.
Grantland Rice, sportswriter

It is no secret that in any pure sense, no world class skier is an amateur. There is no way racers could have lived the lives we did without money.
Jean-Claude Killy, Olympic gold medalist skier

I was lucky. I don't mean in the competition, but in the fact that I had a wife who made decent money and who was just as committed to seeing me win the gold medal as I was. In this country, unless an amateur athlete has a working wife or a wealthy family or a very

tolerant boss, the odds are that he's never going to get the chance to try for a gold medal.
Bruce Jenner, gold medalist decathlon competitor

Let's be honest. The proper definition of an amateur today is one who accepts cash, not checks.
Jack Kelly Jr., Sports Illustrated

There are no longer true amateurs in track.
Adrian Paulen, International Amateur Athletics Foundation president

The Russians are no more professional than the Americans, who give their athletes free college educations.
Avery Brudage, International Olympic Committee president

Trust funds are not necessary anymore. They give the public a false impression that the athletes somehow are still amateur.
Carl Lewis, gold medalist track and field competitor

We're all professionals, rules don't mean anything.
Frank Shorter, champion runner, testifying before the President's Commission on Olympic Sports

Andretti, Mario

(b. Feb. 28, 1940) *Champion race car driver; won Daytona 500, Indianapolis 500, World Formula 1 title*

Mario Andretti was a hell of a race car driver, but he looked like a little girl dribbling the ball.
Bob Netolicky, professional basketball player, referring to a charity game once played between the Indianapolis 500 drivers and the press corps

Angling

Angling is extremely time consuming. That's sort of the whole point.
Thomas McGuane, writer

Anglers are living proof that fish is not brain food.
Randy Voorhees, fisherman and writer

God never did make a more calm, quiet, innocent recreation than angling.
Izaak Walton, writer

The fish is the hunter; the angler is the hunted.
Richard Waddington, Catching Salmon

Soon after I embraced the sport of angling I became convinced that I should never be able to enjoy it if I had to rely on the cooperation of fish.
Spars Grey Hackle, fisherman and writer

There is certainly something in angling that tends to produce a gentleness of spirit and a pure serenity of mind.
Washington Irving, writer

Appearance

I have to believe it was all in the hair.
Michael Douglas, actor, director, producer, to Pat Riley, professional basketball coach, referring to the coach's hair style that Douglas copied for his Academy Award–winning performance in Wall Street

Archery

A bow is a very personal piece of equipment.
Mike Brodeur, champion archer

Every good bow is a work of love.
Saxton Pope, bow hunter and writer

What a glorious weapon the long bow is.
Maurice Thompson, archer and writer

Yew wood was a gift from God to the bowmaker.
Earl Ullrich, attributed by John Strunk, archer

When you pick up a bow to shoot your first arrow, you are partaking in an activity dating back at least 20,000 years. The bow and arrow are pictured in drawings . . . on a cave wall in Spain's Valltorta Gorge.
K. M. Haywood and C. F. Lewis, archers

Arrests

I'd like to refer to this whole thing from start to finish as a real Mickey Mouse operation, but that would be an insult to Mickey Mouse.
Bobby Knight, three-time champion college basketball coach, after being arrested and arguing with police

Art

LeRoy, you're improving.
Weeb Ewbank, Hall of Fame football coach, to artist LeRoy Neiman, after stepping on one of Leroy's paintings during a practice session with a muddy boot

Athletes

All I am is a basketball player. That's who I am and what I am. And when I realized that, it made me feel relieved and happy.
Michael Jordan, professional basketball player & future Hall of Famer

Don't think of him as a dumb jock. Think of him as a smart guy who can kick your butt.
from an ad for Men's Health Magazine

I have the greatest job in the world.
Derek Jeter, professional baseball player

People train much harder than they did before . . . Is there a limit? Athletes don't think that way.
Bill Rogers, marathoner

Players today are faster, stronger and better. This is a different game.
Jason Williams, professional basketball player

The athlete knows he controls what happens to him. He blames no one but himself when things go wrong.
George Sheehan, runner and writer

We're not poets, philosophers, or statesmen. I shoot a ball through a hoop for a living.
Grant Hill, all-star professional basketball player

Attitude

A bad attitude is worse than a bad swing.
Payne Stewart, champion professional golfer

Allus I do is what I please and nobody stops me.
Gorgeous George, professional wrestler

Attention to detail instills pride and discipline.
D. Wayne Lukas, thoroughbred horse trainer

Humor was everywhere—in the good stories one heard, in the quick ripostes and the one-liners, the constant joshing and put-downs,

invariably bawdy and raucous—all of it a hedge against the boredom and regimen.
George Plimpton, sportswriter, writer, and editor

I am not a victim. I am a survivor.
Lance Armstrong, champion cyclist; won Tour de France after surviving his bout with cancer

I like my boys agile, mobile, and hostile.
Alonzo Jake Gaines, college football coach

I feel great!
Pat Croce, professional training guru, National Basketball Association executive and owner

It ain't over 'til the fat lady sings.
Dick Motta, champion professional basketball coach. When his team was down in the finals and it looked as if they might lose, Motta referred to opera, meaning the game wasn't over until the big finish at the end, usually sung by a diva.

It's not whether you get knocked down, it's whether you get up.
Vince Lombardi, professional football player and coach

I learned that if you want to make it bad enough, no matter how bad it is, you can make it.
Gale Sayers, Hall of Fame football player

My motto was always to keep swinging. Whether I was in a slump or feeling badly or having trouble off the field, the only thing to do was keep swinging.
Hank Aaron, Hall of Fame baseball player

The principle is competing against yourself. It's about self-improvement, about being better than you were the day before.
Steve Young, champion football player

When someone tells me there is only one way to do things, it always lights a fire under my butt. My instant reaction is, "I'm gonna prove you wrong."

Picabo Street, Olympic gold medalist skier

You have no control over what the other guy does. You only have control over what you do.

A. J. Kitt, Olympic gold medalist skier

I always thought I was better . . . Anybody who doesn't think that shouldn't be out on the course.

Sam Snead, champion professional golfer

If beating someone as badly and as quickly as I could is having a killer instinct, then, okay, you can call it that.

Don Budge, professional tennis champion

I come to play. I come to beat you. I come to kill you.

Leo Durocher, professional baseball player and manager

I could play with anybody.

Jack Kramer, professional tennis champion, asked how he would do against today's stars

I feel like I came down here as much to get out of the cold weather and to see my friends as anything else. Let's face it, that's not a great attitude to start the year with.

Pam Shriver, professional tennis player

I think human beings that have difficult times think different things at different times. What I had to look at was what was bad in my performance and move forward. I think that's something I have to do from now on.

Hideki Irabu, professional baseball player

I won't let you take advantage of me. I'll kill you before I ever let you take advantage of me.

Kevin Garnett, professional basketball player

My philosophy is you better do it the way you drive your race car: 110 percent.

Max Papis, race car driver

Never go to bed a loser.

George Halas, Hall of Fame owner and coach

No one can throw a fastball past me. God could come down from Heaven, and He couldn't throw it past me.

Ted Williams, Hall of Fame baseball player

Not me. I'm not riding in a white Rolls-Royce.

Leon Hess, sports owner, industrialist and known for being very down to earth, when offered a ride in a white limo at an owners' meeting

People thought I was ruthless, which I was. I didn't give a darn who was on the other side of the net. I'd knock you down if you got in the way.

Althea Gibson, professional tennis champion

What's to worry about? These L.A. goofballs are positively guaranteed to screw up and lose it.

Red Auerbach, National Basketball Association executive, referring to the Los Angeles Lakers in a championship games versus his team, the Boston Celtics (who won)

You didn't beat me. You merely finished in front of me.

Hal Higdon, writer and runner

You can't treat it as any game. Do that and you have a short season. Every game is important, and you always like to start off with a win after all that training.

Gayle Sayers, Hall of Fame football player

You have to be persistent and you have to be dedicated. You have to be hardworking. I've never run into the guy who could win at the top level in anything today and didn't have the right attitude, didn't give it everything he had, at least while he was doing it; wasn't prepared and didn't have the whole program worked out.

Ted Turner, champion yachtsman and baseball owner

You have to strap it on and go get them.

Roger Clemens, profesional baseball player

Audibles

Four set! . . . uh, red, right . . . uh, 22 . . . Ah, shit, son-of-a-bitch, time-out.

Don Meredith, broadcaster and professional football player, during a televised game as the quarterback of the Dallas Cowboys

Auerbach, Red

(b. Sept. 20, 1917) *Champion National Basketball Association coach and executive of the Boston Celtics; won nine NBA titles as coach; won seven more as General Manager*

Fan and foe alike have always agreed on one point—Red Auerbach is undoubtedly the genius of basketball.

Lawrence F. O'Brien, National Basketball Association Commissioner

I've never known anybody who played for him that didn't like him. Of course, I've never known anybody who played against him who did like him!

Bill Russell, Hall of Fame basketball player and coach

Red Auerbach will never be known as a gracious winner.

Freddie Schaus, professional basketball coach of the rival Los Angeles Lakers, a frequent victim in the finals

Autographs

I can't sign it, dear. League rules. Where are you going to be after the game?

Ted Williams, Hall of Fame baseball player to an adoring female fan

I get people knocking me down for an autograph every day.

Tiger Woods, champion professional golfer

Auto Racing

A race car driver's résumé needs to say only one thing—winner.

Benny Parsons, race driver

As a sometime rally driver I have often wondered, in times of great stress or impending accident, just what makes the rally driver tick.

Graham Gauld, writer and racer

The best way to make a small fortune in racing is to start with a big one.

Junior Johnson, champion driver

Driving a race car is like dancing with a buzz saw.

Cale Yarborough, champion driver

Experience is more important than muscle in this business.

Lee Petty, champion race car driver

Everyone loves a Ferrari, even if they hate old man Enzo.

Denis Jenkinson, author and race car journalist

I enjoy racing at high speeds. I am happy when I am running 180 . . . It's my fun as well as my business.

Lee Roy Yarbrough, champion race car driver

In Grand Prix you have to drive ten-tenths most of the time. Nine-tenths isn't good enough.

Graham Hill, champion race car driver

I never felt scared of racing. If I did, I'd quit.

Richard Petty, champion race car driver

In the cutaway cockpit he was clearly visible, arms tensed against the kicking steering wheel, teeth clenched with the sheer effort of controlling this turbulent machine. And you knew as you watched that this was something beyond the reach of ordinary men. This, to me, was motor racing.

F. Wilson McComb, writer

If I can pass someone, I'll do it; I don't care if he is in my other car or if he's Christ Almighty himself. When I am in a race car, I've got one thing in mind: passing *everybody*.

A. J. Foyt, champion race car driver

One thing about great champions in Winston Cup is that the truly great champions are the ones who have won more than one championship.

Jeff Gordon, champion race car driver

On the whole, the Peking-to-Paris race has proved conclusively that the motor-car is a much stronger and more resistant machine than has so far been thought.

Luigi Barzini, Sr., writer, participant in the winning car with driver Prince Borghese, which took 60 days in 1907 (it has not been run since)

People refuse to believe that a man who is wrestling 700 screaming horses, pushing himself up to and beyond the limits of his skill, and betting his life on every turn of the wheel isn't running a lot of profound thoughts through his head.

Mario Andretti, champion race car driver

Sometimes as I sit in the cockpit just before taking off, I wonder just what in the hell am I doing there.

Craig Breedlove, former land speed record holder

Stock car racing is two ends of the world. You win and you're at the very top . . . You blow an engine, you blow a tire, strip a gear, hit a wall, or do one of a thousand freakish things that can keep you from victory and you're a nobody.

David Pearson, champion race car driver

The crashes people remember, but drivers remember the near misses.

Mario Andretti, champion race car driver

The early morning shift is the worst and later with the sun in your eyes. It's the time at LeMans they wreck all the cars. The drivers are tired and the cars start to reach the breaking point.

A. J. Foyt, champion race car driver

The only philosophy that pays off in racing is that you go fast enough to win and slow enough to finish.

Ken Miles, champion race car driver

There's no fifth or tenth. Racing is about winning. That is why I got involved.

Greg Ray, race car driver

There's no secret. You just press the accelerator to the floor and steer left.

Bill Vukovich, champion driver

They really don't make drivers like they used to. That's a fact.

A. J. Foyt, champion race car driver

Until ten years ago nobody made any money in stock car racing. Compared to other professional athletes, drivers didn't make that much money. Owners didn't, promoters didn't.

Humpy Wheeler, racing promoter

What are we going to do, just keep trying to beat each other until we kill ourselves?

Art Arfons, former land speed record holder, to Craig Breedlove, also a former record holder

We didn't have no tickets, no safety equipment, no fences, no nothing. Just a bunch of these bootleggers who'd been arguing all week about who had the fastest car would get together and prove it.

Junior Johnson, champion race car driver

We're not really race drivers because we don't drive in traffic, vary speeds, pass other drivers in traffic, go around corners, but we need all the tools of a good driver—determination and courage and quick reflexes.

Dan "Big Daddy" Garlitz, drag and funny car racer

B

Backups

It's like you're doing a good job at work and the other guy keeps getting the raise.

Allan Bester, professional hockey player

He's the third-string catcher—when is he going to play?

Don Zimmer, professional baseball player and manager, about bullpen catcher Mike Figga, when asked by beat reporters if Figga would get any time on the field

It was like being retired. I'd get eighteen, maybe twenty minutes against the backup center. It was hardly playing.

Bill Cartwright, champion professional basketball player

Bad Day

If you see a defense with dirt and mud on their backs they've had a bad day.

John Madden, champion football coach and Emmy Award–winning broadcaster

I hit the rough, the bunkers, the trees, the gallery, the water . . . You can't make a living doing that.

Tiger Woods, professional golfer, after finishing 11 over par and in last place

I only arrived two days ago, and now I'm going home tomorrow.

Pete Sampras, professional tennis player, ranked #1 in the world, on losing in the opening round of the Swiss Indoors Championship

I should re-enlist in the Army I was so lousy tonight.

Billy Conn, champion professional boxer

When 15 Giants plays netted 1 yard, the suspicion grew on the Giant's bench that something drastic would have to be done to resurrect the team's offense.

Bill Pennington, New York Times, *on the worst offense in the National Football League*

Badminton

Badminton is an attacking game.

Jake Downey, champion badminton player

Badminton is my soul.

Motto painted on Jakarta's largest badminton training center

Every morning I think, God, I'm lucky. The Bureau liked me playing badminton, and my wife loved to play, too. I haven't a complaint in the world.

Joe Alston, champion badminton player and Federal Bureau of Investigation agent

Explosive muscle power is an asset . . . but it is often overshadowed by exceptional reaction time, endurance, recovery of balance, and overall qualities of movement within a small court area.

Barry C. Pelton, writer

In badminton rallies there is constant planning, constant searching for an opening, constant probing for weaknesses.

Frank J. Devlin, champion badminton player

Matches are won or lost on service. It is the one shot that can be practised alone, but sadly there is little evidence of it.

Judy Devlin Hashman, champion badminton player, and C. M. Jones, writer and editor

Suprinto can send a shuttlecock screaming at 200 miles per hour, which makes him a ringer in most any backyard barbecue match.

Steve Rushin, sportswriter, writing about one of the world's best badminton players

The serve in badminton—unlike all other racket games—is essentially a defensive shot.

Frank J. Devlin, champion badminton player

The shuttle is a Prima Donna.

Pat Davis, badminton champion

Top-level badminton is to the game we play at family picnics what the NBA is to H-O-R-S-E in the driveway.

Barry Large, sportswriter

Ballet

In all my years of watching football I can honestly say that I have never once confused football with ballet.

Joan Tisch, wife of Bob Tisch, owner professional football team

The difference between sports and ballet is that in sports you root for somebody. Nobody yells at one of the ballerinas, "Break a bleepin' leg, ya bum."

Mike Littwin, sportswriter

This is sports as ballet, something utterly new and modern, its roots African American, ballet as contested sport. No one, after all, ever guarded Baryshnikov.

David Halberstam, bestselling author of Playing for Keeps, *speaking of Michael Jordan and basketball*

What's the idea of that dance out there. The ballet's downtown, not here.

Leo Durocher, baseball player and manager, to Willie Mays, Hall of Fame baseball player

Barkley, Charles

(b. Feb. 20, 1963) *All-star National Basketball Association player; Olympic gold medalist; league MVP 1993*

What has he done? Nothing but spit on kids, throw people through windows and talk racist when he has a white wife, and talk crazy about black people. He's nobody.

Allen Iverson, professional basketball player

Baseball

A boy's game, with no more possibilities than a boy can master, a game bounded by walls which kept out novelty or danger, change or adventure.

F. Scott Fitzgerald, writer, from a eulogy for his friend Ring Lardner

Alex, my seven-year-old, had the Mark McGwire card I'd bought him in the souvenir shop, holding onto it like it was a winning lottery ticket.

Mike Lupica, sportswriter

Baseball gives every American boy a chance to excel. Not just to be as good as everyone else, but to be better. This is the nature of man, and this is the name of the game.

Ted Williams, Hall of Fame baseball player

Baseball has changed so much from the days when we played that I am fast becoming a stranger to the game.

Bob Gibson, Hall of Fame baseball player

Baseball is a crazy game. Anything can happen.

Fernando Tatis, professional baseball player

Baseball is almost the only orderly thing in a very unorderly world. If you get three strikes, even the best lawyer in the world can't get you off.

Bill Veeck, baseball owner and racetrack operator

Baseball is an 1890 game. It's a peaceful afternoon in the country. What baseball needs to compete is more violence.

Bill Veeck, baseball owner and racetrack operator

Baseball is an allegorical play about America, a poetic, complex, and subtle play of courage, fear, good luck, mistakes, patience about fate, and sober self-esteem . . . It is impossible to understand America without a thorough knowledge of baseball.

Saul Steinberg, writer

Baseball is a worrying thing.

Stan Coveleshi, writer

Baseball is more than just a game. It has eternal value. Through it, one learns the beautiful and noble spirit of Japan.

Suishu Tobita, professional baseball player and manager

Baseball is not a life-or-death situation, and in the big picture, this game is just a small part of our lives. The important thing is to use baseball to help other people.

Ken Griffey, Jr., professional baseball player

Baseball is not the sport of the wealthy, it is the sport of the wage earner.

Bill Veeck, baseball owner and racetrack operator

Baseball is pieces of minutiae that need belaboring.

Bill Scheft, writer

Baseball is so ingrained in Cuba that it has thrived as the "national sport" through 40 years of bitterly anti-American revolution.

Roberto Gonzalez Echevarria, writer

Baseball is the very symbol, the outward and visible expression of the drive and push and rush and struggle of the raging, tearing, booming nineteenth century.

Mark Twain, writer and humorist

Baseball's grip on Japan's collective psyche is due, ultimately, to the fact that it suits the national character . . . baseball provided the Japanese with an opportunity to express their renowned group proclivities on an athletic field . . . Over the years—and despite Oh's home runs—it has been the team aspects of the game, the sacrifice bunt, the squeeze, the hit-and-run, that have come to characterize Japanese baseball.

Robert Whiting, writer, from You Gotta Have Wa

Baseball's summer of '98 provided authentic moments of poetry and passion, the kind of stuff that shines through the crassness and nonsense, to remind us why we still care.

Bob Costas, broadcaster

Baseball's 90% mental. The other half is physical.

Yogi Berra, Hall of Fame baseball player

Baseball was played since the beginning of the nation, hence it was part of the nation.

Roberto Gonzalez Echevarria, writer, referring to the nation of Cuba

Cut me and I'll bleed Dodger blue.

Tom Lasorda, baseball manager

During my lifetime, two events clearly stand out above all others as milestones in the history of batting in baseball: Joe DiMaggio's fifty-six-game hitting streak, and Ted Williams's seasonal batting average of .406. Unfortunately, I missed them both because I was busy gestating during the season of their joint occurrence in 1941.

Stephen Jay Gould, eminent scientist and baseball enthusiast

Every great hitter works on the theory that the pitcher is more afraid of him than he is of the pitcher.

Ty Cobb, Hall of Fame baseball player

Fanaticism? No. Writing is exciting and baseball is like writing.
You can never tell with either
how it will go
or what you will do?

Marianne Moore, poet and baseball fan

For the first hundred years of its existence, baseball had the press of this nation in its pocket. The true story of baseball was never told.

James Michener, Pulitzer Prize–winning author

He's not Mr. October, he's Mr. May.

George Steinbrenner, baseball owner, about Dave Winfield when asked by sportswriters to compare him with Reggie Jackson

I'd walk through hell in a gasoline suit to keep playing baseball.

Pete Rose, professional baseball player and coach

Some kids dream of joining the circus, others of becoming a major league baseball player. I have been doubly blessed. As a member of the New York Yankees, I have gotten to do both.

Graig Nettles, professional baseball player

Hello, Joe? It's Frank. Giants three, Dodgers nothing.

Franklin D. Roosevelt, president of the United States, in a telephone call to Joseph Stalin, dictator, Soviet Union

High school baseball is an education of the heart, the ground is a classroom of purity, a gymnasium of morality; that is its essential meaning.

Suishu Tobita, professional baseball player and manager

If not for baseball, he'd be a bum.

Al Martin, friend of Jason Kendall, professional baseball player

I gave up a lot to play ball. I gave up human relationships. Baseball was my relationship.

Maury Wills, professional baseball player, broadcaster, and manager

I guess I just couldn't believe it. But it's true all right. The flags are down, the lights in the temple are out, and the Harlem River flows lonely to the seas.

Roger Kahn, writer, about the closing of Ebbets Field, after the Dodgers left Brooklyn

I see great things in baseball. It is our game. The American game. It will repair our losses and be a blessing to us.

Walt Whitman, poet

Last year, more Americans went to symphonies than went to baseball games. This may be viewed as an alarming statistic, but I think that both baseball and the country will endure.

John F. Kennedy, president of the United States

Lots of good fans are losing interest in the big leagues because it's a great game but it's being played lousy.

Whitey Herzog, professional baseball player, manager, and executive

Never trust a baserunner with a limp. Comes a base hit and you'll think he just got back from Lourdes.

Joe Garagiola, professional baseball player and broadcaster

Ninety feet between the bases is the nearest thing to perfection that man has yet achieved.

Red Smith, sportswriter

Oh, somewhere in the favored land the sun
is shining bright;
The band is playing somewhere, and some-
where hearts are light,
And somewhere men are laughing, and
somewhere children shout;
But there is no joy in Mudville—mighty
Casey has struck out.

Ernest Lawrence Thayer, writer, from "Casey at the Bat"

One of the strongest points of baseball is that it has room for its critics and those who do not toe the party line. There's a little room for the heretic in the game.

Keith Olbermann, broadcaster

Tell the gentlemen I am glad to know of their coming, but they'll have to wait a few minutes till I make another base hit.

Attributed to Abraham Lincoln, speaking of a group of men coming to convince him to run for the Senate

The strongest thing that baseball has going for it today are its yesterdays.

Lawrence Ritter, writer

The Yankees are baseball.

Joe Torre, professional baseball player and manager, on the Yankees record-winning season

There was ease in Casey's manner as he
    stepped into his place;
There was pride in Casey's bearing, and a
    smile on Casey's face.
And when, responding to the cheers, he
    lightly doffed his hat,
No stranger in the crowd could doubt 'twas
    Casey at the bat.

> *Ernest Lawrence Thayer, writer,*
> *from "Casey at the Bat"*

The romance between intellectuals and the game of baseball is, for the most part, one-sided to the point of absurdity. A large percentage of intelligent Americans evaluate the four hundred men who play major league baseball as demigods. A large percentage of the muscular four hundred rate intellectuals several notches below umpires.

> *Roger Kahn, writer*

Well, that kind of puts the damper on even a Yankee win.

> *Phil Rizzuto, US sports commentator, remark during a Yankee baseball game, on hearing that Pope Paul VI had died*

Well, this year I'm told that the team did well because one pitcher had a fine curve ball. I understand that a curve ball is thrown with a deliberate attempt to deceive. Surely that is not an ability we should want to foster at Harvard.

> *Charles William Eliot, president of Harvard, 1869–1909, reply when asked why he wished to drop baseball as a college sport.*

What's important is that kids discover that baseball is fun—and that it gets to be more fun as you get better at it.

> *Mickey Mantle, Hall of Fame baseball player*

When I began playing the game, baseball was about as gentlemanly as a kick in the crotch.

> *Ty Cobb, Hall of Fame baseball player*

Whenever I decided to release a guy, I always had his room checked first for a gun. You couldn't take chances with some of those birds.

> *Casey Stengel, Hall of Fame baseball manager*

Baseball is a game of race, creed and color. The race is to first base. The creed is the rules of the game. The color? Well, the home team wears white uniforms, and the visiting team wears gray.

> *Joe Garagiola, professional baseball player and announcer, from his book* Baseball Is a Funny Game

Whoever wants to know the heart and mind of America had better learn baseball.

> *Jacques Barzun, writer*

Mexican baseball is exactly like American baseball, except for the extraneous embellishments. They work the hit and run and turn the double-play ball, but they don't sell the hot dog.

> *Peter Golenboch, sportswriter*

Only boring people find baseball boring.

> *Peter Golenboch, sportswriter*

Other sports are just sports, baseball is a love.

> *Bryant Gumbel, broadcaster*

Professional baseball, like any other business, grants no favors. There's more money for the winners, and the way to win is to learn your opponent's weaknesses and play to them.

> *Carol Hughes, sportswriter*

When a poor American boy dreamed of escaping his grim life, his fantasy probably involved becoming a professional baseball player. It was not so much the national sport as the binding national myth.

David Halberstam, writer

You spend a good piece of your life gripping a baseball and in the end it turns out that it was the other way around all the time.

Jim Bouton, professional baseball player
and writer

You've gotta have a lotta little boy in you to play this game.

Roy Campanella, All-star professional
baseball player

You've gotta have b★lls to make it in this league.

Pam Postema, female umpire

Basketball

Any American boy can be a basketball star if he grows up, up, up.

Bill Vaughn, writer

Basketball embodies everything our culture now craves: excitement, speed, dynamic personalities, up-close relationship with stars, the exciting physical nature of the contest, and, of course, the incredible suspense that is possible with each game.

Bill Walton, professional basketball
player and broadcaster

Boys are playing basketball around a telephone pole with a backboard nailed to it. Legs, shouts. The scrap and snap of Keds on loose alley pebbles seems to catapult their voices high into the moist March air blue above the wires.

John Updike, award-winning novelist

When it's played the way is spozed to be played, basketball happens in the air; flying, floating, elevated above the floor, levitating the way oppressed peoples of this earth imagine themselves in their dreams. . . .

John Edgar Wideman, award-winning novelist

Basketball for me has always been a celebration of all the elements in life: the joy of teamwork, the pride of skill development, the enthusiams of the crowd, the running and jumping and cheering and yelling at the refs.

Bill Walton, professional basketball
player and broadcaster

Basketball is the city game.

Pete Axthelm, sportswriter

Basketball is the MTV of sports.

Sara Levinson, National Football League
executive

Guards win games, but forwards win championships.

ÎAnonymous

I couldn't imagine not playing basketball. To me, basketball is what life is all about.

Bill Walton, college and professional
basketball player and broadcaster

It's a fact that the city game is played when and where it was designed not to be played: outdoors, in the sweltering heat, when the gentler games of summer—baseball, tennis, golf, swimming—should rule.

Rick Telander, sportswriter

I haven't been able to slam-dunk the basketball for the past five years. Or, for the thirty-eight years before that, either.

Dave Barry, writer

I love the game because I think it's the one sport where the personal expression of the individual ballplayer comes across the best.

Woody Allen, writer, director, actor

In New York, you can always search and find a player better than you are, to push you to greater things. It is an entire sub-culture built on competition.

Al McGuire, college basketball coach and broadcaster

It's just a game played with a little round ball.

Hot Rod Hundley, professional basketball player

It will be surprising to many to know how little the game has really changed throughout the years. People often believe that much of basketball is completely new, whereas in reality, the things that have been considered of recent development were embodied in the game almost from the very conception.

Dr. James Naismith, the inventor of basketball

Life in basketball has a lot of suffering in it.

Pat Riley, professional basketball player and coach

One thing about the top players in Harlem is that even a 30-point pick-up game is a serious thing. You don't just play the game for the hell of it.

Sonny Johnson, street player, Harlem

Sometimes this game comes down to makes and misses.

Jeff Van Gundy, professional basketball coach

The Game itself is about skills, problems, answers, unselfishness, rotations . . . it all comes back around.

Spike Lee, writer, actor, director

The Good Samaritan . . . was a basketball player who kept throwing passes when he was only two feet from the goddamn basket. You know what God did? He cut him for overpassing.

Bobby Knight, champion basketball coach, to one of his players

There is absolutely no way the best team in the NCAA could even dream of beating the worst team in the NBA . . . You're talking about men vs. boys.

Bill Walton, college and professional basketball player and broadcaster

There's only one way to think about this game and one way to play it. That's all out, foot to the floor, pushing myself as hard as I can for as long as I can. I love playing basketball.

Ervin "Magic" Johnson, Hall of Fame basketball player

This basketball bounces a certain way every time . . . Your behavior must be like a bouncing basketball. I have to be able to predict success based on your behavior and your behavior must be the same every time I call on you.

John Chaney, college basketball coach

This is, above all, a game of movement, of accuracy, of flow.

Harvey Araton, sportswriter

Nobody is going to pay to come out and watch your players run up and down the court in their underwear.

Jerry Adelman, ticket broker, speaking to a National Basketball Association executive in 1960

What is so fascinating about sitting around watching a bunch of pituitary cases stuff a ball through a hoop?

Woody Allen, writer, from Annie Hall

When I get to the NBA, first thing I'm going to do, I'm gonna see my Momma. I'm gonna buy her a house. Gonna get my Dad a Cadillac . . . so he can cruise to the games.

Arthur Agee, age 14, from Hoop Dreams

When Kentucky was upset by Texas Western, with the tenacious defense, disciplined play, and marvelously named players like Big Daddy Lattin and Willie Cager, we were all stunned . . . Maybe I was wrong about the capabilities of black basketball players . . . About a lot of things.

Frank Fitzpatrick, writer, about Texas Western upsetting Kentucky for the national championship. There was not a single player of color on Kentucky. Western Texas started five African Americans, the first team to do so and win a national championship.

When you have played basketball for a while, you don't need to look at a basket when you are in this close. You develop a sense of where you are.

Bill Bradley, basketball player and U.S. senator

Winning in the NBA more often has to do with the psychological qualities than the physical ones.

David Halberstam, writer

You begin by bouncing a ball—in the house, on the driveway, along the sidewalk, at the playground. Then you start shooting: legs bent, eyes on the rim, elbows under the ball . . . No equipment is needed beyond a ball, a rim, and imagination.

Bill Bradley, U.S. senator, champion professional basketball player, and writer

You know what you learn in the NBA? You learn how to play basketball. That's it. The only other thing I learned in my career with the Celtics was how to follow tall men through airports.

Kevin McHale, professional basketball player and executive

You play against other great players and see if you can make things you see out there part of your game. If a new wrinkle works, you use it. A basketball player's game is always under reconstruction.

Ray Haskins, college basketball coach

You smell yourself if you've been playing . . . in the cluster of men lounging around the bench in the middle of the court's open side. Mostly players around the bench, men who've just finished playing the last game of the evening, each one relaxing in his own funk, cooling out, talking the game, beginning to turn it into stories.

John Edgar Wideman, award-winning novelist, college basketball player, from Philadelphia Fire

Batboy

Butch was here before you came, and Butch will be here after you're gone.

Mort Cooper, professional baseball player, to an unidentified rookie, who was needlessly criticizing St. Louis Cardinals' batboy Butch Yatkeman

You're on thin ice. We better win soon or you'll be gone.

Derek Jeter (and other teammates), All-Star professional baseball player, to the batboy during a losing streak, ribbing him that he was bad luck

Becker, Boris

(b. Nov. 22, 1967) *Tennis champion; won Wimbledon, U.S. Open, and Australian Open*

Boris is the kid who, if you tell him not to put his hand in the fire because it's hot, he'll stick his hand right in the fire.

Ian Tiriac, tennis coach

Belmont Stakes

The extra 550 yards could make a big difference.

Elliott Walden, champion thoroughbred trainer

The longest, toughest test of stamina a 3-year-old colt and his trainer can face.

Jerry Izenberg, sportswriter

You don't run this distance but once in a horse's life. There's no telling what will happen.

D. Wayne Lukas, champion thoroughbred trainer

Berra, Yogi

(b. May 12, 1925) *Hall of Fame baseball catcher; played on 10 championship teams, won pennants with both the Yankees and the Mets; three-time American League Most Valuable Player*

He talks OK up there with a bat in his hands. A college education don't do you no good up there.

Casey Stengel, Hall of Fame baseball player and manager

That boy is too clumsy and too slow.

Branch Rickey, baseball executive, on unknown prospect Yogi Berra

Bird, Larry

(b. Dec. 7, 1956) *Hall of Fame National Basketball Association player; 1980 Rookie of the Year; won three NBA championships; 1998 Coach of the Year*

Bird was one of the few white guys who could play what people call the "Black Game."

Dennis Rodman, professional basketball player

He will cut your heart out to win.

Matt Goukas, professional basketball coach, about Larry Bird

He can dominate a game without even taking a shot. He is truly a guy who can make other players better.

Ervin "Magic" Johnson, Hall of Fame basketball player

He will take your heart out, stomp on it, and walk off the court with a sly grin on his face. He won't stop until he whips your ass!

Pat Riley, professional basketball player and coach, to his team before a National Basketball Association finals game

Birdie

I deny the allegations by Bob Hope that during my last game I hit an eagle, a birdie, an elk and a moose.

Gerald Ford, president of the United States

One time at Chattanoga, I hit a real pretty tee shot to the green, and danged if my ball didn't hit a bobwhite in the air and knock it dead. My ball stopped about a foot from the cup and I tapped it in. Only time I ever made two birdies in one hole.

Sam Snead, champion golfer

Blocking

Somewhere in the player's contract, maybe in the fine print, it says, "You're supposed to block."

John McKay, college and professional football coach

The secret is watching the center and going with the snap

Nate Allen, professional football player, about blocking punts and field goals

Blunders

I thought it was a no-brainer.

Chuck Knoblauch, who argued with an umpire about an infraction by a base runner instead of fielding a ground ball, which resulted in a run scoring and the Yankees losing a playoff game

Boats

A boat is a boat, I guess—nothing more than boards and paint and memories. Boards and paint are destined to rot away, but memories are priceless with age.

Larry Dablemont, writer

A small sailing craft is not only beautiful, it is seductive and full of strange promise and a hint of trouble.

E. B. White, writer

Ben Lexcen came up with the greatest innovation in 12-meter yacht design in decades. He deserves all the credit he got and more.

Dennis Conner, businessman and champion yachtsman

Big sea, little boat, out to sea I go.

Molly Mulhern Gross, outdoorswoman, editor, and journalist

Every well-built canoe, yacht or ship, has some individuality, some peculiar trait of its own.

George W. Sears, outdoorsman and journalist

For a vessel to sail easily, steadily, and rapidly, the displacement of water must be nearly uniform along her lines.

George Steers, yacht architect, and builder of America, *the racing yacht for which the America's Cup is named*

Good-bye old girl. God only knows when I shall tread your decks again.

Ben Butler, sailor, politician, and entrepreneur, speaking to America, *the racing yacht for which the America's Cup is named*

Health, south wind, books, old trees, a boat, a friend.

Ralph Waldo Emerson, writer

Her maker had warned me that he would not warrant her for an hour. "She may go to pieces like an eggshell," he said. He builded better than he knew.

George W. Sears, outdoorsman and journalist, about the Sairy Gamp, *a canoe that traveled thousands of miles in the Adirondacks, built by J. Henry Rushton*

It has a picture of a tomato on the front, a mean vicious tomato with blood running from its fangs. It has green vines for hands and they are wrapped around the lighthouse at Cape Hatteras.

Hans Meijer, sailor, who previously had bad luck sailing off of Cape Hatteras

I ought to desist from crusty sailing man's thoughts about "stinkpots." I should try and see such craft not as gas-guzzling noisemakers but as potential nice guys who someday may pull me off a shoal to tow me into harbor when my mast falls down.

Anthony Bailey, writer and sailing enthusiast, about motorboats

It's those dishonest little things, skinned-out hulls to save weight, that can't take it . . . Designers have to change the emphasis from speed to safety.

Ted Turner, yachtsman, baseball owner, about yacht design after the 1979 Fastnet Race

Men who own the biggest boats are always thinking about records.

Roger Vaughn, sailor and writer

Sailing people who live in houses often envy those who live on boats. But those who dwell afloat all year round miss one great thing: the annual pleasure of throwing off a land-based existence in exchange (however briefly) for a seagoing life that will rock them with different demand and buoy them up with different delights.

Anthony Bailey, writer and sailing enthusiast

The lowly skiff might well be called the universal boat.

Edwin Monk, sailor, boat builder, and writer

There is a certain fascination about boat building, in watching a boat gradually take shape, and this particularly so when the results are your own efforts.

Edwin Monk, sailor, boat builder, and writer

There is nothing—absolutely nothing—half so much worth doing as simply messing around in boats.

Kenneth Grahame, writer

The old working craft in which modern sailing craft have their origins have virtually disappeared from the ports of the developed nations.

Bob Bond, sailor, instructor, and writer

Tracing the lines of boats is like tracing the lines of songs. It's a matter of influence. A sheer line or bow profile is transposed, and transformed, personalized and made original.

Douglas Whiynott, writer and sailor

You build someone a boat, and the people who own it become your friends, and they often remain friends for years. You take that away and boatbuilding can be a kind of joyless thing.

Eric Dow, boat builder

Bob Hope

(b. May 29, 1903) *Comedian, movie star*

Never before has anyone swung with so much for so little.

attributed to Winston Churchill about Bob Hope's golf swing, during a charity golf event during World War II

Bodybuilding

Don't get sand kicked in your face.
Charles Atlas (also known as Angelo Siciliano),
bodybuilder, from an ad for his
bodybuilding regimens.

Form is very important. Anyone can go into the gym and lift a weight. The trick is using the proper form to make your muscles give you the results you want.
Sharon Bruneau, champion bodybuilder

I built my American dream one rep at a time.
Bob Paris, champion bodybuilder

Nice business, isn't it, professional bodybuilding? More pimps and whores than Hollywood.
Steve Machalik, world champion bodybuilder

Physically I don't finish a set until I literally can't work the fatigued muscle any longer. I more or less continue until the barbell actually drops from my momentarily paralyzed fingers.
Tom Platz, world champion bodybuilder

Sport or not, bodybuilding as an art, as a science, as a lifestyle, and as a form of entertainment is here to stay.
Fredrick C. Hatfield, writer

The guiding axiom in competitive bodybuilding is "no pain, no gain." As a result, elite bodybuilders frequently joke about being participants in "the sport of masochists."
Bill Reynolds, weightlifting editor and writer

Whatever else I do, I want to always be a kind of ambassador, a preacher for bodybuilding.
Arnold Schwarzenegger, champion
bodybuilder and actor

Whatever it is you do in life, you can never grow in self-esteem unless you get good and pumped first and stay that way. Any time you spend without a pump is time you can never get back again.
Franco Columbo, champion bodybuilder

World governed by a savage force that swallowed me whole from a bookstore in New York City, and did not relent until it had chewed me up and spit me out 80 pounds heavier and 3,000 miles later on a posing dais in Burbank, California. I was swabbed in posing oil and competition color, flexing with all my might, when I came to, a sadder and wiser man.
Samuel Wilson Fussell, bodybuilder

You just haven't lived until you try doing 4 to 6 sets of 100 reps in various quadriceps and hamstring excercises.
Diana Dennis, champion bodybuilder

Books

A major distinction between the athlete of today and those of yesteryear is that the old jocks rarely read books. Today, some even write them.

Howard Cosell, broadcaster

First things first: I can read my own book.
Dexter Manley, professional football player

I haven't read it yet.
Johnny Unitas, Hall of Fame football
player, on his biography

It is all true. But I wish he had come to me. I would tell him so much more.
Primo Carnera, referring to Budd Schulberg's
roman à clef The Harder They Fall, *a novel*
based on Carnera's life

I should've read it.

Charles Barkley, professional basketball player,
All-Star, author

I've dug ditches, lubed jackhammers and manned the graveyard shift at a 7-Eleven. But the worst job I ever had was writing Wayne Gretzky's autobiography.

Rick Reilly, sportswriter, commenting on
Gretzky's reluctance to talk about himself

Three years ago I couldn't spell author. Now I are one.

Don Cherry, professional hockey player

Bowling

One of the advantages bowling has over golf is that you seldom lose a bowling ball.

Don Carter, champion bowler

I'm just tickled to death to get out of the house.

Carl Koch, 100-year-old bowler
who bowled a 199

Good bowling involves repetition.

Mike Aubrey, champion professional bowler

This is the secret of bowling strikes! SQUEEZE the ball at the point of explosion.

Dawson Taylor, champion professional
and amateur bowler

Bowls

There's plenty of time to win this game, and to thrash the Spaniards too.

Sir Francis Drake, admiral and navigator, who
insisted he finish his game of bowls before
fighting the Spanish navy

Boxers

A boxer knocked down is the loneliest guy in the world.

Gene Tunney, champion boxer

A boxer requires a *nob* as well as a statesman does a *head*, coolness and calculation being essential to his second efforts.

Heywood Broun, writer

Boxers, bullfighters and soldiers contract syphilis for the same reasons that make them choose their professions. In boxing most sudden reversals of form, the majority of cases of what is called punch drunkness, of "walking on the heels," are products of syphilis. You cannot name the individuals in a book because it is libelous, but any one in the profession will tell you of a dozen recent cases.

Ernest Hemingway,
Nobel Prize–winnning author

But one thing remains. Jeffries must emerge from his alfalfa farm and remove that smile from Johnson's face. Jeff, it's up to you!

Jack London, rooting for Jim Jeffries, former
heavyweight champion and commonly known
"then" as the "Great White Hope," who lost to
Jack Johnson, the champion. Afterward, London
wrote: "Once again has Johnson sent down to
defeat the chosen representative of the white
race. . . ."

Dempsey was alone and Tunney could never explain himself and Sharkey could never believe himself nor Schmeling nor Braddock, and Carnera was sad and Baer an indecipherable clown; great heavyweights like Louis had the loneliness of the ages in their silence, and men like Marciano were mystified by a power which seemed to have been granted them.

Norman Mailer, Pulitzer Prize–winning writer

Durante in boxing shorts.

Jim Murray, sportswriter and writer, about Luis Rodriguez, boxer

Hardly a blow had been struck when I knew I was Jeff's Master.

Jack Johnson, champion boxer, about the famous Jack Johnson vs. Jim Jeffries match

He was gauche and inaccurate, but terribly persistent.

Heywood Broun, writer, about a forgettable match

He works in the daytime at odd jobs, but what he wants is to walk down the street in the slum where he lives and have the people on the stoops and the guys on the corner recognize him as a man who is a prize fighter. He walks by them sharp in his zoot suit, the satchel in his hand, and they say, "There goes the fighter," and that is his reward.

Jimmy Cannon, sportswriter

I am a fighter who walks, talks, and thinks fighting, but I try not to look like it.

Marvelous Marvin Hagler, champion boxer

I don't want to knock my opponent out. I want to hit him, step away, and watch him hurt.

Joe Frazier, champion boxer

I can't be a poet. I can't tell stories.

Barry McGuigan, professional boxer, when asked why he was a boxer

I haven't got long to go, and I want my family to be around me, happy, on one more Christmas. I won't be here for another. Please, Jack, I want to fight.

Billy Miske, professional boxer, to a boxing promoter; the dying boxer was begging for a fight so that he could buy presents for his family

If fighting is your business, fight!

Grantland Rice, sportswriter

I got into this business, because I got tired of beating up people for free.

Larry Holmes, world champion boxer

I know a good thing when I see it. Fighting is a good thing. It is like gold in that it is found in a nugget cluster of baser metals often buried in the mud.

Budd Schulberg, writer and screenwriter

I'm not boxing anymore. I'm going back to fighting the old-school way. I'm going to walk through guys and destroy them.

Oscar De La Hoya, champion boxer

I was never knocked out. I've been unconscious, but it's always been on my feet.

Floyd Patterson, champion boxer

I was one of the those hungry fighters. You could have hit me on the chin with a sledgehammer for five dollars. When you haven't eaten for two days you'll understand.

Jack Dempsey, champion boxer

Like a dancer, a boxer "is" his body, and is totally identified with it.

Joyce Carol Oates, writer and boxing aficionado

Old fighters react to training the way beautiful women react to scrubbing floors.

Norman Mailer, Pulitzer Prize–winning writer

Prizefighters often are a rough, surly group of men. They use boxing to release rage.

Seth Abraham, HBO executive

So far as the boxing game is concerned the contest next Monday is well named "the fight of the century." These two men, in a class by themselves so far as other fighters go, yet so radically different from each other as to have no salient characteristics in common.

Jack London, author and outdoorsman, writing about the Jack Johnson and Jim Jeffries fight

Someday they're gonna write a blues song just for fighters. It'll be for slow guitar, soft trumpet and a bell.

Sonny Liston, world champion boxer

The closer a heavyweight somes to the championship, the more natural it is for him to be a little bit insane, secretly insane, for the heavyweight champion of the world is either the toughest man in the world or he is not, but there is a great deal of possibility he is. It is like being the big toe of God.

Norman Mailer, Pulitzer Prize—winning writer

Theirs is a lonely sport, at time ugly, brutal, naked. You have to get inside a ring to appreciate how small it is. You wonder how men can ever escape.

Howard Cosell, broadcaster

The uninitiated, the cultivated, the educated don't accept that boxing has existed since pre-Hellenic Greece, and possibly since the time of the pharoahs, because it concedes one musky truth about masculinity: hitting a man is sometimes the most satisfying response to *being* a man. Disturbing, maybe, but there it is.

J. R. Moehringer, sportswriter

The most symbolic battles are no longer, as in the old days of Jack Johnson, Joe Louis, and Ray Robinson, white versus black, nor, as in the sixties and seventies with Muhammad Ali, Joe Frazier, and Ken Norton, black versus black, but rather black versus Latin. No fight could have more appropriately opened the era of the eighties in boxing than the first Sugar Ray Leonard versus Roberto Duran bout.

Gerald Early, sportswriter

They all have their entourages. Every lawyer, every accountant, every hustler is hanging around.

Lou Duva, Hall of Fame boxing trainer

What do you know about prize-fighting, for Christ's sweet sake?

Ernest Hemingway, writer and outdoorsman, to Budd Schulberg, writer and screenwriter, both boxing aficionados

When I see blood, I become a bull.

Marvelous Marvin Hagler, champion boxer

Boxing

After a round of dancing and jabbing, he was hit in the face with a wet sponge. He was rubbed, patted, squeezed and kneaded. Cold water was poured into his trunks. He was harangued, he was reprimanded, and he listened to nothing at all.

Leonard Gardner, novelist, from Fat City

As a younger fighter I was just a boxer. But now my main strength is starting to come. I can tell when I hit someone.

Ricardo Williams, Jr., professional boxer

Benny's an awful smart boxer. All the time he's in there, he's thinking. All the time he's thinking, I was hitting him.

Jack Britton, champion boxer, replying to a question how he beat his opponent Benny Leonard

Boxing is the sport to which all other sports aspire.

George Foreman, champion boxer

Boxing gave Liston an opportunity to meet bigtime hoodlums instead of small time ones.

Attributed to a police officer by Jimmy Cannon, sportswriter

'Cause the referee counted 11.

Gene Fullmer, professional boxer, recounting what his manager replied when he asked why his fight with Sugar Ray Robinson had been stopped; he had been knocked out

Did you keep your chin down?

Cus D'Amato, Hall of Fame boxing trainer, to Jose Torres, champion boxer, who called the trainer after he had been arrested for a street fight

Each boxing match is a story—a unique and highly condensed drama without words.

Joyce Carol Oates, writer

Every talent must unfold itself in fighting.

Friedrich Nietzsche, philosopher

Fighting is the only racket where you're almost guaranteed to end up as a bum.

Rocky Graziano, champion boxer

Float like a butterfly, sting like a bee.

Muhammad Ali, champion boxer

I just knocked him down and that ended the boxing for the night.

Hugh Casey, professional baseball player, about Ernest Hemingway, author and sportsman, during a sparring match

I'll moider da bum.

Tony Galento, heavyweight boxer, when asked what he thought of William Shakespeare

The hardest thing about Prize Fighting is picking up your teeth with a boxing glove on.

Kin Hubbard, humorist and author

The heavyweight championship is, after all, a fairly squalid office.

Murray Kempton, writer

He hits you in the belly and it's like someone stuck you with a hot poker, and left it there.

Billy Soose, professional boxer, about Tony Zale

Honey, I forgot to duck.

Jack Dempsey, champion boxer, to his wife, after losing to Gene Tunney

Hurting people is my business.

Sugar Ray Robinson, champion boxer

It's a terrible sport, but it's a sport . . . the fight for survival is the fight.

Rocky Graziano, champion boxer

It's more important to be a fighter than a sideshow.

Lou DiBella, HBO boxing promoter

I wanted to hit him one more time in the nose so that bone could go right up into his brain.

Mike Tyson, champion boxer, speaking about his fight with Jesse Ferguson

I zigged when I should have zagged.

Jack Ropes, professional boxer

Looking at a fighter who can't punch is like kissing your mother-in-law.

Jack Hurley, boxing promoter

Man, this is a fight, not a rumble.

Evander Holyfield, champion boxer, to Mike Tyson, champion boxer, after the latter bit off part of the former's ear

My toughest fight was with my first wife.

Muhammad Ali, champion boxer

Nobody's marketing minivans to boxing moms, not yet, but it does seem that the sport has become a little more suburban than we remember it.

Richard Hoffer, sportswriter

No dentist ever advised his patient to have his teeth removed by force. So you're not allowed to go into the ring without a mouthpiece. Of course, you become toothless with a mouthpiece, but you usually lose them one at a time.

Jimmy Cannon, sportswriter

Only in boxing do you have that ritual, of two men, nearly naked, exhausted, the smell and taste of each other, after such serious battle, the strange intimacy of that.

Gay Talese, writer

The air was a stink of blueness, sharp with the heat of bodies, and with the weight of puddle beer drying into boards that never knew soap and water, and soured with tobacco spit. Black and gray they huddled on the benches, the sportsmen, with their faces red in rows, regular as match heads, one behind the other, every mouth wide, every eye wild, and there voices mixed in a thickness of sound, an untidiness of raw tone without good thought or sense.

Richard Llewellyn, novelist, from How Green Was My Valley

The bigger they come the harder they fall.

Bob Fitzsimmons, boxer

Boxing has been infested with corruption and gangsterism from the day it began, yet it engages our basic emotions like no other athletic activity.

Howard Cosell, broadcaster

The English scribes were rather indelicate in their descriptions of the contest, implying that both fights were as rehearsed as a Shakespearean play.

Jack Sher referring to two fights between Primo Carnera and Young Stribling

A fight, a piece of writing, a painting or a passage of music is nothing without emotion.

W.C. Heinz, sportswriter, to Floyd Patterson, champion boxer

Sorry? Are you kidding? Boxers are never sorry.

Carmen Basilio, professional boxer

There is a quality about boxing that attaches to no other sport. Well, maybe not boxing; maybe the men who fight, rather than the science itself. They are the most interesting of all athletes, for they seem to have the deepest feelings about life.

Howard Cosell, broadcaster

They are the time-killers, the guys fighting as you come down the aisle to your seat. They are only half seen in their small moments of triumph, and their disgraces are vaguely remembered, like a joke told very late at night when everyone is drunk.

Jimmy Cannon, sportswriter

Bradley, Bill

(b. July 28, 1942) *Olympic Gold Medalist; won two National Basketball Association titles; former U.S. senator*

He dislikes flamboyance, and unlike some of basketball's greatest stars, has apparently never made a move merely to attract attention. While some players are eccentric in their shooting, his shots, with only occasional exceptions, are straightforward and unexaggerated.

John McFee, writer

British Open

Well, you know what they say. The opera is generally not finished until the large woman begins singing.

misquote of Jack Nicklaus at the 1984 British Open, in a statement released by British Open officials

Broadcasters

Like Odysseus at sea, I was drawn by a voice, and I sail in direction of that voice. In other words, I go with Tim McCarver.

Bill Scheft, writer

One of the joys of baseball is the comfort of seeing a familiar face in the booth, and the smugness of feeling superior to that guy.

Bill Scheft, writer

The federal government in all its majesty is worried that sports broadcasters do sinister things, like rooting for the home team.

George Will, writer and part owner of the Chicago Cubs

He could go all the way!

Chris Berman, broadcaster, his signature call, which is an homage to the late Howard Cosell

Let's go to the videotape!

Warner Wolf, sports broadcaster

You could be a thief, a murderer, a gangster, you could run over your wife with your car in the driveway, but you carry around a briefcase and that stock portfolio, and the announcers can't do anything but swoon over you and sing your praises.

Art "Fatso" Donovan, Hall of Fame football player

Broadcasting

The beauty of radio was that you could add color to the game, and be dramatic, and sometimes be over dramatic and build it up . . . You could put all the drama you cared to into a no-hitter, Brock stealing a base, or whatever.

Jack Buck, broadcaster

All you're going to do on radio is talk.

Julius Israel, father of Mel Allen, broadcaster, who was against his son becoming a broadcaster

I don't understand what kind of damn radio that can be if you can't get a score of a ball game on it.

Harry Caray, broadcaster, to a taxi driver who only had a dispatch radio in his cab

If I was this big an asshole when I was playing, shoot me right now.

Jimmy Connors, tennis champion and broadcaster, trying to get interviews at a tennis match

I got nothing better to do that pays me so much.

Don Meredith, professional football player and broadcaster

I like radio better than television because if you make a mistake on radio, they don't know. You can make up anything on the radio.

Phil Rizzuto, professional baseball player and broadcaster

I never understood the value to your broadcasts because I never got to listen, but now I've got to tell you that the one thing that keeps me going is hearing your broadcast.

Lou Gehrig, Hall of Fame baseball player, to Mel Allen, broadcaster, after Gehrig had taken ill and retired from baseball

If I knew what was going through Jack Nicklaus' head, I would have won this tournament.

Tom Weiskopf, champion professional golfer, after being asked on national television what Nicklaus was thinking as he prepared to tee off on the 16th fairway in the final round, as he was driving to win his sixth green jacket at the Masters in 1986; Weiskopf was a runner-up

I think I'll take another bite of my coffee.

Frank Gifford, Hall of Fame football player, broadcaster, while announcing the famous Ice Bowl game

Goooal!

Andres Cantor, broadcaster

People ask me, do you like broadcasting games? And I say, "Yeah, but it's not as good as playing. It's like methadone to a heroin addict."

Tim Green, National Football League player turned broadcaster and writer

You're the professional announcer. I'm just a washed-up, out-of-shape ex-fighter.

Rocky Marciano, world champion boxer, to Howard Cosell, broadcaster

Brushbacks

If the on-deck batter is standing too close to home plate, you brush him back.

Brent Kemnitz, coach of Witchita State, who was suspended for the rest of the season, after one of his pitchers ended the career of an on-deck batter after beaning him

I wouldn't throw at her, but I might brush her back.

Johnny Allen, professional baseball player (pitcher) to Doc Cramer, who said to Allen that he would throw at his own mother

When I came to, I didn't remember anything. After Jeffcoat hit me in the face doctors examined me and said, "What have you got in there?"

Don Zimmer, professional baseball player and manager, about being beaned

Within that unwritten brushback and beanball code, there is a vague by-law: an opposing pitcher cannot be allowed to constantly hit your guys, intentional or not, without being answered; an opposing pitcher should always be held to a high standard of care when projecting a baseball, lest he injure one of your guys.

Buster Olney, sportswriter

Bullfighting

Bullfighting is the only art in which the artist is in much danger of death and in which the degree of brilliance in the performance is left to the fighter's honor.

Ernest Hemingway,
Nobel Prize–winning author

The bull is stronger, but the matador is smarter.

Muhammad Ali, world champion boxer

It is a decadent art in every way and like most decadent things it reaches its fullest flower at its rottenest point.

Ernest Hemingway, Nobel Prize–winning author

I've never seen a corrida where I didn't feel the need to cheer the death of the bull. There's relief on behalf of the matador—that the guy hasn't had his innards unzipped—and you feel an intensely visceral release from a spectacle that combines athletics with blood, blades and mortal danger.

Tony Hendra, writer and humorist

The sexuality of the bullring isn't something aficionados talk about much, perhaps because, from Homer to Hemingway, bulls have tended to be a guy thing. There are few more potent symbols of machismo than a fellow in spangled tights facing down what Tom Lehrer once called "a half-ton of angry pot roast"—and it's a very serious business.

Tony Hendra, writer and humorist

Business

Baseball is too much of a sport to be called a business, and too much of a business to be called a sport.

Philip K. Wrigley, baseball owner

I'd just like to say hello to my attorney, my business partner, my ancillary adviser, my theatrical agent and my publisher. Hi, boys. We're doing fine.

Steve Cady, sportswriter, proposing what athletes panned by the camera on the sidelines should say instead of "Hi, Mom!"

I don't look on football as a career. It's a stepping stone. I know too many ballplayers who were lost when opportunity didn't knock on their door.

Frenchy Fuqua, professional football player

If I could make more money running a supermarket, I'd run a supermarket. My best thing is driving cars . . . It's a business, like any other business.

Richard Petty, champion race car driver

In my time, it was the army generals running Brazil who tried to pick the team. Today, it's the sponsors, the businessmen, the media moguls. The World Cup Finals is the world's biggest TV show.

Carlos Alberto Perreira, champion soccer manager

It's what it aims to be. It's a show. The pros are in the entertainment business.

Red Blaik, champion college football coach

Our main goal is to get people to spend their disposable income with properties associated with the company, whether they're our theme parks, videos, movies or our sports teams. If you've got a dollar, we want it.

Tony Tavares, executive at Disney, which owns several sports franchises

Murdoch and Fox changed the economics of sports when they took football away from CBS.

Robert M. Gutkowski, sports marketing executive

The Champagne has been chilling so long it has frostbite.

Timothy W. Smith, New York Times writer, commenting on the length of negotiations between Evander Holyfield and Lenox Lewis for a unification bout of the heavyweight division

The sports hero must always be on top. If he goes down, he becomes a loser. I quit when I was on top, and the business opportunities came.

Jean-Claude Killy, world champion skier

This is an obit, which is short for obituary. An obit tells of a person who has died, how he lived, and of those who lived after him. This is the obit on the Brooklyn Dodgers.

Dick Young, sportswriter

I'm for sale!

Martina Hingis, women's tennis player, on reaching superstardom and cashing in

These days you have to be a utility player: if you do only one thing, you're not sellable; you have to be able to sing *and* dance.

Joe Favorito, Women's Tennis Association executive

We're still trying to develop a product for him. What we like is that he's a positive role model, reflects a positive image. He's unique.

Michael Jordan, professional basketball player, referring to signing Derek Jeter, professional baseball player, to an Nike Air Jordan contract

When you look at Michael Jordan the business man, you see someone who has cultivated relationships with companies over a long period of time. He has met with their chairmen and has golfed with them, socialized with them and has spent time with them. And he has learned a lot.

Pat Riley, professional basketball player and coach

You can be sold, traded or released at will. You are carried on the books as a depreciable capital asset and exist like a piece of chattal.

Rick Sortun, professional football player

I don't think anyone, unless they're very peculiar, has a relationship with a toothpaste brand. You tell someone to come for a pint and a pie and talk about their team, and they'll knock your door down.

> Peter Draper, group marketing director for Manchester United, comparing brand loyalty to sports loyalties

"Meet me in the garage and take what you want for yourselves," I said to the workmen. They were astonished at what they found there: big piles of bats, balls, gloves, caps, jogging suits, sportswear, tennis rackets, shoes . . . The men looked a little overwhelmed; I guessed they'd never read about this sort of thing in the sports pages.

> Cyndy Garvey, ex-wife of professional baseball player Steve Garvey

Prices are touching the stars!

> Vittorio Cecchi Gori, president, Fiorentina professional soccer club

Butterflies

Anyone here have butterflies?

> Ralph Branca, professional baseball player, to Pee Wee Reese and Jackie Robinson, after being brought in to pitch against Bobby Thompson in the bottom of the ninth, for the pennant

As a professional competitor, I believe that you should have some butterflies and healthy tension before you go out to the mound. You may risk staleness or flatness in your pitching if the adrenaline is not flowing.

> Tom Seaver, Hall of Fame baseball player

I get a few butterflies right when they are introducing our names, but when they throw the ball up, I'm out there playing, and it doesn't matter who it's against.

> Jason Williams, professional basketball player

I think we all get butterflies before we race. I know I did before each of the 176 Grand Prix I competed in.

> Graham Hill, champion race car driver

I was a little nervous out there. It was like any opening day. I don't care how long you played—you always get a little nervous.

> Yogi Berra, Hall of Fame baseball player and manager

Karas always has been ready on Sundays, keyed up so intensely that he vomits just before kickoff time.

> Myron Cope, sportswriter

No matter how long you have been playing, you still get butterflies before the big ones.

> Pee Wee Reese, Hall of Fame baseball player

Some of us shake on the outside, some of us on the inside.

> Roberto Clemente, Hall of Fame baseball player

Tighter than a bullfighter's pants.

> Tommy Holmes, sportswriter, writing about Duke Snider in his first World Series appearance

What's bigger than butterflies? A buzzard? I had a buzzard in my stomach.

> Allen Iverson, professional basketball player

Button, Dick

(b. July 18, 1929) *Two-time Olympic gold medalist figure skater; five-time World Champion; award-winning broadcaster*

Dick Button introduced real athletics in the form of "barrier" high jumps into skating. The strength and virility of his performance simply crashed into the sober circles of the ice world and staged for a moment their conventional ideals . . . He gave to skating its own *raison d'être*.

Nigel Brown, writer and ice skating historian

C

Camping

Thank Heaven there are a few green spots on this green earth that it does not pay to "improve," but they are remote.

George W. Sears, outdoorsman and journalist

The blessed calm of lonely places, where the bright-eyed, wary wood folk come almost to your feet as you sit quietly . . . where the arch rascal man does not intrude; where one may camp for months without seeing a human face or hearing the buzz of civilized racket.

George W. Sears, outdoorsman and journalist

There is a sort of freemasonry among woodsmen that only woodsmen know.

George W. Sears, outdoorsman and journalist

Canoeing

A paddle is a very personal tool.

Robert Kimber, outdoorsman and writer

Canoe races and high-powered whitewater paddling are all well and good. But for me,

what canoeing is really all about is getting out into the big, wild country with a fly rod and some good friends along for the company.

Robert Kimber, outdoorsman and writer

I hope at no distant day to meet independent canoeists, with canoes weighing twenty pounds or less, at every turn in the wilderness, and with no more duffle than is absolutely necessary.

George W. Sears, outdoorsman and journalist

Some people buy these boats and never put them in the water, just keep them in the living room like a work of art.

Mike Faunce, maker of Old Town Canoes

They hardly knew which to admire more, the little craft or the reckless (!) woodsman who would risk his life in such an eggshell.

J. Henry Rushton, canoe builder, about George W. Sears and the canoe he built him, the Sairy Gamp

Toward the end of every long carry, a canoeist strains to spot the glint of water or

the thinning of the canopy that marks the end of the trail.
Christine Jerome, outdoorswoman and journalist

Waterproof bags tend to either be dependable and awkward to use or undependable and easy to use.
Cliff Jacobson, outdoorsman and writer

Career

Having a long NFL career is an accomplishment in itself.
Joe Montana, Hall of Fame professional football player

I guess if I had to describe my career, I'd have to say it's been one of turmoil and happiness.
Richard Neal, professional football player

I wanted to play shortstop for the Yankees. When I would say that in class, teachers would tell my dad that maybe I should think about other careers as well. But it's worked out OK.
Derek Jeter, professional baseball player

It wasn't a career. What it was, was joy and pain, thunder and sunbursts, mountains to climb, rivers to cross and odds to defy.
Jerry Izenberg, sportswriter, about Julie Krone, jockey

Mr. Rodgers, why don't you concentrate more on your vocation rather than your avocation.
the school principal, to Bill Rodgers, champion marathoner, at the school where Rodgers taught for a living

The frightening thing about playing professional football is that it gives you a sense of security. The trouble is that a player enters football when he's about twenty-one. Barring an injury which obviously puts him out earlier, he has a career of ten to fifteen years during which he advances his education only in football.
John Gordy, professional football player

Catcher

A good catcher is the quarterback, the carburetor, the lead dog, the pulse taker, the traffic cop, and sometimes a lot of unprintable things. But no team gets very far without one.
Miller Huggins, champion professional baseball coach

Cell Phones

Using one is disrespectful to other players. Any time you get a chance to talk, you should be talking to other players about baseball.
James Baldwin, professional baseball player, about the banning of cell phones in the White Sox clubhouse

Challenge

Don't catch me after one night.
Pete Rose, professional baseball player, to Tony Gwynn, professional baseball player, both of whom got more than 3,000 hits, after Gwynn got his first major league hit

Hit Sign, Win Suit
Abe Stark, tailor, businessman, politician, from a sign he installed in right field at Ebbetts Field at the base of the scoreboard

I like the challenge. I like the idea of being on more or less even footing with the game. Against my advantages of better eyesight, a rifle, and—I hope—a better mind, the deer match their superior senses of smell and hearing, their intimate knowledge of the cover, and their wonderful alertness.

Ted Trueblood, outdoorsman, editor, and writer

I've never really turned away from a challenge in my career. You can't ever be afraid to do something.

Mike Piazza, All-Star professional baseball player

The idea of such a big challenge intrigued me.

Tom Landry, Hall of Fame football coach, speaking about starting the Dallas Cowboys from scratch in the well-established National Football League

Champions

A champion is one who gets up when he can't see.

Jack Dempsey, champion boxer

A champion is someone who can't settle for second best.

Warren Spahn, Hall of Fame baseball player

A winner never whines.

Paul Brown, champion professional football coach

He's got to improve himself, just like anybody else.

Joe DiMaggio, Hall of Fame baseball player

If you're going to be a champion, you must be willing to pay a greater price than your opponent.

Bud Wilkinson, coach

It's a cockiness really. To be a champion you got to believe so much in yourself you're cocky. You're always trying to play it down, trying not to let your cockiness show, but sometimes it'll show.

Bill White, professional baseball player and American League president

It sounds trite, but I think one must have a reason for being a champion. With most people the reason is a hunger—a hunger for financial gain or a hunger for glory.

Vince Lombardi, Hall of Fame football coach

I would rather be number one and not making any money than number four and making millions.

Pauline Betz, professional tennis champion

Keep your head up; act like a champion.

Paul "Bear" Bryant, Hall of Fame college football coach

Look like a winner and act like a champ all the time. If you win, be gracious. Keep your head on.

James Francis "Jumbo" Elliott, champion track and field coach

Meet the new champ.

Eddie Arcaro, Hall of Fame jockey, introducing rookie jockey Willie Shoemaker, Hall of Fame jockey

My Triple Crown season would have meant nothing, it would have been a waste, unless we got the world championship back.

Mickey Mantle, Hall of Fame baseball player

No team wins the championship holding its breath.

Harvey Araton, sportswriter

Several times I have been threatened with overthrow by phenomenals. On one or two occasions it has been whispered around in such a way as to reach my ears, that importations have been made and it was good-bye to Shrubb. These importations have once or twice materialized. Like deer they would run for a distance and keep me guessing. All of a sudden they would disappear and I, smilingly relieved, would trudge on alone.

Alfred Shrubb, champion runner

Skill alone does not make the champion.

John Devaney, sportswriter, What Makes a Champion?

If you are going to be a champion, you must be willing to pay a greater price than your opponent.

Bud Wilkinson, professional football coach

If you win a championship, you got to go out there next year and prove you're still a champion.

Sam Huff, Hall of Fame football player

I remember when we got our rings . . . I flew out to California after that season and gave it to my father. I didn't need it to prove anything anymore.

Bud Harrelson, professional baseball player

One day we were the laughingstock of baseball, and the next we were champions.

Ed Kranepool, professional baseball player, referring to the 1969 Miracle Mets

There is only a half step difference between the champions and those who finish on the bottom. And much of that half step is mental.

Tom Landry, Hall of Fame football coach

What creates champions is, first, the decision to stay in the sport and work hard. Perhaps nothing more heroic may be involved in this decision than habit, boredom or commitments to friends.

Daniel F. Chambliss, swimming coach and writer

Winning back-to-back championships is tougher than anything because you've got to sustain, and stave off complacency.

Michael Jordan, All-Star professional basketball player

Winning the NBA title is about will, luck, and understanding the *other* guy's game.

Spike Lee, writer, actor, director

You don't get there on natural ability alone. A lot of people are born with natural ability, but few of them become champions.

Chuck McKinley, tennis champion

Championships

After twenty-one years in the major leagues, I still can't recall a game won in extra innings on a botched squeeze play that'd be replayed more times than the Zapruder film.

Durwood Merrill, umpire, after the 1997 American League Championship Series between Cleveland and Baltimore

Every championship, by definition, is historic.

George Vecsey, sportswriter

Finals are about winning or losing; any entertainment that ensues is a welcome side-product which cannot be guaranteed.

David Lacey, sportswriter

I'm not going to tell you what it is that allows you to win at this level. You're going to have to learn it yourself.

Ervin "Magic" Johnson, Hall of Fame basketball player, to Isiah Thomas, professional basketball player, executive, and coach

I played the tour in 1967 and told jokes and nobody laughed. Then I won the Open the next year, told the same jokes, and everybody laughed like hell.

Lee Trevino, champion professional golfer

One gold medal in a championship is ordinary. I wanted to get two golds and be a little different.

Haile Gebreselassie, world champion runner

This is a division championship game. The players will play. You know it's not like there's a dance after the game that we're waiting for, and if there is, I don't have anybody to take. Maybe I'll call Kathleen Turner.

Bill Parcells, professional football coach, responding to a reporter's question about which players would play

To win a championship you've got to do it throughout the whole year.

Jeff Gordon, champion race car driver

When you have a championship team, you have things built into your arsenal to deal with problems.

Greg Ray, race car driver

Winning a championship, even for the stars, is like a stamp of approval. It gives them the feeling that, "Now, I have done it."

Doug Collins, professional basketball coach

Winning the world championship catapulted me to the top. Not only did I make headlines but I was even mentioned in the United States.

Greg LeMond, champion cyclist

You cannot take a seven and win—anytime—during seventy-two holes of title play.

Gene Sarazen, champion golfer

Character

The Battle of Waterloo was won on the playing fields of Eton.

Duke of Wellington, British general and prime minister

As Duke Ellington once said, the Battle of Waterloo was won on the playing fields of Elkton.

Babe Ruth, Hall of Fame baseball player, misquoting the Duke of Wellington

Football doesn't build character. It eliminates the weak ones.

Darrell Royal, National Football League player

My father always told me in the midst of adversity, in the midst of a struggle, "It builds character. Stay strong, be positive, look ahead, don't look back."

Bruce Smith, All-Pro professional football player

Our struggles against aggressors throughout our history have been won on the play-

...ds and corner lots and fields of America.

John Fitzgerald Kennedy, president of the United States

Sport develops not character, but characters.

James A. Michener, Pulitzer Prize–winning author

Sport: If you want to build character, then try something else.

Thomas Tutko, writer

There will never be a day when we won't need dedication, discipline, energy and the feeling that we can change things for the better.

George Sheehan, runner and writer

You don't build character without somebody slapping you around.

Vince Lombardi, Hall of Fame football coach

You have to suck it up, do what you have to do for the team to win.

Patrick Ewing, professional basketball player, about playing hurt

Charisma

Charisma is winning major championships.

Tom Watson, champion professional golfer

Chatter

Mr. Durocher just told me not to talk to you.

Willie Mays, Hall of Fame baseball player, to Roy Campanella, Hall of Fame baseball player, in Mays's rookie year, because Campanella's chatter interfered with Mays's concentration

Cheap Shots

They'll only warn you the first time.

Jack Dempsey, champion boxer, speaking about how you can throw one or two in a fight without being disqualified or losing points

Cheating

Cheating in baseball is just like hot dogs, french fries, and cold Cokes.

Billy Martin, professional baseball player and manager

It's in the mindset of players and managers to cheat whenever they get a chance. They believe it is the equivalent of their First Amendment right in baseball to cheat.

Durwood Merrill, umpire

Chemistry

Chemistry is bullshit. I'll tell you what gives you good chemistry: winning. Losing gives you bad chemistry.

Mike Piazza, professional baseball player

Climbing

A climb is the most human relationship possible with a mountain face.

Harold Drasdo, mountain climber

A couple of years ago I had met a rather unsavory character . . . As our acquaintance dragged on, I discovered that we had much in common. For one thing we were both rather lazy . . . an important quality of the serious climber.

Warren Harding, mountain climber

A day well spent in the Alps is like some great symphony.

George Leigh Mallory, alpinist

A slip was not to be thought of; steadiness was essential.

R.L.G. Irving, mountain climber

A tendency to indulgence, whether in food, mountains, or liquor has, happily, always been a feature of the members of our Club.

Malcolm Slesser, mountain climber

Because it is there.

George Leigh Mallory, alpinist, answering the question, "Why do you climb Everest?"

Because I'm grumpy when I'm *not* climbing.

Doug Scott, climber, when asked why he climbed

Bonatti removed any chances of glory for anyone when he walked all over it by himself in one weekend.

Mick Burke, mountain climber, referring to the feat of climbing Mt. Blanc solo in one weekend by Walter Bonatti, alpinist

Climbers spend money and accept trouble to climb the mountain. They go home and five months later they are thinking about it again. This is the sickness of the alpinist.

Cesar Morales Arnao, climber

Climbing above 8,000 meters . . . any mistake is amplified in rarified air . . . a swallow of hot tea from a Thermos is the difference between life and death.

Anatoli Boukreev, climber and guide

Climbing is a drug, and I need a fix.

Dick Shockley, mountain climber

Climbing is all about facing problems; the better the problems, the more memorable the climb.

Anthony Greenbank, climber and writer

Climbing is more an art than it is a sport.

William A. Read, climber

Climbing would be a great, truly wonderful thing if it weren't for all that damn climbing.

John Ohrenschall, mountain climber

Climb the mountains and enjoy their good tidings. Nature's peace will flow into you as sunshine into flowers. Streams will bring you their freshness and storms their energy, and cares will fall off like autumn leaves.

John Muir, outdoorsman and philosopher

Everest was not mine alone, the highest point on earth, unattainable, foreign to all experience, was there for many boys and grown men to aspire toward.

Thomas F. Hornbein, mountain climber

Every man must seek the pleasures of mountaineering in his own way.

R.L.G. Irving, mountain climber

Even if Mallory and Irvine touched the summit, they didn't make it—that's like swimming to the middle of the ocean.

Ed Viestreo, climber, who did summit Everest

Fear is something that all climbers feel at some time. Without it there would be no caution.

Joe Brown, sportswriter

Forget the hype about the new "extreme" sports; mountaineering has been around for centuries and is clearly the most extreme of all.

Men's Journal

From my deepest and oldest memories, I was always fascinated with the mountains. They had a magical quality about them and climbing was a part of that . . . In climbing you can have a very intense, sometimes spiritual, highly emotional adventure and you can turn around and have another one.

William A. Read, climber

Guiding and climbing are mutually exclusive. I've never been hurt climbing, but when you're guiding, there's always a chance that the client will make a mistake.

Jack Tackle, climber and guide

How free and exultant is the true mountaineer, when he exchanges the warmly glowing atmosphere of the south for the cold and invigorating blasts of the mountain; when he leaves behind him the gentle beauty of the lakes and glories in the savage grandeur of riven rock and contorted glacier.

Edward Shirely Kennedy, alpinist

Hungry! Cold!

Stefano Longhi, alpinist, his last words before he
froze to death on an exposed ledge

I always thought anyone who fell off a mountain simply blacked out or died of fright or by some other means was delivered from consciously suffering such a disagreeable fate. This belief persisted . . . until I fell . . . and proved it wrong.

Peter Potterfield, climber

I awoke to strangely mixed feelings of discomfort and anticipation . . . Suddenly my mind cleared, and I remembered that this was the most important day of all, for it was our turn to start on the long slow upward grind that might, with luck, end on the summit of Everest.

Sir Edmund Hillary, mountain climber, first man
to reach the top of Everest

I can do no more.

Toni Kurz, alpinist, his last words,
died of exposure, suspended in midair
as his ropes knotted up

I closed my eyes and let the sickness spin me away from the bitter realities into unconsciousness. That night the tent became a frozen coffin. We tossed and turned and rolled onto each other through the long, long night.

Jonathan Waterman, climber and writer

I could climb for a million years and still not know why I do it.

Chuck Pratt, mountain climber

I don't expect this climb to make everything right. It'll just feel real good.

Jeff Lowe, climber, talking about how climbing
will not solve life's problems

If anything goes wrong it will be a fight to the end. If your training is good enough survival is there; if not nature claims forfeit.

Dougal Haston, mountain climber

I felt very quiet, very tired. I sat there for more than a half an hour. I took some photographs and I had no fear about getting down. It was very peaceful.

Reinhold Messner, climber, referring to what he
did as the only man to climb Everest alone

I found that climbing was the only thing in life that gave more than momentary satisfaction.

Dougal Haston, mountain climber, when asked "Why do you climb?"

I live not in myself, but I become
Portion of that around me; and to me
High mountains are a feeling, but the hum
Of human cities torture.

Lord Byron, poet

I move like a snail with my home on my back going slowly from place to place, going steadily but always going.

Reinhold Messner, climber, during his climb on Everest alone

I never left a mountain unfinished.

Cesare Maetri, climber

In the United States, great alpinists remain as obscure as chess champions.

David Roberts, outdoor journalist

I think it is not so necessary that a guide chat good, but that he can climb good.

Anatoli Boukreev, climber and guide, was a guide during the Everest disaster of 1996

I think that people that have experiences that are on the edge of life and death want to tell people about them and people want to read about them. Climbing is a real ultimate activity.

Arlene Blum, climber

It is lamentable that whenever a serious accident occurs ... there is generally an outburst of ignorant and foolish criticism. The public are warned against the folly of mountaineering; they are informed that we witfully run unnecessary risks; that we climb almost impossible peaks from a pure spirit of bravado, from a desire to brag of our exploits, or from some other motive of equal silliness and stupidity.

C. E. Matthews, mountain climber

It is not important for me to just climb Everest, but it is a much greater achievement to climb the mountain without using oxygen. I can sit in my home in Italy and know I can climb Everest with a can of oxygen ... Man can reach the moon with the aid of technology, but it is a philosophical question to reach the top of Everest without it.

Reinhold Messner, climber

It is not the role of grand alpinism to face peril, but it is one of the tests one must undergo to deserve the joy of rising for an instant above the state of crawling grubs.

Lionel Terray, mountain climber

It seems to me that the contemplative side of mountaineering can only have an interpretive value, and that the ecstasy of creation can come from action alone.

Giusto Gervasutti, alpinist

It was impossible that a mountain that far away could take up so much of the sky.

David Roberts, climber and writer

K2 has earned over the years a reputation as a killer.

Peter Potterfield, climber and writer

Ms. Pittman was known in certain elevated circles more as a social climber than mountain climber.

Joanne Kaufman, journalist, about Sandy Pittman, who was one of the surviving party during the fatal 1996 Everest climb

Mountaineering was a discovery. There were men, of course, right back through history, who were attracted by individual hills, and went—or tried to go—up them. Just as there were men in Newton's day who watched apples falling, and ate them.

Geoffrey Winthrop Young,
mountain climber

People have climbed from the earliest times . . . but these early venturers went no higher than it was necessary for hunting game or perhaps crystals. The alpine passes were routes for trade or invasion, but the peaks were places of fearsome mystery, the abodes of the gods, devils or dragons.

Chris Bonington, mountain climber

Perhaps we had become a little arrogant with our . . . age of easy mechanical conquest. We had forgotten that the mountain still holds the master card, that it will grant success only in its own good time. Why else does mountaineering retain its deep fascination?

Eric Shipton, mountain climber

Something besides courage and determination is needed to climb a mountain like this. Forgive me if I call it intelligence.

Robert Dunn, climber and writer

Superclimbers are, on the whole, uncheerful about hiking, impatient with the weather, insensitive to the subtleties of landscape.

David Roberts, mountain climber

The age of discovery and conquest has given way to a new period of personal and creative mountaineering.

Robert W. Craig, mountain climber
and writer

The mountain doesn't play games. It sits there unmoved.

Bruce Barcott, climber and writer

The transient population that ends up on the glacier includes serious expedition climbers and raw neophytes on guided climbs, adventurers, dopers, drinkers, and marginally socialized eccentrics looking for an extreme experience.

Peter Potterfield, climber and writer,
about Mt. Everest

The true mountaineer is a wanderer . . . a man who loves to be where no human being has been before, who delights in gripping rocks that have previously never felt the touch of human fingers.

Alfred Mummery, alpinist

There are still a great many walls of rock and ice and a diminishing number of high summits that haven't been touched, but these are going to talented young climbers from every part of the world seeking the untried or that which has not been done. What is creative about these routes and ascents is the style in which they are done.

Robert W. Craig, mountain climber and writer

This time we were without guides, for we had learnt the great truth that those who wish to really enjoy the pleasures of mountaineering must roam the upper snows trusting exclusively to their own skill and knowledge.

Alfred Mummery, alpinist

Today's climber doesn't want to cut himself off from the possibility of retreat; he carries his courage in his rucksack, in the form of bolts and equipment . . . Retreat has become dishonorable, because everyone knows now that a combination of bolts and single-mindedness will get you up anything, even the most repulsive-looking direttissima.

Reinhold Messner, mountain climber

Well, we knocked the bastard off!

Sir Edmund Hillary, mountain climber, to George Lowe, expedition leader, after Hillary became the first man ever to reach the top of Everest

We made it.

Reinhold Messner, climber, after making it to the top of Everest without the aid of compressed oxygen, along with Peter Habeler

"What is the use of going up mountains?" is a question often put. To such I would say: go up a good-sized mountain, and you will know.

Edward Whymper, mountain climber

You find something that is larger than your life and you can take from that and put it into your life. There is such a bonding with people—trusting, sharing, and communicating . . . It makes your life much richer.

Alison Osius, climber

You think of the huge crowds that show up to watch a football game, massive crowds that just go crazy watching a sport, where at the very worst a team is going to gain less points than another. Then you think about some horrendous solo climb where a guy has trained his mind for years and there is nobody at all. If I solo . . . I don't want anybody to watch, because it's absolutely a personal thing.

Todd Skinner, climber

Coaches

Coaches do what works for them, what their personality is.

Jeff Van Gundy, professional basketball coach

Coaches have to watch for what they don't want to see and listen to what they don't want to hear.

John Madden, champion football coach and Emmy Award–winning broadcaster

His peers betray their torment, wincing, grimacing, politicking, intriguing, job-hopping, balding, graying, gaining weight until they flop into the off season like beached whales.

Mark Heisler, sportswriter, about Pat Riley, professional basketball coach

It is much more difficult for coaches now than it ever was. The off season is gone. You're constantly on the job. The pressure to win is constant.

Rich McKay, general manager

Phil Jackson always seems to have a little smirk on his face, as if to say, "I know something the rest of you don't."

David DuPree, sportswriter

There are two kinds of coaches. The kind that have just been fired and the kind that are going to get fired.

Bum Phillips, professional football coach

Coaching

A coach can't hide behind the fact that some players didn't play as well as they could have because that's his job.

Scotty Bowman, champion professional hockey coach

A great manager has a knack for making ballplayers think they are better than they really are.

Reggie Jackson, Hall of Fame baseball player

All I do is take the bows. These are the guys who do all the work.

James Francis "Jumbo" Elliott, champion track and field coach, referring to his two longtime assistants Jim Tuppeny and Jack Pyrah

Barney, what did you do? That's the steal sign!

Leo Durocher, professional baseball player and manager, to Barney Kremenko, sportswriter, after Durocher used the sportswriter to send in signs during a game Durocher had been thrown out of. At one point, Kremenko inadvertently scratched his nose, and a runner was thrown out attempting to steal second.

Behind every half-decent baseball man, there's a better one who took the risk of writing his name in the lineup for the first time.

Whitey Herzog, professional baseball player, executive, and manager

Be reasonable: Do it my way.

sign on desk of John Calipari, college and professional basketball coach

Coaching is easy. Winning is the hard part.

Elgin Baylor, Hall of Fame basketball player

Coaching is teaching. Some coaches try to make what they do sound mysterious and complicated when it's not. . . . to be a good coach, you have to be a good teacher.

John Madden, champion professional football coach, writer, and award-winning broadcaster

Could I be a good coach and lose? To me, that's like asking if a guy can be a good doctor even though his patients keep dying.

Red Auerbach, Hall of Fame basketball coach and executive

He's going to come back and coach for me someday.

Caroll Rosenbloom, owner, about Don Shula, professional football player and coach, whom he would hire and then fire after Rosenbloom's Colts would lose to the Jets

I am going to make a distinction between a coach and a teacher. A teacher or instructor shows you how to do a figure or a particular skating movement. A coach, on the other hand, not only helps you to improve your figure but advises you about your diet, keeps your family away from you when they become bothersome, makes sure you have the right pair of skates, and sees that you get up at the right time for a competition.

Carlo Fassi, figure skating coach

I don't think it's proper to talk about a job or speculate or meet with somebody about a job if the job is filled . . . I wouldn't say it's an unwritten rule in the coaching fraternity because the coaching fraternity doesn't have a lot of rules. But among good people, though, that's the rule.

Dick Harter, professional basketball coach

I'd rather be a football coach. That way you only lose 11 games a year.

Abe Lemons, coach

I don't tell opposing coaches who's starting the second quarter. Why tell them who's starting the first quarter until right before the game starts.

Danny Ainge, professional basketball player and coach

If I had one wish, it would be for Jackie Robinson to be here to see this moment.

Frank Robinson, professional baseball player and first African-American major league manager

If you're losing sleep and you have a knot in your stomach, that means you're probably doing your job.

Bill Walsh, professional football coach

I had the idea that the team could be run by committee, but it's like a business. You need a strong man.

Leon Hess, sports owner

I probably couldn't play for me. I wouldn't like my attitude.

John Thompson, basketball coach

I'm a people coach. People play the game, not X's and O's.

Leeman Bennett, professional football coach

I'm not much of a golfer. I don't have any friends. And, all I like to do the day of a game is go home and be alone and worry about ways not to lose.

Paul "Bear" Bryant, college football coach

I told my coaches, "If the backs don't start running like Chuck Foreman, you're fired."

Dick Vermeil, professional football coach

It's a lot tougher to be a football coach than a President. You've got four years as Presi-

dent, and they guard you. A coach doesn't have anyone to protect him when things go wrong.

Harry Truman, president of the United States

I've heard of managers coming back as part of the grounds crew, or sitting in the front row giving signs, or sitting in the bleachers with binoculars, or standing behind a photographer or a cameraman.

Bobby Valentine, professional baseball player and manager, after being thrown out of a game as a manager, referring to his fine for appearing near the bench after his ejection, disguised in sunglasses and a greasepaint mustache

I want them to use the court to express themselves. But on the other hand, I don't want them to be flip. I don't want to be good old Riley to the players, the guy they could treat as an old shoe.

Pat Riley, professional basketball player and coach

Listen, if you start worrying about the people in the stands, before too long you're up in the stands with them.

Tom Lasorda, baseball manager

Of all the mistakes a coach can make, I think one of the worst is to fall in love with the sound of his own voice. When I see a coach waving his clip board, furiously drawing diagrams, I see a coach who's selling himself to the TV cameras, selling himself to the crowd, when what he should be doing is selling his team.

Red Auerbach, Hall of Fame basketball coach and executive

On most teams the coach worries about where the players are at night. Our players worried about the coach.

> *Art Rooney, owner, about Johnny Blood,*
> *professional football player and coach, about*
> *Blood's infamous lifestyle*

On this team we are all united in a common goal: to keep my job.

> *Lou Holtz, college and professional football coach*

People keep saying that Woody Hayes is a great football coach who overstayed his time. This implies that there was a time when slugging a member of the opposing team was proper coachly deportment.

> *Red Smith, sportswriter*

Some coaches pray for wisdom. I pray for 260-pound tackles. They'll give me plenty of wisdom.

> *Chuck Mills, football coach*

That's a coach's dream, to be able to put our guys against your guys—real gladiator stuff.

> *Erik Howard, professional football player*

The difference is that as a player, you come in, put in your two hours and leave. As a coach, you never really leave; at least your mind doesn't. One of the things I've learned is to keep a pad of paper near the bed so I can write down ideas that come to me in the middle of the night.

> *Kurt Rambis, professional basketball*
> *player and coach*

The job of coaching, rather than yelling at "unruly" kids and constantly pointing out their faults, is to provide an environment in which the racers can learn once and for all that their success depends on disciplining themselves . . .

And if a racer is incapable of disciplining himself, he doesn't belong on the team.

> *Billy Kidd, Olympic silver medalist downhiller*

The players win the matches. Coaches get too much credit and too much blame. I think we deserve credit for an assist.

> *Tom Gullikson, professional tennis*
> *player and coach*

The more you lose, the more positive you have to become. When you're winning, you can ride them harder because their self-esteem is high. If you are losing and you try to be tough, you're asking for dissension.

> *Rick Pitino, college and professional*
> *basketball coach*

The pro game is like being a step-parent: you have the responsibility without the authority.

> *Rick Majerus, college and professional*
> *basketball coach, about the differences*
> *between coaching college and pro*

They can't fire me because my family buys too many tickets.

> *LaVell Edwards, Brigham Young University*
> *football coach and one of 14 children*

To train a champion a coach must be willing to adapt and adjust his or her methods to each skater. That is the key to good coaching.

> *Carlo Fassi, figure skating coach*

I can be out of town in 20 minutes, 30, if I have stuff at the cleaners.

> *Tom McVie, National Hockey League coach*

I can only show you the way. It's up to you to go there.

> *Larry Ellis, track and field coach, to Bob*
> *Beamon, Olympic gold medalist long jumper*

If I was half the coach on the bench that I was in the stands, we'll have no problems.

Bob Plager, professional hockey coach

I've got to coach a guy who won't answer roll, who won't say anything . . . He played well, but it was a bad situation. It was totally against everything that I believed in.

Dan Reeves, professional football player and coach, as an assistant coach, about Calvin Hill's yearlong silence

He can take his'n and beat your'n, or he can take your'n and beat his'n.

Bum Phillips, National Football League head coach commenting on fellow National Football League head coach Don Shula

Have you ever seen a Fellini movie? My life is like a Fellini movie.

George Karl, professional basketball coach

I didn't feel I was properly coaching unless I was butting their heads, pushing them off the line, blocking them on their rears. Football is a show me game, not a preach to me game.

Chuck Knox, professional football coach

If the man tells you there's cheese on the mountain, then you best bring crackers.

Keith Byars, National Football League player on head coach Bill Parcells

If you become paralyzed by the thought that you may be criticized for doing something, you're never going to be the risk taker you need to be as a good coach. Risk taking is part of it. If it doesn't work out, you've got to accept the responsibility for it not working out.

Jeff Van Gundy, professional basketball coach

It takes some time to realize that you are, in fact, World Champion. "World" is such a big word, but when it does begin to sink in you begin to realize what a terrific responsibility you owe to your sport, the people who put you there, and to everybody around you.

Graham Hill, champion race car driver

I teach them how to grab the guy's shirt and step on their toes.

Bob Zawoluk, assistant Lehman College coach

I taught him everything he knows. I didn't teach him everything I know.

Charlie Whittingham, thoroughbred horse trainer, about someone who had worked under him and now was a competing trainer

I was never a rah-rah guy. I was never one of those guys that went around and rah-rahed . . . Rah-rah don't get it done.

Sparky Anderson, professional baseball player and manager

Old coaches never die. They start selling insurance or get promoted to high school principal. Or they ride off to the golf course.

Durwood Merrill, umpire

The greatest horror of coaching is losing.

Joe Schmidt, professional football coach

The player can walk away from losing, but the coach—well, then he should be out . . . he's in the wrong profession.

Joe Schmidt, professional football coach

There is nothing, absolutely nothing, like the feeling of being the coach of a Grand Slam champion.

Nick Bolletieri, professional tennis coach

They forgot to introduce me. Guys were looking at me and saying, "Is this guy a player? Manager? What is he?"

Jeff Van Gundy, professional basketball coach, on his first day as an assistant in the National Basketball Association

To hell with you. I'll see you out begging on the street.

Enrique Soto, coach, in the Dominican Republic minor league to his young players

When a kid has given you the best he has to give, and you have to tell him it wasn't good enough, that's when you ache inside and think maybe there's a better way to make a living.

Vince Lombardi, Hall of Fame coach

When we win, I have no idea why we win. When we lose, I have no idea why we lose. I'm totally confused.

George Karl, professional basketball coach

There's about a foot difference between a halo and a noose.

Bobby Bowden, champion college football coach

You don't get a vote here, son. If you want to get back to the free world, take your things with you.

Vince Lombardi, Hall of Fame professional football coach

Your mother wants you to improve. Your father wants to see you improve. But I just don't give a good goddamn.

Frank Cunningham, crewing coach

You've got ten million dollars worth of players here, so sit down.

Charles Barkley, professional basketball player, to Chuck Daly, coach, at the Olympics during the first Dream Team

College

A school without football is in danger of deteriorating into a medieval study hall.

Vince Lombardi, professional football player and coach

Behind the scenes, millions of dollars flow from booster to assistant coach to player, everyone knows it, everyone's a pimp or a whore.

Kevin Mackey, college and minor league basketball coach

College football is an ugly business.

Mike Tomco, college football player

College football would be more interesting if the faculty played instead of the students—there would be a great increase in broken arms, legs and necks.

H. L. Mencken, humorist and author

College is the fountain of life. You have to drink from it.

John Chaney, college basketball coach

If you find the right junior college kid, he's going to be so thrilled to have a chance to play . . . that he might come in here with a better attitude than the freshman. A junior college kid is older, he's been kicked around a little. He may be a little tougher.

Bobby Knight, champion basketball coach

I hated college football with a passion. I wouldn't walk across the street to see a college game—all those poor guys out there killing themselves for nothing.

Alex Karras, Hall of Fame football player, actor, and broadcaster

It was just the fact that I enjoyed not going to class. That last period of every day had to be taken up with the sport you were participating in, so I ended up going out for every sport throughout the school year. That's how in reality I became involved in so many sports.

Chuck Howley, professional football player, who lettered in five sports in college

I will not permit thirty men to travel four hundred miles to agitate a bag of wind.

Andrew Dickson White, president of Cornell University, who would not allow his football team to travel to play Michigan

I will tour the world for four years, playing tennis for the University of Miami. Then after four years of publicizing your university, you will give me a diploma.

attributed to Bobby Riggs, professional tennis champion and legendary hustler, by Gardnar Mulloy, professional tennis champion, to Dr. Ash, president of University of Miami. Being turned down, Riggs turned professional shortly after.

Jimmy Taylor, the great fullback of the Green Bay Packers, spent four years in college and emerged unscarred by education.

Dick Schaap, sportswriter, best-selling writer, talk show host

My job is to win football games. I've got to put people in the stadium, make money for the university, keep the alumni happy, and give the school a winning reputation. If I don't win, I'm gone.

Frank Kush, college football coach

Otis Sistrunk, from the University of Mars

Alex Karras, professional football player, broadcaster, and actor, during a Monday Night Football game, when asked what college he went to (real answer was none)

Scottsdale Community College Steams are called the "The Fighting Artichokes." That smarty pants name, like the cheerleader in an artichoke costume, is drollery intended to de-emphasize athletics.

George Will, writer and baseball enthusiast

Student athlete is a term susceptible to various definitions. It can mean a biochemistry major who participates in sports, or a Heisman Trophy candidate who is not necessarily a candidate for a bachelor's degree. Some student athletes are more studious than athletic, and vice versa.

Red Smith, sportswriter

Comebacks

I feel like a pussycat off the tee and a gorilla around the greens. I'm not quite there, but I'm not that far away.

Jack Nicklaus, champion professional golfer

I thought I could live off of reputation, and The Game proved me wrong. The Game taught me a lesson.

Michael Jordan, professional basketball player, regarding his first season back in basketball after leaving baseball

It's hard to get rid of the reputation of being a "sore-armer," but you feel in your heart you can make it back to the majors.

Bill Rives, sportswriter, referring to Johnny Beazley, who never made it back to the major leagues

I might say that no one at ringside tried to break my fall.

Jack Dempsey, champion boxer, referring to being knocked clear out of the ring by Luis Firpo, whom he knocked out in the next round

It's like Todd has been frozen for a year-and-a-half. He's thawing out, but it takes time.

Rick Dempsey, professional baseball player and coach, about Todd Hundley

I've had things handed to me and always been able to come through my career pretty quick. But this time I couldn't just come back nonchalant, I had to find the depths of myself to get back.

Chris Antley, professional jockey, and recovering substance addict

The fact that I was in uniform, out there competing, it made the fans see another side of me and allowed them to learn something about recovering from cancer that maybe they'd never see or learn. A man or a woman can come back from cancer and not just exist, but produce at the same level—at a higher level.

Eric Davis, professional baseball player, on coming back from cancer

The mark of the great player is his ability to come back. The great champions all have come back from defeat.

Sam Snead, champion professional golfer

This is something I've waited for for almost two years. I was getting a lot of ribbing from the guys before practice, guys asking me if I remembered how to get into my stance. And that felt great, too, because I felt a part of the team again.

Brian Williams, professional football player, who took two years to recover from an eye injury

When is the last time I contended? Heck, I don't think I could have contended for my club championship the last couple of years.

Paul Azinger, champion golfer, coming back from cancer

You have no choice about how you lose, but you do have a choice about how you come back and prepare to win again.

Pat Riley, professional basketball player and coach

Commissioner

I always dreaded this day would come and the day is here.

Gary Bettman, National Hockey League commissioner, speaking of the retirement of Wayne Gretzky

Oh-h-h, my yes, I would love to be the hockey commissioner. But I don't know if I have the qualifications. You see, I can't skate.

Tiny Tim, musician, sports fan, when asked by a reporter if he would like to be the National Hockey League commissioner

Competition

A competitor will find a way to win. Competitors take bad breaks and use them to drive themselves just that much harder. Quitters take bad breaks and use them as reasons to give up. It's all a matter of pride.

Nancy Lopez, champion professional golfer

After eight years in the NFL, I'm convinced that the only thing that separates chumps from champions is the individual's competitive drive.

Joe Montana, Hall of Fame professional football player

Compete against yourself, not others.

Peggy Fleming, Olympic gold medalist skater and broadcaster

Competing in athletics helps you face problems. In sports, you have to fight for everything you get. Nobody is going to hand you anything.

Betty Meade, champion squash player

Competitive sports teach and reaffirm for the players all the positive values of life.

Harvey S. Wiener, writer and swimmer

Hole it. I'm giving you nothing but hell today.

Gene Sarazen, champion golfer, to Walter Hagen, champion golfer, at the Professional Golfers Association championship

I am really happiest playing golf, playing tennis, playing a game, being in competition, doing something—I really come alive. That kind of life is fulfilling for me. I get a kick out of that.

Bobby Riggs, professional tennis champion and legendary hustler

I could not shrink from a challenge. If the chance was there and if—no matter how difficult it appeared—it meant winning. I was going to take it. It was the sweetness of the risk that I remembered, and not its dangers. You must play boldly to win.

Arnold Palmer, champion professional golfer

I know quite a few players who have the ability to do more. I have worked hard to be where I am. They need to work harder.

Steffi Graff, champion professional tennis player

I'm telling you, you cannot one-up t/

Debbie Thomas, Olympic silver meda/ skater, about Katarina Witt, Olympic gold medalist figure skater

I'm very competitive. I want to be the best player in the world. To be that, you have to beat the best.

Annika Sorenstam, professional golfer

In golf, I'd rather Bobby Jones beat me eight and seven than for me to beat some duffer nine and eight. I've never got any fun out of beating second-rate opponents.

Dev Milburn, college football player, one of the Four Horsemen

I started racing before I ever had my driver's license. I'd be out there racing kids my age, and their dads would be out their tuning up their engines trying to make the cars run faster, and my dad was usually racing with the stock cars. I wasn't competing with the other kids, but with their dads.

Alan Kulwicki, race car driver

It is the battle, the contest, that counts, not the score. If two meet, one must win and one must lose. But they can both have a great afternoon!

Dev Milburn, college football player, one of the Four Horsemen

I've always felt that competition, stripped to its essence, is a battle of will. Skills, conditions, even luck may vary. Only one thing remains constant: break an opponent's will and you'll beat him every time.

Jim Brown, Hall of Fame football player

I would just say that we have a need to compete. It's as natural as sleeping or eating. We have a need to excel.

Ted Turner, champion yachtsman
and baseball owner

Look, if my mother put on a helmet and shoulder pads and a uniform that wasn't the same as the one I was wearing, I'd run over *her* if she was in my way.

Bo Jackson, professional baseball
and football player

Ski racing chose me—I was thrown into it because it was all around me. And because I discovered I had a strong, competitive spirit, I stayed with it.

Jean-Claude Killy, Olympic gold
medalist skier

There's no denying the pleasure of kicking your compadres' collective butts.

Fred Matheny, cyclist and writer

We Americans are a competitive race. We bet on anything. We love to win.

George S. Patton, U.S. general

We knew if we weren't in awe of them we could play them.

Kevin Ault, college basketball player

What, me help another discus thrower? I would make recommendations that would be very difficult for him to follow—have him concentrate on something that had absolutely no relation to his problems.

Al Oerter, Olympic champion discus thrower

When you step on that field, you cannot concede a thing.

Gayle Sayers, Hall of Fame football player

When we're on the road, they are like my family. But when qualifying starts, they are the opposition.

Dario Franchetti, automobile racer, about some of
his friend/competitors

You are never really playing an opponent. You are playing yourself, your own highest standards, and when you reach your limits, that is real joy.

Arthur Ashe, champion tennis player
and writer

Composure

The ballplayer who loses his head, who can't keep his cool, is worse than no ballplayer at all.

Lou Gehrig, Hall of Fame baseball player

People have said it's going to be a boxing match, a rumble in the jungle. It's hard to play body to body and not get into a skirmish. But a cool head has to prevail.

Chris Childs, professional basketball player

Concentration

Concentration is the ability to think about absolutely nothing when it is absolutely necessary.

Ray Knight, professional baseball player
and manager

I never hit a careless shot in my life. I bet only a quarter but I play each shot as if it were for a championship. I concentrate as hard for a quarter as I do for a championship.

Walter J. Travis,
professional golfer

The secret of shooting is concentration.
Bill Bradley, basketball player and U.S. senator

You think of the ball *first,* and *then* what's coming for you down the field. Reverse the order, and you've got yourself a fumble.
Tommy Watkins, professional football player

Confidence

All of a sudden, I lacked that confidence and that energy it takes to be any athlete.
Julie Krone, professional jockey

Coach, after all the shit we've been through, there is no way we lose tonight.
Michael Jordan, professional basketball player, to Bobby Knight, college coach, a note taped to Knight's blackboard before the Gold Medal game in the 1980 Olympics

Confidence is a lot of this game or any game. If you don't think you can win, you won't.
Jerry West, Hall of Fame basketball player and executive

Confidence is everything. From there, it's a small step to winning.
Craig Stadler, champion professional golfer

I always thought I could play pro ball. I had confidence in my ability. You have to. If you don't, who will?
Johnny Unitas, Hall of Fame football player

I don't consider myself a lesser known. . . . When I'm playing with Norman or Fred Couples, I feel I'm as good as them. If you don't, you don't belong out here.
Scott McCarren, professional golfer

I knew I was going to be a champ when I was ten.
John Newcombe, champion tennis player

I really lack the words to compliment myself today.
Alberto Tomba, Olympic gold medalist skier

No one can guard me one-on-one. I'm not afraid of anyone in this league.
Allen Iverson, professional basketball player

What you're thinking, what shape your mind is in, is what makes the biggest difference of all.
Willie Mays, Hall of Fame baseball player

Whenever he was able to impart his confidence, that part of the game just sparkled.
Frank Clarke, football player, about Tom Landry, Hall of Fame coach

I knew I wasn't going to be average.
Chamique Holdsclaw, basketball player

The ones who believed in themselves the most were the ones who won.
Florence Griffith-Joyner, Olympic medalist track and field competitor

Without confidence a golfer is little more than a hacker.
Bobby Jones, champion golfer

Confrontation

He can run, but he can't hide.
Joe Louis, champion boxer, about Billy Conn, before a title bout

Consistency

My dad taught me about the importance of consistency. He told me if you're consistent, you can last longer.

Ken Griffey, Jr., professional baseball player

This game is like the N.C.A.A. tournament. Coaches rise up and win one now and then, but there's only one John Wooden. I think I have proved I can sustain that high level of excellence, and I believe we're going to be this good for a long time.

D. Wayne Lukas, thoroughbred horse trainer

Consolation Game

Consolation affairs attract all the attention of a bunion at a nudist colony.

Blackie Sherrod, sportswriter

Control

Control the elements, control what's inside of you.

John Chaney, college basketball coach

To me the game is a question of control: control yourself, control your emotions, control of your opponent.

Fred Perry, professional tennis champion

Corbett, Gentleman Jim

(b. Sept. 1, 1866; d. Feb. 18, 1933) *World Heavyweight Champion, 1892–1897*

I honestly think he is better than Benny Leonard. He's the greatest thing I have ever seen in the ring. I learned plenty.

Gene Tunney, champion boxer, speaking after an exhibition match with the aging, ex-champion Corbett (Leonard was a then top-ranked contender)

Cosell, Howard

(b. Mar. 25, 1920; d. Apr. 23, 1995) *Broadcaster of* Monday Night Football *and* Wide World of Sports

Everything you've ever heard about Howard Cosell, good and bad, is true. But it's probably understated.

Roy Firestone, broadcaster

Arrogant, pompous, obnoxious, vain, cruel, verbose, a show off. I have been called all of these. Of course, I am.

Howard Cosell, broadcaster

A voice that had all the resonance of a clogged Dristan bottle.

1973 Year Book, Encyclopedia Brittanica

Get that nigger-loving Jew bastard off the air. Football is an American game.

Anonymous letter received by ABC during the first year of Monday Night Football *about Howard Cosell*

If Howard Cosell was a sport, it would be Roller Derby.

Jimmy Cannon, sportswriter

I tell it like it is. Howard Cosell tells it like Roone Arledge wants it told.

Harry Caray, broadcaster

Courage

The miracle isn't that I finished . . . The miracle is that I had the courage to start.

John Bingham, runner and writer

To uncover your true potential you must first find your own limits and then you have to have the courage to blow past them.

Picabo Street, Olympic medalist skier

Crenshaw, Ben

(b. Jan. 11, 1952) *Champion golfer; won two Masters*

He can't keep his ball in the fairway. I've told him that he might have a tan like mine if he didn't spend so much time in the trees.

Lee Trevino, champion professional golfer

Crew Chief

As crew chief, I have one philosophy—to be everyone's friend. I like to be one of the guys, but at the same time I have to be the boss too. I like to treat them like I wanted to be treated when I was doing their job.

Andy Petree, crew chief

Cricket

April: This is the time of year when the sentimental cricketer withdraws his bat tenderly from its winter bed and croons over it, as if it were a Stradivarius or a shoulder of mutton.

R. C. Robertson-Glasgow, sportswriter

Athletics, unlike cricket, is a sport in which individual brilliance can be measured, regardless of the quality of the competition.

Peter Lovesey, writer

Call me sad, but like a substantial minority of other Scots, I actually enjoy cricket.

Neil Robertson, sportswriter, columnist

Cricket is the only game where you are playing eleven of the other side and ten of your own.

G. H. Hardy, mathematician

For a cricket fan America is a sporting Sarah.

Tunku Varadarajan, writer

Half the charm of cricket is its ever changing patterns.

T. Baily, Championship Cricket

I couldn't bat for the length of time required to score 500. I'd get bored and fall over.

Dennis Compton, writer

England lacked—why do I use the past tense, let us say it lacks—gumption, guts, class, technique, battle, ability, panache, sinew, courage, pride, passion, determination, vim and depth. The team is a mournful gaggle of trundlers and plodders, which will be blown away, game after game. . . .

Tunku Varadarajan, professor of law and sportswriter, speaking of the England team before an international test match

I do love cricket—it's so very English.

Sarah Bernhardt, actress

I have always looked upon cricket as organized loafing.

William Temple, Archbishop of Canterbury

I tend to believe that cricket is the greatest thing that God ever created on earth . . . certainly greater than sex, although sex isn't too bad either.

Harold Pinter, playwright

It's a funny kind of month, October. For the really keen cricket fan, it's when you realize your wife left you in May.

Dennis Norden, comedian

It's as exciting as mailing letters.
Pat Hayden, professional football player and
Rhodes scholar

Like the British Constitution, cricket was not made; it has "grown."
Neville Cardus, English Cricket

Is there life after cricket?
Marvin Cohen, The Time Factor

Cricket is a team game of individual encounter.
J. M. Kilburn, cricketer

A fast bowler who doesn't get results has no future.
John Snow, cricketer

On the day I can't play cricket anymore, I'll do as them Romans did—I'll get into a 'ot bath and cut my ruddy throat!
Cecil Parkin, cricketer

The bowler's Holding, the batman's Willey.
attributed to a BBC broadcaster by Steve
Rushin, sportswriter, referring to a match
wherein the opposing players were Michael
Holding and Peter Willey

The new woman is taking up cricket evidently with the same energy which has characterized her other and more important spheres of life.
Cricket magazine, in 1895

There is no such thing as a crisis in cricket, only the next ball.
W. R. Grace, cricketer

There's no use hitting me there, there's nothing in it.
Derek Randall, cricketer, after being hit on the
head by a bouncer from Dennis Lillee

They came to see me bat not to see you bowl.
W. G. Grace, cricketer, at a famous match in
which he was bowled first ball

Polite baseball.
K. A. Auty, cricketer and writer

Croquet

Depend upon it, croquet is the game of the future. It wants writing, though.
George Eliot, novelist

He has the true croquet spirit. He trusts no one but himself; never concedes—no matter far behind he may be—and hates his opponents with an all-enduring hate.
Moss Hart, playwright and screenwriter, on
Darryl Zanuck, movie producer

In some people's minds croquet is a quaint and literally gentle Victorian game in which good sportsmanship and polite manners carry the day. Yet to anyone who has played the game often, the inaccuracy of this image is as close at hand as your favorite mallet.
Christopher R. Reaske, writer and
croquet player

I would rather see our youth playing football with the danger of an occasional broken collarbone than to see them dedicated to croquet.
John Cavanaugh, president
Notre Dame University

Kahn's course was flat and as smooth as a billiard table.
Harpo Marx, actor, speaking about
Otto Kahn's croquet lawn

Keep your temper and remember when your turn comes.

A. Rover, writer and croquet player

Recently a Connecticut couple married thirty-three years, got a legal separation, the man explaining "his wife was not aggressive enough in croquet mixed-doubles."

Dynamic Maturity, *1974*

Rutherford B. Hayes also liked to play croquet on the White House lawn, but even there the Democrats would not let him alone. They charged he had squandered six dollars of taxpayers' money for a set of fancy boxwood croquet balls.

Roger Butterfield, historian

Talbott's estate was particularly prized for its glass-smooth croquet court. One evening in the late 1920's, in a scene worthy of Gatsby, several of the Round Table's diehard croquet fanatics fought off the falling darkness by driving their cars through the shrubbery to the perimeter of the course. In the crosshatch of beams their headlights threw on the lawn, they played all night.

James R. Gaines, writer, referring to the wits of the Algonquin Round Table

The ingenuity of man has never conceived of anything better calculated to bring out all the evil passions of humanity than the so-called game of croquet . . . Our forefathers early recognized the insidious wickedness of the game and rooted it out.

Living Age *magazine, in 1898*

The ladies will very much oblige all their associates in croquet by avoiding long dresses, which are continually dragging the balls about over the ground greatly to the annoyance of the players and disturbance of the game.

A. Rover, writer and croquet player

There are really two great moments for a croquet player, aside from winning the game. The first is when he is introduced to croquet. The second is when he feels he is good enough to order his own mallet with his initials on top of the handle.

Peter Maas, writer

The workmen have come out . . . to mow the lawn into perfect smoothness, and make it as even as we trust the paths of the players may be through life.

Harper's Weekly, *in 1871*

When staying with Sir Edward Cassel he was often pitted against the Duchess of Sermoneta, who was not only extremely pretty but also a very bad player so that a game with her always put him in a good mood.

Christopher Hibbert, historian, referring to King Edward VII, of England

Crying

I remember sitting in the corner of the locker room, crying my head off.

Dave Meggyesy, professional football player and political activist, addressing a loss and the question of whether athletes cry

Curling

It is the broom that wins the battle.

Rev. John Kerr, curler

Cycling

A lot of Americans regard European racing with too much reverence.

Kent Gordis, American cyclist

An Army from Mars could invade France, the government could fall, and even the recipe for sauce Bernaise be lost, but if it happened during the Tour de France nobody would notice.

Red Smith, sportswriter

As I get into the countryside, I have the feeling that nobody else exists. The world is there for me, and as I cycle on, everything happening around me seems specially put there by nature for my personal enjoyment.

Jean-Claude Killy, Olympic gold medalist skier

Cycling is necessarily a constant series of descents.

H. G. Wells, writer

Everybody says how hard a marathon is, but twenty-five thousand people show up for one in New York. Only two hundred people can enter the Tour de France, and it takes years to get there because you can't just sign yourself up for it.

Greg LeMond, champion cyclist

Fix a man's bike and he'll ride for a day,
Teach a man to fix his bike and he'll ride
　　forever.

Attributed to anonymous by Allen St. John,
cyclist and writer

Get a bicycle. You will never regret it if you live.

Mark Twain, writer and humorist

Hurrah, hurrah, for the merry wheel,
With tires of rubber and spokes of steel;
We seem to fly on the airy steeds
With eagle's flight in silent speed.

Wheelman, a turn of the century cycling journal

I have always struggled to achieve excellence. One thing that cycling has taught me is that if you can achieve something without a struggle it's not going to be satisfying.

Greg LeMond, cyclist

If I had never had cancer, I would never have won the Tour de France. I'm convinced of that. I wouldn't want to do it all over again, but I wouldn't want to change a thing.

Lance Armstrong, champion cyclist, winner of
Tour de France, cancer survivor

I'll tell you what racing's about. It's about suffering. It's about pain—racing hurts.

Andrew Juskaitis, cyclist and writer

It's professional cycling and the killer instinct comes out after 170 miles.

Jackie Simes, U.S. cycling team director

It would not be at all strange if history came to the conclusion that the perfection of the bicycle was the greatest incident of the nineteenth century.

Detroit Tribune, *in 1896*

Look at it closely and you'll see that a bicycle frame has more triangles than a *Dynasty* rerun.

Allen St. John, cyclist and writer

Many a woman is riding to the sufferage on a bicycle.

Elizabeth Cady Stanton, suffrage leader

Most people underperform because their training lacks purpose. They don't have a plan, so they ride too hard or too easy.

Massimo Testa, champion cyclist

My job was to work for Hinault. He was the only rider on our team with a shot at the win and we had to make sure he had minimum effort throughout the race. That meant bringing back break aways and making sure that at the end of the race we kept up a good pace.

Johnathan Boyer, cyclist

My job is to help the team. We're here to protect the yellow jersey, and I'm here to protect it.

Frankie Andreu, professional champion cyclist

Nowadays, if there is an elopement, a stagnation in the peanut market, a glut in smoking tobacco, or a small attendance at the theaters, everyone who is a loser points to that bicycle and says, "You did it."

Bicycle World, *in 1898*

Quite a number of our young men, who formerly were addicted to stupid habits, and seeking of nonsensical distractions and vulgar pleasures, are now vigorous, healthy, energetic, and for the sake of this extraordinary machine submit themselves to an ascetic rule of life, and, induced by taste and passion, acquire habits of temperance, the imperative desire of quiet and regular living, and most important of all, the steady exercise of self-control.

Henri Desgranges, founder of the Tour de France, in 1895

Ride lots.

Eddy Merckx, cyclist

Sprinting is a function of three elements—fast pedaling, the power to turn the big gear and your position in the group.

Fred Matheny, writer and cyclist

The fellow who is ambitious to ride a century every Sunday belongs in the category with the prize pie eater and the one who enters gorging and guzzling contests.

The New York Herald, *1890s*

There is something uncanny in the noiseless rush of the cyclist, as he comes into view, passes by, and disappears.

Popular Science, *in 1891*

The notion of transforming this recreation into a mode of mass transit is PC looniness of legendary proportion.

Brock Yates, cyclist

The Tour de France may be finished, but it feels as though no one told my body.

Frankie Andreu, cyclist and writer

This is the home of the yellow jersey.

Stuart O'Grady, champion cyclist, his home answering machine message

Thoughtful people . . . believe that the bicycle will accomplish more for women's sensible dress than all the reform movements that have ever been waged.

Demerarest's Family Magazine, *in 1895*

Threadless streeters, sleeveless jerseys, clipless pedals. Why does the bike biz have this penchant for naming things after things they aren't?

Don Cuerdon, cyclist and writer

What do you call a cyclist who doesn't wear a helmet? An organ donor.

David Perry, cyclist and writer

Wheelies looked impressive when you were 12, and they still look cool today. But even if you're on a circus-clown career track, wheelies are more than just flashy stuff—they're mighty useful besides.

Andrew Juskaitis, cyclist and writer

When you're out peddling, you smell the blossoms blooming, feel your heart pumping, and remind yourself that life is good.

Shair Karin, cyclist

Your legs will turn to rubber after three days. You'll get the worst case of crotch rot you can possibly imagine. And some lonesome lumberjack is gonna see you ride by in those tight black shorts and those purple shoes, and he's gonna chase you down, and make you squeal like a pig.

Bike shop manager to David Nolan,
outdoor journalist, when the latter
told the former he was going to be
biking through the Canadian wilderness

Darts

You don't have to be a beer drinker to play darts, but it helps.

Anonymous

Dawkins, Darryl

(b. Jan. 11, 1957) *National Basketball Association All-Star; famous for shattering backboards during NBA games*

Everyone knows he used to call himself "Chocolate Thunder." But on the nights he didn't play well we used to call him "Chocolate Blunder."

Michael Ray Richardson, professional basketball player, teammate

Daytona 500

It's the largest picnic in the world.

Peter Golenboch, sportswriter

Death

As a traveling sportswriter, Death has been a constant companion on the road. This can be vexing, especially when Death gets the aisle seat on airplanes.

Steve Rushin, sportswriter

Can you believe it, Joy? Can you believe this shit?

Brian Piccolo, professional football player, to his wife, Joy, as he lay dying of cancer. He was dead three hours later.

Crikey—he's the heir to the throne . . . If he crashes, I'll be the heir to the bloody Tower.

Graham Hill, champion race car driver, trailing his own Formula 2 car being driven by Prince Charles, at over 160 mph

Death? I give it a quick, glancing thought.

Juan Manuel Fangio, champion race car driver

Everybody wants to go to heaven, but nobody wants to die.

Joe Louis, champion professional boxer

Every good hunter is uneasy when faced with the death he is about to inflict.

José Ortega y Gasset, philosopher

I don't want to find out I've lost my reflexes when I'm in a race car. I want to be ahead of that.

Arie Luyendyk, race car driver

If I close my eyes and meditate, I can still see them.

Jimmy Murphy, assistant soccer manager, about eight soccer players from the 1958 Manchester United team who died in a snowy plane crash at Munich Airport

It is so pleasant to sit and do nothing—and therefore so dangerous. Death through exhaustion is—like death through freezing—a pleasant one.

Reinhold Messner, mountain climber

It hurts when you lose friends. But, this is our business. Death and injury are part of the sport.

A. J. Foyt, champion race car driver

I love you. Sleep well, my sweetheart. Please don't worry too much.

Rob Hall, mountain climber and guide, his last words via radio and satellite to his wife, as he froze to death on the side of Everest

It's been a good 'un.

Don Meredith, professional football player and broadcaster, to a fellow passenger when it was thought his flight was going to crash

Mummy—a plane has crashed in fog at Arkley golf course on its way from Marseilles to Elstree . . . They think Daddy's dead.

Damon Hill, son of Graham Hill, champion race car driver; the child reported it to his mother during a dinner party. He had seen it on television.

Now you will not swell the rout
Of lads that wore their honors out,
Runners whom renown outran
And the name died before the man.

A. E. Housman, poet

The casualty rate is three or four times higher than any other sport. Last year, we had nine deaths, quite a few broken backs, and quite a few paralyzed.

Eddie Arroyo, jockey

The championships were canceled due to the death of the entire American team in a plane crash at Brussels.

United States Figure Skating Association Press Guide, entry for the 1961 champion, in its list of champions

The plain truth is that I knew better but went to Everest anyway. And in doing so I was a party to the death of a good many people, which is something that is apt to remain on my conscience for a very long time.

Jon Krakauer, outdoorsman, mountain climber, journalist

The others are all dead—I am too weak to push the button on the radio any longer—this is my last transmission—goodbye.

Elvira Shataeva, mountain climber, who was the last of eight Russian women climbers lost during the ascent of the High Pamirs

Well, this should be interesting.

Dr. Tom Waddell, Olympic decathlon competitor and gay rights activist, died of AIDS, his last words

When I can't play tennis anymore, I'll die.

Bill Tilden, professional tennis champion, who played the day before he died

When men take up a dangerous sport some must expect to die.

> Yachting World *magazine, referring to the 1979 Fastnet Race*

You always feel bad when your fellow yachtsmen drown. But you never can really be completely prepared for what nature has in store.

> *Ted Turner, champion yachtsman and baseball owner*

You just have to treat death like any other part of life.

> *Tom Sneva, champion race car driver*

You know the risks, you accept them. If a man can't look at danger and still go on, man has stopped living. If the worst ever happens—then it means simply that I've been asked to pay the bill for the happiness of my life—without a moment's regret.

> *Graham Hill, champion race car driver, the last words of his autobiography, which he was writing when he was killed in an airplane accident*

Decisions

Like throwing the ball out of bounds. All the crowd knows is that the ball was thrown out of bounds. A quarterback knows that his receiver was covered.

> *Y. A. Tittle, Hall of Fame quarterback*

Dedication

Most of my time was spent racing, so I did miss out on some of the things the other kids did. But I never have regretted it.

> *Jeff Gordon, champion race car driver*

Defeat

Defeat creates orphaned thoughts.

> *Madeleine Blais, writer*

Losing is no disgrace if you've given your best.

> *Jim Palmer, baseball player*

The taste of defeat has a richness of experience all its own.

> *Bill Bradley, Hall of Fame basketball player and U.S. senator*

You never really lose until you stop trying.

> *Mike Ditka, football player and coach*

Defense

Any time your defense gives up more points than a basketball team, you're in trouble.

> *Lou Holtz, college and professional football coach*

The art of defense is really an art based on hard work.

> *Bill Russell, Hall of Fame basketball player and coach*

Tonight we played defense like the Washington Generals trying out for the next Harlem Globetrotters game.

> *Rick Pitino, professional basketball coach and collegiate champion coach, remarking on a poor showing by his Boston Celtics after being blown out by the mediocre New Jersey Nets*

Dempsey, Jack

(b. June 24, 1895; d. May 31, 1983) *World Heavyweight Champion 1919–1926*

His complete intent was an opponent's destruction. He was a fighter—one who used every trick to wreck the other fighter. Yet outside the ring, Jack is one of the gentlest men I know.

> *Grantland Rice, sportswriter*

I don't know why I did that. I guess it was just instinct. But later, I thought to myself, "My God, they could have shot or stabbed me."

> *Jack Dempsey, world champion boxer, discussing how he knocked out two muggers with his bare hands when he himself was already a senior citizen*

I'll take on Dempsey any time in any street he wants to name. I'll knock him out for nothing.

> *Harry Willis, a.k.a. the Brown Panther, the black boxing champion whose shot at Dempsey and the championship was blocked by racism*

More than any other individual, Jack Dempsey created big-time sports in America.

> *Roger Kahn, best-selling writer*

The public suddenly saw him in a new light, the two-handed fighter who stormed forward, a flame of pure fire in the ring, strong and native, affable, easy of speech, close to the people in word and deed and feeling.

> *John Lardner, writer*

Whenever I hear the name, Jack Dempsey, I think of an America that was one big roaring camp of miners, drifters, bunkhouse hands, con men, hard cases, men who lived by their fists and by their shooting irons and by the cards they drew.

> *Jim Murray, sportswriter*

Designated Hitter

I'll soften my answer by just saying that it's appalling.

> *A. Bartlett Giamatti, Major League Baseball comissioner*

It relieves the manager of all responsibility except to post the lineup card on the dugout wall and make sure everybody gets to the airport on time.

> *Red Smith, sportswriter*

Desire

Ever to be the best and to surpass others.

> *Achilles in* The Odyssey, *by Homer*

I have got to make it here. I just can't go back to Louisiana and Arkansas. I've been there and I know what's there.

> *Lou Brock, Hall of Fame baseball player, about making the major leagues*

I haven't run as fast as I can, I haven't spoken as well as I can, and I haven't written as well as I can. If you take any less than that view, you're finished.

> *George Sheehan, runner and writer*

It doesn't matter about your coach so much if you have the desire to win. You got to have it. It's not boring if you're winning.

> *Hank Kashiwa, downhiller, U.S. ski team*

Somebody asked me, "Does this place owe you one?" I don't believe in things getting owed to you. I think you go out there and you play well enough to get them yourself.

> *Greg Norman, champion golfer*

There is no way you will ever be a great player unless *you* want it.

> *Bobby Knight, champion college basketball coach*

Who wants to play in a game that means nothing?

> *Roberto Clemente, Hall of Fame baseball player*

You can make a man hustle by fining him. But you can't teach him desire. It's there or it isn't.

> *Johnny Keane, professional baseball manager*

You would have to take a stun gun or whatever and shoot him to get him off that court. He's going to leave it all out there.

> *Jeff Van Gundy, professional basketball coach, about Patrick Ewing, who played an entire game with a torn Achilles tendon in the playoffs and out-scored and out-rebounded the opposing player to lead the team to a win*

Determination

If desire is what we want and dedication is the price we pay to get what we want, then determination is what keeps us there.

> *Dennis Green, professional football coach*

It's not whether you get knocked down, it's whether you get up.

> *Vince Lombardi, Hall of Fame professional football coach*

They're going to beat me, a good fake has got to beat me, but the thing is not to give up.

> *Night Train Lane, professional football player*

DiMaggio, Joe

(b. Nov. 25, 1914; d. Mar. 8, 1999) *Hall of Fame baseball player; won 10 World Championships; holds all-time record for hitting safely in a game—56 games*

Joe, put on a uniform—they can use you.

> *Henry Kissinger, U.S. secretary of state to DiMaggio after a Yankee playoff loss in the 1990s*

Where have you gone Joe DiMaggio
A lonely nation turns its eyes to you.

> *Paul Simon, singer and songwriter, from the song "Mrs. Robinson"*

DiMaggio even looks good striking out.

> *Ted Williams, Hall of Fame baseball player and champion fisherman*

DiMaggio's streak is the most extraordinary thing that ever happened in American sports.

> *Stephen Jay Gould, writer*

He was the perfect Hemingway hero ... His grace and skill were always on display, his emotions always concealed.

> *David Halberstam, writer*

It was so wonderful, Joe. You've never heard such cheering.

> *Marilyn Monroe to her then husband, Joe DiMaggio, after appearing in front of troops in Korea. DiMaggio replied simply: "Yes I have."*

I would like to take the great DiMaggio fishing. They say his father was a fisherman.

> *Ernest Hemingway,* The Old Man and the Sea

This son of Italian immigrants gave every American something to believe in. He became the very symbol of American grace, power and skill.

William Jefferson Clinton, president of the United States

Diving

Hockey players get hit in the face with a puck and they get fifty stitches and then come out and play the rest of the game. You only have four stitches, and you only have to do two dives.

Ron O'Brien, U.S. Olympic diving coach, to Greg Louganis

The irony about divers is that, like dancers, we were never the healthiest lot.

Greg Louganis, Olympic gold medalist diver

Doctors

I'd like to find me a plastic surgeon and have my face redone. I'd play a year in college, get drafted number two overall in the NFL draft, take the league's money, put it in the bank, and then have the plastic surgeon restore my original face.

Dexter Manley, professional football player, who was banned for life by the National Football League for substance abuse

If the doctors had told me that I might die playing football, I'd have asked them what the chances were—"Give me the odds, Doc"—that's how much I wanted to play.

Jack Youngblood, professional football player

I have two good doctors—my right leg and my left.

Anonymous

Get your ass out of my office, Dr. Dayton. You've got ten minutes to clean your shit out of my locker room and ten more minutes to get off campus. I'll mail your last check.

Paul "Bear" Bryant, Hall of Fame college football coach, to the team doctor of the Texas A&M, whom he felt was too protective of players

Medicine is just about life and death. Sports is more important than that.

Andrew Edgar, philosopher

The joker got funny and said he found urine in my whiskey. I fired him.

Ty Cobb, Hall of Fame baseball player

Dog Shows

How many other times a year do you get to see dogs with better haircuts than their owners?

Linda Stasi, journalist

I am struck by an irony central to the lot of a purebred dog: As it attains the hallmarks of its breed, it seems to simultaneously relinquish its basic dogginess, until it is less a dog . . .

Jean Hanff Korelitz, journalist

I took her to a show in New Jersey when she was 6 months and 3 days old to get her used to shows—the car, the throwing up, the night in the motel—and she hated it. Every time we picked her up she peed on us. Then we took her to Maine, and she liked it a little better. . . .

Nonie Reynders, owner-handler of Norwich terriers

She's never shown better. People say she's better the second time around. She's the Tina Turner of Dogs.

Michael Canalizo, handler of Afghan hound Ch. Tryst of Grandeur, commenting that she was one of the favorites to win the show after not being on the dog show circuit for two years

She's not getting married or anything. She's a showgirl so she's going to have a string of affairs.

Fran Sunseri, owner of Salilyn 'N Erin's Shameless (a.k.a. Samantha), a Springer spaniel, winner of the 2000 Westminster Kennel Club Dog Show, when asked what the dog was going to do, as she was being retired from the ring

The bitch is back! After two years of male domination, the venerable Westminster Kennel Club awarded its top award last night to a Norwich terrier bitch. . . .

Gersh Kuntzman, writer

The participants are extremely competitive people. That dog out there is an extension of your ego. There's a lot of backbiting—"That dog's had plastic surgery," which is illegal, or "That judge is fixed." You don't see many good losers.

Michael Stern, writer

This is a dog show, after all.

Roger Caras, announcer, writer, humane activist, after a German shorthair pointer relieved itself in the ring during the Westminster Kennel Club Dog Show

TV is going to the dogs tonight: USA is televising the "Westminster Dog Show," while Fox is presenting yet another blood-and-mayhem sweeps special.

David Bianculli, media critic and columnist

Welcome to the . . . Westminster Kennel Club Dog Show, where the dogs don't act like dogs, the people sometimes fight like them.

Rick Hampson, journalist

Double Plays

These are the saddest words—
Tinker to Evers to Chance.
Picking forever our gonfalon bubble,
Causing a Giant to hit into a double,
Words that are heavy with nothing but trouble,
Tinker to Evers to Chance.

Frank Adams, sportswriter

Draft (the)

In pro football the college draft is what makes good teams great, as the youngsters imbue a team with their youth and enthusiasm, pushing the veterans to play harder, and sometimes pushing them out.

Peter Golenboch, sportswriter

It's sure different. I don't want to make a habit of it.

Jerry Krause, team executive, after being in the National Basketball Association lottery for the first time, a season after winning the championship six out of the previous eight years

I was a very late draft choice of the Mittendorf Funeral Home Panthers. Our color was black.

George Will, author and baseball enthusiast, about his Little League draft

We avoided guys who could play the piano.

Paul Brown, football coach and team owner

We don't take underclassmen.
Red Auerbach, basketball executive, on why the Celtics passed on Julius Erving

We would have moved up to take a sexier player, but we were very cautious about doing something just to be sexy.
George Seifert, professional football coach

Whenever you draft, your chances of being wrong are much greater than being right. Every time you take a player, you leave behind six hundred or so others, and chances are that some of them will turn out to be better than the guy you took. No matter how you slice it, the numbers are against you.
Bill Tobin, team executive

Drinking

Colonel Jacob Ruppert makes millions of gallons of beer and Ruth is of the opinion that he can drink it faster than the Colonel and his large corps of brewmasters can make it. Well, you can't! Nobody can!
"Gentleman" Jimmy Walker, mayor of New York, speaking at a banquet honoring Babe Ruth, where he admonished him for his drinking, whereupon Ruth swore not to abuse alcohol anymore, and went on to have one of his best seasons

Drugs

A guy strung out on cocaine cares about setting an example for kids? He cares about stuffing his nose with cocaine. Period.
Jim Brown, Hall of Fame football player

All I really need to know about drugs is that you can't take them and play golf.
Nancy Lopez, champion professional golfer

America discovered cocaine for the first time in the mid-70s. Back then cocaine was the drug you heard about. It was Donna Summer and Barry White and disco music and limousines and *Hollywooooood*.
Thomas "Hollywood" Henderson, professional football player and recovery counselor

Being responsible for yourself, about knowing why you get high an' why you don't need to get high. You know what I'm sayin'? Some guys don't know that they don't need to get high.
Dirk Minnefield, professional basketball player

Drugs are very much on the scene in professional sports today, but when you think about it, golf is the only sport where the players aren't penalized for playing on grass.
Bob Hope, comedian and actor

How many great athletes need to die or have their careers ruined before they get the message? I don't respect anyone who uses drugs. It's so obvious that drugs do nothing but debilitate your mind and your body and, no matter who you are or how old you are, drugs will destroy you sooner or later.
Larry Bird, Hall of Fame basketball player and coach, from a statement issued after the death of Len Bias

I'd always tried to be the best at anything I did . . . I was the best drug addict going. I took great pride in doing it right.
Maury Wills, professional baseball player, broadcaster, and manager

I don't know. I never smoked Astroturf.
Tug McGraw, professional baseball player, when asked if he preferred grass or Astroturf

If I don't make it to the NBA, I'm gonna be a drug dealer. Somehow I gotta get me a Lexus. Whatever it takes.
Booger Smith, high school basketball player, the opening line of the documentary Soul in the Hole

If track is serious about ridding the sport of illegal drugs, then a separate organization is needed, whose only duty is to catch cheaters, regardless of the potential media impact.
Steve Holman, Olympic runner

I got caught in Seoul, lost my gold medal, and I'm here to tell people in this country it's wrong to cheat, not to take it, and it's bad for your health. I started taking steroids when I was nineteen years old because most of the world-class athletes were taking drugs.
Ben Johnson, champion track and field competitor, who was stripped of an Olympic gold medal for testing positive for steroid use

I had good results without doping, but pressure from the sponsors forced me to jump the gun. It was a personal decision . . . I have made a mistake.
Alex Zulle, champion cyclist

In the quest for the winning edge, the advantage over one's opponent, many athletes have opted to dig deeper into their pharmaceutical grab bag.
Fredrick C. Hatfield, writer

It's terrible for the sport but in a strange way it may be good for the sport. This tells all the riders that no matter how much of a star you are,

no matter what race you are leading, you can be caught and punished if you are using drugs.
Bernard Thevenet, champion cyclist and broadcaster, about the drug crackdowns in the European tours

I've got enough problems keeping myself under control without putting some shit in my body that's supposed to make me wild. I do all right on that without any help.
Dennis Rodman, professional basketball player

My high comes from victory. Sports are my drugs.
Jean-Claude Killy, Olympic gold medalist skier

Never has a urine sample been given with such enthusiasm.
Dan Jansen, Olympic gold medalist speed skater, after "holding it in" so that he could deal with a throng of reporters after his last Olympic gold medal

The poor horse got to his feet and galloped for ten miles away from the course; a lucky thing for the trainer, because the horse was not found in time to be given a saliva test.
Dick Francis, champion jockey and novelist, referring to a horse that fell and then ran off a track and away after being given a dose of performance-enhancing drugs

What you had was a thirty-nine-year-old male, 6-foot-5, in excess of 300 pounds, a healthy individual, took one shot of heroin and basically dropped dead as a result.
Bruce Glassrock, Plano, Texas, police chief, on the death of Mark Tuinei

I am a rich man. Just look at my arms. All of my money is in my veins.
Earl Manigault, Harlem playground basketball legend and ex-convict

We won it at the fitba and cocaine's the fitba player's drug. It doesnae stey in the system for long so ye can beat the random tests. So it has to be charlie. It's only appropriate that the money should stay in the game.

Irvine Welsh, Scottish novelist, from
Trainspotting

Dunks

From this day on you shall refer to that historic tribute to interplanetary strength as "Chocolate Thunder Flying, Robinzine Crying, Teeth Shaking, Glass Breaking, Rump Roasting, Bun Toasting, Wham Bam, Glass Breaker I Am Jam." Hopefully, that will satisfy everyone who has been bugging me to put a name on that dunk.

Darryl Dawkins, professional basketball player

He stays up so long he has to file a flight plan with the FAA when he dunks.

Darryl Dawkins, professional basketball player,
referring to Michael Jordan

The 360-windmill was just the warm-up act, a perfect score that put Carter in catch-me-if-you-can mode. For the rest of them playing the Washington General Dunks to Carter's Globetrotters, it was enough to just sit back and hope for a miss that just didn't happen.

Chris Young, sportswriter, referring to the 2000
National Basketball Association
All-Star Slam-Dunk Contest

When Darryl broke that backboard, it was one of the greatest things I ever saw happen in sports history.

Joe Namath, Hall of Fame football player,
referring to Darryl Dawkins, professional
basketball player

When Darryl jammed that dunk, he didn't just break the rim off the backboard—that backboard exploded.

Neil Funk, sportswriter

Durocher, Leo

(b. Jul. 27, 1905; d. Oct. 7, 1991) *Major League Baseball manager; won one World Series and three pennants*

Durocher played people, not colors.

Bill White, baseball player and league executive

He's no Boy Scout, but he understands people. You'll get no special favors from him, but neither will anybody else.

Monte Irvin, professional baseball player

Earnhardt, Dale

(b. Apr. 29, 1952; d. Feb. 18, 2001) *Champion race car driver; won NASCAR seven times; won Daytona 500*

Dale was a lot of fun to race against because he had a cockiness about him. He was full of himself, but there was a funness about him. He enjoyed driving race cars, had a good time doing it.

Jeff Hammond, crew chief

Eating

There are two opposing schools about breakfast. If you knew you were not going to be into fish for two or three hours, a good big breakfast would be the thing. Maybe it is a good thing anyway but I do not want to trust it, so drink a glass of vichy, a glass of cold milk and eat a piece of Cuban bread, read the papers and walk down to the boat. I have hooked them on a full stomach in that sun and I do not want to hook any more that way.

Ernest Hemingway, Nobel Prize–winning writer

Edge (the)

If somebody wants to get an edge on me, they'll have to search for the cracks themselves. They will have to find that advantage themselves. I'm not going to give it to them.

Chuck Knox, professional football coach

There's the guy who says, "Even if I go Oh for three, when I get home I'm just Dad." It sounds to me like they're taking too many Oh for threes. I guess I'm a little afraid of losing that edge.

Mike Piazza, professional baseball player

Effort

Because there might be somebody out there who's never seen me play before.

Joe DiMaggio, Hall of Fame baseball player, to Jimmy Cannon, sportswriter, after Cannon asked him why he played so hard in games after the pennant had already been won

Cinderella never worked this hard.
> *Rick Pitino, college and professional basketball coach, responding to how it felt to be a "Cinderella" team*

Doing your best is more important than being the best.
> *Shannon Miller, Olympic gold medal–winning gymnast*

Don't let anyone outwork you.
> *Attributed to Derek Jeter's father, by Derek Jeter, professional baseball player*

He looked like a big, fat pussy toad out there.
> *George Steinbrenner, baseball owner, about Hideki Irabu, pitcher*

If I do something, it must be 100 percent. There can be no 99.9.
> *Dominik Hasek, professional hockey player*

I just can't sit there and expect the ball to come to me because that makes me easy prey for defenders.
> *Ronaldo, professional soccer player*

I like to see people work . . . Whatever you do, do well. You should be the best you can.
> *William Talbert, professional tennis champion*

I'm just a ball player with one ambition, and that is to give all I've got to help my ball club win. I've never played any other way.
> *Joe DiMaggio, Hall of Fame baseball player*

Industry is not the expenditure of shoe leather. It is having ideas—ideas about the job you hold, how to improve it and yourself.
> *Branch Rickey, baseball executive*

It's not about the market, it's about winning and playing good, you know, that's all that counts.
> *Latrell Sprewell, professional basketball player*

I wish to hell I'd never said the damn thing. I meant the effort . . . I meant having a goal. I sure as hell didn't mean for people to crush human values and morality.
> *Vince Lombardi, Hall of Fame football coach, referring to his famous quote: "Winning isn't everything, it's the only thing."*

My father always told me if I trained hard and took it seriously, my time would come.
> *Ricardo Williams, Jr., professional boxer*

No ballplayer gives 100 percent on every play. He can't. But if you don't on a crucial play, one that loses you a game, oh, geez, it tears you up inside.
> *Rick Casares, professional football player*

No, you grunted. When you grunt you made an effort, and it counts.
> *Sam Snead, champion professional golfer*

People come out to see you perform and you've got to give them the best you have within you.
> *Jesse Owens, Olympic gold medal–winning runner*

When your nose is bleeding and your eyes are black and you are so tired you wish your opponent would crack you on the jaw and put you to sleep, fight one more round remembering that the man who fights one more round is never whipped.
> *"Gentleman" Jim Corbett, champion professional boxer*

You big, dumb son-of-a-bitch, why don't you go in and take that uniform off and go home, for chrissake? You're out here screwing around, with an eleven-run lead . . . You're gonna lose the game, at least you're not gonna get credit for the win, somebody else is on the Dodger team, so why don't you just take that uniform off, because you're not pitching.

Jackie Robinson, Hall of Fame baseball player, to Don Newcombe, when Newcombe was admittedly "experimenting" with a few pitches with a comfortable lead and suddenly loaded up the bases with Ralph Kiner in the box

You should learn a lesson from this smaller guy. He was determined and he really tried hard.

Jesse Owens, Olympic gold medalist track and field competitor, to a group of youngsters, referring to a pint-sized Carl Lewis, Olympic gold medalist track and field competitor, at the Jesse Owens meet

Ego

It is the great word of the twentieth century. If there is a single word our century has added to the potentiality of language it is ego. . . . Muhammad Ali begins with the most unsettling ego of all.

Norman Mailer, Pulitzer Prize–winning writer

The only players I hurt with my words are ones with inflated opinions of their ability.

Bill Parcells, National Football League head coach

Elliott, James Francis "Jumbo"

(b. 1915; d. 1981) *National Collegiate Athletic Association champion track coach*

He holds the all-time record for attendance at weddings and funerals.

Jim Tuppeny, track and field coach, at the legendary track coach's own funeral

There is an old saying, "There are no irreplaceable men on this earth." To me, that is not quite true. Ask the hundreds who knew and loved him.

Jack O'Reilly, stadium announcer, broadcaster, and track and field historian

Emotion

Emotion only stays with you a short period. What you want is a sustained effort of performance.

John Chaney, college basketball coach

Endorsements

American Express. Don't steal home without it.

Wesley Snipes, actor in Major League

I'd rather get Gatorade poured on me than bust my butt selling it.

Bill Parcells, professional football coach

I want to take some time off and do more endorsements.

Oscar De La Hoya, champion boxer

Of the many accolades in sports the right to design your own athletic shoe for the world's top sneaker company is pretty special.

Leigh Gallagher, journalist

Endurance

Believe you can do it. Think no other way but "Yes you can." The human body is capable of considerably more physical endurance than most of us realize.

Paul Reese, Cross USA runner

My strength is being the last man standing.

Robyn Benincasa, extreme athlete, adventure racer

Enthusiasm

If your work is not fired with enthusiasm, you will be fired with enthusiasm.

John Mazur, professional football coach

Equestrian

Clearly it helps to have some gypsy blood, as I must have, in order to enjoy moving around the globe with six horses, two trucks, a trailer, an assortment of motorcycles, bicycles, and better than one hundred pieces of "luggage." Logic, common sense, and practicality must not be essential, for they seem to be missing from my repertoire, else I long since would have stayed home.

Deidre Pirie, champion team driver

Dressage may not strike the uninitiated as a very dramatic sport, but like so many of the really good things in life, it can easily become an acquired taste.

Sandy Pflueger, champion equestrian

Every little boy has a dream. Some dream of pitching in a World Series, some of playing in the Super Bowl. My dream was to ride in the Olympic Games.

Greg Best, Olympic silver medalist

He's everything a horse should be. He's just waiting for me to deliver the ride.

Alice Debany, show jumper, about The Natural, a horse she was riding

He wanted to be a good horse. And now he's a winner, and there aren't a lot of horses that want to win the way he does.

Lisa Jaquin, Olympic equestrian, speaking about her horse For The Moment, who went to win the grand prix of the Los Angeles International

I had to realize that if you didn't win a ribbon in the finals, it didn't mean you aren't a good rider, and if you do win a ribbon it doesn't mean you're going on to greatness.

Kate Chope, show jumper

I love my horses. I love to ride. And I love to win.

Debbie Dolan, show jumper

We have heard the allegations regarding the alleged acts of violence to horses for insurance purposes . . . The well-being of horses at the Winter Equestrian Festival, and of horses everywhere, is our primary concern. We offer our total cooperation with the police and the FBI in any investigation they may choose to conduct and should there be any truth to these allegations, we hope the investigations will lead to the arrest of anyone involved.

Gene Misch, chairman of the Winter Equestrian Festival, regarding the famous equestrian insurance fraud case

Whenever anyone asks them what I did, they say, "Oh, she plays around with horses."

Lisa Jaquin, Olympic equestrian, speaking of her family

Winning at Devon is different from winning every place else. Even placing well here is better than winning at other shows.

David W. Hollis, rider and journalist

Equipment

At one time, I had sixteen different rackets with my name on them . . . A computer goes to work. No racket had won so many major tournaments.

Jack Kramer, professional tennis champion, on the best-selling tennis rackets of all time, the Jack Kramer model

The old glove is dead. The Richie Ashburn model for left-handers, veteran of 10,000 baseballs, has expired at the age of 23.

Ray Fitzgerald, sportswriter, in a column when the glove was taken out of production

What you need is a suit of armor. I haven't got none of those around.

Friday Mcklem, equipment manager Detroit Lions, to George Plimpton, writer posing as a free agent quarterback

Era

There will never be another period like those Twenties . . . There were a lot of first-rate competitors . . . there were millionaire sportsmen around who had interest in all sports. If you thought you could make your point, those were the days to prove it.

Gene Tunney, champion boxer

Equipment Managers

We're the mothers of the organization. We do every thankless task. We pack for them, we clean up after them. If we didn't, they'd up with two left shoes.

Mick McCord, equipment manager, fo . . .

Excuses

No excuse in the world counts for squat.

Mark Schubert, U.S. Olympic swimming coach

Execution

I think it's a good idea.

John McKay, college and professional football coach, responding to a question as to what he thought of his team's execution

Executives

An ability to see beyond the obvious is vital for a general manager.

Mike Wise, sportswriter

A real executive goes around with a worried look on his assistants.

Vince Lombardi, Hall of Fame football coach and executive

Coaches get fired everyday, but a GM can be dumb and last forever.

Doug Moe, professional basketball player and coach

I'm not going to beg anyone to coach this team.

Dave Checketts, franchise executive, after Pat Riley had left the New York Knicks

It's never one loss or a losing streak. That's not how you make the decision.

Dave Checketts, franchise executive, about firing other executives or coaches

In order to run an efficient organization there has to be a Dictator.

Al Advise, owner, football

I've never wanted to sit in a fancy luxury box. I'm in the same seat every game, right in the midst of the crowd. And I'm there because I want to be there.

Red Auerbach, Hall of Fame basketball coach and executive

Front office brilliance in baseball is rarer than a triple play.

Roger Angell, writer

No athletic director holds office longer than two unsuccessful football coaches.

Bob Zuppke, Illinois University football coach

The problem is, they have so many selfish, egotistical people in upper management who think they know more about baseball than Branch Rickey.

Attributed to unknown/former Baltimore Orioles executive

Exercise

Any kind of exercise, is generally better than no exercise at all. Walking is better for you than sitting in front of a television set and playing a sport is better for your health than just being a spectator.

Arnold Schwarzenegger, champion bodybuilder and actor

Exercise has always been my form of meditation. I draw great strength from it, physically as well as emotionally and intellectually.

Dr. Tom Waddell, Olympic decathlon competitor and gay rights activist

Exercise is bunk. If you're healthy, you don't need it; if you are sick, you should take it.

Henry Ford, United States industrialist

Exercise is king. Nutrition is queen. Put the two of them together and you have a kingdom.

Jack Lalanne, fitness guru

I have never taken any exercise . . . and never intend to take any.

Mark Twain, writer

What time does the dissipation of energy begin?

Lord Kelvin, physicist

Expectations

Problems begin when expectations exceed ability.

Johnathan Beverly, runner and writer

Most of us find something frightening about surpassing our own or another's expectations, and this fear usually keeps us from doing it.

Timothy Galloway, writer

The expectation I feel here has risen and rightfully so because we have won. And that's the way it should be. I don't ever want to be a part of any organization that doesn't have high expectations.

Pat Riley, professional basketball player and coach

When I came up, Casey told the writers that I was going to be the next Babe Ruth, Lou Gehrig and Joe DiMaggio all rolled into one. Casey kept bragging on me and the newspapers kept writing it, of course, and I wasn't what Casey said I was. I don't mind admitting that there was incredible pressure on me because of what Casey was saying, and the fans were expecting so much, which I wasn't able to deliver.

Mickey Mantle, Hall of Fame baseball player

You have to expect things of yourself before you can do them.

Michael Jordan, champion professional basketball player

Experience

I value every single game I ever coached. Based on my experience over thirty years in the league, eighteen as a coach, you value every game. And if you don't value it, the players won't value it.

Pat Riley, professional basketball player and coach

Extreme Sports

A harmless and enjoyable walk across England.

Alfred Wainwright, Cross UK walker

Extreme athletes are the sporting industry's answer to our insatiable hunger for anything anti-establishment.

Joanne Chen, writer

Few people have reached the top in the sport of triathalon. Fewer still have been able to maintain that position.

Scott Tinley, champion triathlete

I encourage all of you . . . triathletes to reach for your goals, whether they be to win or just to try. The trying is everything.

Dave Scott, champion triathlete

I felt so good when I crossed the finish line. People who saw me on TV thought I was spaced out . . . All I did was go beyond [my previous] limit.

Julie Moss, champion triathlete, after the 1982 Ironman triathlon

I saw the Ironman for the first time on television in 1982, when Julie Moss fell and crawled across the finish line . . . People were crying and cheering. I thought, "This is incredible."

Mark Allen, champion triathlete

I like to sit on top of my BASE objects for a while, just to look at all those creatures walking to work and stressing.

Thor Alex Kappfjell, BASE jumper

It's no secret that triathlons would be much larger if they didn't have that swim part.

Terry Laughlin, triathlete

I was never the "sweat when no one sees you" kind of person, but I really wanted to test my limits.

Tammy Street, competitive deep freediver

Many dedicated endurance athletes don't need to be told what to do—they need to be told what not to do

Scott Tinley, champion triathlete

Race day is harvest time—that's when you reap the benefits.

Mark Allen, triathlete

Technically, these guys did not run entirely from coast to coast contiguously, because they crossed the Hudson River and Mississippi River by ferry.

Paul Reese, Cross USA runner, who covered both rivers by running across bridges and ran the

entire United States at age 73, speaking of
early runs

The feeling I get at the starting line is that it's over—all the hard work and training are over: The race is the fun part.

Julie Moss, champion triathlete

There are a lot of guys that have more jumps than I have, but when I do jump, I make a point of jumping from special objects in special places.

Thor Alex Kappfjell, BASE jumper

The X Games is about performing at the very highest standards of the modern mixed-climbing game. Not stewing in a tent, freezing your hands at 20,000 feet, or living on freeze-dried yak droppings.

Will Gadd, extreme mixed-climber

My favorite BASE jump is always the last one I've done.

Marta Empinotti, BASE jumper

When all is said and done, the only pressure you have is what you generate for yourself.

Paula Newby-Fraser, eight-time Ironman
champion

When it's good, it's really good. And when it's bad, it's still pretty good.

Scott Tinely, champion triathlete, comparing sex
and pizza to the Ironman triathlon

Failure

Every athlete has to deal with his past failures.

Dan Jansen, Olympic gold medalist speed skater

I can accept failure, but I can't accept not trying.

Michael Jordan, professional basketball player

For every Michael Jordan, there's an Earl Manigault. We can't all make it. Somebody has to fail.

Earl Manigault, Harlem playground basketball legend, and ex-convict

I have figured out that part of the reason I do the things I do, and cannot seem to conquer that one word—myself—is because . . . is because . . . I am a coward.

Floyd Patterson, champion boxer, on why he insisted on leaving arenas in disguise after losses

Fame

Celebrity is a privilege. It is not a right.

Grant Hill, professional basketball player

Great stars that knew their days in fame's bright sun. I heard them trampling to oblivion.

Grantland Rice, sportswriter

I had pro offers from the Detroit Lions and the Green Bay Packers, who were pretty hard up for linemen in those days. If I had gone into professional football, the name Jerry Ford might have been a household word today.

Gerald R. Ford, president of the United States, former center for the University of Michigan

I walk out in the morning, and the UPS guy tells me to go get 'em or something. It's fine, but . . . there's definitely something to be said for anonymity.

Mike Piazza, professional baseball player

I . . . went to the ESPYs, the ESPN sports awards . . . and was simply amazed when famous athletes asked me for *my* autograph. That just doesn't happen to speed skaters.

Dan Jansen, Olympic gold medal speed skater

Mama raised us never to think we're better than anybody else. All the publicity doesn't make you a better person because it's only there for a short time.

Lee Roy Selmon, professional football player

No longer four sous, but one. What a solemn lesson lay in the fall of price! Fate conveys her pronouncements even through the cries of street vendors. Our popularity had fallen seventy-five percent in two hours.

Luigi Barzini, Sr., writer, participant in the Peking-to-Paris race, where he rode in the winning car with Prince Borghese, driver

Oh my gosh, I can't believe I did that. They probably think I'm a real dingbat.

Shannon Miller, Olympic gold medalist gymnast, after mistaking warning motorists as adoring fans and driving the wrong way down a one-way street

Smart lad, to slip betimes away
From fields where glory does not stay
And early though the laurel grows
It withers faster than the rose.

A. E. Housman, poet

There are always thousands of kids around the village, and they all want autographs. After signing a few hundred books, it's easy to brush the kids off or break the monotony by signing yourself as "Bing Crosby" or "Satchel Paige," but if you're square with the small fry . . . you'll discover they'll open doors for you that make your Olympic trip twice as interesting.

Bob Mathias, gold medalist decathlon competitor, politician, and actor

This is the toll of fame: it is always there—always demanding.

Bill Furlong, sportswriter

Family

I got two daughters, one 4 months and one 17 months. It's so much easier to be playing football than taking care of them. Now that's a real job. People ask if I change diapers. I say, "Are you kidding me? I'm the diaper man."

Jesse Armstead, professional football player

I guess we've been Cup crazy the last few years.

Steve Yzerman, professional hockey player, whose wife bore him two children during the playoffs in consecutive years

I had never been there for Bump—or for many of my children. I wasn't home when he was born. I wasn't home to watch him play ball or graduate from school or celebrate his birthday. I was always playing ball.

Maury Wills, professional baseball player, broadcaster, and manager

I love hopping in that car and being home in about two hours. It's the most exciting thing in my life right now. I'm getting back to being a son to my mother, and that's a bond you can't replace with all the money and fame in the world.

Kerry Collins, professional football player

My family is the most important thing to me. I love basketball, but I need my family around me.

Karl Malone, professional basketball player

My life is strange (it has always been strange!), but I feel a lovely calm these days, and a great deal of that comes from being with you and Mom—and watching you grow.

Dr. Tom Waddell, Olympic decathlon competitor and gay rights activist, who wrote this in his journal for his young daughter before he died of AIDS

The kids like to call to hear their father's voice.

Jeannie Fischer, wife of Scott Fischer, mountain climber, who had died a year earlier on Mt. Everest, and whose voice was still on the family's answering machine

My sister's expecting a baby, and I don't know if I'm going to be an uncle or an aunt.

Chuck Nevitt, North Carolina State basketball player, explaining to his coach why he appeared nervous at practice

The prudent climber will recollect what he owes to his family and his friends.

C. E. Matthews, mountain climber

They can't understand why I can't stay home with them all the time. Why just the other day Bobby Jr., told my wife, Joanne, to take my suitcase away from me.

Bobby Hull, Hall of Fame hockey player

Fans

All that a spectator gets out of the game is fresh air, the comical articles in his program, the sight of twenty-two young men rushing about in mysterious formations, and whatever he brought in his flask.

Robert Benchley, humorist, writer and screenwriter

Anyone at the stadium can lose his life. Take the match that Mexico lost to Peru, two–one. An embittered Mexican fan shouted in an ironic tone, "Viva Mexico!" A moment later he was dead, massacred by the crowd.

Ryszard Kapuscinski, journalist

As a people, we count on going to the ballpark or the arena hungry. For three hours we sit there, gorging ourselves like ancient Romans.

Wells Twombly, sportswriter

Fans are the only ones who care. There are no free-agent fans who say, "Get me out of here. I want to play for a winner."

Dick Young, sportswriter

Fifteen Years of Lousy Football.

A banner on a plane that flew over Giants Stadium, in New Jersey

For the real fan, sports are life—and death.

Mike Littwin, sportswriter

Having to watch the Yankees 42 games in one year is the Red Sox fan's equivalent of the Witness Protection Program: it's no way to live, and if you're lucky, no one will find you.

Bill Scheft, writer, a Boston Red Sox fan who lived in New York City

In most European countries, football-related violence is currently a predominantly internal problem, with the majority of incidents occurring at club-level matches, while supporters of the national team abroad are generally better-behaved. The English are an obvious exception to this rule.

Executive Summary, Fan Violence report, Social Issues Research Centre, Oxford, UK

I apologize to the spectators that it was over so quickly. But if it continues like this at the French Open, I'll be happy.

Martina Hingis, professional tennis player, referring to a match she won in 42 minutes, sweeping her opponent 6-1, 6-0

I don't think about a big home run or a big play in the field. I think about warming up in left field and looking out behind the stadium and seeing thousands of people rushing into the ballpark for the first pitch.

Art Shamsky, professional baseball player

I'm beginning to see that the real source of the madness is the unconsciousness of the crowds. I mean, I've been trying to blame the players, the coach, the owners, and the Commissioner for the ugliness, but really WIN OR BE KILLED is a thing in a culture. These fans today were murder.

Arnold J. Mandell, sports psychiatrist

In ancient Rome, citizens befuddled by the complexities of the waning empire found in battles waged by the gladiators precisely the simplistic relief from the government problems of their day.

James Michener, Pulitzer Prize–winning author

In each home, team affiliation was passed on from father to child, with the crucial moments in a team's history repeated like the liturgy of a church service.

Doris Kearns Goodwin, writer and historian

If I have a bad game and they boo me, that's fine. I make the big money. I'll take the blame. But if I take a shot and it doesn't go in, and they boo me? It's ridiculous.

Antoine Walker, professional basketball player

If you make plays and the team wins, the fans will be fine. I don't worry about the fans.

Donovan McNabb, professional football player

If you're a Cleveland Indians fan, that's how it goes: no justice, only irony.

Scott Raab, sportswriter

I'm standing there in the gift shop trying to buy a magazine when this woman starts screaming my name. I didn't even turn around. It was so annoying and embarrassing. There were 15 people in the store staring at me.

Lindsay Davenport, tennis player

It's the kind of place where you can be a successful neurosurgeon, but if you were a lousy football player, people still look at you funny.

Geno DeMarco, Geneva College football coach on local fans

Insufferable ass loses for Reds!

Jimmy Powers, sportswriter, suggesting a headline after a fan leaned over and interfered with a ball in fair play, which the umpire ruled an automatic home run

I owe the public nothing . . . I refuse to be nice to the kiddies.

Bill Russell, Hall of Fame basketball player and coach

I've never been to Maracana, and there is no way you could ever get me to go there. Just to think of all those stinky, sweaty men shouting curse words, fighting and pouring beer and urine all over each other makes me nervous.

Leticia Carvalho de Almeida, Brazilian female soccer fan

The fans finally got what they wanted. They got Allie Sherman fired and they got it with the power of song, with "Good-bye, Allie" serenade that had become a lynch chant wherever the Giants played and lost.

Gene Roswell, sportswriter

The fans have had their hearts broke too often. Come through for them one day, that's nice. Blow it the next, and you're a bum all over again.

Marty Barrett, professional baseball player

Maury, we just wanted you to know that our last name is Wills and we named our little boy Maury, after you. We want to thank you, Maury.

Attributed to unknown fans at Dodger Stadium, by Maury Wills, professional baseball player, broadcaster, and manager

New Yorkers are fanatical fans. Even with the harshest New York fans, though, they're pretty forgiving.

Al Leiter, professional baseball player

Nowhere else in the country do people spit at you, throw bottles at you, throw quarters at you, throw batteries at you and say, "Hey, I did your mother last night—she's a whore."

John Rocker, controversial professional baseball player, about New York fans

On the morning of the start, it seems incredible to relate, there must have been two thousand people on the dock (which I thought would collapse into the seas). This enormous crowd of well-wishers and the merely curious walked back and forth . . . The people came to see this strange breed of men about to set off on a great adventure, the first part of which would keep them at sea for almost two months.

Hal Roth, yachtsman

Parisians like tennis, but they love *la cuisine* more.

Yannick Noah, champion professional tennis player

Please, please get a hit. If you get a hit now, I will make my bed every day for a week.

Doris Kearns Goodwin, writer and historian

Professional sports add something to the spirit and vitality of a city . . . A winning team can bring a city together, and even a losing team can provide a bond of common misery.

Bill Veeck, baseball owner and racetrack operator

Quite a few of them start with, "you big asshole."

Joe Schmidt, professional football coach, quoting his fan mail

Roger has stolen my fans.

Mickey Mantle, Hall of Fame baseball player, about Roger Maris, after Maris was booed

Sports owners have always been scum. Players have always been greedy. The average fan has always been treated like crap.

Mike Lupica, sportswriter

The dream is not for the player. It is for the fan, the worshipper without whom there would be no professional game at all. It is for the lover of the game who doesn't really know what it's like out there on the field, and never *will* know.

Danny Blanchfowler, professional soccer player

The old Dodger fans were the kind of people who picket. The old Giant fans would be embarrassed to do anything so conspicuous, but they were the kind of people who refuse to cross picket lines. Yankee fans are the kind of people who think they own the company the picket line is thrown around.

Murray Kempton, Back at the Polo Grounds

The real stars of the Cubs were the fans. The players change, but the fans stay.

Stuart Gordon, theater and film director and producer

There's a new television show called *thirtysomething, Cowboysnothing.*

Anonymous, reported by Peter Golenbock, sportswriter

These frenzied spectators literally overwhelmed him, swarming round, shouting, yelling, dancing and jumping about like madmen. Those who got near him slapped and banged him on the back, yelling as they did so, "Good!" "Splendid!" "Glorious!" Thus they continued until all the little remaining breath in George's body was well-nigh beaten out of him.

account from an unnamed newspaper about Walter Goodall George's victory in a running event with William Cummings in England in 1886

The Yankees were the "Bronx Bombers," whose pinstriped uniforms signified their elite status, supported by the rich and successful, by Wall Street brokers and haughty business men. The Dodgers were "dem Bums," the "daffiness boys," the unpretentious clowns, whose fans were seen as scruffy blue collar workers who spoke with bad diction. The Giants, owned since 1919 by the same family, the Stonehams, were the conservative team whose followers consisted of small business men who watched calmly from the stands, dressed in shirts and ties, their identity somewhat blurred, caught, as they were, between the Yankee "haves" and the Dodger "have-nots."

Doris Kearns Goodwin, writer and historian

They booed Holzman, DeBusschre and Reed. I guess I'm in good company.

Al Bianchi, Knicks executive

This community doesn't want academic excellence. It wants a gladiatorial spectacle on a Friday night.

Dorothy Fowler, high school teacher, in Odessa, Texas

We are here for the purpose to win for the fans. That is who we work for.

Roberto Clemente, Hall of Fame baseball player

We had the opening-day upper-deck brawl to end all brawls—a brawl so spectacular, a brawl that went on so long, a brawl that spilled over so many rows of blue seats, it actually brought the baseball game to a brawl-gaping halt.

Jayson Stark, sportswriter, referring to a fight in the stands that actually stopped the game, in an opening day game between the Phillies and Braves in Philadelphia

We're not looking for trouble. It's all in fun. But these people take it personal. It's the fifth inning and we're already in our third section.

Bobby Kline, Mets fan, who along with his rowdy buddies went to Veterans Stadium to root for his team loudly amidst the Philly faithful

We've got an undertaker with us from Utica, so you don't have to worry, you can hit him as hard as you like.

Anonymous fan to Rocky Graziano, before a championship bout

When fans come to the ballpark, damn it, every last one of 'em is a manager.

Whitey Herzog, professional baseball player, executive, and manager

When we were on the bench, we would look up into the stands and count the people.

Larry Grantham, professional football player on the terrible New York Titans, whose games went largely unattended

When we were uptown we got a lot of fat broads who, when they got tired of beating up their husbands, came to the Garden looking for a fight. Or we got West Side hookers on the make.

Anonymous New York Knickerbockers executive

You can't compare Brooklyn fans with any other . . . It was OK if they wanted to holler against their own. But they didn't want strangers to do it.

Gil Hodges, professional baseball player and manager

We were in Dallas together in 1960 when [Landry] coached the Cowboys and I coached the Texans. We got along very well. But there was a lot of confusion because of the teams' names, and I used to get a lot of his mail, and he would get a lot of mine. If I got a letter and it was someone saying something negative about the Cowboys, I would seal it back up and send it to him. The ones that said good things about the Cowboys, he never saw.

Hank Stram, Hall of Fame football coach and broadcaster

Without Tittle the Giants couldn't go from Grand Central to Times Square on the subway.

Irwin Shaw, best-selling author, attributed to his next-door neighbor

You wolves been howling for blood all year. Maybe this'll shut you up.

John King, professional baseball player, pitcher, as he threw fifty chunks of meat into the stands

Fatigue

Fatigue makes cowards of us all.

Vince Lombardi, Hall of Fame football coach

Fats, Minnesota

(b. Jan. 19, 1913; d. Jan. 18, 1996) *Infamous and brash pool player and trick shot artist; portrayed in the motion picture* The Hustler *by Jackie Gleason (who was taught by Fats's arch nemesis Willie Mosconi)*

He starts playing for two dollars a game, and pretty soon the butcher and baker are playing for a hundred bucks a game and they never saw a pool table before that.

Anonymous pool hustler about Minnesota Fats, legendary pool player

"Hustler" is another word for "thief," and "Minnesota Fats" is another word for "phony."

Willie Mosconi, world champion pool player

He's probably never been to Minnesota.

Willie Mosconi, world champion pool player

Fear

Correct form is the forerunner to good performance, and the early cure of fear.

Branch Rickey, baseball executive

Do I have fear? I've asked myself that question a million times and come up with a million answers.

Shanny Shanholtzer, downhiller, U.S. ski team

Fear? A downhiller with fear? If I had fear, I wouldn't race.

> *Karl Schranz, champion downhiller*

Fear is your best friend or your worst enemy. It's like fire. If you can control it, it can cook for you; it can heat your house. If you can't control it, it will burn everything around you and destroy you.

> *Cus D'Amato, boxing trainer*

Fear of failure, especially in our success-oriented society, is a common malady that afflicts us all in one degree or another. The thing to do is simply recognize it for what it is, then treat its symptoms. Fear of failure manifests itself as tension.

> *Eric Evans, Olympic kayaker and outdoorsman*

He was kind of staring . . . It was as if he knew something bad was about to happen.

> *Ed "Too Tall" Jones, professional football player, about Craig Morton in a Super Bowl loss*

I always ran through fear—of being beaten. It brought out the best in me, being terrified of being beaten.

> *Shirley Strickland De La Hunty, Olympic medalist track and field competitor*

I'd love to play baseball, even now, but I have this one great fear, you see: I'm afraid of the ball.

> *Tiny Tim, musician, sports fan*

I guess I'm more afraid of being afraid than actually being afraid.

> *Ted Turner, yachtsman and baseball owner*

In a sense, fear became a friend—I hated it at the time but it added spice to the challenge and satisfaction to the conquest.

> *Sir Edmund Hillary, mountain climber*

It is never possible to conquer fear, but it can be subdued for a time. Watch the great athlete work at his craft and you see someone who has known fear before and will know fear again, but who goes about his job fearlessly. This is the courage of an athlete and it is towering to behold.

> *Roger Kahn, sportswriter*

Those moments when I went from calmness to curiosity to worry to panic (I have always feared drowning) . . . Why seek them? Perhaps not only to have stories to tell, but also to make sense of the stories we already know.

> *Andrea Barrett, sailor and kayaker*

To taste fear . . . and choke it down is a continuing act of bravery.

> *Roger Kahn, sportswriter, referring to the constant brushback pitches thrown at Gil Hodges, and his ability to stand at the plate*

When everything is working perfectly, I'm no more afraid than I am driving the family car on a highway. When something goes wrong, it scares the hell out of me.

> *Fireball Roberts, champion race car driver*

Fencing

Dueling at the drop of a hat was as European as truffles and as American as mom's apple pie.

> *Barbara Holland, writer*

Fencing came to me out of the blue, one of those quirks of fate. But it must have been a pretty strong quirk. I came to the sport not so much by choice as by pure necessity.

> *Ralph Faulkner, fencer*

For as long as I have known, the throwing of bouts has been going on in fencing.

Lev Rossochick, sportswriter

For the screen, in order to be well photographed and also grasped by the audience, all swordplay should be so telegraphed with emphasis that the audience will see what is coming. All movements—instead of being as small as possible, as in competitive fencing—must be large.

Fred Cravens, competitive fencer and stunt coordinator, attributed by Nick Evangelista, fencing instructor

In fencing you lose a lot. We tell them "Stop crying; life is going to be this way."

Peter Westbrook, Olympic bronze medal fencer and fencing coach

It is customary for profligates to learn the art of fencing.

London edict, 1286 A.D.

It is the fencing master's strict moral duty toward his artistic ancestors to see to it that centuries-old traditions are respected, honored and enforced.

Aldo Nadi, fencer

It's not necessarily who's hitting first, but who is hitting correctly.

Eric Perret, writer

The entire secret of arms consists of only two things: to give, and not to receive.

Molière, Le Bourgeois Gentilhomme

The sabre is a cavalry weapon, so your target is a mounted man from the waist up; and it's an edged weapon, so you're not limited to poking—you get to wing the thing. It leaves welts. Foil and epee fencers say it's for barbarians.

Eric Perret, writer

World Cup bouts are for sale, and an unscrupulous few go that route.

Don Lane, Canadian fencing team

You can't go nowhere, you can't fight with anybody, unless you have good footwork. It's impossible. You can't do nothing without good footwork.

Peter Westbrook, Olympic bronze medal fencer and fencing coach

Field Goals

It was a good game . . . if you like field goals.

Don Meredith, professional football player and broadcaster

Twenty-two straining giants in perfect condition fight for fifty-nine minutes. Then some European runs onto the field, kicks a fifteen-yard field goal, wins the game, and shouts, "Hooray!"

Alex Karras, professional football player, broadcaster, and actor

Field Hockey

Field hockey is preeminently a game of swift and fluid movement . . . more a passing game than a dribbling and dodging game.

Wendy Lee Martin, field hockey coach and player

It's not too much to say that the character of the playing surface determines the level of play possible in this game—just as it does in baseball or billiards.

Wendy Lee Martin, field hockey coach and player

The true elegance of field hockey is the team passing game. Unfortunately, many players are remembered for their dribbling skills instead of their passing skills because it appears to be more spectacular.

Elizabeth Anders, Olympic field hockey player and college field hockey coach

Fielding

Although he is a very poor fielder, he is also a very poor hitter.

Ring Lardner, sportswriter

Don't let it hit you on the coconut, Maxie!

Dick Groat, baseball player and manager, warning second baseman Maxvill not to botch an easy pop-fly hung up in midair

Etten's glove fields better without Etten in it.

Joe Trimble, sportswriter, about Nick Etten, professional baseball player

I fought the wall, and the wall won.

Dmitri Young, professional baseball player, after dropping a fly ball when he ran into the outfield wall

Fights

Here I am, come out and get me.

Tommy Lasorda, professional baseball player and manager, to Hank Bauer and Billy Martin, from the mound, as a Kansas City pitcher, after knocking down three batters in a row

If they took away our sticks and gave us brooms, we'd still fight.

Phil Esposito, former professional player and executive

If you see European hockey, there are no fights, and it's boring.

Eddie Johnston

I have never liked it when guys on my team have gone out and fought somebody after I got hit.

Steve Yzerman, professional hockey player

I'll kill you. You remember that, I'll kick your ass! You've got a good team and you don't need that edge! That's why I told my kid to knock your f★★★★★★ kid in the mouth!

John Chaney, college basketball coach, to John Calipari, college coach, after an altercation between the two

I'm low on sticks, and I didn't want to lose one on his head.

Mike Richter, on not swinging at Tie Domi, who was fighting with one of his teammates

Sometimes people ask, "Are hockey fights for real?" And I say, "If they weren't, I'd get in more of them."

Wayne Gretzky, Hall of Fame professional hockey player

They key is to be fast with your dukes. First, you get him with a good shot. The gloves come off right away—that's automatic—then you get him with the first punch.

John Ferguson, professional hockey player

We don't want anybody to be fighting for no reason. We don't want anybody to get kicked out because that's not professional. But, if that's what we have to do, then we're going to have to do it.

Antonio Davis, professional basketball player

We're the last of the gladiator teams.

Isiah Thomas, professional basketball player, executive and coach, about being part of the Detroit Pistons

Finley, Charles O.

(b. Feb. 22, 1918; d. Feb. 19, 1997) *Major League Baseball owner (won three World Series); also owned National Hockey League and American Basketball Association teams*

Charles O. Finley is as vulgar as spit. I think he's beautiful.

Charles McCabe, sportswriter

A combination of Machiavelli and Billy Graham.

Charles McCabe, sportswriter

Firings (coaches)

It's like a marriage. You're not going to fight with your lover when you're having sex and having a good time. But as the marriage goes on and goes on and you get used to each other, you get set in your ways and this and that.

Michael Cooper, professional basketball player, referring to the departure of Pat Riley, professional basketball player and coach

Try to exercise, eat better, try to do some fun things with my wife.

Tom Davis, college basketball coach, on what he was going to do after he was fired

You've taken my team away from me.

Tom Landry, Hall of Fame professional football coach, after coaching the Dallas Cowboys to 20 straight seasons with a winning record, on the day he was fired

Fishing

Abating in his flurry, the whale once more rolled out into view; surging from side to side; spasmodically dilating and contracting his spout-hole, with sharp, cracking, agonizing respirations. At last, gush after gush of clotted red gore, as if it had been of purple lees of red wine, shot into the frightened air; and falling back again, ran dripping down his motionless flanks into the sea. His heart had burst!

Herman Melville, novelist, from Moby-Dick

After toiling and watching and creeping about for the greater part of a day, with scarcely any success, in spite of all our admirable apparatus, a lubberly country urchin came down from the hills with a rod made from a branch of a tree, a few yards of twine, and, as Heaven shall help me! I believe a crooked pin for a hook, baited with a vile earthworm—and in half an hour caught more fish than we had nibbles throughout the day.

Washington Irving, writer

All great fishermen go to bed early.

Ted Williams, Hall of Fame baseball player and world-class fisherman

All men are equal before trout.

Herbert Hoover, president of the United States

Although the thrill of fishing is catching the fish, the greatest challenges any captain faces are often keeping the crew focused, making sure the vessel remains mechanically sound, and returning safely to port.

Linda Greenlaw, swordfish boat captain

Angling is somewhat like poetry, men are to be born so.

Izaak Walton, writer

95

Angling may be said to be so like the mathematics, that it can never be fully learnt.

Izaak Walton, writer

As a big game fisherman, I never saw a sailfish that didn't look better in the ocean than on somebody's line—or wall.

Grantland Rice, sportswriter

At the outset, the fact should be recognized that the community of fishermen constitute a separate class or subrace among the inhabitants of the earth.

Grover Cleveland, president of the United States

Casual observers are apt to think that people who scrinch along brooks swatting mosquitoes and getting their seats wet are just trying to escape these tension-producing atomic days; nothing could be further from the truth. The creep'n'crawl society is dedicated to the proposition that small streams operate on the short-term payment plan.

A. J. McClane, outdoorsman and writer

Cruelty disguised as a sport! Fishing is the vice of the shirker and the rummy. No-works, ashamed of their laziness, cover it up by doing their loafing with a fishing line in their hands.

Jimmy Cannon, sportswriter

Fishing, if a fisher may protest,
Of pleasures is the sweetest, of sports the
best,
Of exercises the most excellent,
Of recreations the most innocent,
But now the sport is marred, and wott ye
why?
Fishes decrease, and fishers multiply

Thomas Bastard, writer (1598)

Fish in the water are always larger than fish out of the water.

Randy Voorhees, fisherman and writer

Fishing is a test of character, but it's a test you can take over and over as many times as you want.

John Gierach, fisherman and writer

Every healthy boy, every right-minded man, and every uncaged woman, feels at one time or another, and maybe at all times, the impulse to go 'a fishing.

Eugene McCarthy, writer, politician

Fishing is a jerk at one end of the line waiting for a jerk at the other end.

Mark Twain, writer

Fishing is an Art, or at least, it is an Art to catch fish.

Izaak Walton, writer

Going all over the world doesn't make you a top fisherman, it makes you a top traveler.

Lee Wulff, outdoorsman and writer

Good fishing never stops. There are only times when in some places it is better than in others.

George Fichter, fisherman and writer

How capricious is the memory of anglers! I cannot remember the name of my first dog, my first schoolteacher, or the first girl I kissed . . . but I can remember the correct name of the first trout stream I ever fished.

M. R. Montgomery, outdoorsman and writer

I do it because it won't be done much longer. I fish with my hands, well, jus' 'cause I can.

Patrick Mire, grappler (or hand fisherman)

I have done a little research with waitresses, bellhops, and bartenders. The waitresses say that fishermen abuse them most and tip with a miser's caution.

Jimmy Cannon, sportswriter

I have found repeatedly, of late years, that I cannot fish without falling a little in self-respect. I have tried it again and again. I have skill at it, and, like many of my fellows, a certain instinct for it, which revives from time to time, but always when I have done I feel that it would have been better if I had not fished.

Henry David Thoreau, philosopher and writer

I have had a marlin sound four hundred yards straight down, all the rod under water over the side, bent double with that weight going down, down, down, watching the line go, putting on all pressure possible on the reel to check him, him going down and down until you are sure every inch of line will go. Suddenly he stops and you straighten up, get onto your feet, get the butt in the socket and work him up slowly, finally you have a double line on the reel and think he is coming to gaff and then the line begins to rip out as he hooks up and heads off to sea just under the surface to come out in ten long, clean jumps.

Ernest Hemingway,
Nobel Prize–winning author

I have never caught a fish on a first cast, nor have I ever made a first cast without thinking I would catch a fish.

Ellington White, writer

I have to admit that those golden trout sure are small. But then I ask, How big exactly

does a nugget of true gold have to get before it is of true value?

Thomas McIntyre, outdoorsman and writer

If Satch and I were pitching on the same team, we'd cinch the pennant by July 4, and go fishing until World Series time.

Dizzy Dean, Hall of Fame baseball player,
referring to Satchel Paige,
Hall of Fame baseball player

I spent a season in my new craft fishing on the coast, only to find I did not have the cunning to bait a hook.

Joshua Slocum, sailor, first modern sailor
to sail around the world alone

It is impossible to avoid the conclusion that the fishing habit, by promoting close association with nature, by teaching patience and by generating or stimulating useful contemplation, tends directly to the increase of the intellectual power of its votaries and through them to the improvement of our national character.

Grover Cleveland, president of the United States

Just sort of estimate 'em, son. For some inscrutable reason, the Lord made fish light and women heavy.

Havilah Babcock, outdoorsman and writer,
attributed to his father about never
weighing a fish

Most trout fisherman I know, in these later days of greatly heightened fishing pressure on streams, where the anglers appear to outnumber fish, approach their sport with the attitude of the gambler who, on being told that the roulette wheel was crooked, said: "I know, but what can I do? It's the only wheel in town?"

Arnold Gingrich, outdoorsman and writer

No fish is more humbling than a big tailer who ventures into glass-calm shallows—a mere presence that dares you to make the first move.

A. J. McClane, outdoorsman and writer

No misanthrope, I must nevertheless confess that I like and frequently prefer to fish alone. Of course in a sense all dedicated fishermen must fish alone; the pursuit is essentially a solitary one; but sometimes I not only like to fish out of actual sight and sound of my fellow addicts, but alone in the relaxing sense that I need not consider the convenience or foibles or state of hangover of my companions. . . .

Robert Traver, outdoorsman and writer

Nothing quite properly prepares you for the look of your first California golden trout you take from a creek and hold in your hand . . . What he most looks like as he flutters in your hand is a terrible drink or a goddamned Technicolor sunset!

Thomas McIntyre, outdoorsman and writer

One of the attractions of wading into a stream is that you become a part of the world of the trout, salmon, or steelhead that you seek.

Joan Salvato Wulff, outdoorswoman, broadcaster, and writer

People may fish in different ways, for different species, and for different reasons, but we all connect as anglers. The language of fishing cuts across all differences.

Jim Brown, fly-fisherman and collector of antiquary fishing equipment

Rainbow trout fishing is as different from brook trout fishing as prizefighting is from boxing.

Ernest Hemingway, Nobel Prize–winning author

Salmon, male and female, are called cocks and hens, I learn from my books. The salmon appears to be a very odd fish.

William Humphrey, outdoorsman and journalist

Somehow I feel that all the elements and all life, whether human or otherwise, are directly related, so much so that anyone who is sincerely enraptured by the wonders of nature stands very close to the great beyond. To such souls fishing is an outlet to the feelings, a surcease from life's trials.

Edward C. Janes, fisherman and writer

Sometimes, after staying in a village parlor till the family had all retired, I have returned to the woods, and, partly with a view to the next day's dinner, spent the hours of midnight fishing from a boat by moonlight, serenaded by owls and foxes, and hearing from time to time, the creaking note of some unknown bird close at hand.

Henry David Thoreau, philosopher and writer

Sometimes you think you've got the fish caught and cleaned, and he slips back into the water.

Charlie Whittingham, thoroughbred horse trainer

The gods do not deduct from man's allotted span the hours spent in fishing.

Babylonian proverb

The minds of anglers are usually as crammed as their fishing vests although not necessarily with information that will enlighten non-anglers.

M. R. Montgomery, outdoorsman and writer

The minnow was thrown as a fly several times, and, owing to my peculiar, and hitherto unpublished, methods of fly throwing, nearly six pennyworth of the triangles came off, either in my coat-collar, or my thumb, or the back of my hand. Fly fishing is a very gory amusement.

Rudyard Kipling, Nobel Prize–winning author

The real angler knows his sport transcends every limitation of economics, class and culture. In my own hometown, fishing was the only place the doctor, the alcohol welder, the priest, the barber, and the town bum could meet on equal footing.

Thomas McGuane, writer

The real lessons of fishing are the ones that come after you've caught the fish. They have to do with solitude, gratitude, patience, perspective, humor, and the sublime coffee break.

John Gierach, fisherman and writer

The red tide now poured from all sides of the monster like brooks down a hill. His tormented body rolled not in brine, but in blood, which bubbled and seethed for furlongs behind in their wake. The slanting sun playing upon this crimson pond in the sea, sent back its reflection into every face, so that they all glowed to each other like red men.

Herman Melville, writer

The rest of the world's trout may be taken in summer, to the sounds of birds and the pleasant hum of insects, but the steelhead—the big, sea-going rainbow of the Northwest coasts—is winter's child.

Paul O'Neil, outdoorsman and writer

These are my tarpon, but you may play with them.

Jake Jordan, fisherman

The true sportsmen among anglers is the trout fisherman, who wades right into the fish's territory and battles it out hand to hand, taking an honest man's chance of being swept down the rapids and bashed against the rocks.

Red Smith, sportswriter

The whole madness of Opening Day fever is quite beyond me: it deserves the complexities of a Jung or a Kafka, for it is archetypal and rampant with ambiguity. And still you would not have it.

Nick Lyons, outdoorsman, writer, and publisher

There are a dozen justifications for fishing. Among them is the importance to the political world. No political aspirant can qualify for election unless he demonstrates he is a fisherman, there being twenty-five million persons who pay annually for a license to fish.

Herbert Hoover, president of the United States

There certainly is something in angling, if we could forget, which anglers are apt to do, the cruelties and tortures inflicted on worms and insects, that tends to produce a gentleness of spirit, and a pure serenity of mind.

Washington Irving, writer

There is no use in walking 5 miles to fish when you can depend on being just as unsuccessful near home.

Mark Twain, humorist and writer

This is where they painted spots on him and taught him to swim.

Meade Schaeffer, angler and artist, commenting on a fishing village, Roscoe, New York

Throw your bread upon the water and a carp will beat you to it.

Hugh E. Keogh, sportswriter

To capture the fish is not all of fishing. Yet there are circumstances which make this philosophy hard to accept.

Zane Grey, writer

To celebrate Opening Day on the Beaverkill is a little like observing Christmas in Bethlehem.

Red Smith, sportswriter

Upon finishing his residency in tropical medicine, he got married, went on a fishing honeymoon to Ireland, returned to London, where he set his wife up in a flat in South Kensington, and shipped out to Nairobi. There he spent the next twenty-five years, returning home on three months' leave every year to fish, and to see his wife.

William Humphrey, outdoorsman and journalist, referring to a fishing companion

Your three- or four-pound sophomores smack resoundingly. But your real fish, your juggernauts, your deans and full professors sort of roll ponderously and engulf your lure.

Havilah Babcock, outdoorsman and writer

You will search far to find a fisherman to admit that a taste for fishing, like a taste for liquor, must be governed lest it come to possess its possessor.

Sparse Grey Hackle, writer

Fixing

I'm forever blowing ball games . . .

Ring Lardner, writer, (sung to the tune of "I'm Forever Blowing Bubbles"), about Claude Williams, one of the conspirators in throwing the 1919 World Series

This series is fixed. You can have it—I'm going to the race track.

Champ Pickens, event promoter, speaking about the 1919 World Series

Fly-fishing

Anyone can tie a fly and name it after himself, but the trick is to create one that will be used consistently by other fishermen.

Nelson Bryant, writer

Down in Maine, when they say "fly-fishing only" they mean fly-fishing only the way a gentleman would fish, for fish only a gentleman would fish for. In other words, casting dry flies to trout or salmon and—if one must, wets, too, though the latter act is regarded as questionable at best, somewhat akin to picking up chicken wings with one's fingers.

Ted Williams, Hall of Fame baseball player and world–class fisherman

Fly-fishing is easy to learn, like calculus or the golf swing.

Randy Voorhees, fisherman and writer

Fly-fishing is probably the final refinement in angling. In no other fishing is the balance of tackle so vital. This is the system that really lets you test the limits of your equipment and skill.

Ray Bergman, fisherman and writer

Fly-fishing takes you to spectacular places and gives you a reason for being there that is far more compelling than just looking at the scenery. You become a participant rather than a spectator, the creatures of the water world become an extension of those things you care about . . . It is difficult to feel lonely when you are "out fishin'."

Joan Salvato Wulff, outdoorswoman, broadcaster, and writer

Fly-fishing. There was a small stream up behind our house, with brook trout. I taught myself how to fly-fish—learned practicing on the brook trout—and got to be pretty good at it.

Greg LeMond, champion cyclist, when asked what he did when he wasn't racing

Fly rods are like women; they won't play if they're maltreated.

Charles Ritz, writer and sportsman

For years my fly-casting technique has compared, rather banally I might add, to an old lady fighting off a bee with a broom handle.

Patrick F. McManus, outdoorsman and writer

In August the multitudes run to the beaches by hordes, the politicians return to their conventions and their drums and flags and slogans, most of the sporting magazines turn to hunting, the city turns deathly gray and dry and hot and anxious, and I begin to hear the last chords of the fly-fisherman's year.

Nick Lyons, outdoorsman, writer, and publisher

In our family there was no clear line between fly-fishing and religion.

Norman Maclean, A River Runs Through It

It's funny how we always expect that, in the wilderness, innocent fish will pounce greedily on any fly. It does happen, of course, but in my experience there have been just as many occasions when I had to eat humble pie.

A. J. McClane, outdoorsman and writer

No pursuit on earth is so burdened by arcane lore as fly-fishing, beside which brain surgery and particle physics are simple backyard pastimes.

Charles Kuralt, broadcaster and writer

Presenting a fly to a fish moving through the water is like shooting game birds; you must lead the target to make the interception.

Joan Salvato Wulff, outdoorswoman, broadcaster, and writer

The angler can have no cold nor discomfort nor anger, unless he be the cause himself. For he can lose at the most only a line or hook, of which he can have a plentiful supply of his own making.

Dame Juliana Berners, Treatise of Fishing With an Angle, *written in 1496*

Until man is redeemed, he will always take a fly rod too far back.

Norman Maclean, writer

When I first started fly-fishing it was largely because of casting, that incredible suspension of the line overhead, the sweeping curve following, in a delayed reaction, the motion of the rod. The point of all other fishing was to bring home meat, but with a fly line the process itself was the purpose. The elegance of casting justified the endeavor, regardless of the catch.

Wayne Fields, outdoorsman and writer

While it is true that flowing rivers create difficulties for the fly-caster, these are trivial compared to the problems faced by the trout.

M. R. Montgomery, outdoorsman and writer

Focus

I just went out and tried to do my best because I wanted to do my best, not because I was focused the whole time on winning. If you focus on winning, you have to focus on other people. I would focus solely on doing my best.

Greg Louganis, Olympic gold medalist diver

I'm just focused on what I have to do, not why I was brought here.

Latrell Sprewell, professional basketball player

I'm not going to relax. Now is the time to be even more focused, more positive, more serious, to make sure things go in the right direction.

Corey Pavin, champion professional golfer

I try not to get too caught up in thinking about the task ahead. I just do what has to be done. I have the belief in myself that what I'm doing is right. Then I let the rest happen.

Eamonn Coghlan, world champion miler

None of us can relax until we get to the final, lift the cup and take it back to Brazil.

Ronaldo, professional soccer player

Too many golfers get concerned about what others do and forget to do what they have to do to play the game.

Sam Snead, champion golfer

With a chance to win, Durocher was hardly fit to live with. He could only see one thing—the pennant. He wouldn't settle for anything less, wasn't interested in anything less, and wouldn't talk about anything less.

Russ Hodges, broadcaster

The conventions of the ring demand that a fighter in training become a monk. For months at a time, he hardens his body on road-work and beefsteak, and practices an enforced loneliness—even (tradition has it) sexual loneliness—better to focus the mind on war.

David Remnick, writer

My plans are all Dempsey.

Gene Tunney, champion boxer, who shunned a few lesser, easy fights, because he wanted to become champion

When you're riding, only the race in which you're riding is important.

Bill Shoemaker, Hall of Fame jockey

You've got 45 minutes left in your dream. If you don't use this time wisely you're going to go home and be sad about it.

Tony DiCicco, soccer coach, U.S. women's World Cup team

Food

Carrots may be good for my eyes, but they won't straighten out the curve ball.

Carl Furillo, professional baseball player

I eat what I eat and I weigh what I weigh.

George Foreman, champion boxer

If we're not willing to settle for junk living, we certainly shouldn't settle for junk food.

Sally Edwards, Ironman triathlete and writer

Most of the top runners I know feel the same way about diet. They're skeptical about nutrition being the prime element in racing success, but they like to check each other's grocery lists. Just in case.

Don Kardong, runner and writer

Some days you want broccoli, other days Hostess Ding Dongs. Don't ask why.

Scott Tinely, champion triathlete

Sometimes I wonder whether I run high mileage so I can eat like this, or do I eat like this so I can run high mileage?

Bill Rodgers, champion runner, speaking of his favorite snack of mayonnaise and chocolate chip cookies

Take me out to the ball game,
   take me out to the crowd.
Buy me some peanuts and Cracker Jack,
I don't care if I ever get back.

lyrics from "The Old Ball Game"

Take away the hot-dog and all its attendant comestibles, such as peanuts, popcorn, Cracker Jacks and egg salad sandwiches, and you'd have a different country.

Wells Twombly, sportswriter

Together they are capable of devouring any two Chinese restaurants east of Shanghai on the same night. That they have not yet succeeded is not for lack of trying.

Jerry Izenberg, sportswriter, on professional football players and roommates Erik Howard and John "Jumbo" Elliott

Football

As a reflection of American life, the most popular sport in America is professional football: brutal, precise, competitive, and highly standardized. In football, as in much of American society, the competitor is The Enemy, and the all-consuming passion is to win, often at any cost.

Dr. Ross Thomas Runfola, sportswriter

At the base of it was the urge, if you wanted to play football, to knock someone down, that was what the sport was all about, the will to win closely linked with contact.

George Plimpton, writer and editor

You go outdoors to play football. You go in the house to get warm.

Bud Grant, professional football coach

Football is a game designed to keep coal-miners off the streets.

Jimmy Breslin, journalist

Football is unique and good. Where else in life do you see dedication and teamwork and spirit? People enjoy it because it is reassuring to them to see good things.

Woody Hayes, college football coach

Football is not a game but a religion, a metaphysical island of fundamental truth in a highly verbalized, disguised society, a throwback of 30,000 generations of anthropological time.

Dr. Arnold Mandell, sports psychologist

Football players, like prostitutes, are in the business of ruining their bodies for the pleasure of strangers.

Merle Kessler, writer

Forget touchdowns, I played football for the chance to hit another man as hard as I could—to fuck him up, to move through him like wind through a door. Anybody who tells you different is a liar.

Elwood Reid, writer

Due to its ingredients . . . courage, mental and physical condition, spirit and its terrific body contact which tends to sort the men from the boys . . . football remains one of the great games of all time.

Grantland Rice, sportswriter

I do believe that my best hits border on felonious assault.

Jack Tatum, professional football player

In a universal sense, football is so insignificant, it's ridiculous.

Pat Hayden, professional football player

I never realized what it meant to take a team from a warm climate into the ice-box area of the Midwest. To my sorrow, I found out twice in three years.

George Allen, professional football coach, reply on losing his second cold weather Conference championship.

If their IQ's were lower, they would be geraniums.

Russ Francis, professional football player, on defensive linemen

If you've never been tackled by L.T. [Lawrence Taylor], don't feel bad about it. Believe me, there are better things you can do with your time.

Eric Dickerson, professional football player

Is it normal to wake up in the morning in a cold sweat because you can't wait to beat another human's guts out?

Joe Kapp, professional football player

It's not the fact that men love football that makes modern woman want to scream . . . It's the assumption that she is incapable of loving it too.

Sally Jenkins, writer

It would be a real misfortune to lose so manly and vigorous a game as football.

Theodore Roosevelt, president of the United States

Let's face it, you have to have a slightly recessive gene that has a little something to do with the brain to go out on the football field and beat your head against other human beings on a daily basis.

Tim Green, professional football player, broadcaster, and writer

Football is a game played down in the dirt, and always will be.

Steve Owen, champion professional football coach

Football is the closest thing we have to the Christians and the lions.

Dan Jenkins, best-selling author

Men are clinging to football on a level we aren't even aware of. For centuries, we ruled everything, and now, in the last ten minutes, there are all these incursions by women. It's our Alamo.

Tony Kornheiser, writer

Monday Night Football.

Camille Paglia, writer and feminist, when asked what was her favorite television show

Professional football is no longer a game. It is a war. And it brings out the same primitive instincts that go back thousands of years.

Malcolm Allison, writer

Pro football is like nuclear warfare. There are no winners, only survivors.

Frank Gifford, professional football player

The prevalent nature of the professional football player is that of soldier of fortune. He's trained and willing to bust people up.

Jim Brown, Hall of Fame football player

We're basically a save-the-whales-team; we can't turn down big people who can play.

George Young, professional football executive

When it comes to football, God is prejudiced—toward big, fast kids.

Chuck Mills, professional football player

Football is, after all, a wonderful way to get rid of your aggressions without going to jail for it.

Heywood Hale Broun, writer

Football is the quintessential American sport: lots of violence punctuated by committee meetings.

George Will, political analyst and baseball aficionado

Football isn't a contact sport, it's a collision sport. Dancing is a contact sport.

Vince Lombardi, National Football League Hall of Fame coach

The best thing in football was to really pop someone. One of the great joys of my life was to get a bead on a guy and really put him out.

John Gordy, professional football player

The head coach can be considered the general, and his assistants the butt-kicking drill instructors, along with the whole coterie of trainer-medics, physicians, waterboys and office helpers. In addition the President can come to the war zone and see how his boys are doing.

Rick Sortun, professional football player

A boy who doesn't like contact shouldn't play football, because he isn't going to change.

Red Blaik, former college football coach

Some guys might play pro football for the money alone, but after two years they're gone. This is just too punishing a sport to play just for money.

Rick Casares, professional football player

To me, no football player is too young, no football player is over the hill, no football player is dumb. They are all smart enough, all champions—if I and my coaches are good enough to teach them.

Chuck Knox, professional football coach

Western supremacy in football is a triumph of the middle-class over the rich.

Knute Rockne, Hall of Fame college football coach

When I played football I was turning people onto violence, competition and greed.

Chip Oliver, professional football player

Women get pleasure and empowerment from subverting and making fun of football. In part because it's clear to them that it's an all-male institution that celebrates exclusively male values, such as brutality and aggression.

Dr. Margaret Carlisle-Duncan, human kineticist

You'll know, because you'll be looking out of your ear hole.

Ronnie Barnes, trainer, to David Meggett, professional football player, referring to what in the National Football League is called an "Official NFL hit"

You've got to be a son-of-a-bitch to play this game right.

Carl Brettschnieder, professional football player

Ford, Gerald

(b. Jul. 14, 1914) *president of the United States; played football at University of Michigan; avid golfer*

Be careful, Jerry! You're going to hit a Democrat.

Tip O'Neill, speaker of the House (Democrat), to President Ford (Republican) at a celebrity golf tournament

There are forty-two golf courses in the Palm Springs area and nobody knows which one Ford is playing until after he hits his tee shot.

Bob Hope, comedian and actor, on the former president

It's not hard to follow Jerry Ford on the golf course, you just follow the wounded!

Bob Hope, comedian and actor, on the former president

Four Horsemen

Outlined against the blue-gray October sky, the Four Horsemen rode again. In dramatic lore they are know as Famine, Pestilence, Destruction and Death. These are only aliases. Their real names are Stuhldreher, Miller, Crowley and Layden.

Grantland Rice, sportswriter, writing about the famed starting Notre Dame football backfield

Fox Hunting

A chance-bred hound is like a chance-bred race horse; he may be very good at his work, but he is worthless for breeding. Not being carefully bred himself, the faults of his progenitors are certain to be reproduced in the offspring.

Lord Willoughby de Broke, master of the Warwickshire Hunt

Hounds that run forward and frequently examine the discoveries of others when they are casting about and hunting have no confidence in themselves, while those who will not let their cleverer mates go forward, but fuss and keep them back, are confident to a fault.

Xenophon, philosopher, pupil of Plato

Hunting literature has never, or so it seems to me, dwelt sufficiently on the charm of foxhounds. Their purely professional qualities are extolled—nose, tongue, speed, endurance—but nothing is said for their social gifts. Or, for example, the charm of the reception that, in their own domain, the bitch-pack will accord to a friend.

Edith Oenone Somerville, master of Foxhounds, West-Carbery

If hunting were based on exclusiveness it would have perished long ago.

William Bromley-Davenport, sportsman and politician

In that word 'unting what a ramification of knowledge is compressed.

R. S. Surtees, writer and foxhunter

It's not that I loves the fox less, it's that I loves the 'ound more.

R. S. Surtees, writer and foxhunter

Just before she sank, a few horses and hounds got loose and jumped over board, and one of the hounds, seeing a horse swimming near it, managed to scramble onto its back, apparently immediately recognizing it as a friend. The hound was rescued.

Philip K. Crowe, environmentalist, outdoorsman, and writer, referring to the sinking of a ship that was transporting horses and hounds for hunting to India, when the ship sank

Never had the fox or hare the honor of being chased to death by so accomplished a huntsman; never was a huntsman's table graced by such urbanity and wit. He could bag a fox in Greek, find a hare in Latin, inspect his kennels in Italian and direct the economies of his stables in French.

Peter Beckford, hunter and writer, about William Somerville, hunter

Subscription packs are productive of more energy and less cavailling than private packs; every man feels his interest at stake both summer and winter and will look to things all the year round, instead of lounging carelessly out during the season, leaving the breeding and protection of foxes, the propitiation of farmers and other etceteras to the private owners of the hounds, who in all probability leaves it to the huntsman . . . A subscription pack makes every man put his shoulder to the wheel, not only to keep down expense, but to promote sport.

R. S. Surtees, writer and foxhunter

The ducks flew up from the Morton Pond
The fox looked up at their tailing strings,
He wished (perhaps) that a fox had wings. . . .

G. D. Armour, poet, from Reynard the Fox

The English country gentleman galloping after a fox—the unspeakable in full pursuit of the uneatable.

Oscar Wilde, writer

There can be no more important kind of information than the exact knowledge of a man's own country; for this as well as for more general reasons of pleasure and advantage, hunting with hounds and other kinds of sport should be pursued by the young.

Plato, philosopher

They're not dogs, they're hounds. And they don't bark, they tongue.

Evelyne Hoover, field master, Pickering Hunt, to a person who complained about barking dogs

When hounds come out of cover and dwell on the line of the fox, it always appears to me that they are, so to speak, timing and making sure that the scent of the fox is really that of a fox. If all foxes smelt the same, why should they dwell? . . . I have seen hares . . . hunted by staunch foxhounds who themselves would never dream of hunting hare if they knew what they were doing.

M. F. Berry, journalist and foxhunter

When men seek in cover for a fox and the hounds happen to find him, then the hunter rejoicest for the exploit of his hounds . . . If the hounds put up a fox while drawing for hare, a warning must be blown that there is a thief in the wood.

Edward, Duke of York, grandson of Edward III, master of hounds

A fox has . . . a large amount of reasoning faculty in his beautiful head, the very expression of his eye tells it, and it is further proved by the impossibility of the stuffer or preserver of beasts and birds to give the specimen its crafty and observant expression; it is also beyond the power of the painter.

Grantly Berkley, Member of Parliament, author, and foxhunter

My life divides into three parts. In the first I was wretched; in the second ill at ease; in the third hunting.

Roger Scrunton, media personality,
writer, foxhunter

Of all the things in this world, Fox-hunting is the most difficult to explain to those who know nothing about it.

Lord Willoughby de Broke, outspoken
foxhunter

When you're on a horse, hunting foxes, you're back in time, like you're in the 1700's or 1800's. You're not thinking about the real world. You don't have cell phones.

Shepherd Ellenberg, real estate investor
and foxhunter

The upland and copses, which at the end of August had still been green islands among the black fields plowed ready for winter corn, and the stubble had become golden and lurid red islands in a sea of bright green autumn crops. The gray hare had already changed half its coat, the foxes' cubs were beginning to leave their parents, and the young wolves were bigger than dogs. It was the best time of year for the chase.

Leo Tolstoy, novelist, from War and Peace

Freshmen

Freshmen get nothing but abuse . . . but plenty of that.

Knute Rockne, college football coach

Fumbles

I told Ricky to forget about the fumbles. What was I going to do, jump on him?

Mack Brown, Texas A&M coach, speaking
about Rick Williams's fumble after breaking
all-time rushing and all-time all-purpose yards
college career marks and rushing for 250 yards
in his final game

The only time I would ever get the ball is when there is a mistake. So the less I get the ball the happier I am.

Tom Mack, professional football player, offensive
lineman

Future

OK, so we don't intend to win this year, maybe not even next year. It's the future we're concerned with.

Chuck Knox, professional football coach, after
having traded away four star players

The future is now.

George Allen, professional football coach

Gaijin

The old isolationist thinking is still prevalent here. Gaijin are useful as scapegoats when things go wrong. But they are not really welcomed by the baseball establishment.

Takenori Emoto, writer

We're mercenaries, pure and simple. Our job is to do well and let the Japanese players have the glory and take the blame when things go bad.

Leon Lee, professional baseball player

You're an outcast no matter what you do. You go 5-for-5 and you're ignored. You go 0-for-5 and it's, "Fuck you, Yankee go home."

Warren Cromartie, professional baseball player

Gambling

A fool and his money are soon parted, usually before they run by the second half of the daily double.

Kelso Sturgeon, Guide to Sports Betting

A gambler is nothing but a man who makes his living out of hope.

William Bolitho, writer

But there, right there, the beast quit. Quit dead, do you hear? Two other horses went S-W-O-O-S-H and passed him at the finish. I was down to a bus ticket.

Tiny Tim, musician, sports fan

Everybody loves a gambler, until he loses.

Vince Lombardi, Hall of Fame football coach

For sure the best poker player will be my utility infielder and he'll be taking money off my All-Star shortstop. It always works like that.

Joe McCarthy, professional baseball player and manager

I believe it is more moral for government to legalize gambling than it is to force people to gamble in the unregulated and ruthless domain of organized crime.

Howard Samuels, first OTB (Off-Track Betting) head

I bet on a horse at ten-to-one. It didn't come in until half-past five.

Henny Youngman, comedian

I can't stand to look at a team that hasn't beaten the spread and thinks it's won.

Pete Axthelm, writer and broadcaster

I didn't necessarily know about horses more than the next guy, but I might have known a little more about playing. I never was afraid to bet.

Art Rooney, owner, Pittsburgh Steelers, who won approximately $200,000–$300,000 in one day at Saratoga

Information, sound information, is what you need at a racetrack.

Arnold Rothstein, gambler, fixer of the 1919 World Series

It matters not who wins or loses, but how you cover your points.

Steve Cady, sportswriter

I went to bed Charles Barkley and I woke up Pete Rose.

Charles Barkley, professional basketball player, after being fined $5,000 by the National Basketball Association for making a side bet with Mark Jackson (then of the Knicks) about who would win the game

Money won is twice as sweet as money earned.

Paul Newman in The Color of Money

Organized baseball has a phobia about gambling. The parks are policed to prevent it, the clubhouse bulletin boards have placards that shout in bold print the penalties meted out to players and club employees caught at it, and the most witless jockeys of the dugout know better than to joke about fixing games.

Lee Allen, sportswriter

The better the gambler, the worse the man.

Publius Syrus, Roman historian

The horseplayer doesn't consider himself a horseplayer. He thinks he can break the habit anytime he wants to. The shylocks know he's hooked forever.

Jimmy Cannon, sportswriter

The horseplayer who insists on wagering large amounts of money on the sure things must live and die broke.

Kelso Sturgeon, Guide to Sports Betting

Of all the human emotions none is so productive of evil and immorality as gambling.

Charles-Maurice de Talleyrand, statesman and writer

The urge to gamble is so universal and its practice is so pleasurable, that I assume it must be evil.

Heywood Broun, sportswriter

The best thing in the world is to win at the racetrack. The second best thing is to lose at the racetrack.

Old racetrack aphorism, attributed by William Murray, writer

There was, shall we say, a bookie element in Boston, and I thought everyone who asked me about my health was a gambler. Men would call up and say they were taking their sons to the games so they wanted to make sure I was okay. They were just checking.

Bill Russell, Hall of Fame basketball player

What you did was gamble. In those early days . . . I guess we all gambled.

Chandler Harper, golfer

You beat someone gambling, you don't have to feel sorry for him. He wouldn't be gambling if he didn't know what the hell he was doing, you understand, or thinks he knows what he's doing.

Minnesota Fats, legendary pool player

You don't need a lot of money at the track, you need winners.

Gerry Okuneff, professional handicapper

It was a complete oversight on my side.

Hansie Cronje, South Africa cricket team captain and star, who took payoffs from bookmakers, after admitting to the government that he had taken an additional $100,000 he had not admitted to earlier

He is called Hot Horse Herbie because he can always tell you about a horse that is so hot it is practically on fire, a hot horse being a horse that is all readied up to win a race, although sometimes Herbie's hot horses turn out to be so cold they freeze everybody within fifty miles of them.

Damon Runyon, writer

You're blind! You're a crook! You're robbing me!

Walter Matthau, actor, to the different umpires and referees who appeared on as many as fifteen televisions in his home, during his many gambling binges

Garagiola, Joe

(b. 1926) *professional baseball player; broadcaster*

When Joe was playing baseball, he could never hit a curve. Well, he can now. His slices are majestic.

Bob Hope, comedian and actor, about Joe Garagiola

Gehrig, Lou

(b. June 19, 1903; d. June 2, 1941) *Won six World Series; second all-time games played (2,130); two-time League MVP*

Don't feel badly, Lou. It took twenty-one hundred thirty games to get you out, and sometimes it only takes fifteen minutes to get me out of a game.

Lefty Gomez, professional baseball player (pitcher), to Gehrig, after he took himself out of a game for the first time

They better get Gehrig out of there before somebody kills him. I pitched him inside, across the letters today—just once! If Gehrig saw that ball he couldn't move away from it. The ball went through his arms . . . not over or under 'em, but through his arms!

Jo Krakaukas, professional baseball player, speaking of Gehrig's final at-bats

Gibson, Bob

(b. Nov. 9, 1935) *Hall of Fame baseball pitcher; two-time Cy Young Award winner; won two World Series*

Gibson pitches as though he's double parked.

Vin Scully, broadcaster

He'd knock you down just for having bad breath.

Joe Garagiola, professional baseball player and broadcaster

Gibson, Josh

(b. Dec. 21, 1911; d. Jan. 20, 1947) *Hall of Fame baseball player; played in Negro Leagues; called the "Babe Ruth of the Negro Leagues"*

If they had ever let him play in a small place like Ebbets Field or the old Fenway Park,

Josh Gibson would have forced baseball to rewrite the rules. He was, at the minimum, two Yogi Berras.

> *Bill Veeck, baseball owner and thoroughbred racetrack operator*

Gipp, George

(b. Feb. 8, 1895; d. Dec. 14, 1920) *All-American college football player*

Gipp is no football player. He's a runaway son-of-a-bitch!

> *John J. McEwan, college football coach*

Rock, I know I'm going . . . but I'd like one last request . . . Someday, Rock, sometime—when the going isn't so easy, when the odds are against us, ask Notre Dame to win a game for me—for the Gipper. I don't know where I'll be then, Rock, but I'll know about it and I'll be happy.

> *attributed to George Gipp, a dying college football player, by Knute Rockne, college football coach, and recounted by Rockne for the legendary 1928 Notre Dame–Army football game*

Gleason, Jackie

(b. Feb. 26, 1916; d. June 24, 1987) *Comedian, actor, sportsman, and avid golfer*

He has the only cart with a bartender.

> *Bob Hope, comedian, actor*

When he gets into a sand trap, the sand has to get out.

> *Bob Hope, comedian, actor*

Goalie

Being goalie is a much bigger responsibility than anyone else on a team, but it's something I really like about this job. I've always liked responsibility.

> *Dominik Hasek, professional hockey player*

Guys strike out all the time in baseball, but if a goalie misses one, the world is over.

> *Murray Bannerman, professional hockey player*

Right now he feels like he's stopping a basketball and right now we feel like we're shooting at a lacrosse net.

> *Wayne Gretzky, Hall of Fame hockey player, on Dominik Hasek, hockey goalie*

What goaltenders are afraid of is being scored on.

> *Lorne Worsley, professional hockey goalie*

You're the last line of defense. Any way you can, no matter what part of your body you use, you keep the ball out of the net.

> *Mark Morris, professional soccer player*

Goals

It's so special to score goals—it's the home run.

> *Ron Coron, hockey executive*

You have to have stepping-stone goals that are within reach. Once you keep getting up those stepping-stones, you'll reach the pinnacle of your goals and your dreams.

> *Dominique Dawes, Olympic gold medalist gymnast*

Golf

A controlled shot to a closely guarded green is the surest test of any man's golf.

> *A. W. Tillinghast, writer*

All my life I've been trying to make a hole in one. The closest I ever came was a bogey.

Lou Holtz, college football coach

First you teach a golfer to hook the ball by using his hands and arms properly. Then you teach him how to take the hook away by using his body and legs properly.

Harvey Pennick, professional golf
instructor and coach

Getting in a water hazard is like being in a plane crash—the result is final. Landing in a bunker is similar to an automobile accident—there is a chance of recovery.

Bobby Jones, champion
professional golfer

Give me the fresh air, a beautiful partner, and a nice round of golf, and you can keep the fresh air and the round of golf.

Jack Benny, comedian and actor

Golf and sex are the only things you can enjoy without being good at.

Jimmy Demaret, champion golfer

Golf: a game in which you claim the privileges of age, and retain the playthings of childhood.

Samuel Johnson, writer

Golf combines two favorite American pastimes: taking long walks and hitting things with a stick.

P. J. O'Rourke, writer and journalist

Golf gives you an insight into human nature, your own as well as your opponent's.

Grantland Rice, sportswriter

Golf is a game that has drawn . . . together and created a special fraternity among the celebrities of show business, sports, and politics.

Bob Hope, comedian, actor

Golf is a good walk spoiled.

Mark Twain, humorist and author

Golf is in the interest of good health and good manners. It promotes self-restraint and affords a chance to play the man and act the gentleman.

William Howard Taft, president of
the United States

Golf is the most fun you can have without taking your clothes off.

Chi Chi Rodriguez, champion professioal golfer

Golf is the reason for being. We work so that we may live, and we live so that we may play the game.

E. Parker Yutzler, Jr., amateur golfer

Golf is twenty percent mechanics and technique. The other eighty percent is philosophy, humor, tragedy, romance, melodrama, companionship, camaraderie, sussedness, and conversation.

Grantland Rice, sportswriter

Golf is played almost entirely between your ears.

Seve Ballesteros, champion professioal golfer

Golf may be played on Sunday, not being a game within view of the law, but being a form of moral effort.

Stephen Leacock, humorist

Golf seems to me an arduous way to go for a walk. I prefer to take the dogs out.

Princess Anne of Great Britain

Grip it, and rip it!

John Daly, champion professioial golfer

Humiliations are the essence of the game.

Alistair Cooke, writer and historian

I am happy to learn that half the people taking up golf today are women. I shudder to imagine the bad advice those women are getting from husbands and fathers and boyfriends, most of whom should keep their minds on their own vexations of their own game.

Harvey Pennick, golf coach and writer

I am the captive of my slice
I am the servant of my score.

Grantland Rice, sportswriter

If you wish to hide your character, do not play golf.

Percey Boomer, teaching pro

I don't say my golf game is bad, but if I grew tomatoes, they'd come up sliced.

Miller Barber, champion professional golfer

I look at a golf course as a huge waste of pastureland.

Karl Malone, professional basketball player

In the fell clutch of grip and stance
I've often winced and cursed aloud.

Grantland Rice, sportswriter

I regard golf as an expensive way of playing marbles.

G. K. Chesterton, writer

I still enjoy the ooh's and aah's when I hit my drives. But I'm getting pretty tired of the aw's and uh's when I miss the putts.

John Daly, champion professional golfer

If you are caught on a golf course during a storm and are afraid of lightning, hold up a 1-iron. Not even God can hit a 1-iron.

Lee Trevino, champion professional golfer (thrice hit by lightning himself)

The income tax has made liars out of more Americans than golf.

Will Rogers, entertainer and humorist

In golf, you don't lose to another guy. You lose to the golf course, or you lose to yourself.

Glenn Laydendecker, professional tennis player

It is nothing new or original to say that golf is played one stroke at a time. But it took me many years to realize it.

Bobby Jones, champion professional golfer

The peculiar thing about this game—any game really, but this game far more than most—is, the more you fight it, the more it eludes you.

Braxton Dodson, to his son, James Dodson, writer

This game, you never lick it.

Harold Sanderson, professional golfer

It is the fashion these days to speak of golf as a kind of religious experience, a doorway to the spiritual side of man, an egress to the eternal. My father was a man of faith, but I don't think he viewed the golf course as a path to God. He thought golf was a way to celebrate the divinity of life, the here and now, and simply the best way to play.

James Dodson, writer

In good company there is no such thing as a bad golf course.

> *James Dodson, writer*

No game designed to be played with the aid of personal servants by right-handed men who can't even bring along their dogs can be entirely good for the soul.

> *Bruce McCall, writer*

One of the nice things about the Senior Tour is that we can take a cart and a cooler. If your game is not going well, you can always have a picnic.

> *Lee Trevino, champion professional golfer*

Rail-splitting produced an immortal president in Lincoln, but golf hasn't produced even a good A-1 congressman.

> *Will Rogers, entertainer and humorist*

Republican religion. That's why so many men worship it on Sunday morning.

> *attributed to Kristen Cress by James Dodson in* Final Rounds

The golf swing is like a suitcase into which we are trying to pack one too many things.

> *John Updike, novelist and critic*

The mystery of golf is that nobody can master it. You can shoot a good score today, but can you do it tomorrow?

> *Curtis Strange, champion professional golfer*

There are only two things in the world you gotta do with your head down—golf and praying.

> *Lee Trevino, champion professional golfer*

There are two things that made golf appealing to the average man . . . Arnold Palmer and the invention of the mulligan.

> *Bob Hope, comedian and actor*

There is the fantasy, indulged by every hacker on his pillow, of playing with Nicklaus or Palmer.

> *Alistair Cooke, writer and historian*

The spice of golf, as of life, lies in variety.

> *Robert Hunter, writer and golfer*

The very summer in which I at last, acting on an old suggestion of my genial publisher, settle to the task of collecting my scattered pieces about golf turned out to be an unhappy one for my game.

> *John Updike, novelist and critic*

The woods are full of long drivers.

> *Harvey Pennick, golfing instructor and philosopher*

Through golf you get to know the inside of people.

> *Willie Turnesa, golfer*

What golf develops best is masochism.

> *Bruce McCall, writer*

What other people may find in poetry, I find in the flight of a good drive.

> *Arnold Palmer, champion professional golfer*

You can talk to a fade, but a hook won't listen.

> *Lee Trevino, champion professional golfer*

Golf Clubs

A good driver is a hellava lot harder to find than a good wife.

> *Lee Trevino, championship professional golfer, married three times*

Actually, the only time I ever took out a one-iron was to kill a tarantula. And it took a seven to do that.

Jim Murray, sportswriter

Damn the car. My golf clubs are in the trunk. The best set I ever had.

Lawrence Taylor, Hall of Fame
professional football player,
responding to the news of
his car being reported stolen

When I first got to playing, the clubs I used were made out of coat hangers.

Walter Stewart, golfer

When practicing, use the club that gives you the most trouble, not the one that gives you the most satisfaction.

Harry Vardon, professional golfer

Golf Courses

Every hole should be a demanding par and a comfortable bogey.

Robert Trent Jones, Jr.,
golf course architect

Putting greens are to courses what faces are to portraits.

Charles Blair McDonald,
golfer and writer

The ardent golfer would play Mount Everest if somebody put a flagstick on top.

Pete Dye, golf course designer

The strategy of a golf course is the soul of the game.

Robert Trent Jones, Jr.,
golf course architect

Gordon, Jeff

(b. Aug. 4, 1971) *Won Daytona 500; NASCAR Rookie of the Year; three-time Winston Cup champion*

He's not just the driver of the future. He's the driver of the *immediate* future.

Dale Janett, writer

Graduation

I'm going to graduate on time, no matter how long it takes.

Senior basketball player at the
University of Pittsburgh

Grand Slams (tennis)

If ever there was a first family of Wimbledon it is the Sterry-Cooper alliance. Since the early days of 1894 there has always been a Sterry or Cooper in the All England Club. They are as ubiquitous as strawberries and cream.

Gwen Robyns, writer

Like clockwork, their sorority meets once a year, every year, on the red clay of Paris, in springtime. For the past decade, Steffi Graff, Monica Seles, and Arantxa Sanchez Vicario have exerted a virtually monopoly on the French Open. The older they get, the nicer it is to slide along on the clay and let the surface do their walking for them.

Robin Finn, sportswriter

The All England Lawn Tennis and Croquet Club's Championship at Wimbledon is the greatest show on earth. It is an anachronism . . . it is a bland mixture of English garden party atmosphere with hard-core professional organization.

Gwen Robyns, writer

The first day of a Grand Slam . . . is a renewal: friendship and flings may begin or spring up again; someone new on the tour may turn some heads. At the very least, gossip will crop up in the locker rooms and in every corner of the players' lounge.

John Feinstein, writer, Hard Courts

The U.S. Open is tennis at its most gladiatorial. The spectators are an amalgam of the knowledgeable and ignorant, the drunk and the sober, the crude, rude and reserved.

H. A. Branham, writer

To be the U.S. Open champion is the greatest feeling you could have. And to try and do it again is what you live for. If these guys aren't living for that, something is wrong.

Pete Sampras, professional tennis champion

When you look back on the greatest tennis players of all time, you look at the number of Grand Slam tournaments they have won; the ranking is something everyone just takes for granted. In my mind the major titles are the most important thing.

Pete Sampras, professional tennis champion

Grange, Red

(b. June 13, 1903; d. Jan. 28, 1991) *Hall of Fame football player; All-American college football player*

On the field, he's the equal of three men and a horse.

Damon Runyon, writer

Grass Courts (tennis)

It is not the speed of grass that does guys in, but the unpredictability.

Arthur Ashe, tennis Hall of Famer

Greatness

A truly great player makes the worst player on the team good.

*Oscar Robertson, Hall of Fame
basketball player*

He's taking his stubbornness and turning it into a positive. He's not too old . . . He's just stubborn and competitive, because that's what great players are made of.

*Allan Houston, All-Star basketball player,
referring to teammate Patrick Ewing*

I am still the greatest player in the world. I just didn't perform well that night.

*Ronaldo, professional soccer player, after
a loss in the World Cup*

Jordan's swagger, Gretzky's grace and Elway's determination were not dulled by age or eroded by exposure.

Richard Hoffer, sportswriter

I don't know anything about greatness. That's for others to decide.

Richard Petty, champion race car driver

There won't be another Jordan. There won't be another Gretzky.

Jaromir Jagr, professional hockey player

We were of the same era. We were the two top players of our league. In my heart I have always felt that I was the better hitter than Joe, which was always my first consideration, but I have to say that he was the greatest baseball player of our time.

Ted Williams, Hall of Fame baseball player

When I watch myself on film, sometimes I don't even believe some of the things I do.

Walter Payton, Hall of Fame football player

When you're as great as I am, it's hard to be humble.

Muhammad Ali, champion boxer

You have to win everywhere to be a great player.

Gary Player, champion professional golfer

Gretzky, Wayne

(b. Jan. 26, 1961) *Hall of Fame hockey player; won four Stanley Cups; 10-time National Hockey League scoring champion; holds 61 National Hockey League records*

He played hockey like a chess master, several steps ahead of everyone else.

E. M. Swift, sportswriter

He was able to turn on a dime like no one else.

Mario Lemieux, Hall of Fame hockey player

He was the greatest [player] in the history of his sport, perhaps the single most innovative North American athlete since Babe Ruth. He changed his game.

George Vecsey, sportswriter

He was the kind of guy who got to know the clubhouse people, the stickboys. With older people it was always Mister.

Scotty Bowman, professional hockey coach

His passion to be the best player in the world is what drove him. He never had a game where afterward you would say, "Wayne looked a little flat tonight."

Mike Keenan, professional hockey coach

I heard people say he was the Michael Jordan of hockey. Horsepuck. Jordan was the Gretzky of basketball.

Rick Reilly, sportswriter

No person in sports has done as much for their sports as you have done for yours.

Gary Bettman, National Hockey League Commissioner, to Wayne Gretzky

The Edmonton Oilers without Wayne Gretzky is like *Wheel of Fortune* without Vanna White.

Attributed by Joel Stein (sportswriter) to Canadian House leader

Wayne Gretzky was a hockey artist in a sport often stereotyped for brute force and violent intimidation, using his stick as a paintbrush and his skates as dance slippers.

Joe Lapointe, sportswriter

Gymnastics

Competing is my favorite part of gymnastics. I just love being out there. I love the challenge.

Shannon Miller, Olympic gold medalist gymnast

Everyone is focusing on "You're an Olympic champion," but it's a lot more than that. We are representing our sport. We have a larger role to play.

Kerri Strug, Olympic gold medalist gymnast

Gymnastics is an expression of my innermost emotions, my response to love and care with which I have always been surrounded in my life.

Olga Korbut, Olympic gold medalist gymnast

Gymnastics makes me feel good about myself—knowing I can set goals and accomplish them, organize my time, and please lots of people.

Shannon Miller, Olympic gold medalist gymnast

Gymnastics taught me how to be focused and disciplined, which helped me prepare for life.

Kerri Strug, Olympic gold medalist gymnast

I don't want to be responsible one day for any young woman coming up to me and saying, "You robbed me of my childhood."

Al Fong, gymnastics coach

In gymnastics, one "off" movement and you're ruined.

Kerri Strug, Olympic gold medalist gymnast

I've never been very strong in the vault, which is probably why I didn't like it. But I've worked on it and I've got it under control. But even if you do it a million times, once you get into a competition situation, anything can happen.

Amanda Borden, Olympic gymnast

I'm mad on the platform. I want myself to be violent. Otherwise, I wouldn't be competitive.

Nelli Kim, Olympic gold medalist gymnast

I was never thinking of the score. You can't . . . You must do the exercise, because the score will come.

Nadia Comaneci, Olympic gold medalist gymnast

I weighed ninety-eight pounds and I was being called an overstuffed Christmas turkey. I was told I was never going to make it in life because I was going to be fat. I mean, *in life.*

Kristie Phillips, Olympic gymnast

Ninety percent of gymnastics is the mental ability to perform when the time comes.

Kurt Thomas, Olympic gymnast

The four-inch-wide apparatus requires nerves of steel and unwavering dedication.

Susan Vinella, journalist

There is an instant after you have released your grip on the apparatus when you are in the air, free. There is no feeling like it.

Yuri Titov, world champion gymnast

These girls are like little scorpions. You put them all in a bottle and one little scorpion will come out alive. That scorpion will be a champion.

Bela Karolyi, Olympic gymnastics coach

This isn't golf.

Bela Karolyi, Olympic gymnastics coach, referring to the seeming age limit there is on gymnastic careers

We rarely ask what becomes of Olympic gymnasts when they disappear from view. We don't want to see them parade past us with their broken bodies and mangled spirits.

Joan Ryan, writer

Hall of Fame

A man never gets to this station in life without being helped, aided, shoved and prodded to do better. I want to be honest with you; the players I played with and the coaches I had . . . they are directly responsible for my being here.

Johnny Unitas, Hall of Fame professional quarterback

Whitey and Mick both made the Hall of Fame and I didn't. I wasn't a bad influence on them, they were a bad influence on me.

Billy Martin, professional baseball player and manager

Handball

Anybody involved with handball has a childish mind.

Morris Levitsky, handball aficionado

Handballers share a camaraderie unique to the handball community.

George J. Zafferano, handballer and writer

Human hands are to the handball player as the racket is to the tennis player.

Wayne McFarland and Philip Smith, authors

It is the only game in which you *dive* headfirst on concrete.

Michael Disend, writer

The one-wall game originated along the beaches of New York, where bathers found hitting a tennis ball against the open walls of the bath houses with their hands an excellent game . . . New York City is considered the stronghold of the one-wall game.

Michael Yessis, writer

The origin of throwing or striking a ball against a wall and chasing after its crazy rebound is rather obscure and lost in antiquity.

George J. Zafferano, handballer and writer

The time to start using the off hand is sooner rather than later.

Wayne McFarland and Philip Smith, writers

Hazing

It's good for them. It embarrasses a little, but relieves them a lot. Makes them part of the group.

Vince Lombardi, Hall of Fame coach, talking about rookie hazing in pro football

Heart

Holyfield's biggest asset, or course, was his ticker. He doesn't know how to quit . . . Without a doubt, he has the biggest heart I've ever encountered in this business, which is why he's such a great champion.

Mills Lane, district court judge and boxing referee

Heroes

Each of our idols are [sic] unique; yet each of them experienced life in ways that illuminate the history and culture of their times. Although not all of them came up swinging or dribbling from the slums, their stories suggest how sports empowers not only individuals, but whole classes, races, and generations of people—even those, perhaps especially those, who have been denied the full opportunities of American life. . . . Because their lives helped shape our values, our habits, the content of our character, no full understanding of America is possible without an understanding of its sports idols.

Robert Lipsyte and Peter Levine, from their book
Idols of the Game

Every athlete is a role model, whether they want to be or not. You have to recognize that position.

Dale Earnhardt, champion race car driver

Heroes and cowards feel exactly the same fear. Heroes just react to it differently.

Cus D'Amato, Hall of Fame boxing trainer

My dad was my biggest hero, but they haven't made a poster of him yet.

Derek Jeter, professional baseball player

One sign of a hero is if you feel enhanced simply when talking about him—recounting his feats, recalling a time when your own little life was touched by his.

Roger Rosenblatt, sportswriter

We could hear what the ballplayers said to one another as they ran onto the field and could watch their individual gestures and mannerisms as they loosened up in the on deck circle. There come to earth, were the heroes of my imagination, Snider and Robinson and the powerful-looking Don Newcombe.

Doris Kearns Goodwin, writer and historian

High School

Life really wouldn't be worth livin' if you didn't have a high school team to support.

Bob Rutherford, realtor and fan

Today, more civic loyalty centers around [sic] high school basketball than around any other one thing. No distinctions divide the crowds which pack the school gymnasium for home games, and which in every kind of machine crowd the roads for out-of-town games, North Side and South Side, Catholic and Kluxer, banker and machinist—their one shout is 'eat 'em, beat 'em Bearcats.

Robert and Helen Lynd, sociologists

Hiking

The only thing predictable about bears is that they are unpredictable.

> *Craig Medred, writer and camper/hiker*

Hope and the future for me are not in lawns and cultivated fields, not in towns and cities, but in the impervious and quaking swamps.

> *Henry David Thoreau, philosopher and writer*

One should always have a definite objective, in a walk as in a life—it is so much more satisfying to reach a target by personal effort than to wander aimlessly.

> *Alfred Wainwright, Cross UK walker*

Puny man pitted against the elements. A flyspeck of humanity out there alone, somewhere in an endless waste of ice and water, snow and gale, staving off death hour after hour—or waiting for it numb and half frozen, with cold begotten resignation.

> *Ben East, sportswriter*

The necessity of relying on one's own skill and judgment for comfort and safety is one of the many attractions of wilderness travel of all kinds.

> *Raymond Bridge, outdoorsman and journalist*

You can't see anything from a car; you've got to get out of the goddamn contraption and walk, better yet crawl, on hands and knees, over the sandstone and through the thornbrush and cactus. When traces of blood begin to mark your trail, you'll see something, maybe.

> *Edward Abbey, naturalist and writer*

Hitting

But you don't have to go up in the stands and play your foul balls. I do.

> *Sam Snead, champion golfer, to Ted Williams, Hall of Fame baseball player and fisherman, arguing which was more difficult, to hit a moving baseball or a stationary golf ball*

Every time he hits the ball, it's like he waits to break it. I'm pulling for him. He's the man.

> *Mark McGwire, professional baseball player, commenting on Sammy Sosa*

Frank caught the ball and was trying to get across the field when Chuck Bednarik nailed him. Chuck weighed about 240 pounds and hung Frank out on his arm, just clotheslined him and smacked him on the chin . . . They took him to the lockeroom on a stretcher, and I remember going back to the huddle and everybody saying, "It's all over for Frank, no way he can survive that hit."

> *Sam Huff, Hall of Fame professional football player, referring to the play in which Chuck Bednarik almost ended Frank Gifford's career. Gifford came back a year later*

I don't need to hit a home run anymore. I only have to hit a single. I do everything for the team. I just want to win.

> *Sammy Sosa, professional baseball player*

If you want to be a great hitter, don't go to the movies. It ruins your eyes.

> *Rogers Hornsby, Hall of Fame baseball player*

Get it in the air.

> *Ted Williams, Hall of Fame baseball player and world class fisherman, was famous for telling hitters to make sure their swing was on an upward slant against the pitcher's downward velocity*

Here comes Jim Brown through a hole and I'm right there to meet him. I hit that big sucker head-on and my gear came down and cut my nose and my teeth hit together so hard the enamel popped off. He broke my nose, broke my teeth, and knocked me cold.
Sam Huff, Hall of Fame professional football player, about Jim Brown, Hall of Fame running back

Hit 'em like you live—hard and in the alleys.
Reggie Smith, professional baseball player and coach

Hit the ball carrier harder than he hits you.
Ray Nitschke, Hall of Fame football player

In America the big thing is that you want to hit something. I used to walk around in my tennis clothes with a racket all the time and ask everyone, "Do you want to hit?"
Fred Perry, professional tennis champion

It's a lot easier hitting a quarterback than a little white ball.
Bubba Smith, professional football player, on why he preferred football to golf

It took me seventeen years to get three thousand hits in baseball. I did it in one afternoon on the golf course.
Hank Aaron, Hall of Fame baseball player

Keep your eye on the ball and hit them where they ain't.
Wee Willie Keeler, professional baseball player

Once my swing starts, I can't change or pull up. It's all or nothing at all.
Babe Ruth, Hall of Fame baseball player

Say you get four at bats; that's twelve strikes a game. If you can't hit four hard, you're not in the right business.
Mike Piazza, professional baseball player

Stand your ground and take your lumps.
Yogi Berra, Hall of Fame baseball player and manager

That guy can hit me in the middle of the night, blindfolded and with two broken feet to boot.
Don Newcombe, professional baseball player, about Tommy Heinrich

The more hitters we have in this game, the better it is for the game. Listen, when you're coming towards the park and you're two blocks away, and you hear a tremendous cheer, that isn't because someone has thrown a strike. That's because someone has hit the ball.
Ted Williams, Hall of Fame baseball player

With old-timers, whether it be baseball players or fighters, the ability to hit goes last.
Grantland Rice, sportswriter

When he hits you, he buries you.
Walt Michaels, professional football coach, about Greg Buttle, professional football player

When I hit a guy, I'll hit him in the throat—he doesn't have pads on there.
Conrad Dobler, professional football player

You don't think and hit at the same time.
Yogi Berra, Hall of Fame baseball player and manager

You can eliminate a guy with a big hit. Some guys, if you get them with a big pancake hit, they disappear the rest of the game.

Brian Burke, Vancouver Canucks
general manager

Hockey

By the age of 18, the average American has witnessed 200,000 acts of violence on television, most of them occurring during Game 1 of the NHL playoff series.

Steve Rushin, sportswriter

I just loved the game. It gave me so much. All I ever wanted to do was be a hockey player, and then give something back when I retired.

Willie O'Ree, professional hockey player, first
African-American hockey player

He who lives by the cheap shot dies by the cross-check.

Stan Fischler, hockey commentator and historian

Hockey belongs to the Cartoon Network, where a person can be pancaked by an ACME anvil, then expanded—accordion-style—back to full stature, without any lasting side effect.

Steve Rushin, sportswriter

Fighting has been part of hockey for 50 years. It'll be with us another 50. Count on it.

John Ferguson, professional hockey player

It's hard to believe . . . that hockey methodically set out to make the games more physical, more damaging to players, more breathtaking to the increasing number of

warm-climate fans who did not grow up skating on ice and appreciating finesse. Yet the high sticking and the league's relentless merchandising of thumping checks feels something like a trend.

Robert Lipsyte, writer

It would be a better game if it were played in the mud.

Jimmy Cannon, sportswriter

I went to a fight the other night and a hockey game broke out.

Rodney Dangerfield, comedian and actor

No other team sport in recorded history accepts fighting as such a crucial aspect of the game.

Dr. Ross Thomas Runfola

People talk about skating, puck handling and shooting, but the whole sport is angles and caroms, forgetting the straight direction the puck is going, calculating where it will be diverted, factoring in all the interruptions.

Wayne Gretzky, Hall of Fame hockey player

The problem with hockey is that there's too much hockey and not enough fighting.

Ira Berkow, sportswriter, sarcastically discussing
the physical play of the Philadelphia Flyers

There aren't any black hockey players; they play football or baseball.

Jackie Robinson, Hall of Fame baseball player
and first African-American major league baseball
player, to William O'Ree, first African-American
National Hockey League player

We get nose jobs all the time in the NHL, and we don't even have to go to the hospital.

Brad Park, professional hockey player

We're not the smartest group of guys, but we are the most down-to-earth group of guys.

> *Dixon Ward, professional hockey player*

We take the most direct route to the puck and we arrive in ill humor.

> *Bobby Clarke, professional hockey player and team executive*

You could have a house party with two hundred people and have more room than you have in the crease.

> *Grant Fuhr, professional hockey player*

I can sympathize with Canadians whose noses are out of joint. How would Americans feel if the baseball commissioner was Japanese?

> *Bob McKenzie, columnist, writing about the Americanization of hockey, which Canadians feel is their national sport*

Hogan, Ben

(b. Aug. 13, 1912; d. July 25, 1977) *Champion golfer; won four U.S. Opens, two Masters, two PGAs, and one British Open*

He was as grim as a rattlesnake.

> *Gene Sarazn, champion golfer*

I don't say Ben's the greatest golfer in the world or the greatest swinger of a golf club, but nobody ever worked like him.

> *Babe Didrickson Zaharias, champion professional golfer*

Hollywood

I broke into Hollywood the old-fashioned way: I knew somebody.

> *Jim Brown, Hall of Fame football player*

I empathized with the plight of the man/monster who didn't want to hurt anybody and just wanted to be left alone to live his life. I understood his anger and reveled in his power and strength and the way that his tormentors would ultimately bow down before him when he eventually lost his temper.

> *Lou Ferrigno, champion bodybuilder, professional football player, and actor, star of* The Incredible Hulk *TV series*

I just can't stand the thought of her kissing another man, let alone being in bed with someone, even though I know it's only for the cameras.

> *Ronaldo, professional soccer player, about his girlfriend Suzanna Werner, who has made several movies and television cameos*

I love acting . . . All you do is look in the camera, smile, and lie with charm. I learned how to do that watching Don King promote fights.

> *Tex Cobb, professional boxer and actor*

My wife's been trying to talk me into doing movies once baseball is over, but I've seen what it's like, long 14- 15-hour days. I think this job's probably more fun.

> *Matt Williams, professional baseball player*

Home (games)

I don't think home court means a lot until it gets to a deciding game. In a deciding game, I think it's a huge factor.

> *Jeff Van Gundy, professional basketball coach*

Home Run Heard Round the World

I jumped and skipped around the bases like I was half nuts. Gee whiz, I kept saying, gee whiz! I guess you could call me an "accidental hero."

Bobby Thompson, professional baseb all player, who hit the Home Run Heard Round the World

I literally went berserk when he hit the homer. I threw the cards in the air, kicked the table, and kept yelling, "He did it! He did it!"

George Plimpton, writer and editor

Now it is done. Now the story ends . . . the art of fiction is dead. Reality has strangled invention.

Red Smith, sportswriter

Safe prediction: the home run that Bobby Thompson of the New York Giants hit off Ralph Branca of the Brooklyn Dodgers on October 3, 1951, will forever remain the quintessential moment in baseball history.

David Lehman, writer and historian

Seldom does the stuff of myth, of fact and of interborough history come together more exactly.

David Lehman, writer and historian

That was the single greatest moment probably in sports in my lifetime.

Woody Allen, writer, director, actor

The Giants win the pennant, the Giants win the pennant, the Giants win the pennant! I don't believe it, I don't believe it, I don't believe it!

Russ Hodges, broadcaster

Home Runs

I just felt if I got a strike to hit, I would hit it out . . . it really wasn't one of my greatest.

Hank Aaron, Hall of Fame baseball player, on his 715th home run, breaking Babe Ruth's all-time record

I just wish I could have enjoyed it as much as Sammy Sosa and Mark McGwire enjoyed it last year.

Hank Aaron, Hall of Famer, speaking about chasing Babe Ruth's record and the hate mail that interfered with enjoying the pursuit

I must admit when Reggie Jackson hit that third home run and I was sure nobody was listening, I applauded into my glove.

Steve Garvey, Hall of Fame baseball player, who played on the losing side

That ball got out of here in a hurry. Anything going that fast better have a damn stewardess on it—don't you think?

Kevin Costner, actor, in Bull Durham

The ball sailed so high that when it came down it was coated with ice.

Bill McGeehan, sportswriter, writing about one of Babe Ruth's home runs

There is nothing harder to do in all of sports than hitting a home run.

Ted Williams, Hall of Fame baseball player and champion fisherman

Nothing

Ted Williams, Hall of Fame baseball player, when asked what he was thinking about during his last at-bat, when he hit a home run

Honesty

Honesty is as important in fishing as it is in golf.

Randy Voorhees, fisherman and writer

Hope

If you have hope, there's a light at the end of the tunnel. Hope makes you better. The air in the locker room is different when you have hope.

Dixon Ward, professional hockey player

I'm a football fan, and we're still in the first quarter. Let's keep going awhile and we'll see where we are around halftime.

Jimmy Vasser, automobile racer

It ain't over 'til it's over.

Yogi Berra, Hall of Fame baseball player and manager

It's just a matter of hoping nobody comes and gets you. There's no use looking back.

Chris Antley, professional jockey, on being ahead in the homestretch

When the astronauts walked on the moon I figured we had a chance to win. Nothing seemed impossible after that.

Tug McGraw, professional baseball player

You gotta believe.

Tug McGraw, professional baseball player

Horseback Riding

The horse is such a beautiful animal. When you're on him, in control of him, moving with him as one, it is a beautiful feeling. The best is when you're almost getting him to know what you want to do.

Steve Cauthen, jockey

It doesn't matter what you do in the bedroom as long as you don't do it in the street and frighten the horses.

Daphne Fielding, playwright,
The Duchess of Jermyn Street

It takes a good deal of physical courage to ride a horse. This, however, I have. I get it at about forty cents a flask, and I take it as required.

Stephen Leacock, journalist

Horses

A horse may have the look of eagles, but I've never seen yet an eagle who could run.

Charlie Whittingham, thoroughbred horse trainer

Anyone who's not happy with the job I'm doing can pick up their horses and leave tomorrow.

Woody Stephens, thoroughbred horse trainer

A race horse must be judged in three directions—speed, stamina and time—the time he lasts.

Grantland Rice, sportswriter

Did any other horses besides Charisma ever get left out in the middle of the night in a strange field in a lightning storm during a horse competition?

Susan Cox, U.S. district attorney, during the trial of Marion Hulick and George Lindemann, Jr. for the murder of Charisma and insurance fraud. The horse was murdered that night.

Don't say anything bad about a horse until it's been dead ten years.

Charlie Whittingham, thoroughbred horse trainer

Get yourself a good horse, son, and you'll dine with kings.

Charlie Whittingham, thoroughbred horse trainer

He's about as much as it costs to run my airplane for a while.

Jimmy Stone, businessman and thoroughbred owner, about his horse, Menifee

Horses are like people. Some kids don't mature until college.

Arthur Hancock III, owner, speaking of how sometimes you discover what a horse has in big races

Horses are more important to me than most people.

Mary Bacon, jockey

Horses can certainly race every two weeks, and in some cases even more than that. The velocity is going to be higher among horses of talent. They're running on the edge.

Dr. Larry Bramlage, veterinarian

I feel as a horse must feel when the beautiful cup is given to the jockey.

Edgar Degas, painter, after seeing one of his paintings sold at auction

I never saw Man o' War but I'd bet my money on Citation if they ever hooked up. Right now, if they blow the bugle where he's buried, Citation would break out of the grave and beat what's around.

Jimmy Cannon, sportswriter

It's not the money. It's not some genius on a computer figuring marriages made in heaven. It's the horse. You've got to have the horse.

D. Wayne Lukas, thoroughbred horse trainer

I've talked to thousands of horses . . . but not in their tongue apparently.

Grantland Rice, sportswriter

Men are generally more careful of the breed of their horses and dogs than of their children.

William Penn, preacher & founder of Pennsylvania (1644–1718)

Nothing brings out the prick in a man faster than his first good horse.

Francis Dunne, professional steward

Power is in controlling the blood, not the money.

Steve Crist, sportswriter, about the power of breeders

That was one big horse. I had to get a stepladder to attach the wire to his ear.

Tom "The Sandman" Burns, professional horse assassin, referring to the electrocution of show horse Belgium Waffle, owned by Tammie Bylenga Glaspie, who was convicted of mail fraud for collecting the insurance money

The mistake everyone was making was breeding those classic distance mares to a classic distance horse.

D. Wayne Lukas, thoroughbred horse trainer, referring to the lack of speed in the equation

There's no blue book on horses.

Richard Baily, supposed horse trainer, murdered Helen Brach, and con man who duped would-be horse owners

They have an unusual relationship. They're buddies. They have a window between their stalls, and they stand there and look at each other. They like each other. And both have a shot to win.

Bob Baffert, thoroughbred horse trainer, on two fillies he entered in the Preakness Stakes

We all buy our feed at the same place, and use the same veterinarians. It's all the horses. All we can do is screw up.

David Whitely, thoroughbred horse trainer

We thought a few times, maybe we ought to quit paying the bills for this horse.

Bob Lewis, owner of thoroughbred Charismatic, surprise Kentucky Derby winner

When a horse doesn't run his race, there's a reason.

Seth Hancock, owner and breeder

You can lead a horse to water
    But you can't make him drink.

Anonymous proverb

You can't mourn the horse that got away.

Richard Mandella, trainer

You may have my husband, but not my horse. My husband won't need emasculating, and my horse I won't have you meddle with.

D. H. Lawrence, writer, from his novel St. Mawr

Horse Racing

A horse is worth $50 and what the traffic will bear.

John Nerud, thoroughbred trainer and owner

By the end of the year he'll be running in Omaha.

D. Wayne Lukas, thoroughbred horse trainer, about a horse that did not measure up

Claiming horses is like trying to make a living by going through people's garbage cans.

Lefty Nickerson, thoroughbred horse trainer

Did you ever notice, old pal, in the race
    track's dizzy spin
There are ninety ways a horse can lose—but
    only one way to win?

Grantland Rice, sportswriter

Don't tell me who a horse is by. Tell me who he can run by. Unless a foal is born with two heads or three legs, there's no way of knowing that he's a no-account when the farm turns him over to the trainer.

John Nerud, thoroughbred horse trainer and owner

The first question I was always asked—invariably, everywhere—was how I found horse racing compared to baseball. My answer—invariably, everywhere—was that, fans excluded, you meet a nicer brand of human being in racing.

Bill Veeck, baseball owner, racetrack operator

Hell, I'm not a horseman.

Bob Lewis, thoroughbred owner, whose horses won two Kentucky Derbys

Horses don't know the odds.

Nick Zito, thoroughbred horse trainer

If he had his way, he'd enter the Budweiser Clydesdales in a race.

Jerry Berger, about friend Bob Lewis, thoroughbred owner, who made his fortune in the beer business with Budweiser

If he runs on the lead, he'll finish at Kennedy Airport.

Alfredo Callejas, thoroughbred horse trainer

If I believed in reincarnation, I'd come back as a second guesser.

Carl Nafzger, thoroughbred horse trainer

It's time to be quiet and let the horse run.

Elliot Walden, thoroughbred horse trainer

The horses were ready to run, but track officials said there was nothing for them to run for.

Fred S. Buck, Horse Race Betting. Referring to New York racetrack official who had absconded with association bankroll

If you want a friend on the race track, buy a dog.

Jerry Izenberg, sportswriter

I knew it for a "dog," a horse which hated racing.

Dick Francis, champion jockey and novelist

It's a quick way for a rich man to get his name in the newspapers. It's like buying a baseball team. There's always going to be someone with too much money who we can get interested in horse racing.

John Nerud, thoroughbred horse trainer

It's not how many races you win that counts, but that you win the good ones.

Charlie Whittingham, thoroughbred horse trainer

I want to destroy the two myths about racing that I think have kept ninety percent of the public from ever attending. First, that racing is an elite sport dominated by fourth-generation snobs who think fans are an intrusion.

Second, that racing is a sport that attracts unemployed degenerates and creepy old men who have nothing better to do with their time.

Robert Brennan, racetrack owner

Some horses have extraordinarily strong preferences for one or two tracks, or for left-handed or right-handed courses only, or for hard or soft going, or for sun on their backs, and a wise trainer does not try to lay down an opposite law. Put a horse on a track he likes, on going he likes, with a jockey he likes, and he will be worth a stone and ten lengths by the finish.

Dick Francis, champion jockey and novelist

Stupid horses . . . are exasperating. They will not put themselves right before a fence, and they resist their jockey's efforts to do it for them.

Dick Francis, champion jockey and novelist

The farm wasn't for me. It was too laid-back and too slow. It was the racetrack I loved. I loved getting the *Racing Form* and handicapping the racing. I wanted to be where the action was—around the track, on the go and with the horses.

Elliott Walden, thoroughbred horse trainer

The horses and their keepers sleep through the night, awaiting the early dawn of a new day with its quota of hope, of promise, of providing for every hard knocker in the world a possible pot at the end of a glorious rainbow.

William Murray, writer

The losing jockey blames the owner, trainer, track, and horse while the trainer indicts the jock, owner, program seller, and stewards and the owner views the business as a Communist plot.

Phil Jackman, sportswriter

This business has always been about dreams.

D. Wayne Lukas, thoroughbred horse trainer

This is a sport where the horses tend to sound alike and the jockeys, for all their courage and skill, are existentially cast in supporting roles.

Harvey Araton, sportswriter

This sport features the highest of the highs and the lowest of the lows.

Al Michaels, broadcaster

When it comes to busting for that opening it's all largely instinct. You've got a split second to decide. You are right or you are wrong. You can't wait.

Eddie Arcaro, jockey

While all of racing is a bet, each race is a sport.

Frank Deford, sportswriter

Year in and year out, the *Racing Form* has maintained a special status in American journalism. Besides being the most expensive U.S. daily, it is also one of the oldest.

Fredrick C. Klein, writer

One after another the fresh horses for the coming race made their appearance, for the most part English racers, wearing horsecloths, and looking with their drawn up bellies like strange, huge birds.

Leo Tolstoy, novelist

It was a glorious sight, and the come and go of the quick little hoofs, and the incessant

salutations of ponies that had met before on other polo grounds and racecourses were enough to drive a four-footed thing wild.

Rudyard Kipling, novelist

The changing room for jockeys was warm and gay like a busy little nursery. Jockey's valets, with the air of slightly derelict family butlers, had been ironing in their shirtsleeves since seven in the morning.

Enid Bagnold, novelist, from National Velvet

Howe, Gordie

(b. Mar. 31, 1928) *Hall of Fame hockey player; played in five decades; number two on all-time goals (801) and points (1,850)*

Mr. Howe, before I die, please tell me how you can skate so gracefully down the ice, with three or four hockey players in front of you, and still manage the puck so magnificently. Tell me, Mr. Howe, how are you able to stick control the puck so beautifully in that kind of situation?

Tiny Tim, musician, sports fan,
to Johnny Carson when asked
who he would want at his deathbed

Hull, Bobby

(b. Jan. 3, 1939) *Hall of Fame hockey player; All-Star; prodigious scorer*

He's so powerful that defensemen don't want a piece of him—they don't want to take him head on.

Glenn Hall, professional hockey player

Hull dominates all thought about the game; he changes its traditions and shapes its rules.

Bill Furlong, sportswriter,
The Price of Fame for Bobby Hull

Humor

There is no room in baseball for a clown.

*Chuck Dressen, professional baseball
manager, to Bob Uecker, player
and later broadcaster*

Hunting

A bird-eating dog is worse than an egg-sucking hound or a stump-sucking mule. Whatever the seven deadly sins of dogdom are, bird-eating is deadliest.

Havilah Babcock, outdoorsman and writer

A brash young shooting guest informed me over her second drink that preserve shooting was as artificial as patronizing a brothel. She hadn't shot on a preserve and I have never visited a brothel so neither of us were too well qualified to discuss it.

*George Bird Evans, hunter, outdoorsman, and
writer*

Africa is flesh and blood, and the hunt is ever a love affair.

Isak Dinesen, novelist

All hunters should be nature lovers.

*Theodore Roosevelt, president of the United
States*

As hunting tools, the bow and arrow are enjoying something of a renaissance these days, though Robin Hood and Hiawatha, were they around, would hardly recognize the instruments for all of their twentieth-century refinements.

John G. Mitchell, writer

Bracing against the predawn chill in a duck blind with my father was one of the most vivid memories of growing up in Eastern Arkansas. Similar mental snapshots have been created across our nation for centuries as parents have introduced their children to the beauty of our wildlife through hunting and fishing.

Blanche Lambert, U.S. congresswoman

Each autumn when the nights grow longer than the days and the aspens turn to gold on the hillsides, I am faced by an annual dilemma: Should we explore some new area or should we hunt once more in the old, familiar spot?

Ted Trueblood, outdoorsman, editor, and writer

Even a dog of general purpose breed cannot be expected to work properly unless he is correctly trained.

Michael Brander, sportsman and writer

Except for the early years of my childhood, I can't remember a time when the handling of fly rods and shotguns has not made for magic moments in my life.

Richard Wentz, outdoorsman and writer

Far from the truth lay the antique assumption that man had fathered the weapon. The weapon, instead, fathered the man.

Robert Ardery, scholar

For a man who's bred to hunting
Must forever be that way.

Archibald Rutledge, poet

For many people throughout history, the most seductive voice of Mother nature at special times of the year has been the invitation to join the hunt.

*James A. Swan, environmentalist,
outdoorsman, and writer*

He could train a dog with less exertion, and with less expense to the English language, than any other man I have ever known. I verily believe he could take a full-blooded July hound and turn out a passable bird dog in six weeks.

Havilah Babcock, outdoorsman and writer

He hunted big game all throughout the United States and Canada, water fowl on the Chesapeake Bay, and rabbits in the Catskill Mountains of New York. His true love, however, was on party boats, where the camaraderie meant as much as the full cooler.

Vincent T. Sparano, sportsman, about
George H. Hass, sportsman,
editor, and writer

Hounds and houndsmen are not like you and me. A hound is not made for bringing you the Sunday paper, honoring a point, or retrieving a gadwall. He is made for trailing and running larger mammals, treeing them, or baying them on the ground and catching them, to hold for the hunter. Houndmen, if they are true houndmen, would rather run their dogs in the woods than spend an all-expense-paid weekend in Paris, France.

Thomas McIntyre,
outdoorsman and writer

Hunting can become almost an obsession, as evidenced by garages filled with boats and decoys, gun cabinets, engraved shotguns, hunting dogs, trophies on the walls, stacks of sporting magazines, wildlife paintings and carvings, stacked bales of hay in backyards for archery practice—camouflage for water fowl, wild turkey, and archery deer seasons, and bright orange for hunting big game with a rifle.

James A. Swan, environmentalist,
outdoorsman, and writer

Hunting is a complex affair with roots too deep to be pulled up and examined. If a hunter is asked to explain his sport, he can no more rationalize hunting than he can describe emotion.

John Madson and Ed Kozicky, writers

Hunting is a glorious sort of vice working its narcotic with all the efficacy of the ubiquitous poppy.

Colonel Charles Atkins, outdoorsman

Hunting is almost anything the hunter wants to make of it—including not pulling the trigger at the last minute.

Roger Caras, broadcaster,
animal rights advocate, and writer

Hunting is the oldest, and by all odds the most diversified, sport known to man. The chase began long before the dawn of recorded history. It is the only sport, born of grim necessity, which now continues as a recreation enjoyed by millions.

The New Hunter's Encyclopedia

Hunting is what an animal does to take possession, dead or alive, of some other being that belongs to a species that is basically inferior to its own. Vice versa, if there is to be a hunt, this superiority of the hunter over the prey cannot be absolute.

José Ortega y Gasset, philosopher

I am a hunter, too, but slowly the hunting has become more important than the shooting . . . I was raised in the hunting tradition, but even in me something has begun to happen; there is a voice of warning of coming scarcities, there is an apprehension for the future; there is a fear of the unknown qualities of majorities soon to govern the land.

Dayton O. Hyde, writer

I am truly moved at these moments. I really don't understand them completely. I know I am participating in life.

Ted Nugent, musician, outdoorsman, and hunter

I am very fond of hunting and there are few sensations I prefer to that of galloping over these rolling, limitless prairies, rifle in hand, or winding my way among the barren, fantastic and grimly picturesque deserts of the so-called Bad Lands.

Theodore Roosevelt, president of the United States, conservationist, and outdoorsman

I can take a good deal, but I won't have my dog called down.

E. Annie Proulx, writer

If I could shoot a game bird and still not hurt it, the way I can take a fly trout on a fly and release it, I doubt if I would kill another one. This is a strange statement coming from a man whose life is dedicated to shooting and gun dogs.

George Bird Evans, hunter, outdoorsman, and writer

I have observed that the more bungling and inept a hunter is, the more likely he is to find fault with a dog.

Ted Trueblood, outdoorsman, editor, and writer

In conversation I have never heard anybody call a woodcock anything but a "woodcock," although sometimes, when we're hunting woodcock exclusively and don't expect to flush grouse, we might refer to them simply as "birds." When we miss them, we usually call them sonsofbitches.

William G. Tapply, outdoorsman, sportsman, and writer

In some strange way the birds we kill fly on forever. Perhaps its the broken arc, the interrupted parabola, the high zig through the alders that never quite made it to zag—all those incompletions crying out to be consummated. But something there is that keeps them airborne if only in our hearts, their wings forever roaring at the base of our trigger fingers.

Robert F. Jones, outdoorsman and writer

In the act of hunting, a man becomes, however briefly, part of nature again. He returns to the natural state, becomes one with the animal, and is freed of the existential split: to be part of nature and to transcend it by virtue of his consciousness.

Erich Fromm, psychologist

I shot him nine times with a .220 Swift. . . . One time I hit him in the face and took away his lower jaw and still he didn't die. He just bled and began to snap fruitlessly with half a face at his own dragging guts.

Robert Ruark, writer, about using enough gun to kill your prey

It is not essential to the hunt that it be successful.

José Ortega y Gasset, philosopher

I was never successful in outwitting antelope on the several occasions when I pitted my craft and skill against their wariness and keen sense, always either failing to get within range or else missing them.

Theodore Roosevelt, president of the United States, conservationist, and outdoorsman

Man and dog have articulated in each other their own styles of hunting, and this represents the height of hunting.

José Ortega y Gasset, philosopher

Neither in body nor in mind do we inhabit the world of those hunting races of the Paleolithic era, to whose lives and life way we nevertheless owe the very form of our bodies and structures of our minds. Memories of their animal envoys still must sleep, somehow, within us; for they wake a little and stir when we venture into wilderness.

Joseph Campbell, philosopher and historian

No sportsman can ever feel much keener pleasure and self-satisfaction than when, after a successful stalk and good shot, he walks up to a grand elk lying . . . in the cool shade of the great evergreens, and looks at the massive and yet finely molded form.

Theodore Roosevelt, president of the United States, conservationist, and outdoorsman

Only good shots—or gentlemen—should hunt together. Learn leisureliness alone. The beginner must work out his own salvation, and the fewer spectators present to witness the infamy and psychoanalyze his failures the better.

Havilah Babcock, outdoorsman and writer

On rare occasions, novice hunters have stalked another hunter who is gobbling. There is no need for that kind of nonsense.

Experienced hunters know that it is almost impossible to stalk a wild tom successfully.

Nelson Bryant, outdoor writer

Over the centuries man and his dog have hunted together and, though the shotgun and the rifle have replaced the bow and the spear, few of the basic methods of hunting have altered.

Michael Brander, sportsman and writer

Storytelling began with Stone Age hunters sitting around the campfire recounting their deeds.

Stephen E. Ambrose, historian

The big-game rifle is the weapon of romance and, when a man picks one up, he becomes for the moment a pioneer, an explorer, a wilderness hunter, a present-day Daniel Boone.

Jack O'Connor, sportsman, outdoorsman, and writer

The chase is among the best of all national pastimes; it cultivates that vigorous manliness for the lack of which in a nation, as an individual, the possession of no other qualities can possibly atone.

Theodore Roosevelt, president of the United States, conservationist, and outdoorsman

The chase is the thing. The game in the hand is not much more than a reminder of the pleasurable efforts expended on its taking.

Larry Koller, outdoorsman, editor, and writer

The difference between mere killing and a glorious sport is the manner in which you do it—over thrilling dogs, in magnificent country and with a reverence for the game.

George Bird Evans, hunter, outdoorsman, and writer

The hunter, beset too long by the moralizer, will point to the slaughterhouse with an enigmatic look. Of course, he has a point. A great many well-hunted deer and quail die better in this country, at least, than cows, sheep, pigs, chickens, ducks, turkeys, and horses do.

Roger Caras, broadcaster, animal rights advocate, writer

The hunter's life, with its adventures and dangers, must have been of tremendous importance for the evolution of man. It was a touchstone of intelligence, courage and skill.

G. H. R. von Konigswald, scholar

The hunter's vision is itself a part of nature . . . His eye roves across a landscape which is itself living. The hunter in man lives an eventful life, a present, sound filled pulse which collectively is the dynamic, oral, traditional society, where the poet is historian and men are bound in myth and music to a generous and religious existence.

Paul Shephard, environmentalist and outdoorsman

The kill matters. And the manner of the kill matters. All else is trivial, for nothing else is final.

Robert Elman, outdoorsman and writer

The licensed hunter kills only a tiny fraction of the game in Africa. In fact, the fees he pays are in most cases the sole revenue the government can rely on to pay the warden. The poachers and the advance of agriculture are the real enemies of wildlife.

Philip K. Crowe, environmentalist, outdoorsman, and writer

The mere size of the bag indicates little as to a man's prowess as a hunter and almost nothing as to the interest or value of his achievement.

Theodore Roosevelt, president of the United States, conservationist, and outdoorsman

The only reason I played golf was so I could afford to hunt and fish.

Sam Snead, champion professional golfer

The pursuer cannot pursue if he does not integrate his vision with that of the pursued. That is to say, *hunting is an imitation of the animal.*

José Ortega y Gasset, philosopher and hunter

The pointing dog is a refinement, unlike any other canine. Only the hunting dog has so strong a tie with the hunter, a partnership through thousands of years. When the chukar calls are silenced by the hunter's nearness and their exact location is unknown, the dog is no mere possession or servant but a full-fledged partner and collaborator.

Charles F. Waterman, outdoorsman and writer

The reward is in the hunt.

Ted Trueblood, outdoorsman, editor, and writer

The wonderful, silent ease with which hunting elephants negotiate jungle has always been a source of wonder to me . . . I had already loaded my rifle and now swung the barrel around ready for action. The bull had winded us, however, and even though I saw his head, and a great head it was, the angle was not right, and before the elephant could be maneuvered into a better position, he made off down the mountain.

Philip K. Crowe, environmentalist, outdoorsman, and writer

pockets is an adequate number for an
out. For hunting, on the other hand,
lot more.

Patrick F. McManus, sportsman and writer

Upland shooting is at its highest level when
the bird-dog-gun triad is balanced by a gun
and a dog worthy of the bird.

George Bird Evans, hunter,
outdoorsman, and writer

When I go hunting with him, he does that as
hard as he plays football.

Bud Holmes, attorney, about Walter Payton, Hall
of Fame football player

When some of my friends have asked me
anxiously about their boys, whether they
should let them hunt, I have answered, yes—
remembering that it was one of the best parts
of my education—make them hunters,
though sportsmen only at first, if possible,
mighty hunters last, so that they shall not find
game large enough for them in this or any
vegetable wilderness—hunters as well as fishers of men.

Henry David Thoreau, writer and philosopher

Winter is a greater hunter than man will
ever be.

Thomas McIntyre, outdoorsman and writer

You can practice calling with a record, and
pick up calling tips from authorities, but it is
the wild turkey himself, ultimately, who
teaches you really how to call.

Thomas McIntyre, outdoorsman and writer

Any fool, without encountering the smallest
modicum of risk, can murder a bull elephant

at 200 yards with a lung shot. This is not elephant hunting, but elephant killing.

Peter Hathaway Capstick, big game
hunter and writer

Hunting big, dangerous game is an excellent
method of cultivating one's own fatalism.
People die from the slightest error, while
others survive without a scratch the most
mind-boggling acts of idiocy.

Peter Hathaway Capstick, big game
hunter and writer

Hustle

Good things happen to those who hustle.

Chuck Noll, professional football coach

Hype

As in a Super Bowl, there can be more hype
than substance in the Subway Series, more
newsprint and bluster than worthiness.

Buster Olney, sportswriter

The hype is there, but the game is all the
same.

Greg Maddux, professional baseball player

Who knows? Amid world beating hearts
The Tumult and the Shouting starts.

Grantland Rice, sportswriter

You could say that he's been underpromoted,
but you would be tragically understating the
case.

Cedric Kushner, boxing promoter, about Sugar
Shane Mosley

I

Indianapolis 500

A man can be a splendid race driver, but if he doesn't compete at Indianapolis, he is nothing. If he doesn't win at least once at Indianapolis, well, there always is the insinuation that maybe something was lacking.

Mario Andretti, champion driver

This is the Indianapolis 500, a gigantic, grimy lawn party, a monstrous holiday compounded of dust and danger and noise, the world's biggest carnival. . . .

Red Smith, sportswriter

Iditarod

It's a bad place to get lost. From here to anywhere is a long, long way, and help is hard to find.

Craig Mildred, sportswriter

Those who live in dog country dissect the Iditarod's entry list like the Yankees batting order on Opening Day.

*Brian Patrick O'Donoghue,
political columnist and sled racer*

Individuals

I got fed up with team sports, which I played as a kid—football-soccer and cricket—I was an individual.

*Fred Perry, professional
tennis champion*

Society loves conformists. I'm not a conformist. I'm a big believer in individuality, in freedom.

Pam Postema, female umpire

Injuries

All right, no limping. If you have to limp, don't scrimmage. If you want to scrimmage, don't limp.

Red Blaik, college football coach

A piece of scenery fell on me. I'm a stagehand at the Metropolitan Opera. You can't make a living as a referee.

*Arthur Mercante, Jr., referee, replying to a
question about his injured hand*

A thigh. A neck. A leg. Is it an anatomy class? A butcher's inventory? It's the National Football League's injury report!

Ira Berkow, sportswriter

Being apart from the team. That may have been the toughest part.

Brian Williams, professional football player, commenting on being out of football for two years due to an injury to his eye

Chris Childs spit a tooth into his hand and fixed a menacing stare on Dikembe Motombo, who trotted away innocently.

Selena Roberts, sportswriter, referring to Chris Childs, professional basketball player, after being elbowed by Motombo, a sharp-elbowed center

I didn't do this operation for golf. I did it for quality of life, so that my wife, Barbara, didn't have to put up with me having my hip dominating my life.

Jack Nicklaus, champion professional golfer

I don't feel like "the man." I feel like less than a man.

Chris Childs, professional basketball player, on being injured during the playoffs

I'm a good candidate for a knee replacement.

Steve Williams, a.k.a. Stone Cold Steve Austin, professional wrestler

I'm going to become a ventriloquist. I'll get a little football player and put him up on my knee.

Dan Dierdorf, professional football player and broadcaster, through clenched teeth after his jaw had been broken

I'm more likely to get hurt bumping into things around the house.

Walter Payton, Hall of Fame football player

It collapsed like a folding chair.

Rebecca Lobo, professional basketball player, about injuring her knee

It is Monday morning, and all over the land the bill is being presented to some large, tough men for playing so fearlessly with the equation of mass times velocity; only the backup quarterback bullets out of bed on recovery day.

Mark Kram, sportswriter

It's from all those people kissing your ass.

Pete Sheehy, clubhouse manager, to Joe DiMaggio, after he asked Sheehy if he had injured his butt

It looked like a piece of sausage.

Mitch Libonati, hotel employee, who found the remains of Holyfield's ear

I've added a scar on my knee. That's all.

Jason Seahorn, professional football player

I've busted up my body and scarred myself and gotten burned—I've got scars I'll carry to the grave—just to make some money.

A. J. Foyt, champion race car driver

I was doing a floater, and I came down sort of awkward on my heel. I hit it hard enough to break my fibula and tibia. If it weren't for my board, I would have drowned. I was in that much pain.

Jason Buttenshaw, surfer

My back is sore, my knee is sore, my hand is sore, and I have bruises on both my feet.

Erik Howard, professional football player

My catcher, Mr. Berra, is wearing a lemon on his thumb.

Casey Stengel, Hall of Fame baseball player and manager, referring to a lemon Yogi's mother insisted he wear on his injured thumb for three days, contrary to Yankee physician's orders to treat it otherwise

Nobody is hurt. Hurt is in the mind. If you can walk, you can run.

Vince Lombardi, professional football player and coach

One of the things that happens is you watch the team and suddenly you're saying "they" instead of "we" because in the middle of it all, you feel invisible again.

Joe Morris, professional football player

Progressively and inexorably, as I moved through high school, college and pro leagues, my body was dismantled. Piece by piece . . . as the organization and competition increased, the injuries came faster and harder.

John McMurtry, professional football player

Sometimes it's so hard for me to move, it feels like I'm standing in cement.

Rik Smits, professional basketball player, after trying to play through a broken toe

This is a human body, and we don't always expect 100 percent.

Lornah Kiplagal, marathoner, after being forced to withdraw after a bout of bronchitis

To a new life where knees do not throb and tendons do not ache at dawn and the ghostly potential for permanent disability no longer

rides just an errant hoofbeat off your right shoulder.

Jerry Izenberg, sportswriter

Two long half-moon scars ran down either side of his knee, which no longer had the outlines of a kneecap, but seemed as shapeless and large in his leg as if two or three handfuls of socks had been sewn in there.

George Plimpton, writer, referring to the knees of Gil Main, professional football player

Young lady, try my left arm—I think you'll find I'm still alive.

Tex Hughson, professional baseball player, to a nurse trying to take his pulse on one of his arms where the muscles had grown so big they were choking off the blood supply

Years of training. Hours of dreaming. And knowing it all came down to an unfortunate, untimely, unbelievable stroke of bad luck.

Don Kardong, runner and writer, speaking about the Olympics and injuries

You were supposed to depersonalize your body, it wasn't your leg, it was "the leg."

Rick Sortun, professional football player

You don't worry about injuries this time of year. We're in a pennant race. If you can walk, you can play.

Davey Johnson, champion baseball manager, to Wally Backman, player, and team doctor, when the doctor told him that Backman might have a broken leg and it should be x-rayed

You should sue your legs for non-support.

Dan Reeves, professional football head coach and player, to Dandy Don Meredith, professional football player, referring to the latter's bad knees

Inspiration

Ability may get you to the top, but it takes character to keep you there.

John Wooden, basketball coach

Ain't no man can avoid being born average, but ain't no man got to be common.

Satchel Paige, Hall of Fame baseball player

He who is not courageous enough to take risks will accomplish nothing in life.

Muhammad Ali, boxer

Keep Mendoza in the bullpen.

Don Zimmer, professional baseball player and manager, speaking words of encouragement to starting pitcher Hideki Irabu, about Mendoza, whom he'd forced from the rotation

Talent is God-given, be humble; fame is man-given, be thankful; conceit is self-given, be careful.

Anonymous (quoted often by John Wooden)

The big thing is not what happens to us in life, but what we do about what happens to us.

George Allen, professional football coach

You always have to focus in life on what you want to achieve.

Michael Jordan, basketball player

Intelligence

Nobody in football should be called a genius. A genius is a guy like Norman Einstein.

Joe Theismann, football commentator and former player

Why would anyone expect him to come out smarter? He went to prison for three years, not Princeton.

Dan Duva, boxing promoter, on Mike Tyson hooking up again with promoter Don King

I told him, "Son, what is it with you? Is it ignorance or apathy?" He said, "Coach, I don't know and I don't care."

Frank Layden, Utah Jazz president, on a former player

We weren't the tallest, fastest, or best jumpers. We were just the most intelligent team I've ever seen.

Walt "Clyde" Frazier, Hall of Fame basketball player and broadcaster, talking about the championship New York Knicks teams of the late 60s and early 70s

Interpreters

There's only one thing wrong with my interpreter. He can't speak English.

Attributed to an American baseball player in Japan, by Robert Whiting, writer

Irving, Julius (Dr. J)

(b. Feb. 22, 1950) *Hall of Fame basketball player; won two championships (one ABA and two NBA); All-Star; one of only three players to score more than 30,000 career points; broadcaster*

My coach said to me, "Marvin, stop watching the gut . . . stop idolizing him."

Marvin Barnes, professional basketball player

J

Jackson, Shoeless Joe

(b. July 16, 1889; d. Dec. 5, 1951) *Major League Baseball player; lifetime .356 batting average; banned from the game as one of the Chicago "Black Sox" who threw the 1919 World Series*

I copied my swing after Joe Jackson's. His is the perfectest.
> *Babe Ruth, Hall of Fame baseball player*

Say it ain't so, Joe!
> *Attributed to a little boy after Jackson was accused of conspiring to throw the 1919 World Series*

Jackson, Reggie

(b. May 18, 1946) *Hall of Fame baseball player; won five World Series*

There isn't enough mustard in the world to cover Reggie Jackson.
> *Darold Knowles, professional baseball player*

When you unwrap a Reggie bar, it tells you how good it is.
> *Catfish Hunter, professional baseball player*

Jockeys

A bad rider can't do what you tell him and a good one won't listen to you anyway.
> *Charlie Whittingham, thoroughbred horse trainer*

Every steeplechase jockey has two ambitions. One is to ride more winners than anyone else in one season, and become Champion Jockey for that year. The other is to win the Grand National at Aintree.
> *Dick Francis, champion jockey and novelist*

G-Man, give me a shot.
> *Chris Antley, jockey, to Gary Stevens, jockey, during the Preakness, where Antley was trapped on the inside with Charismatic by Stevens's Stephen Got Even, to which Stevens replied, "Go ahead, little buddy." Charismatic won the race.*

He was hungry. He had a passion to get back into it. He's always been a great rider—a great finisher that fit that horse.
> *D. Wayne Lukas, thoroughbred horse trainer, about Chris Antley, jockey*

If I did not enjoy riding horses that do not win I could not be a jockey. No one could. It is a hard life in some ways, but the pleasures of riding by far outweigh the knocks; and every jockey thinks the same, for if he did not, he would change to another job.

> *Dick Francis, champion jockey and novelist*

If it is possible to inherit so vague a quality as a wish to be a jockey, I did so. My father was a jockey, and his father also.

> *Dick Francis, champion jockey and novelist*

No secret is so close as that between horse and rider.

> *William Shakespeare, playwright and poet*

Lady jockeys? Well, they do more for the silks than the boys do.

> *Bill Veeck, baseball owner and racetrack operator*

She was all jockey and no lady until after the race was won.

> *Jerry Izenberg, sportswriter, about Julie Krone, jockey*

There is no quicker way for a jockey to go out of business. He must either find a way to live with his fear or quit.

> *Roger Kahn, sportswriter*

You've got to make sure the horse thinks you're a part of him.

> *Eddie Arcaro, Hall of Fame jockey*

Johnson, Jack

(b. Mar. 31, 1878; d. June 10, 1946) *Heavyweight Champion of the World 1908–1915; first African-American boxing champion*

I grew to love the Jack Johnson image. I wanted to be the rough, tough, arrogant, the nigger white folks didn't like.

> *Muhammad Ali, champion boxer*

Johnson was magnificently defiant, and defiantly magnificent.

> *David Remnick, writer and editor*

Jordan, Michael

(b. Feb. 17, 1963) *Won six National Basketball Association championships; six-time National Basketball Association Finals MVP; Rookie of the Year*

He painted his own masterpiece on the ceiling of basketball's Sistine Chapel, and he didn't need a scaffold to lift him there. Michael Jordan can fly.

> *Ray Sons, sportswriter, after Jordan scored 63 points in an All-Star game*

He's the simplest, purest player who plays the game.

> *Jerry West, Hall of Fame basketball player and team executive*

In my prime I could have handled Michael Jordan. Of course, he would be only 12 years old.

> *Jerry Sloan, professional basketball player and coach*

Jesus in Nikes.

> *Jason Williams, professional basketball player*

Jordan has created a kind of fame that exceeds sports; he is both athlete and entertainer. He plays in the age of the satellite to an audience vastly larger than was possible in the past and is thus the first great athlete of the wired age.

David Halberstam, writer

Michael Jordan is in Paris. That's better than the Pope. It's God in person.

France-Soir, *French newspaper*

Michael Jordan is one of the greatest athletes in any sport in any era, and all of us are fortunate that we saw him play, because the greats are like that—spectacularly individual. Singular in approach. There will never be another one truly like him.

Spike Lee, writer, actor, director

That was God disguised as Michael Jordan.

Larry Bird, Hall of Fame basketball player and coach

The only thing I thought—Michael Jordan left too early. I've got kids who idolize him. I wish he was still playing.

Wayne Gretzky, Hall of Fame hockey player, about Michael Jordan's retirement

You don't bring your wife and children to the game when he comes to town 'cause he'll embarrass you.

Mark Jackson, professional basketball player, on Michael Jordan

K

Kayaking

A kayaker needs to know and become familiar with all the idiosyncrasies of water on the move.

Jay Evans, Olympic kayaker and outdoorsman

I know how to spell the word relax, but it's not something I do very often. When I get in a sea kayak and leave the shore, it's one of the few times that I can really enjoy the ultimate escape—away from faxes, phones, voice mail, and time commitments.

Deb Shapiro, kayaker

Loose hips save ships.

Attributed to anonymous by Shelly Johnson, kayaker and journalist

Sea kayaking gives a person the opportunity to venture on to a wild, unpredictable expanse in a craft that moves solely by the strength of their arm, directed by their experience and knowledge.

Derek C. Hutchinson, canoeist, kayaker, and journalist

The correct hip-flick makes the roll almost effortless.

Raymond Bridge, outdoorsman and journalist

The kayak . . . cuts no groove and leaves no scar. The same stretch of water can be paddled every day but the surface may never be the same twice.

Derek C. Hutchinson, canoeist, kayaker, and journalist

The kayaker relies on his or her paddle as much as on the boat.

Raymond Bridge, outdoorsman and journalist

There was nothing else to be done except lash the two kayaks together side by side, stiffen them with snowshoes under the straps, and place the sledges athwart them, one before, one behind.

Fridtjof Nansen, kayaker, speaking about his legendary experience with Hjalmer Johansen, on the Arctic Ocean

This is a sport that requires technique. Women tend to be better listeners, so they develop better technique.

Judy Harrison, publisher of
Canoe and Kayak Magazine

Thoreau was right: rivers are a constant lure to the adventurous instinct in mankind. If Henry were alive today, he would pursue that lure with the modern recreational kayak.

Jay Evans, Olympic kayaker
and outdoorsman

When you sit in the cockpit of your boat, you are at eye-level with the world around you: a curious harbor seal, a magnificent sea cliff of forbidding granite, a horizon line as the sun breaks free for the day. This vantage point is breathtaking in its intimacy.

Shelly Johnson, kayaker and journalist

Kentucky Derby

Churchill Downs crackles with the anticipation of what will be over in a few minutes. It is not so much the prospect of a good horse race that the Derby crowd looks forward to, as to that of instant history.

Steve Crist, sportswriter

Horses seem to thrive in Kentucky in the springtime.

Nick Zito, thoroughbred horse trainer

I don't care if she never wins another race or if she never starts another race. She has won the greatest race in America and I am satisfied.

Harry Payne Whitney, owner of Regret,
winner of the 1915 Kentucky Derby

The stretch looked like a cavalry charge.

Joseph Durso, sportswriter

When you win the Derby, everybody goes over there to Pimlico to beat the Derby winner. But to the guys crying about the size of the field, I'd say, "Don't enter."

D. Wayne Lukas, thoroughbred horse trainer

Kickers

How many guys we got in this league—1500? Well, that means there are 1,495 guys he can't lick.

Bill Parcells, professional football coach, referring
to his kicker, who had told the media he wanted
to get in some hits during an upcoming game

I am a kicker, but I'm tough. On kickoffs, I'll barrel through there and knock those runners right on my fanny.

Errol Mann, professional football player

I was flabbergasted. I thought he meant my punting. But he clarified it. He said, "Why are the Giants so terrible?"

Dave Jennings, professional football player and
broadcaster, when asked "Why are you so
terrible?" on a radio talk show

Kicking

That young 'un can't be doing that all by himself. He's got to be getting some dang help from somewhere. Let's get us some of them balls to take back home.

Bum Phillips, professional football coach, who
accused Oakland of filling Ray Guy's football
with helium, because his kicks went
so high and so deep

King, Billie Jean

(b. Nov. 22, 1943) *Tennis champion; won six Wimbledons, four U.S. Opens*

King gave the women's game credibility, not by winning the Grand Slam singles titles but by beating Bobby Riggs in the infamous "Battle of the Sexes" match.

John Feinstein, writer

On the court, she's an evil, merciless bastard. Totally ruthless. She'll do everything and anything within the rules to win.

Frank Hammond, tennis referee

King, Don

(b. Aug. 31, 1931) *Famous boxing promoter*

Looks black, lives white, and thinks green.

Larry Holmes, world champion boxer

Knight, Bobby

(b. Oct. 25, 1940) *Champion college basketball coach; won three NCAA basketball titles; Olympic gold medalist basketball coach (1984)*

Bob Knight is unique. In another time, he would have been a superb general. He never made it past private in the Army, but he has proved himself to be a fantastic leader throughout his career. He may well be the last of the coaching dictators.

Al McGuire, champion college basketball coach and broadcaster

You know, there were times, when if I had a gun, I think I would have shot him. And there were other times when I wanted to put my arms around him, and hug him, and tell him that I loved him.

Isiah Thomas, professional basketball player

Knockouts

I knew it was all over then. I saw his cheekbone cave in.

Jack Dempsey, champion boxer, speaking of an opponent

Krone, Julie

(b. July 24, 1963) *All-time winningest female jockey; won Belmont Stakes*

She is a jock in both senses of the word—a jock as in an athlete, with agility and courage and a consuming need to beat your brains in regardless of the game we're playing, and a jock as in shorthand for jockey, rider of four-footed things that weigh a dozen times her hundred pounds.

Bill Lyon, sportswriter

Lacrosse

In a sport like lacrosse there is continuous movement, a flow that exhilarates the player and arouses the spectator.

Mike Keenan, champion
hockey coach

It is a beautiful game—above all, for the skill of stick handlers in throwing and catching either long, looping passes or balletlike shorter ones.

Bob Scott, champion college coach

Lacrosse may be called a madman's game, so wild it is.

New York Herald Tribune

When I play lacrosse it makes me feel like I am playing the game with all of my ancestors. It also makes me proud that it was our people who gave lacrosse to the world. For these reasons, lacrosse is more than just a game.

Chief Irving Powless, Jr.,
Onondaga Nation

Landry, Tom

(b. Sept. 11, 1924; d. Feb. 13, 2000) *Hall of Fame professional football coach; All-Pro defensive back; won two of five Super Bowl appearances; third all-time winningest coach (270)*

He was known as Ol' Stone Face, and on the sideline it was easy to see why. However well or poorly the Dallas Cowboys were playing, Coach Tom Landry's expression under his snap-brim fedora never changed. But that's the way he wanted it.

Dave Anderson, sportswriter and writer

He helped build one of America's premier sports organizations, but I think that as a coach—both offensively and defensively— he was an incredible innovator. He was ahead of the learning curve on both sides of the ball.

Calvin Hill, All-Pro professional football player

He's the man that pretty much molded me into the man I am today.

Tony Dorsett, Hall of Fame professional
football player

He shaped my philosophy on everything. I followed his philosophy on football and how he handled himself on and off the field. He was a tremendous influence on me.

Dan Reeves, professional football coach, who took two different teams to a total of four Super Bowls, professional football player

He wasn't just about building football teams. It was about building men of character. Many of the things he did were to teach us important lessons about our success in life after football.

Drew Pearson, All-Pro professional football player

He was so stable, so consistent. He never got excited. He never got down. Tom was just stable. He didn't show great emotions when things were going right and he didn't show great dejection when things were going wrong. I think that made him a great leader.

Lee Roy Jordan, Hall of Fame football player

He will be remembered for many special reasons, including his record as a coach, the innovations he brought to our game, and the personal integrity he displayed.

Paul Tagliabue, National Football League commissioner

It was always difficult playing against him because he did things differently. We always had to go against the 4–3 flex defense. I don't think any coach ever figured out how to contain that flex defense. It was a tremendous defense. It still surprises me that nobody plays the flex today.

Ron Jaworski, All-Pro quarterback and broadcaster

Ours is a land that prides itself on sports' achievement, but never in the history of sports in this state has there been anything larger and more captivating than the mighty reign of Landry and the Cowboys.

Randy Galloway, sportswriter and writer

There was somewhat of a shyness about him, but he was always there when you needed him. I don't know anyone who didn't have respect for him as a person. As a human being, coach Landry is right there among the very best. There's nothing phony about him.

Roger Staubach, Hall of Fame quarterback

They were different than anybody else we played, and it took a lot of preparation to play them. They had good players in their scheme, but their defensive scheme was always so much different than anybody else. It took a while to get the players to know what they were doing.

Chuck Noll, Hall of Fame football coach, won four Super Bowl titles

The thing I remember about Tom is how completely confident he was without being cocky. I remember one time when Tom presented the defensive game plan for that particular week, and Sam Huff asked what if they do something other than you just described, and Tom said, "Sam they won't."

Wellington Mara, National Football League owner

When you played for him, he's the boss. When I coached for him, he was the boss, too, but when you played for him there was a fear in there.

Mike Ditka, Hall of Fame professional football player and Super Bowl–winning coach

A reporter asked me once if I'd ever seen Tom Landry laugh. 'No,' I answered, 'I only played nine years."

Jerry Glanville, professional football player and head coach

Lanier, Bob

(b. Sept. 10, 1948) *Hall of fame basketball player; eight-time All-Star; coach*

Lanier played defense in his sleep. I call him Mr. Sweet Hands. The referee could look right at him holding you, and he wouldn't see it.

Darryl Dawkins, professional basketball player

Lardner, Ring

(b. Mar. 6, 1885; d. Sept. 25, 1933) *Newspaper columnist, humorist, and novelist*

Over the years the sports page has been hyped as a literary showcase. Its first writing star was Ring Lardner.

Benjamin DeMott, writer

Ring was closer to being a genius than anyone I've ever known. He had a sense of humor that was sometimes beyond this world. He was tall, dark and slender and was never what you'd call loquacious.

Grantland Rice, sportswriter

Last Place

Actually, I don't ever recall them not being in last place.

Bob Wolff, Hall of Fame broadcaster, referring to the Washington Senators

Leadership

"Leadership is a matter of having people look at you and gain confidence, seeing how you react," he once said, alluding to his Cowboys players. "If you're in control, they're in control."

Tom Landry, Hall of Fame football coach and all-pro football player

A lot of parents think kids ought to learn responsibility from work, and I've always said, "Baloney." Kids learn leadership and organization from games, from having fun.

John Madden, professional football coach and commentator

I believe in leadership. And I definitely believe I am a leader. But I believe I lead by example.

Mike Piazza, baseball player

If they were Indians back in the early days of this country, Lawrence would be the emotional war counselor who leads the braves into battle. But Banks would be the tribal chief. When you have two personalities like that in one linebacking corps, it's a coach's dream.

Bill Parcells, professional football coach, about Lawrence Taylor, Hall of Fame football coach, and Carl Banks, professional football player

I guess I don't talk much, but I think a man can set an example for his team by his actions on the field.

Harmon Killebrew, professional baseball player

Leaders have a different look from followers. They get it sometime while being potty-trained or tumbling around a kindergarten playroom. . . . People who don't get it early never do.

Harvey Manning, mountain climber

Leadership is getting people to do something they shouldn't be able to do.
Al Roberts, college football player

Listen, I'm a leader. If anyone gives me trouble in a huddle—I don't care who they are—I'm going to sting them.
Terry Bradshaw, Hall of Fame football player

You lead by example.
Alvin Dark, professional baseball player

Lee, Spike

(b. Mar. 20, 1957) *Comedian, writer, actor, director, sports fan*

Sometimes he opens his mouth a little too much and gets the *other* guys going.
Reggie Miller, professional basketball player

Le Mans

Le Mans has to be the most dangerous race in the world. It is one long accident looking for a place to happen.
Mario Andretti, champion driver

Liebling, A. J.

(b. May 31, 1904; d. Dec. 29, 1963) *Columnist, sportswriter, humorist*

The problem for Liebling and for the *New Yorker* must have been how to sell a blood sport like boxing to a genteel, affluent readership to whom the idea of men fighting for their lives would have been deeply offensive; how to suggest boxing's drama while skirting boxing's tragedy. It is a problem, that for all his verbal cleverness, Liebling never entirely solves.
Joyce Carol Oates, writer

Life

A life is not important, but for the impact it has on other's lives.
Jackie Robinson, Hall of Fame baseball player

Desperate situations are not necessarily our proudest moments, and are difficult to describe truthfully.
B. M. Annette, mountain climber

Each of us has to discover his own path—of that I am sure. Some paths will be spectacular and others will be peaceful and quiet—who is to say which is the most important?
Sir Edmund Hillary, mountain climber, first to scale Everest

Golf is golf and life is life, and blurring the line between the two can be disastrous.
Laura Baugh, professional golfer, recovering alcoholic

I might have had a tough break, but I have an awful lot to live for.
Lou Gehrig, Hall of Fame baseball player, who was afflicted during his playing days with amyotrophic lateral sclerosis, an incurable disease

I'm old, I'm bald, and I'm short not only in stature but also in patience with those unwilling to give their best effort. . . . Life's nothing but one continual battle from start to finish. We come into it kicking, and if we've got an ounce of gumption, we go out the same damned way.
Mills Lane, district court judge and boxing referee

I'm not going to turn around and be a golfer again just because I had hip surgery. I've got other things to do.

Jack Nicklaus, champion professional golfer

In life, not just basketball, the key is to be able to control the little things. No human being is capable of overcoming all the big things in life, the things that aren't in your control. . . . A person is an idiot if he doesn't manage the things he can't manage.

John Chaney, college basketball coach

I swing big with everything I've got. I hit big or I miss big. I like to live as big as I can.

Babe Ruth, Hall of Fame baseball player

I know that I'm never as good or bad as any single performance. I've never believed my critics or my worshippers, and I've always been able to leave the game at the arena.

Charles Barkley, professional basketball player

Life is like boxing. You've only got so many punches to throw, and you can only take so many.

George Foreman, champion boxer

Life hangs by a very thin thread and the cancer of time is complacency. If you are going to do something, do it now. Tomorrow is too late.

Pete Goss, champion solo sailor and writer

Life is truly a balancing act. In one hand you hold your running, and in the other, you hold your job, your family and other tasks and challenges that you face on a daily basis. For all the things that are important in your life, you have to find that balance.

Joan Benoit Samuelson, marathoner

The people who I know who BASE jump all love life, and because they do they're pretty reflective about it. When you put yourself in such dangerous situations, where one mistake will kill you, it makes you think.

Thor Alex Kappfjell, BASE jumper

The solution to any problem—work, love, money, whatever—is to go fishing, and the worst problem, the longer the trip should be.

John Gierach, fisherman and writer

"There's nothing left to do!" is a common cry you hear from all sorts of young people and it's sad in a way because you know the speaker must be closing his eyes to the adventurous opportunities that still abound. The world is full of interesting projects—if you have the imagination and resourcefulness to seek them out. Finding new adventures has never been a problem in my life—the big difficulty is finding the time to do them.

Sir Edmund Hillary, mountain climber, first to scale Everest

Trying to achieve goals in life shouldn't prevent you from enjoying life.

Max Papis, automobile racer

We do have choices, we do have control, but in the end we are going to have only one life unfold. In that sense you have to know when to relax and stop worrying about it.

Eammon Coghlan, champion runner

Limits

Know your limits and listen to your body. Find your own rhythm and stick to it.

Bobby Julich, cyclist

Lineman

Usually for linemen the only recognition you get is from your mother and your wife.

Korey Stringer, defensive lineman, football

Locker Room

If you are not a player, but some peripheral member of the tennis establishment—a promoter a writer or a pretty girl or even just some hanger-on, or a friend of a friend—it is easy to get into the Player's Tea Room. Either you give the old guard at the bottom of the stairs a pound or two the first day or you can climb over a little fence from the press balcony.

Arthur Ashe, Hall of Fame tennis champion and writer

If you go into rooms where athletes change their clothes as much as I do you would be disgusted by the way the place smells. The customary odor of the locker room is a healthy one and is dominated by liniments, sweat, soap melting in the hot waters of the showers.

Jimmy Cannon, sportswriter

Locker rooms that wrestlers use are very different from any other—dingy and small and dirty, and always with this distinctive smell, a body smell that's worse than anything you find in places where football players and baseball players have been. I don't know why.

Alex Karras, Hall of Fame football player and professional wrestler

That's so when I forget how to spell my name, I can still find my #%@# clothes.

Karas Grimson, Chicago Blackhawks left wing, who kept a color photo of himself above his locker.

Sometimes all I get is a large closet. Sometimes I dress in the first-aid room.

Barbara Jo Rubin, jockey, referring to the fact that most tracks didn't have separate locker rooms for male and female riders in the beginning

The competitors' lounge at the All England Club is the meat market of the world of tennis.

Gwen Robyns, writer

There were rats in pretty nearly every building, including our locker room. The rats would chew on the leather shoulder pads at night, and we'd come back the next day and find their teeth marks.

Don McIlhenny, professional football player

The philosophy of the locker room . . . physical strength and the ability to withstand pain are the most positive virtues. Women are things. Bookish people and little people are suspect.

Rick Sortun, professional football player

Years ago the competitors' lounge at Wimbledon had, in theory, been the sacrosanct preserve of players and their guests. But, in practice, it had always been a throbbing hive of hustlers, racquet dealers, clothing reps, agents, tournament directors, assorted groupies, gofers, and camp followers.

Michael Mewshaw, writer

Lombardi, Vince

(b. June 11, 1913; d. Sept 3, 1970) *professional football player and coach*

He went from warm to red hot. You could hear him laughing or shouting for five blocks.

Wellington Mara, National Football League Hall of Fame owner

Vince fears high winds make every forward pass a gamble. To Vincent T. Lombardi gambling on a football field is a crime against nature.

Red Smith, sportswriter

Losing

As soon as I was in front I started praying for someone to pass me. It was a horrible realization . . . Instead of running it out of them, I was running it out of me.

Eamon Coghlan, champion runner, about losing in the Olympics

Athletes seem to have a much healthier attitude. There's a difference between a good loser and learning how to lose. I was never a good loser, but losing teaches you something.

Betty Meade, champion squash player, amputee

Every time you win, you're reborn; when you lose, you die a little.

George Allen, professional football coach

I despise losing and would do anything to avoid it.

Michael Jordan, professional basketball player

I didn't have to run that extra mile, didn't have to spar that day, I could have stayed up that night in camp and watched the late show . . . I could have fought tonight in no condition.

Floyd Patterson, champion boxer, his thoughts after the second Patterson–Liston fight, which he lost

I'd lost to him the first four times. I was beating him 7-5, 3-0 and he walked off the court. He didn't even give the satisfaction of beating him.

John McEnroe, professional tennis champion, about Jimmy Connors

I hate to lose. Hate, hate, hate to lose.

George Steinbrenner, owner, New York Yankees

I never learned how to lose.

Jim Ryun, track athlete

I slept like a baby—I woke up and cried every two hours.

Fred Taylor, professional football player, after a loss

I used very, very poor judgment and I'm man enough to admit that.

John A. Kelly, champion marathoner, after pressing too early in a race, wearing himself out and losing the race to Ellison Brown, who eventually beat him with an unexceptional time

I was overconfident. I overestimated my powers at the time, and I underestimated hers. Now, when you do that in any competitive event, it is a big mistake.

Bobby Riggs, professional tennis champion and legendary hustler, about losing to Billie Jean King in the "Battle of the Sexes" match

With the Red Sox, the past is always the present. If it's not Babe Ruth's departure, it's Bucky Dent's home run.

Dave Anderson, New York Times, regarding historical playoff losses by the Boston Red Sox

Washington: First in war, first in peace, last in the American League.

Anonymous, regarding losing franchise, the Washington Senators

The hardest part of losing is knowing you have failed those who are depending on you.
Johnny Roach, professional football player

Let's call the whole thing off.
Dr. A. Harry Kleinman, ringside physician to the referee, at the Jerry Quarry–Joe Frazier heavyweight bout. Quarry lost.

Losing is the great American sin.
Jerome Holtzman, writer

Sometimes when you go out on the court, you have a feeling of being useless and you know everything is doomed.
Rosie Casals, champion tennis player

We couldn't make a basket, we couldn't rebound, and we didn't play defense. You might say we put it all together.
Bill Fitch, professional basketball coach

My baseball career spanned almost five decades—from 1925 to 1973, count them—and in all that time I never had a boss call me upstairs so that he could congratulate me for losing like a gentleman. When you're playing for money, winning is the only thing that matters. Show me a good loser in professional sports, and I'll show you an idiot. Show me a sportsman, and I'll show you a player I'm looking to trade.
Leo Durocher, professional baseball player and manager

Nice guys finish last.
Leo Durocher, professional baseball player and manager

The minute you start talking about what you're going to do if you lose, you've lost.
George Schultz, secretary of state

They just made us look lousy.
Ron Greschner, professional hockey player, referring to the Montreal Canadiens defeating the New York Rangers

Wait 'til next year.
Anonymous, attributed as Brooklyn Dodger fan lament

We wuz robbed—we should have stood in bed.
Joe Jacobs, boxing trainer, after his fighter, Max Schmeling, lost to Jack Sharkey

When you're not winning any matches since two months, it feels like you'll lose forever.
Yevgeny Kafelnikov, professional tennis player

Winning is one thing. They don't remember their victories as much as their losses. Losing is a more powerful energy for them.
Vic Braden, tennis commentator, on John McEnroe and Jimmy Connors

You either get a good trip or a bad trip. Today we got the nightmare trip.
Gary Stevens, professional jockey

Louis, Joe

(b. May 13, 1914; d. Apr. 12, 1981) *World Heavyweight Champion 1937–1949; longest continuous reign by any world champion*

Everybody loved Joe. From black folks to redneck Mississippi crackers, they loved him.
Muhammad Ali, champion boxer

He was a credit to his race—the human race.

Jimmy Cannon, sportswriter

He carried in a sense so many of our hopes, maybe even our dreams of vengeance.

Maya Angelou, poet

His name was Joe Louis and he was black and he was simply the greatest heavyweight fighter who ever lived. He could fend like Johnson and jab harder than Tunney and punch like Dempsey at Toledo.

Budd Schulburg, writer and screenwriter

I remember Joe Louis as a kid. Every time he was in a fight the whole family gathered around the radio. . . . When Joe Louis fought, the whole black neighborhood came to a standstill.

Maury Wills, professional baseball player, broadcaster, and manager

Louis was the anti–Jack Johnson. His talent was so undeniable and his behavior was deferential that in time he won over even the Southern press. . . . Unlike Johnson, Louis knew his place. He offended no one.

David Remnick, writer and editor

Nobody trained like Joe Louis. He always wore white knit trunks with a white tank top and black boxing shoes with white socks. He was all business.

Lou Duva, Hall of Fame trainer

Save me, Joe Louis. Save me, Joe Louis. Save me, Joe Louis.

Last words of a prisoner condemned to die in a gas chamber, reported by Martin Luther King, as the pellets were being dropped in

Love (of the game)

Do it because you love it. Don't do it because you want to make a lot of money at it. If you do it because you love it . . . everything else will fall into place.

Wayne Gretzky, Hall of Fame hockey player

I'm a firm believer that people only do their best at things they truly enjoy. It's difficult to excel at something you don't enjoy.

Jack Nicklaus, golfer

The reasons I was playing the game have always been the same. The game was all I cared about; it never felt like a job.

Dennis Rodman, professional basketball player

There's a love of the game in this city that is very difficult to put into words. You start off when you're very young and you never get it out of your system. You might get married to a woman, but basketball is still your first love.

Willie Hall, street basketball player, Harlem

You've got to love what you're doing. If you love it, you can overcome any handicap or the soreness or all the aches and pains, and continue to play for a long, long time.

Gordie Howe, hockey player

Luck

Dame Fortune is a cock-eyed wench, as
 someone's said before,
And yet the old Dame plays her part in any
 winning score.
Take all the credit you deserve, heads-up in
 winning pride,
But don't forget that Lady Luck was riding
 at your side.

Grantland Rice, sportswriter

Everything in a game happens by chance, so what you're doing is trying to make your own breaks.

Nate Allen, professional football player

First you've got to be good, but then you've got to be lucky.

"Lighthorse Harry" Cooper, golfer

Good luck is what is left over after intelligence and effort have combined at their best.

Branch Rickey, baseball executive

If I knew what it was, I'd take it with me every week.

Meg Mallon, professional golfer, when asked why she had been so lucky

If you don't get lucky, you just sit there like a big dork.

Don Nelson, professional basketball coach, speaking of the National Basketball Association lottery

Luck is the residue of design.

Branch Rickey, Hall of Fame baseball executive

Luck means a lot in football. Not having a quarterback is bad luck.

Don Shula, professional football coach

Smart is better than lucky.

Alvin Clarence Thomas, from Titanic Thompson

Sometimes you have to have good breaks.

Jose Maria Ozabal, champion golfer

You can play very well and lose, or play very badly and win. Things can happen. And you know what? That's just the way it goes.

Carl Eller, professional football player

Lukas, D. Wayne

(b. Sept. 2, 1935) *Champion thoroughbred horse trainer; won Preakness five times, Kentucky Derby four times and Belmont four times*

He's a coach and he pushes his athletes—and that's the nature of the game. The thing about him is he's got energy and goals.

Carl Nafzger, thoroughbred horse trainer

He's got his opinions and they come out quick. He wants you to hear them and listen to them. But I believe he has earned that right for all he's done for the game.

John Nerud, thoroughbred horse trainer

Madden, John

(b. Apr. 10, 1936) *Professional football coach; won Super Bowl; award-winning broadcaster*

John is a dominating personality. He can get people to stay with a bad game longer than anyone.

Barry Frank, agent

McEnroe, John

(b. Feb. 16, 1959) *Tennis champion; won U.S. Open four times, won three Wimbledon titles*

The guy is an artist. There's no one in the game quite like him.

Gerry Armstrong, professional tennis umpire

Majors, The (golf)

Most distressing to those who love the game of golf is the applauding and cheering of misplays or misfortunes of a player. Such occurrences have been rare at the Masters but we must eliminate them entirely if our patrons are to continue to merit their reputation as the most knowledgeable in the world.

Bobby Jones, champion golfer, note printed on the back of every Masters ticket since the 1930s.

Most of the time, professional golfers are playing for money. It is how they are measured by the end of the year. But four times a year, the money becomes completely irrelevant. They are playing for history.

John Feinstein, writer

Only one player will prevail, and considering the caliber of names at the top, the magnitude of the event and the difficulty of the course, the winner will have to overcome one of the greatest challenges of his career. But then, isn't that what a major is supposed to be about?

Clifton Brown, sportswriter

Playing in the U.S. Open is like tippy-toeing through hell.

Jerry McGee, golfer

The Masters doesn't begin until the back nine on Sunday.

John Feinstein, writer

The week of a major just has a different feel to it than other weeks. There's more tension during the practice rounds. You pay more attention to the golf course and the greens than to whatever bets you may have going.

Tom Watson, champion golfer

Management

It's like a child doing something bad at the dinner table. You send him to bed without dinner, but he's back down for breakfast in the morning.

George Steinbrenner, baseball owner, on rehiring Gene Michael, executive

Risk is something general managers live with every day.

Selena Roberts, sportswriter

Managing

A manager's job is simple. For 162 games you try not to screw up all that smart stuff your organization did last December.

Earl Weaver, baseball manager

I don't happen to think that a manager is a significant influence in major-league baseball. For the most part managing a team is a farce. One wearies of their studied idiosyncrasies, the spitting of the tobacco, the hitching of the belt, all the rest of the nonsense that goes with conducting a game that's juvenile enough to be totally understood by eight-year-olds in Little Leagues.

Howard Cosell, broadcaster

Managing is getting paid for home runs that somebody else hits.

Casey Stengel, baseball manager

Managing is like holding a dove in your hand. Squeeze too hard and you kill it; not hard enough and it flies away.

Tom Lasorda, baseball manager

Once there was a theory that devising strategy, dictating and alternating tactics, matching wits with the licensed genius across the way were part of the manager's job and that his degree of success in these areas accounted for his ranking in his profession.

Red Smith, sportswriter

Mantle, Mickey

(b. Oct. 20, 1931; d. Aug. 13, 1995) *Hall of Fame baseball player; won 7 of 12 World Series; won Triple Crown batting title; three-time league MVP*

He is the only baseball player I know who is a bigger hero to his teammates than he is to the fans.

Clete Boyer, professional baseball player

Mickey Mantle had those dual qualities so seldom seen, exuding dynamism and excitement but at the same time touching your heart—flawed, wounded. We knew there was something poignant about Mickey Mantle before we knew what poignant meant.

Bob Costas, broadcaster

Mickey Mantle just was everything. At my bar mitzvah I had an Oklahoma accent. And I think I once told my parents, "Play me or trade me."

Billy Crystal, comedian

Mickey was like Marilyn Monroe. He didn't have to be the greatest ballplayer. He had that charisma.

Hank Aaron, Hall of Fame baseball player, about Mickey Mantle, Hall of Fame baseball player

Shoot, if he'da told me, I'da give him first base.

Satchel Paige, Hall of Fame pitcher, telling sportswriters after the game what he thought of Mickey Mantle bunting to try to get on base

There were days when Mickey Mantle was so darn good that we kids would bet that even God would want his autograph.

Bob Costas, broadcaster

Maradona, Diego

(b. Oct. 30, 1960) *Champion soccer player; led team to two World Cup finals; won 1986 World Cup*

He was the most naturally talented player ever—a cheat, a drug-user, but on his best playing days, a magician with a ball.

Jimmy Burns, author

Pele had almost everything; Maradona has everything. He works harder, does more and is more skillful. Trouble is that he'll be remembered for another reason. He bends the rules to suit himself.

Sir Alf Ramsey, soccer executive

Sadly, you can't keep a good man down, nor Diego.

Terry Badoo, CNN soccer analyst and writer

Marathons

After every experience, it's natural to reflect that you might have done better. Only after a marathon can I say I have given everything.

Kenny Moore, champion marathoner

I wanted to try a marathon.

Grete Waitz, champion marathoner, when asked why she had come to her first New York City Marathon

Often, the enjoyment is the training before and the memory after.

Doug Kurtis, marathoner

Rejoice. We conquer!

attributed to the Athenian runner who ran from the plains of Marathon all the way to Athens to announce the Greek victory over the Persians, and then died

The marathon is the ultimate endurance test. Oh, sure, people sometimes go longer than that. But 26 miles 385 yards is where racing ends and where ludicrous extremes begin.

Joe Henderson, runner and writer

The winners run at speeds equaled or surpassed by no more than a handful of runners ever in the world. As important for me was the fact that more than fifteen thousand people from sixty-eight countries compete in our race.

Fred Lebow, organizer of the New York City Marathon

To succeed in the marathon at a very high level of competition you have to live in a very stable environment. You need people to support you and help you out. If you don't have this kind of backing, you're not going to make it.

Bill Rodgers, champion marathoner

Too many runners attempt the marathon much too early in their careers and then become ex-runners.

Robert Eshich, college running coach

To understand the marathon is to run it a lot . . . You really can't know it until you've felt the other side of it. That's the only way it's possible.

Bill Rodgers, champion marathoner

Marketing

If you're not the way the NBA wants you to be, you pay the price. If you look at the players they market, they have that nice, goody-two-shoes image. If you don't have it, you fall by the wayside.

Rod Strickland, National Basketball Association player

Marching Band

The critics agreed the Yale band was two steps faster than Harvard's.

Red Smith, sportswriter

The majorettes, their black-and-white costumes falling just below their buttocks, twirled and beckoned as the band—fifty-four clarinetists, fifty-one flutists, thirty-six coronetists, twenty-six trombonists, twenty-five percussionists, eighteen saxophonists, fourteen French Horn players, nine baritone players and nine tubaists—belted out "Boogie Woogie Bugle Boy." The color guard waved its flags to "Barbara Ann."

H. G. Bissinger, author

The marching band, brassy and brisk whether or nor it was led by an amazing baton-twirler of either sex, is an essential feature of a major college football. Its pregame entrance and half-time maneuvers represent a distinctive, indigenous American pop art form.

Leonard Koppett, writer,
The Avant-Gardes of 'Music'

The players tried to take the field,
   the marching band refused to yield,
do you remember what was the deal,
   the day, the music died?
Don McLean, musician, "American Pie"

Marriage

I fought Sugar Ray six times; I only beat him once. This is my sixth marriage and I ain't won one yet—so I figure I'm due.

Jake LaMotta, world champion boxer

I guess to be honest you just get use to them not being part of your life. You just have to build a life around yourself and then when they come back . . . there are sometimes a bit of an adjustment, depending on how long they've been away for. But overall it just sort of happens, you just slot back into good old routines.

Kylie Wetzell, partner of Adrian Cashmore, New Zealand rugby player

Look down at the field, and there was Steve at first base. How many games, how many years had she been sitting there? When Steve had waved to me in the crowd, was it really me he was waving at?

Cindy Garvey, ex-wife of professional baseball player Steve Garvey, upon seeing her husband's mistress for the first time

When he didn't remember our anniversary, I knew he was OK.

> *Lisa McCaffrey, wife of Ed McCaffrey,*
> *professional football player,*
> *referring to a concussion*

When you divorce baseball, someone once said, baseball divorces you.

> *Danielle Gagnon Torrez, ex-wife of professional*
> *baseball player Mike Torrez*

You've got to time your babies for the off-season and get married in the off-season and get divorced in the off-season. Baseball always comes first.

> *Liz Mitchell, wife of professional*
> *baseball player Paul Mitchell*

Masculinity

He treats us like men. He lets us wear earrings.

> *Torrin Polk, University of Houston receiver, on*
> *his coach John Jenkins*

To me being tough includes going into corners without phoning ahead to see who's there.

> *Ted Lindsay, professional hockey player*

Masters, The

Something magical happens to every writer who goes to the Masters for the first time, some sort of emotional experience that results in a search party having to be sent out to recover his typewriter from a clump of azaleas.

> *Dan Jenkins, writer*

Maturity

A lot of players don't really mature until their early 30's, or mid-30's and at that point they really break out.

> *Jim Furyk, professional golfer*

Even though I think I'm mature on the football field, I'm still a kid. If there's a good play, I'll jump up and down on the sidelines.

> *Gary Parris, professional football player*

Every player goes through a maturation period where they develop and improve.

> *Alonzo Mourning, professional basketball player*

I made some mistakes—my immaturity is the one thing that sticks out—but I've learned a lot. Sometimes that takes time.

> *Kerry Collins, professional football player*

Mays, Willie

(b. May 6, 1931) *Hall of Fame baseball player; played in 24 All-Star games; also known as "The Say Hey Kid"*

There have been only two geniuses in the world. Willie Mays and Willie Shakespeare.

> *Tallulah Bankhead, actress*

This game was invented for Willie Mays a hundred years ago.

> *Ray Sedecki, professional baseball player*

When you watched Willie Mays play baseball, it wasn't like watching anyone else play baseball. That was a style that was sensational, and he was so electrifying. Every time he came up, every time he was on base, every time a ball was hit to the outfield, there was a moment when you waited for him to do something, and so many times he did it. It's so hard to do that in baseball.

Woody Allen, writer, actor, director

Media (the)

Good. You won't be able to put my picture in the media guide.

Leon Hess, sports owner, when told by his public relations staff that they could find no pictures of him anywhere in the organization

I forgot some appointment twelve years ago and *Sport* magazine hasn't let up on me since.

Ted Williams, Hall of Fame baseball player to Ed Linn, sportswriter

If you're famous in America the media will exploit you. The media is also America's safeguard. A lot of them are bastards, but I'd rather have those bastards than no media at all.

Jim Brown, Hall of Fame football player

I'm rapidly getting to the point now where I don't care about the interviews or anything anymore. I guess from a business point of view every bit of publicity you can get is good, but it's just not worth it to me. You get sick about talking about the same thing over and over again.

Alberto Salazar, champion marathoner

I think playing my first match was great. But the media is really sort of out of control.

Jennifer Capriati, professional tennis player, after her first professional tour match

I thought they were a sport magazine, not the *National Enquirer.*

Jim Pierce, father of Mary Pierce, professional tennis player, after a scathing article about him appeared in the magazine

I told him, "Don't buy the papers tomorrow. You're not going to like what you read."

Bill Parcells, professional football coach, about Phil Simms after a bad game

It would be impossible to overstate the degree to which sports-talk radio is shadowed by the homosexual panic implicit in the fact that it consists almost entirely of out-of-shape white men sitting around talking about black men's buff bodies.

David Shields, writer

Maybe this isn't a good time to have you doing undercover surveillance work.

Attributed to Federal Bureau of Investigation managers, by Joe Alston, champion badminton player, after the undercover surveillance FBI agent was featured on the cover of Sports Illustrated

That box over there, you know, people pass judgment on players, athletes, and people in general by what they see on TV.

Alonzo Mourning, professional basketball player

Too bad, America, but you missed one of the greatest basketball shows on Earth.

Attributed by Michael Berg, writer, to Sports Illustrated, *about the American Basketball Association's last championship series, which was not televised*

You have to show the winner pass the finish line, and then cut to the jubilation, but when there was the developing story as soon as the race was over . . . then all you can do is cover it.

Curt Gowdy, Jr., television producer, about Charismatic's dramatic loss in the Belmont Stakes and subsequent injury

Mental

Certainly the difference between winning and losing, between the winner and the runner-up, is always a mental one.

Peter Thompson, professional golfer

If you don't sharpen up your minds at a young age, you'll never be sharp at all. If you don't spend quality time doing what you're supposed to be doing now, you can't look forward to doing what you think you should be doing later on.

John Chaney, college basketball coach

I learned a long time ago, you can't let outside forces get inside your head and affect how you play.

Allan Houston, professional basketball player

I'm about five inches from being an outstanding golfer. That's the distance between my left ear and my right.

Ben Crenshaw, champion professional golfer

In order to be eligible to play, it was necessary for him to keep up his studies, a very difficult matter, for while he was not dumber than an ox, he was not any smarter.

James Thurber, writer, cartoonist, about an offensive lineman from Ohio State University

Ninety percent of the game is half mental.

Yogi Berra, Hall of Fame baseball player and manager

Raw power was giving way, at least a little, to cunning. More than ever, headwork won ballgames.

Burt Solomon, writer

Success is 90% physical and 10% mental. But never underestimate the power of that 10%.

Tom Fleming, runner and writer

The good Lord was good to me. H[e gave me] a strong body, a good right arm a[nd a weak] mind.

Dizzy Dean, Hall of Fame baseball player and broadcaster

The simpler I keep things, the better I play.

Nancy Lopez, champion professional golfer

The key is being able to endure psychologically.

Greg LeMond, champion cyclist

The mind is the limit. As long as the mind can envision the fact that you can do something, you can do it—as long as you really believe 100 percent.

Arnold Schwarzenegger, champion bodybuilder and actor

You've got fast feet. But there are millions of people who have fast feet. The people who win races are the ones with fast brains.

Ross Kitt, father of A. J. Kitt, champion downhiller, to Kitt before a big race

Minor Leagues

The CBA has been a proving ground for players, coaches, and referees. The CBA has been instrumental in the development of many of the people you see in prominent positions all over the NBA.

Rod Thorn, National Basketball Association league executive speaking of the Continental Basketball Association

The CBA is only a bounce away from the NBA.

Kevin Mackey, college and minor league basketball coach, favorite recruiting and motivating line for players in the Continental Basketball Association

If you're playing here for money you're playing for the wrong reason. You could be further on in your career if you're out there working at something else.

Gerald Oliver, assistant coach, Continental Basketball Association

The NBA is sirloin, medium rare; the CBA is a double cheeseburger, ketchup only. The NBA is a best-selling novel; the CBA is a feature in the *National Enquirer*. The NBA is fantasy; the CBA is reality.

Bob Ryan, sportswriter, comparing National Basketball Association to Continental Basketball Association

You know in high school, how your parents came to the games and your girlfriend and friends? In pro ball, those people aren't around anymore. In Fort Myers, you look up in the stands and there's 200 or 300 people, and you don't know any of them. You're alone and you're fighting for a job that only 5 percent of the people get.

Shane Gunderson, minor league baseball player

Don't worry kid, you'll be back.

George Steinbrenner, owner, New York Yankees, to Bernie Williams, All-Star Major League Baseball player, early in Williams's career

Mistakes

Be quick, but never hurry.

John Wooden, basketball coach

Can't afford to miss, or you get beat.

Ben Hogan, champion golfer

His right name was Frank X. Farrell, and I guess the X. stood for "Excuse me." Because

he never pulled a play, good or bad, on or off the field, without apologizing for it.

Ring Lardner, sportswriter and novelist, from Alibi Ike

I accept the fact that I am going to miss it sometimes. I just hope I miss it where I can find it.

Fuzzy Zoeller, champion professional golfer

If you make a mistake, you die.

Todd Skinner, mountain climber

I sometimes think about what we're doing out here and how hard some people work at it and then when it isn't happening, some player will say to me, "I'm sorry, coach, but I'm trying," and I'll tell him exactly what my father told me: you don't get any medals for trying.

Bill Parcells, professional football coach

Joe Frazier did not come out smokin'. Jerry Quarry did. It was Quarry's mistake.

Roy McHugh, sportswriter, referring to Quarry's loss in the fight

Most coaches hate preventable mistakes as much as I did. Somebody asked Don Shula if it wasn't a waste of time to correct a small flaw. "What's a small flaw?" Don wanted to know.

John Madden, professional football coach and commentator

Oh my God! I'm on the ice! What am I doing down here?

Michelle Kwan, medal-winning Olympic skater, after falling on the ice during the 1997 U.S. National Championships

She didn't win; I gave it to her. I hit so many errors. It was absolutely absurd.

Serena Williams, professional tennis player, speaking of a loss to Martina Hingis

The man who complains about the way the ball bounces is likely to be the one who dropped it.

Lou Holtz, professional football coach

We did something we should never do. We took it for granted.

Jenni Meno, pairs skater (with Todd Sand), after losing at the National Championships in which they were heavy favorites

When all is said and done, as a rule, more is said than done.

Lou Holtz, college football coach

When you make a mistake, there are only three things you should ever do about it; 1) admit it; 2) learn from it; 3) don't repeat it.

Paul "Bear" Bryant, professional football coach

Money

Good stockbrokers are a dime a dozen, but good shortstops are hard to find.

Charles O. Finley, baseball owner

I don't like money, but it quiets my nerves.

Joe Louis, champion boxer

I'd rather play for pay than run for fun.

Mel Gray, professional football player

I really don't like to talk about money. All I can say is that the Good Lord must have wanted me to have it.

Larry Bird, Hall of Fame basketball player and coach

I'm sick of people talking about money, money, money all the time.

Shaquille O'Neal, professional basketball player

Money isn't everything, but it's way ahead of whatever is in second place.

attributed to unknown by Mario Andretti, champion race car driver

People make too big a deal about the money. Some guy was complaining to me, and I told him, "Hey, if you don't like it, take your kids to see *Riverdance.*"

Mike Piazza, professional baseball player

The beauty of money is that money can buy what the farm can't grow.

William C. Rhoden, sportswriter

The difference in Namath and me is that when you make the money he makes, they say you're ruggedly handsome. When you make the money I make, they say you have a big nose.

Jim Valvano, college basketball coach

The only reason I'd go to the NBA is if someone throws funny money—players' money—at me.

Jim Calhoun, college basketball coach

The pressures that are generated these days are not confined to jumping clear rounds, producing a brilliant extension or going fast. These days, we have pressures from sponsors, owners, and organizers that were unheard of a few years ago. The reason is simple—money.

Jane C. Wofford, champion equestrian show jumper

The winner gets $100,000 and the loser goes home and sits on his ass and does nothing.

> *Bobby Riggs, professional tennis champion*

They both knew how to spend the green stuff but neither knew anything about conserving it.

> *Grantland Rice, sportswriter, speaking of Bill Tilden and Babe Ruth*

This is terribly embarrassing for me to admit, but money makes me happy . . . But maybe if you never had money you're more inclined to use it just to remind yourself that you've got some.

> *Arthur Ashe, Hall of Fame tennis champion and writer*

Those boys playing football get their $2 or $3 million up front, and if they don't have a good day, they are not out anything. They still get paid on Monday. If we don't win, we don't get paid on Monday.

> *Richard Petty, champion race car driver*

We have the highest-paid orange juice squeezer in the world.

> *Frank Graham, Jr., baseball executive, pointing out Roy Campanella, National League Most Valuable Player, who sat at nights in spring training with the kitchen staff, squeezing oranges*

We took ALL the money.

> *Woody Stephens, horseracing trainer, his favorite saying*

When I read the sports pages these days I think I'm reading the *Wall Street Journal*.

> *Dan Jansen, Olympic gold medalist speed skater, referring to player's salaries and other sports business dollars*

When they say it's not about money, it's always about money.

> *George Young, football team executive*

When you're fighting, you're fighting for one thing: money.

> *Jack Dempsey, champion boxer*

When you spend what we've spent on talent, to be a .500 team is unacceptable. Period.

> *Dave Checketts, franchise executive, about the New York Knicks, one of the highest-salaried teams in history*

Yes, it is forever about the money. Sports teaches you that eight days a week, making virtues of greed and lust, littering its fields with the currency of betrayal.

> *Ian O'Connor, sportswriter*

You go between horses for money, not for fun.

> *Eddie Arcaro, jockey*

You wasted your money.

> *Bill Russell, Hall of Fame basketball player and coach, responding to Seattle Supersonics owners, who pleaded with him ("But Bill, we paid a million dollars for him") not to release Jim McDaniels.*

Motherhood

I left my babies to go compete against girls half my age.

> *Laura Baugh, professional golfer and recovering alcoholic, referring to times in her life when golf was all she had*

Motivation

I like praise. But if I'm doing bad, I want to hear about it. That's what drives you.

> *Kobe Bryant, professional basketball player*

It was a violent game. I don't mean there were any fights—but they were desperate and they were committed and they were more motivated than we were.

Pat Riley, professional basketball player and coach, referring to the Kentucky vs. Texas Western championship game. Riley played for Adolph Rupp at Kentucky. Texas Western was the first team to start five African Americans and win a national championship.

True motivation is not getting people to play their potential. True motivating is getting people to play beyond their potential.

Rick Pitino, college and professional basketball coach

You can only whip the mule so much before the mule turns around and says I've had it.

Kurt Rambis, professional basketball player and coach

Moving

We didn't care if the team moved here from Hartford, we don't care if they win or lose while they're here, and we don't care when or where they'll go if they pack up and leave.

Dennis Rogers, columnist, about the Hurricanes playing in Raleigh, North Carolina, after they had moved from Hartford

171

N

Nagurski, Bronco

(b. Nov. 3, 1908; d. Jan. 7, 1990) *Hall of Fame football player; All-American college football player*

I believe that 11 Nagurskis could beat 11 Granges or 11 Thorpes.

Grantland Rice, sportswriter

Namath, Joe

(b. May 31, 1943) *Hall of Fame football quarterback; won Super Bowl III; club owner; actor*

The Joe Namaths of the world are meaningless. They come and go, fleeting figures of passing glamour. You'll find them in the sports tomes but not in the history books.

Howard Cosell, broadcaster

A saloon keeper, from Beaver Falls, Pennsylvania.

Red Smith, sportswriter

National Association for Stock Car Auto Racing

Bloody black magic.

Alan Jones, champion Formula 1 racer, commenting on stock car racing

There is no way growing up in the thirties and thinking in the nineties this is where we are going to be.

Junior Johnson, champion stock car racer

The very words "stock car" are an acute bit of merchandising con, a deadpan form of mislabeling.

John S. Radosta, sportswriter

Negotiations

He was waiting to sign his new deal and he needed something to drive, so I took care of him. I told him before he brought it back to clean and service it.

Alonzo Mourning, professional basketball player, talking about fellow player Mark Strickland

I'd walk into the owner's office to talk contract and I'd say, "Hi ya, partner."

Joe DiMaggio, Hall of Fame baseball player, asked what he might be worth in today's free agent market

If you believed my side, I'm worth $2 million. If you believed theirs, I should be back in pee-wee hockey.

Ken Wregget, professional hockey player

I never tried to be bigger than the organization. I sacrificed my chance for free agency from time to time to help them with contract extensions that gave them salary cap room. This time, I had an idea what I deserved, and they met me halfway.

Jesse Armstead, professional football player

He wants Texas back.

Tommy Lasorda, Dodger manager, when asked what terms Mexican-born pitcher Fernando Valenzuela wanted in his upcoming contract negotiations

If our first pick was a contract holdout for 20 minutes, that would be too long.

Al Lerner, owner, speaking of how the Cleveland Browns got first-round draft choice Tim Couch to sign before their time on the draft clock was up

I got a million dollars worth of free advice and a very small raise.

Ed Stanky, professional baseball player

KISS MY ASS.

Auggie Busch, baseball owner, sent this telegram to Frank Lane, general manager, who was holding out for contract extension

Loyalty is a one-way street. They got to want you. You got to want to stay.

Tony Gwynn, professional baseball player

Maybe Hiromitsu can bleach his hair blonde and put on blue contact lenses. Then maybe he'll get the salary he deserves.

Wife of Hiromitsu Ochai, professional baseball player, who won Japan's Triple Crown, but still made less than half of what American players were paid

On the basis of what they're offering, I could play four or five games.

John Riggins, professional football player

That boy in there has a lawyer with him and he doesn't need one.

Unidentified basketball executive, referring to negotiations with then rookie Bill Bradley

Then Mr. Gehrig is a badly underpaid player.

Joe DiMaggio, Hall of Fame baseball player, to Ed Barrow, general manager, when Barrow remarked that Gehrig in his peak years didn't make as much money as what DiMaggio was negotiating for

We're just kind of dancing, but we haven't kissed yet.

Isiah Thomas, professional basketball player, coach, executive, and broadcaster, about his negotiations with the Washington Wizards basketball team

Negro Leagues

As the eighth commissioner of baseball . . . I apologize for the injustice you were subjected to. Every thinking person in this country agrees. Your contribution to baseball was the finest because it was unselfish.

Fay Vincent, Major League Baseball commissioner, addressing the Negro League reunion at the Baseball Hall of Fame

I have played against a Negro All-Star team that was so good, we didn't think we had an even chance against them.

Dizzy Dean, Hall of Fame baseball player

Nicklaus, Jack

(b. Jan. 12, 1940) *Champion golfer; won six Masters; four U.S. Opens; three British Opens*

He's been on a 30-year lucky streak.

Frank Beard, professional golfer on Jack Nicklaus

If Nicklaus tells you an ant can pull a bale of hay, don't ask any questions, just hook him up.

Lee Trevino, champion golfer

Nicknames

That's better, anyway you look at it, than someone calling you a shoeshine boy.

Sal "The Barber" Maglie, professional baseball player, who was asked what he thought of the nickname he'd been given by opposing teams, referring to the constant brushback pitches he threw

Night Clubs

Nobody ever goes there anymore—it's too crowded.

Yogi Berra, Hall of Fame baseball player and manager

No-Hitter

A million-to-one shot came in. Hell froze over. A month of Sundays hit the calendar. Don Larsen today pitched a no-hit, no-run, no-man-reach-first game in a World Series.

Shirley Povich, sportswriter

Notre Dame

RUM + VODKA + IRISH = FIGHT

Red Smith, sportswriter

Half the world loves Notre Dame and the other half seems to hate us. . . . I couldn't begin to tell you where it all started but I can tell you that there aren't many people unemotional and objective about us.

Richard W. Conklin, associate vice president, University of Notre Dame

Offense

I got used to getting touches and cutting and creating and anticipating what I could do next to get easier shots. Here, I'm not allowed to do that. I'm not used to an offense that's focused on one individual. The biggest adjustment has been standing out there, waiting to catch and shoot threes. That's not my style.

Scottie Pippin, professional basketball player

Those big tough guys on defense want to play our strength against their strength. I'd rather play our strength against their weakness.

Bob McKittrick, professional football coach

What's creative about throwing the ball into some big bruiser and watching him bull his way to the basket?

Don Nelson, professional basketball coach

Officials

A bald, mumbly judge from Reno.

David Remnick, writer, describing fight referee Mills Lane

Boo the players, but leave the referees alone. They're doing a difficult job well and they don't need 5,000 assistants.

Scotty Morrison, referee-in-chief, National Hockey League

Go out through your dugout. I don't want you crossing the field and showboating in front of the crowd.

Ed Hurley, umpire, to Dan Dressen, baseball coach, after throwing him out of a game

I did the first Frazier–Ali fight. Twenty-eight years later my son does another heavyweight championship. It's like two bookends.

Arthur Mercante, Sr., Hall of Fame referee

Imagine the job description: you're to run around in the mud on a Saturday afternoon and accept the malicious abuse of up to 40,000 people for ninety minutes plus injury time. Pay negligible.

Nicholas Royle, writer

Judges are supposed to be unbiased, and if you believe that I have a bridge to sell you.

Debbie Thomas, Olympic medalist figure skater

The trouble with referees is that they just don't care which side wins.

> *Tom Canterbury, college basketball player*

There are good judges and there are judges who you will feel are not as capable; in the long run of a career, they seem to balance out.

> *Carlo Fassi, figure skating coach*

The referee won't stop the clock now unless they draw blood.

> *Doug Collins, professional basketball player and broadcaster*

This here official, JoJo Guerra, should be put in jail.

> *Pat Petronelli, Marvin Hagler's co-manager, referring to the judge who scored the Hagler–Leonard fight 10-2 in favor of Leonard*

To me, sports is a rental business and it's an entertainment business.

> *Wayne Huizenga, baseball and football owner*

With the introduction of the referee the crudeness of "The Noble Art" passes over into the relative sophistication of boxing.

> *Joyce Carol Oates, writer*

You wanna know the chief quality a ref has gotta have in the NBA? That's a pair of elephant balls.

> *Jason Williams, professional basketball player*

Officiating

As the referee, you've got to reside over this licensed wrath while keeping a tight rein on order. That's the job, keeping up with the pounding action, slipping in and out of that specter of unmitigated furor and confusion, prying apart hundreds of pounds of frustration, rage and fury.

> *Mills Lane, district court judge and boxing referee*

If the referee's not going to take care of it, you got to take care of it.

> *Tim Harding, professional basketball player*

I thought about it and I thought about it, and I decided it was the right thing to do. Let the chips fall where they may.

> *Mills Lane, boxing referee, who disqualified Mike Tyson for biting off a piece of Evander Holyfield's ear*

I'm not allowed to comment on lousy officiating.

> *Jim Finks, New Orleans Saints general manager*

It's all right, but what we need in Yorkshire–Lancashire matches is no umpires—and fair cheating all around.

> *Maurice Leyland, cricketer*

Mother, may I slug the umpire,
May I slug him right away?
So he cannot be here, Mother,
When the clubs begin to play?

> *attributed to anonymous by Bill Mazer, broadcaster*

There were 2,200 calls last weekend, and how many are we talking about?

> *Dick Hantak, head of officiating, National Football League*

The greatest accolade is silence.

> *Dolly Stark, basketball official*

The officials could see it better than I could. I was too busy fighting.

Floyd Patterson, champion boxer, after losing his first fight on points

What does it take to be a good referee? Beats the hell out of me. No one thinks any referee is good.

Richie Powers, basketball official

What you learn about the job, though, is that you can never predict what will happen. The most innocuous, innocent match can blow up at any time, anywhere. You always have to concentrate totally because you never know where a problem is going to come from.

Gerry Armstrong, tennis umpire

When the bell rang to end the twelfth round, both of them continued slugging it out. And when I stepped in to break it up, Bowe nailed me with a solid shot to the back of the head. I'm getting too old for that shit.

Mills Lane, district court judge and boxing referee

Why did you wait until the second half?

attributed to South American soccer fans, when a referee was kicked to death by irate fans of the home team, which was losing the match

You're a rookie official. I don't talk to rookie officials.

Norm "The Dutchman" Van Broklin, Hall of Fame professional football player and professional football head coach, to a league official during a game. He did not talk to the official the entire game.

Olympics

Citius, altius, fortius. . . . swifter, higher, stronger.

Olympic motto

First time I ever slept on my back. Had to, or that medal would have cut my chest.

Muhammad Ali, world champion boxer, gold medalist

"Going for the gold" is a good expression. It's not caution. It's abandonment.

Frank Carroll, figure skating coach

Hitler was there every day, watching. He looked like Charlie Chaplin sitting up there, him and the fat guy, Goering.

John A. Kelly, champion marathoner and Olympic runner

I'm absolutely positive that it does work if you're wining and dining judges and bringing them in, buying them dinners and stuff. But it's up to the individual judges to spot if they're being played for suckers or if it's genuine.

Alex McGowan, Olympic figure skating coach

I'm glad they were able to continue the games. What they're about is peace and sportsmanship.

Shannon Miller, Olympic gold medalist gymnast, after the bombing in Atlanta during the Olympics

I really just hoped to make the finals. Winning the medal was just . . . extra.

Amy Chow, Olympic gymnast

It was a lifetime of training for just 10 seconds.

Jesse Owens, Olympic gold medalist track and field competitor

I wish there were two gold medals, but it wouldn't mean as much if there were two gold medals.

Michelle Kwan, Olympic medalist figure skater, after losing to Tara Lipinski in the Olympics

I would say that going to the Olympics and winning a gold medal is a far greater challenge than defending the America's Cup, because, first of all, there's a lot more people you're competing against. There was a total of, I think, only seven boats in the entire America's Cup, whereas in the Finn class at the Olympics there are probably five to six hundred sailors who try for a slot.

Ted Turner, champion yachtsman
and baseball owner

The great global festival of sinew and sweat.

Red Smith, sportswriter

The most important thing about the Olympic Games is not winning, but taking part.

Pierre de Coubertin, sportsman and educator

The Olympics are a dinosaur, running out of cities . . . If you use the politics of a nation to judge whether or not you compete with that nation, you might as well say that international sport is dead.

Sebastian Coe, champion runner

Medals are more important than times. Medals stay forever. Times change.

Rosa Mota, Olympic gold medalist marathoner

No athlete wins Olympic medals based entirely on the coach's direction. I believe that the coach contributes only 30 percent of what it takes to become a champion. The other 70 percent is the skater's will, determination, intelligence, and ability to compete.

Carlo Fassi, figure skating coach

Nobody ever beats the decathlon. You might set a record and kick the hell out of it one day, but you know it will always be there, waiting for you to try again, telling you, "Okay you son of a gun, try and get me this time."

Bruce Jenner, Olympic gold medalist
decathlon competitor

No one can ever imagine what it's like to stand on the podium and be called one of the world's greatest athletes. What I do in football, I just do it, but nothing will compare to that.

Bob Hayes, champion Olympic sprinter and
professional football player

Olympic Village was under siege. Two men lay murdered and eight others were held at gunpoint in imminent peril of their lives. Still the games went on.

Red Smith, sportswriter

Once the gun goes off, there isn't a lot of thinking, just instinct.

Bonnie Blair, Olympic gold medalist speed skater

The Olympic year is a very trying period, and most athletes have problems afterwards, sometimes as long as a year or two. It just knocks you off track.

Ekaterina Gordeeva, Olympic gold medalist pairs
skater

The self-appointed, self-perpetuating kangaroo court that calls itself the International Olympic Committee.

Red Smith, sportswriter

These Olympics, probably more than any before, are showing a lot of little girls it's okay to sweat, it's okay to play hard, and it's okay to be an athlete.

Lindsay Davenport, champion tennis player,
about the 1996 Olympics

The sport is bigger than the man. Any man. Nobody ever shaped the decathlon in his own image.

Bruce Jenner, Olympic gold medalist decathlon competitor

Winter Olympians are the hibernating animals of sport. Every few years we stick our noses out of our caves, venture into the cold to skate, ski, luge, or knock a hockey puck around, then disappear again, into the forest or the North Pole or wherever it is we go until another Olympics roll around again.

Dan Jansen, Olympic gold medalist speed skater

Part of the charm of the Winter Olympics is that ice skating and all the rest of those Olympic sports completely disappear for four years at a time.

Dan Jenkins, writer and best-selling author

On the Road
You just can't sit in your room at the hotel watching CNN.

Monica Seles, champion professional tennis player

Opportunity
We're the only ones who have a chance.

Jim Valvano, champion college basketball coach, when asked if he thought his team had a chance in the championship game against the heavily favored University of Houston Cougars, during an improbable run through the NCAA Men's Basketball Tournament in which his team won

Owners
Charles Comisky was not only the meanest skinflint in baseball, but a man who could cruelly flaunt his wealth, while treating those who brought it to him as peons.

Stephen Jay Gould, scientist and baseball enthusiast

Getting money out of those people—track owners—is like trying to squeeze a lemon dry.

Eddie Arroyo, jockey

I admit he's the greatest ticket seller in the history of sports, but I'm not going to pay him $4 million a year. I'm just not going to do it.

Jerry Reinsdorf, basketball and baseball owner, about Michael Jordan, for whom he eventually paid much more

I don't earn as much as a utility infielder, but baseball is my game and I can't let one or two high-priced players drive me out of it.

Bill Veeck, baseball owner and racetrack operator

I have owners who don't mind spending the $25,000 it costs to fly a horse across the country for a big race. They know they'll usually make more money than that by running.

D. Wayne Lukas, thoroughbred horse trainer

I'm going to write a book, *How To Make A Small Fortune In Baseball*—you start with a large fortune.

Ruly Carpenter, baseball owner

Irsay had been dealing with San Diego and the Raiders, and he'd gotten mad at them. You want John Elway? . . . You're going to get John Elway—twice a year on another team. I'm just thankful we got him 16 times a year—on our side.

Dan Reeves, professional football coach

I say to our trainers, "I won't try to tell you how to train horses, just don't tell me how to sell beer."

Bob Lewis, thoroughbred horse owner, winner of two Kentucky Derbys

Just a fad—passing fancy.

Philip Wrigley, baseball owner, on baseball played after dark under the lights

Make no mistake. This decision was not easy.

Robert Kraft, on moving the New England Patriots from Foxboro, Massachusetts to Hartford, Connecticut and taking a sweetheart deal

Maybe all the owners should do like Charlie—run the team on the phone from Chicago and make the decisions after consulting cab drivers and the guys in the barbershop.

Bill Cutler, baseball executive, talking about Charles O. Finley, Major League Baseball owner

My, God. I've heard the story of all that sweat and sacrifice of how he made his money, five hundred times.

Bill Dauer, about Charles O. Finley, Major League Baseball owner

Running a two-car team was my main preoccupation in 1975 and I recommend it as a surefire way of getting ulcers.

Graham Hill, champion race car driver

Those first few years my brother used to go to school—at Fordham Prep—with a handful of tickets to give away, and I'd give them away at grammar school.

Wellington Mara, Hall of Fame football owner

Owning the Yankees is like owning the Mona Lisa.

George Steinbrenner, owner

Remember, half the lies they tell about the Dodgers aren't true.

Walter O'Malley, baseball owner

The ironic thing is that I've never seen [Al Davis] and Darth Vader in the same place.

Howie Long, professional football owner, about Al Davis

The most beautiful thing in the world is a ballpark filled with people.

Bill Veeck, baseball owner and racetrack operator

This is the ultimate ego play for a wealthy New York investor.

Marc Ganis, a sports consultant, on the prospect of buying the New York Jets

We can't hopscotch franchises around the country. We have built this business in the trust of the fans. If we treat them as if it doesn't count, it isn't going to wash.

Art Modell, football owner, speaking out against the proposed move of the Rams from Los Angeles to St. Louis. Modell would also later move his franchise from Cleveland to Baltimore, despite sellout crowds for his team.

Wellington Mara . . . cloaks himself in the piety of Saint Patrick's and behaves as if his ownership derives from the Vatican.

Howard Cosell, broadcaster

When you come right down to it, the baseball owners are really little boys with big wallets.

Harold Parrott, writer

You could make more money investing in government bonds. But football is more fun.

Clint Murchison,
football owner

You like being with the Yankees? We'll, let me give you two tips. You wear your hat like a Yankee and you call me sir.

George Steinbrenner, owner, New York Yankees,
to Shane Spencer, rookie

Pain

If you're gymnast something is always hurting, but you still train. You just have to learn to live with discomfort.

Mary Lou Retton, gymnast and
Olympic gold medalist

I hate to say it, but it's true—I only like it better when pain comes.

Frank Fletcher, professional boxer

I knew at the time I was damaging myself, but I made a decision. I said, "Look, you are going to have arthritis and you are going to have pain—what do you want to do? Do you want to stop now and have the pain, or can you live it?"

Dr. Tom Waddell, Olympic decathlon competitor
and gay rights activist

I know how the pain of cycling can be terrible: in your legs, your chest, everywhere. You go into oxygen debt and fall apart. Not many people outside cycling understand that.

Greg LeMond, cyclist

It is an aspect of training, but a subtle aspect. I don't think about it much.

Jim Ryun, track athlete

Pain is a given. I don't try to fight the pain or pretend it's not there. In fact, I give into it. But only for a little while.

Ric Munoz, marathoner,
HIV-positive for 12 years

Races always evoke some dread about pain that will come. But we can't escape the fact that the more discomfort we can accept in a race, the faster we will run. Successful racing means *courting the pain.*

John Elliott, runner

The man who can drive himself further once the effort gets painful is the man who will win.

Roger Bannister, runner

There has never been a great athlete who died not knowing what pain is.

Bill Bradley, professional basketball player
and U.S. senator

This is the best feeling there is.

> *Pat Fischer, professional football player*

Thrust against pain, pain is the purifier.

> *Percy Cerutty, Australian Olympic coach*

We train through the winter in deep snow and ice. Our slogan is "Pain is good, more pain is even better."

> *Matt Carpenter, mountain runner*

When you win, nothing hurts.

> *Joe Namath, Hall of Fame football player*

Palmer, Arnold

(b. Sept. 10, 1929) *Champion golfer; won four Masters, two British Opens, and one U.S. Open*

There are dozens on the pro tour who would be as good as Palmer if they had his outlook. But you can't put something into a man that isn't there.

> *Ed Furgol, professional golfer*

Parents

As a footballer, I wasn't even his shadow. At the most, he inherited my passion for soccer. His class? . . . That's the divine gift.

Nelio, father of Ronaldo, professional soccer player

He has taught me to follow in his footsteps as a boxer, and to learn from his mistakes in life.

> *Floyd Mayweather, Jr., professional boxer, whose father was once a number one contender and then went to jail later on for drugs*

I could beat on other kids and steal their lunch money and buy myself something to eat. But I couldn't steal a father. I couldn't steal a father's hug when I needed one.

> *Bo Jackson, professional baseball and football player*

I don't reckon I regret it. When he wins, he can have it, but he ain't gonna have it given to him.

> *Lee Petty, champion race car driver, who had his son's win in a race nullified, because he hadn't fulfilled the requisite number of laps. The victory instead went to himself.*

I'm so sorry I ever heard of tennis because it cost me my family. I spent years grooming her. Now she's got $4 million in the bank and I don't have enough to fill up my tank at the gas station.

> *Jim Pierce, father of Mary Pierce, professional tennis player, who has a restraining order against her father*

It's amazing. I thought I knew my father really well. But there were things in the book about him—what he felt about the game—that I never knew.

> *Cal Ripken, Jr., professional baseball player, who read his father's posthumously published book*

It was like one of those karate pictures when the pupil has to fight the master. He was strong. He got tired and quit, but I learned a lot and respected him even more afterward.

> *Ricardo Williams, Jr., professional boxer, referring to a boxing match he had at the age of fourteen with his father, retired boxer, Ricardo Williams, Sr.*

My Daddy was a race car driver, so I became a race car driver. If he'd been a grocer, I might have been a grocer . . . But he was a race car driver, so here I am.

> *Richard Petty, champion race car driver*

Oh, what a feeling! I'll never forget this as long as I'll live. I want to thank my mother for buying me my first pair of skates.

Harry Sinden, hockey coach, after his Philadelphia Flyers won the Stanley Cup

The cops won't take you; the fire department won't take you. The only thing you'll be able to do is drive a cab.

Matty Ferrigno, father of Lou Ferrigno, champion bodybuilder, professional football player, and actor

There's a lot of people in this sport that live through their kids. We'll never do that.

Jack Lipinski, father of Olympic gold medalist figure skater Tara Lipinski

When it would rain, we'd go under the boardwalk and I'd throw to him. In the apartment we rented, I'd move the furniture out and he would hit Wiffle Balls.

Vince Piazza, father of Mike Piazza, professional baseball player

When I go home to visit my parents these days, both of them still perky into their eighties with a social calendar more advanced than my own, it doesn't take my dad long to get started about the modern game. I'm old enough now to realize that we've had almost the same conversation for close on thirty-five years.

Steve Grant, writer

Passing
I like to throw the ball. To me, the pro game *is* throwing. I may be wrong, but putting the ball in the air is the way to win.

Y. A. Tittle, Hall of Fame quanterback

It doesn't matter how simple or fancy a pass is. The only good pass is one that is caught by its target.

Red Auerbach, Hall of Fame basketball coach and executive

Passing is the most important fundamental in lacrosse.

Jim Hinkson, champion lacrosse coach

Ten years from now, they won't even talk about my goal scoring; it'll just be my passing.

Wayne Gretzky, Hall of Fame hockey player

Wendell [Ladner] was the only guy I ever met who could throw a bad pass to himself. He'd throw it and go get it, throw it and go get it.

Steve Jones, professional basketball player

Passion
Maybe it's wasn't talent the Lord gave me. Maybe it was the passion.

Wayne Gretzky, Hall of Fame hockey player

As long as it's still fun, which it still is, as long as I'm still passionate, which I still am, and as long as I am still competitive, which I hope to be, then I'll be around.

Lance Armstrong, champion cyclist, winner of Tour de France, and cancer survivor

Patience
Bob Knight was many things: brilliant, driven, compassionate—but not patient.

John Feinstein, writer

As long as my pitchers throw strikes, I'll have patience. But when they start walking people and getting behind—I don't need that.

Lou Pinella, professional baseball player and manager

Today, I just told myself, "You have 64 more holes to get it back." I'm going to be patient in this tournament.

Tiger Woods, champion golfer

Payroll

As Phil Rizzuto and Whitey Ford raised the World Championship banner, Shepard proudly announced, "The flag we are about to raise is a symbol of courage, conviction and everlasting truth." He forgot to mention the 1999 Yankees' $86 million payroll, the highest in baseball.

William C. Rhoden, sportswriter

Pelé (Edson Arantes do Nascimento)

(b. Oct. 23, 1940) *Soccer player; won three World Cups*

Brazilians who travel report that they are asked about Pele by people who would not know where to find Brazil on a map.

Janet Lever, sociologist and writer

His name and tales of his talents have spread throughout the world . . . Barely civilized African tribes that play soccer with human skulls supposedly shout "Pele!" as they play.

Chuck Cascio, writer

Pele's ability when receiving a high-cross is particularly fascinating to watch. He lets it ride off his chest, pivots, and takes a thunderous shot at the goal. Or the next time, he may deflect the ball behind the oncoming

defender and follow up at top speed to create a split-second opening for himself.

Hubert Vogelsinger, writer

Pele's fame is of global proportions. He has visited eighty-eight countries, met two popes, five emperors, ten kings, seventy presidents, and forty other chiefs of state. Biographies of Pele have been translated into more than 100 languages.

Janet Lever, sociologist

Pele is the greatest sportsman of all time in all sports.

Ian Woosnam, North American Soccer League commissioner

Pele won't finish the World Cup. It's amazing he hasn't gone mad.

attributed to a French journalist, by the Sunday Times History of the World Cup, *after Pelé was brutally cut down by a Bulgarian midfielder named Zhechev*

The wonderful thing about watching Pele is that he represents soccer in its purest form, soccer as it should be played. All the facets of the game are there, embodied in one man, all of them beautifully balanced to produce soccer perfection.

Paul Gardner, sportswriter

To me you are still a little boy, but everyone else seems to think you're grown up. Maybe I am wrong. Maybe I shouldn't stand in your way if this is really a chance for you.

Pelé's mother, saying goodbye when he went to play professional soccer in Brazil at the age of fifteen

When you talk about Pele you break out a box labeled "Superlatives" and roll out all the euphemisms. When Pele plays he makes straight news coverage obsolete. Pele never jumps, he always soars; he never runs, he always darts; he never outhustles his opponent, he victimizes them; he never kicks, he always blasts; he is never led, he always leads.

Chuck Cassio, writer

Penalties

You're going to get it whether you return it or not, so you might as well hack somebody once in a while.

Steve Yzerman, professional hockey player

Performance

Don't try to perform beyond your abilities—but never perform below them.

Frank Robinson, baseball player and manager

What do I think of his performance?! That's a helluva question!

Tommy Lasorda, professional baseball manager, being asked about Dave Kingman's performance against his team, after he had eight RBIs in one night

Physically Impaired Athletes

Have a dream, make a plan, go for it. You'll get there, I promise.

Zoe Koplowitz, marathoner, afflicted with multiple sclerosis

Running on an artificial leg at full speed is like driving backward at 55 miles per hour, using only your rearview mirror to guide you.

Thomas Bourgeois, champion runner, below-the-knee amputee

When I am running, I feel everything is in sync. Even my mechanical leg becomes a part of me.

Sarah Reinersten, marathoner, above-the-knee amputee

Pitching

Anyone can light it up for one or two starts. To do it over the course of a year, you have to be a superstar.

Joe Torre, champion professional baseball player and manager, referring to Roger Clemens's drive for a record number of wins without a loss

A perfect pitcher is an impossible concept, as long as major league hitters remain capable of hitting perfect pitches.

Bob Gibson, Hall of Fame baseball pitcher

A pitcher will take any little advantage he can today, and I don't blame him. I'd pitch in front of the rubber when I had a chance. I never used a cut ball much, but I wasn't to proud to.

Preacher Roe, professional baseball player

As a rule, pitchers can't bunt, can't hit, can't field, can't run and can't slide. The only thing they can do is throw the ball longer and harder than anyone else.

Maury Wills, professional baseball player, broadcaster, and manager

Baseball's roadside is littered with the careers of terrific rookie pitchers who quickly dissolved into rusty, dented mediocrities.

Daniel Okrent, sportswriter

Every hitter likes fastballs, just like everybody likes ice cream. But you don't like it when someone's stuffing it into you by the gallon. That's what it feels like when Nolan Ryan's thrown balls by you.

Reggie Jackson, Hall of Fame baseball player and executive

Every pitcher has to be a little in love with death.

Bill Lee, professional baseball player

Good pitching will always stop good hitting and vice-versa.

Bob Veale, professional baseball player

He calls it his Hall of Fame pitch because it puts some pitchers in Cooperstown before their time.

Ken Griffey, Sr., professional baseball player and coach, about Durwood Merrill, umpire

He talks too much. He talks like he's Bob Gibson. I'm the only guy who can't hit him.

Charlie Hayes, professional baseball player, about pitcher Todd Stottlemyre

His arm has been scanned and prodded and manipulated and sliced.

Buster Olney, sportswriter, about David Cone's arm

I'm gonna send every one of those sons-of-bitches on their backs . . . there was always that lousy talk about me choking up and never being able to win the big ones. But I never had a teammate of mine tell me that I couldn't protect him with that baseball when it was time for somebody to be sent right on his ass.

Don Newcombe, professional baseball player

I never throwed an illegal pitch . . . Just once in a while I used to toss one that ain't never been seen by this generation.

Satchel Paige, Hall of Fame baseball pitcher

In the politically correct, number-crunched, no-salt-added modern facsimile of baseball, there is no place for an older pitcher to whom the game, any game, was a war.

Lonnie Wheeler, writer

It's lonely out there.

Rick Cerone, professional baseball player, catcher, after fulfilling a childhood fantasy and pitching one inning in a real game at Yankee Stadium

It's not just the one he throws out there that just falls off the table. It's the sounds. There's the grunt of the fastball, and then there's the sound of that fastball away.

Bobby Valentine, professional baseball player and manager, talking about the pitching of Roger Clemens

I've never heard a crowd boo a homer, but I've heard plenty of boos after a strikeout.

Babe Ruth, Hall of Fame baseball player

Just a bit outside.

Bob Uecker, professional baseball player, announcer, and actor, in Major League, describing a wild pitch

Nothing. No movement, no jerk, no reach . . . That kind of thing isn't always appreciated, but it makes or breaks a pitcher.

Tim Belcher, professional baseball player, pitcher, speaking about good catchers

Stand on the rubber and read the writing on the mitt. Total focus. Shut the world out.

Jan Reid, sportswriter

Strikeouts are boring—besides that, they're fascist. Throw some ground balls. More democratic.

Kevin Costner, actor, to his pitcher,
in Bull Durham

That last one sounded a little low.

Lefty Gomez, professional
baseball player, to an umpire on
a third called strike
by Bob Feller, pitcher

There is nothing quite like the feeling of expectation on the morning of the day or night that you are scheduled to pitch.

Tom Seaver, Hall of Fame
baseball player

The mound is my personal zone. During those moments on the pitching rubber, when you have every pitch at your command working to its highest potential, you are your own universe.

Bill Lee, professional
baseball player

The Tigers might be hurt, but I'll ya one thing, the pitchers all over the league will improve.

Casey Stengel, Hall of Fame baseball manager,
commenting on Detroit's big slugger
Harvey Kuenn, being called up in
front of the draft board

Pitino, Rick

(b. Sept. 18, 1952) *NCAA, NBA basketball coach*

This guy is not a real person, he's a rattlesnake.

Peter Vecsey, sportswriter

Playbook

My college playbook was like a Dr. Seuss book. With the 49ers, it's like a cookbook.

Terrell Owens, wide receiver, professional
football player

Play Calling

Baby, no one sends in plays for Francis.

Fran Tarkington, Hall of Fame football player,
when asked who called his team's plays

I think you can hit Warfield on a down-and-in pattern.

Richard M. Nixon, president of the
United States, to Don Shula, Hall of Fame
football coach

No, we ain't gonna play that. We're gonna kick their butts.

Lee Roy Jordan, Hall of Fame football
player, waving off a defense called
in from the sidelines

Playing Time

The two most important things to athletes: playing time and money.

John Paxson, champion professional
basketball player

Playoffs

In the playoffs, there are no lay-ups, so when guys get in the paint they're usually getting hacked.

Latrell Sprewell, professional basketball player

It was what I expected. Challenging, nerve-racking at times, exhilarating at times. Just

191

like every playoff game I've ever been a part of.

Kurt Rambis, professional basketball player and coach

The team I was with last year is home watching us right now, and I'm in the playoffs. I'm having fun.

Marcus Camby, professional basketball player

We can't think about the playoffs. We would not even accept a bowl bid at this time.

Dan Henning, professional football coach

Where else would you want to be in October, except here?

Derek Jeter, professional baseball player

You need to be a little bit lucky in the playoffs.

Yanic Perreault, professional hockey player

Politics

Beyond the happy rhetoric, our hockey triumph didn't validate our system any more than defeats in other years had undermined our way of life.

Pete Axthelm, author, referring to the 1980 victory of the U.S. Olympic hockey team over the Olympic team from the U.S.S.R.

Durwood, you might not realize this, but you just hung up on Marlin Fitzwater.

George W. Bush, politician and baseball owner (later, 43rd U.S. president), to Durwood Merrill, umpire, after the latter hung up the phone on the press secretary to George H. W. Bush, U.S. president, thinking it was a prank phone call. President Bush wanted a real umpire's windbreaker to throw out the first pitch at a Texas Rangers game, his son's team

Glad to meet ya, Mr. Vice Prez. Love ya, but didn't vote for ya.

Don Meredith, football player and broadcaster, to Vice President Spiro T. Agnew

I did all I could to make Coolidge president.

Ring Lardner, sportswriter, to Warren G. Harding, U.S. president, after accidentally knocking down a tree limb that fell on the then president

I made a technical critique, one that I still deeply believe. This left has really gone all the way. But let's get real—with the country in the condition it's in, does it seem serious to transform a soccer critique into a state affair?

Silvio Berlusconi, former Italian prime minister and opposition leader, media magnate and owner of AC Milan, referring to criticisms he made of Dino Zoff, champion goalie and coach of the Italy 200 team, just after Italy's heartbreaking loss to France in the 2000 European championship. Zoff immediately resigned after Berlusconi's criticisms and the constitutional government criticized Berlusconi for trying to use the loss to advance his own political gain.

In our political system that is sometimes impossible, unless you're willing to sell your soul. It's like playing football with eleven men on your team and thirty-three on the other. You're forever running into a stone wall.

Bob Mathias, gold medalist decathlon competitor, politician, and actor

It's better than "Pomp and Circumstance."

Joe Torre, professional baseball player and manager, to Bill Clinton, U.S. president, and Hillary Clinton, first lady, at a ceremony honoring the World Champions, as Torre approached the podium and the band played "Hail to the Chief"

The box score always adds up—politics never does.

James Reston, journalist and author

The White House needs a little less Vince Lombardi and a little more Abraham Lincoln.

Dave Meggyesy, professional football player and political activist

This is sport. More important things are waiting for us off the court.

Vlade Divac, professional basketball player, a citizen of the former Yugoslavia, whose family and friends were caught up in the war in Bosnia

Well, I don't think he'd enforce a rigorous curfew.

George Will, political columnist and baseball aficionado, to Roy Firestone, television interviewer, after he was asked what kind of baseball manager Senator Ted Kennedy would be

Whether in sports or politics, competition in and of itself is good.

Bill Bradley, Hall of Fame basketball player and U.S. senator

You travel around Texas with me, and everyone wants to talk about Nolan Ryan.

George W. Bush, governor of Texas and baseball owner

You've got to stick your butt out more, Mr. President.

Sam Snead, champion professional golfer, to Dwight D. Eisenhower, U.S. president, giving the president a lesson.

Polo

The sport of kings.

Anonymous

Man is a ball tossed onto the field of existence, driven hither and thither by the chaugan-stick of destiny, wielded by the hand of Providence.

Persian proverb

No sport, save possibly steeplechasing and football, is so good a school . . . as polo.

George S. Patton, U.S. general

Polo irritates people in a way that other sports don't. One reason my be the subtle sense emanated of a private game in which spectators are not so much welcomed as endured.

Frank Milburn, writer

Polo Grounds

The return of the Polo Grounds to the National League was like the raising of a sunken cathedral.

Murray Kempton, sportswriter, about the 1962 New York Mets debuting of Polo Grounds after the Giants moved to San Francisco

Pool

By rights it should be a reasonably easy game. . . . No one is allowed to block or tackle you to prevent you from getting to the ball. No one can move the balls to make them harder to hit.

Steve Mizerak, champion pool player and beer pitchman

If you know a good player who is tempted by pool hustling, introduce him at once to a career guidance counselor, a psychotherapist or a surgeon who does lobotomies.

Robert Byrne, champion pool player and writer

It is a game of infinite variables. . . . True excellence is rare and vanities are punished.

Jim Harrison, novelist, from Just Before Dark

It is impossible to imagine Goethe or Beethoven being good at billiards or golf.

H. L. Mencken, critic, humorist, author

Let us to billiards.

William Shakespeare, from Antony and Cleopatra

Petty thievery is a more profitable job than pool hustling.

Robert Byrne, champion pool player, columnist, and writer

Sex after ninety is like trying to shoot pool with a rope.

George Burns, comedian, actor

Some people meditate, others paint. I shoot pool.

Laura Shepard, champion pool player

The human race divides itself neatly into two different groups—those who love pool and those who don't. Neither understands the other and often doesn't care to.

Mike Shamos, champion pool player

The trouble with shooting pool is that it's no good if you don't win.

Paul Newman, in The Color of Money *(written by Walter Tevis)*

There are 350 varieties of shark, not counting loan or pool.

L. M. Boyd, writer

When I realized that what I had turned out to be was a lousy, two-bit pool hustler and drunk, I wasn't depressed at all. I was glad to have a profession.

Danny McGoorty, champion pool player and hustler

You can put two eight-year-olds on a pool table and go to Europe for a week. Those kids will still be at the table playing pool.

Minnesota Fats, legendary pool player, hustler, trick shot artist

To play billiards well was a sign of an ill-spent youth.

Herbert Spencer, philosopher

Post Season

In the post season, teams play for forty minutes.

Tyrone Grant, college basketball player

Potential

I just want to realize my potential. That would be a victory in itself.

Steve Bartkowski, professional football player

Practical Jokes

How could you do that to that poor little animal!

Art "Fatso" Donovan, professional football player, finding a dead groundhog in his bed after sneaking in late from breaking curfew

I knew he would have killed me if he caught me.

Cale Yarborough, champion race car driver, about Little Joe Weatherly, after he put a live, defanged rattlesnake in Weatherly's lap while he was getting ready to race.

My God, what is it?

Adolph Rupp, college basketball coach, upon smelling a dead skunk underneath his chair during a game against South Eastern Conference rival Mississippi State.

Practice

A football player has certain responsibilities. Practice is one of them. You'd have no kind of team if the players didn't report to practice.

Joe Schmidt, professional football player

An hour of hard practice is worth five hours of foot-dragging.

Pancho Segura, professional tennis player

Concentration is why some athletes are better than others. You develop that concentration in training. You can't be lackadaisical in training and concentrate in a meet.

Edwin Moses, medal-winning track star

For the best part of eighteen years I've averaged a round a day. That's three hundred and sixty rounds of golf times eighteen, or six thousand, five hundred and seventy rounds . . . a lot of walking . . . a lot of shots. I've worked . . . I've worked like hell.

Babe Didrickson Zaharias, Olympian and champion golfer

It's not necessarily the amount of time you spend at practice that counts; it's what you put into the practice.

Eric Lindros, professional hockey player

The more I practice, the luckier I get.

Gary Player, champion professional golfer

There aren't any tricks. It's hard work and pain and loneliness. But you can come back. That's what I want everybody to know—you can come back.

Gale Sayers, professional football player

There's no such thing as natural touch. Touch is something you create by hitting millions of golf balls.

Lee Trevino, champion professional golfer

To so many players, practice is like a pause between their cell-phone conversations.

Marty Conlon, professional basketball player

You play the way you practice

Pop Warner, professional football coach

You hit home runs not by chance, but by preparation.

Roger Maris, professional baseball player

For every pass I ever caught in a game, I caught a thousand in practice.

Don Hutson, National Football League player

Practice, practice, practice.

Paul Hornung, Hall of Fame football player, response to a question asking how he could play so well despite being notorious for breaking late-night curfews

Practice wasn't a right but a privilege.

John Vargas, coach, U.S. national water polo team

Rock used to load us down with extra-heavy practice gear. On Saturday, when we climbed into game suits we felt like four Lady Godivas. Actually we were four pounds lighter on Saturday than on weekends.

Elmer Layden, college football player,
one of the Four Horsemen, speaking of
Knute Rockne, coach

I won't do it on Thursdays because I don't get paid to do it on Thursdays.

Alex Karras, Hall of Fame football player,
discussing his practice habits

You can learn twice as much about the tune of your boat in two hours of practice sailing as you can for the same time on the race course, with its tactical distractions.

Mike Fletcher, sailor and journalist

Predictions

I guarantee it.

Joe Namath, Hall of Fame football player,
regarding a Jets victory over the Baltimore
Colts in Super Bowl III

This team has a chance of going all the way. So did the *Titanic*.

Jim Murray, sportswriter

We're going to turn this team around 360 degrees.

Jason Kidd, upon his drafting to
the Dallas Mavericks

Prefontaine, Steve "Pre"

(b. Jan. 25, 1951; d. June 1, 1975) *All-American track and field runner; National Collegiate Athletic Association champion*

Pre inspired a whole generation of American distance runners to excel. He made running cool.

Alberto Salazar, marathon runner

Preparation

Hours of running stadium steps, hours of rowing on ergometers, hours of lifting weights and work in the tanks had come down to a few minutes of racing.

Devin Mahony, coxswain

How many successful people have you ever heard say, "I just make it up as I go along?" I can't think of one.

Mike Ditka, professional football coach

Everyone wants to win on game day. Every coach and player walks on the field fired up and raring to go. But if they have not put in the time to prepare during the week, they will fall flat on their faces.

Joe Gibbs, professional football coach

In football and in business preparation precedes performance.

Bill Walsh, professional football coach

The will to win is grossly overrated. The will to prepare is far more important.

Bobby Knight, champion college basketball coach

The will to win means nothing without the will to prepare.

Juma Ikangaa, champion marathoner

When you start the Daytona 500, that car doesn't know when it was built. As long as you've done it right and on the line, that's all that counts. But the earlier you build it and the more time you take with it, the more you test it, the greater the odds you are going to get it right.

Alan Kulwicki, race car driver

Press (the)

I've never known a football writer who ever had to stand up to a blitz.

Joe Namath, Hall of Fame football player

We don't turn on the TV anymore. We unplugged it. We don't buy any New York newspapers.

Chuck Knoblauch, professional baseball player, after an error cost the Yankees a playoff game in 1998

Pressure

Make or miss, win or lose? Not many people can say they've been in that situation, and now I have.

Allan Houston, professional basketball player, who scored the game-winning basket in the playoffs to win a first-round series, with a last second shot

There's always pressure to perform.

Scott Brosius, professional baseball player

To me the pressure is game to game, inning to inning, batter to batter, pitch to pitch, and it's that way May, June, September—any month.

Roberto Clemente, Hall of Fame baseball player

When you face an elimination game, you can go one of two ways. You can start looking for scapegoats or you can rally behind each other.

Brendan Shanahan, professional hockey player

When you play in a World Series, you either accept the challenge and do better than you normally do, or the pressure gets to you and you fall beneath your normal level.

Red Rolf, professional baseball player

Pride

The proudest day of my life wasn't the day I won the 500 or when I won my first USAC title or the Daytona 500 or Sebring. It was April 15, 1964—the day I became an American citizen. More than most people, I understand the meaning of the words "Only in America."

Mario Andretti, champion race car driver

You've got to look at it like when you were back in high school, when you had the pride, you were glad and proud to put on the jersey, you were a Brave, or whatever you were.

John Starks, professional basketball player

Prizes or Prize Money

I may buy the Alamo and give it back to Mexico.

Lee Trevino, champion golfer, replying to a question regarding how he'd spend the prize money after winning the U.S. Open

When someone offers you two million dollars you don't spit in their face.

Ivan Lendl, champion tennis player, referring to accepting an invitation to the Grand Slam Cup

When you get $180,000 to win a race, how can you be disappointed in time?

Laz Barrera, jockey

Professionals

Being a professional athlete is just being a big kid.

Larry Csonka, Hall of Fame football player and broadcaster

I found out pretty quickly that pro football ideals are in the gutter. These men are supposed to be the best, but I found they were pretty hung up on money, booze, and sex.

Chip Oliver, professional football player

Now, how would you define a track athlete who spends all of his or her time training and competing, is paid to appear in meets, paid bonuses for good performances, paid to wear certain shoes, paid to say good things about corporate sponsors? Unless you are totally naive and incredibly ignorant, or unless you have reason to twist the truth, "professional" would have to be your answer.

Carl Lewis, Olympic gold medalist track and field competitor

Professional football is a damn tough way to make a living. And when it's all said and done, that's precisely what the game is—a job.

Johnny Sample, professional football player

The guy who says he'd give it all up to play this game for free? I'm like, "Yeah, go right ahead." The fact is, this game is just too hard. You can't do it for nothing.

Phil Simms, professional football player and broadcaster

We ought to pay attention to the world of professional sports. What happens at the elite levels makes its way into our culture.

Lucy Danziger, sports magazine editor

You have to perform at a consistently higher level than others. That's the mark of a true professional.

Joe Paterno, college football coach

Promoters

It ain't the number of seats you got, it's the number of asses in 'em.

George Gainford, boxing manager

Prostitutes

This is the baddest cat in the world, and I'm with your husband and five hookers!

Muhammad Ali, world champion boxer, to Nancy Seaver, wife of Tom Seaver, Hall of Fame baseball player

When they saw it was Edwin, I think they felt, "This is a nice fish to fry."

Gordin Baskin, manager of Edwin Moses, after he was arrested for soliciting for prostitution

Where's the good stuff? I want it all.

Darryl Strawberry, professional baseball player, to an undercover policewoman posing as a prostitute

Putting

A bad putter is like a bad apple in a barrel. First it turns your chipping game sour. Then it begins to eat into your irons. And finally, it just eats the head off your driver.

Sam Snead, champion professional golfer

A good putter is a match for anyone. A bad putter is a match for no one.

Harvey Pennick, golf teacher

I don't know anyone else who putts with a swizzle stick.

Bob Hope, comedian and actor, referring to Jackie Gleason

It wasn't a misread, it was a bad putt.

Annika Sorenstam, professional golfer

I was the world's worst putter.

William "Wild Bill" Melhorn, professional golfer

I've played with some of the best players in the world . . . and the difference between their game and my game is about four putts a round. Nothing else. But it's everything.

Dana Quigley, champion golfer

The mistake I made was becoming a wrist putter.

Sam Snead, champion golfer

There are very few truths about putting. You get the ball in the hole, and it doesn't matter how.

Arnold Palmer, champion professional golfer

When a player holes a crucial short putt, or rolls one in from sixty feet, it is on the green—on the "dance floor," as golfers like to say—where he punches the air and does a little jig of celebration.

Al Barkow, writer

You can always recover from a bad drive, but there's no recovering from a bad putt. It's missing those 6-inchers that causes guys to break up their sticks.

Jimmy Demaret, champion professional golfer

Quarterbacks

A quarterback doesn't come into his own until he can tell the coach to go to hell.

Johnny Unitas, Hall of Fame football player

Get more open—I'm getting old.

Dan Marino, quarterback, to Lamar Thomas, professional football player (receiver)

If a survey was taken, I think you'd find more injuries happen to a quarterback while standing in the pocket than by taking off with a ball.

Steve Grogan, professional football player

One day I throw the ball like Roger Staubach, one day like Roger Rabbit.

Mike Winchell, college football player

There was no mistaking a professional quarterback's throw—one had the sense, seeing it come, of a projectile rather than a football.

George Plimpton, writer

Quitting

I learned, one, you shouldn't ever quit. And I learned, two, you'll never be able to explain it to anybody.

Jim Ryun, track athlete

No más, no más. No more box.

Roberto Duran, champion boxer, refusing to continue fighting Sugar Ray Leonard, champion boxer

The Jets haven't been worth the aggravation, but I'd be damned if I ever quit. I'll never sell.

Leon Hess, owner of the perennial American Football Conference East doormat New York Jets

The first time you quit, it's hard. The second time, it gets easier. The third time, you don't even have to think.

Paul "Bear" Bryant, Hall of Fame college football coach

R

Race Walking

Thirty-seven soft-shoe shufflers in their underwear crowded up to the starting line for the 20,000 meter walk—a sprint of about twelve and a half miles.

Red Smith, sportswriter

Racism

Are you crazy, man? You can get electrocuted for that! A Jew looking at a white girl in Kentucky?

Muhammad Ali, world champion boxer, to Dick Schaap, sportswriter, regarding a comment by Schaap about a pretty woman on a street corner in Louisville, Kentucky

As a kid, I carried the sousaphone in my school marching band. Believe me, I'm used to being noticed.

Thurl Bailey, professional basketball player, who is an African American and Mormon

As a black youngster I would say to myself, "Josh Gibson was just as good—if not supe-
rior to—Yankee Bill Dickey . . . Satch Paige is just as good as the Yankee Red Ruffing . . . then why can't they play in the big leagues?"

Art Rust, Jr., sportswriter

Baseball is America's sport and has to reflect what is going on in America.

Dave Winfield, professional baseball player, referring to African Americans not getting managerial and front office positions

Hey, Jewboy, you aren't going to win any gold medals!

Unnamed U.S. Olympic swimmer to Mark Spitz, Olympic gold medal swimmer

I don't give a damn about the color of a man's skin. I'm only interested in how well or how badly he plays this game.

Leo Durocher, professional baseball player and manager

I don't have any regrets about not playing in the majors. At that time the doors were not open only in baseball, but in other avenues that we couldn't enter. They say I was born too soon; I say the doors were opened up too late.

James Bell, Hall of Fame baseball player and Negro Leagues star

I don't want to be the best black golfer ever. I want to be the best golfer ever.

Tiger Woods, champion professional golfer

If it had not been for the wind in my face, I wouldn't be able to fly at all.

Arthur Ashe, champion tennis player and writer

It can now be honestly doubted that the boys from the Hookworm Belt will have the nerve to foist their quaint sectional folklore on the rest of the country.

Stanley Woodward, sportswriter, speaking of a strike contemplated by some professional baseball players upon the introduction of Jackie Robinson into the major leagues

Little boy's playing great out there. Just tell him next year not to serve fried chicken at the dinner. Or collard greens or whatever the hell it is they serve.

Fuzzy Zoeller, champion golfer, about Tiger Woods, for which he later apologized

The argument that blacks are physically superior to whites is merely a racist ideology camouflaged to appeal to the ignorant, the unthinking and the unaware.

Harry Edwards, sociologist and motivator

The hate mail won't be thrown away yet. We still have hatred in the country and we need to be reminded.

Hank Aaron, Hall of Fame baseball player, speaking about the hate mail he got when he broke Babe Ruth's all-time home run record

This is the United States of America and one citizen has as much right to play as another. The National League will go down the line with Robinson whatever the consequences.

Ford Frick, National League president

This isn't revolution, it's evolution. The need for better players at all positions has overtaken the need to preserve the myth of white dominance and heroism embodied by the quarterback.

William C. Rhoden, sportswriter, about the first draft in which three African-American quarterbacks were taken in the first round

Hemus, that's a goddamn cheap Jew hit and you're a goddamn Jew hitter!

Attributed by Solly Hemus, professional baseball player, to Warren Spahn or Lew Burdette regarding a "cheap single" during a regular season game

Hey, no Mexicans allowed on this course!

Chi Chi Rodriguez, champion golfer, to Lee Trevino, champion golfer—both are Hispanic

How can it be the great American game if blacks can't play? Hell, we sell beer to everyone.

Auggie Busch, baseball owner

I ain't got no dog-proof ass!

Sonny Liston, champion boxer, responding to comments about his not participating in civil rights marches

If I were black, I'd be just another center who plays well. . . . I want to be judged for my play, not my color. I don't deserve any medals for my color.

Bill Walton, Hall of Fame basketball player

If I weren't earning more than $3 million a year to dunk a basketball, most people on the street would turn and run in the other direction if they saw me coming.

Charles Barkley, professional basketball player

If you're a basketball player, a movie star, or an entertainer, it's more acceptable for you to cross racial boundaries. If you're just a normal, everyday person, people look at you like you're doing something wrong.

Dennis Rodman, professional basketball player

I have seen many Negro players who should be in the major leagues. There is no room in baseball for discrimination. It is our national pastime and a game for all.

Lou Gehrig, Hall of Fame baseball player

I've seen hate mail in a lot of situations. I've never seen anything like that, never. It was tragically unfair and just plain wrong.

Bud Selig, baseball owner and commissioner, speaking about the hate mail Hank Aaron received as he was about to break Babe Ruth's all-time home run record

It's hard being black. You ever been black? I was black once—when I was poor.

Larry Holmes, champion boxer

No one can say how many Negro champions were barred from practically all fields.

Grantland Rice, sportswriter

No one questions the color of a run.

Bobby Bragan, baseball executive

The South African government considered me too activist, a latent troublemaker. The fact that I had once made a flip offhand remark to the effect that an H-bomb should be dropped on Johannesburg may have caused the government to arrive at this conclusion.

Arthur Ashe, Hall of Fame tennis champion and writer

We played in a time when black people were supposed to stick together, so I asked Gibby one time why he always threw at the brothers. He said, "Because they're the ones who are gonna beat me if I don't."

Dick Allen, professional baseball player

When I began to sound off, I was portrayed as a wise-guy, uppity nigger.

Jackie Robinson, professional baseball player and first African-American major-league player

When you talk about racism in basketball, the whole thing is simple: a black player knows he can go out on a court and kick a white player's ass.

Dennis Rodman, professional basketball player

Racquetball

You are in control of your racquetball destiny when you are serving because the serve is the only shot in racquetball that you initiate and control.

Ed Turner, writer, and Marty Hogan, champion racquetball player

Rankings

If you win Wimbledon and the Open you've won the two biggest tournaments of the year. I think that makes you No. 1, no matter what the computer says.

Martina Navratilova, champion tennis player

really isn't a number one tennis player, ... At any given time there's maybe five ... ... .op players who are interchangeable in the top spot. I'm good, but I'm not an unequivocal number one. Things change too fast to make that kind of judgment.

John Newcombe, champion tennis player

Being No. 1 puts a lot of pressure on you. Everybody is always gunning for you. Every time you go out to play a match you feel as if you have to protect something. Even so, it's better than being No. 2.

Rod Laver, champion tennis player

Reality

Ten of you guys, out of two hundred, will play varsity basketball in high school. If you're lucky, one of your guys might play division one college basketball. Those are the odds—maybe even less than that.

Grant Hill, professional basketball player, warning kids to study and make something of themselves through academics

There are so many guys I know who had the intelligence to do almost anything, but all they thought about was basketball. And then when basketball didn't work out, they had nothing to turn to.

Charles Barkley, professional basketball player

Things are never quite as good as they seem. Things are never quite as bad as they seem. In between falls reality.

John Calipari, college and professional basketball coach

Rebounds

Every time a shot goes up, I believe that the rebound is mine. I really believe it. I go after every ball because I believe it belongs to me.

Moses Malone, professional basketball player

I don't believe in boxing out. My idea about rebounding is just to go get the damned ball.

Charles Barkley, professional basketball player

I never thought I'd lead the NBA in rebounding, but I got a lot of help from my teammates—they did a lot of missing.

Moses Malone, professional basketball player

I never want to score. Never. I want to rebound.

Dennis Rodman, professional basketball player

What's rebounding? A dog can go after a ball. If that's what they want me to do, I'll do that.

Jason Williams, professional basketball player

Receiving

A wide receiver just has to be flexible and give the quarterback a break.

Sammy White, professional football player

I can throw the ball 100 yards, and one of these days I'm going to throw the ball all the way back down the field.

Harold Carmichael, professional football player

It's like a gunfight: When you draw, you don't have time to look, only to react.

Bobby Hammond, professional football player, about receiving punts and kickoffs

People talk about big targets but what the passer wants is an open target.

Harold Jackson, professional football player

Records

He could break all the records before he's through.

Gil Hodges, professional baseball player and manager, speaking about rookie Nolan Ryan

How do you run a world record? You compress all your baser urges into one minute and forty-two seconds of running.

Peter Coe, father of Sebastian Coe, champion runner

I can't believe I did it. Seventy home runs. It's absolutely amazing—I am in awe of myself right now.

Mark McGwire, professional baseball player, after setting the new mark for most home runs in one season

My feeling is that as long as the record stands, fine, I'm happy . . . But it won't last forever. Some young guy will come along and he won't be one bit impressed.

Bruce Jenner, gold medalist decathlon competitor

Perhaps there is no such thing as an unbeatable performance but for a reasonable facsimile thereof, Beamon's leap of 29 feet 2¹/₂ inches at the Mexico City Olympics October 1968, does nicely.

Red Smith, sportswriter, about Bob Beamon's all-time record broad jump

Records are made to be broken.

Fred Lieb, sportswriter, quoting the old saying

Records don't drive me. I'm going to do whatever I can to help the team, plain and simple. It doesn't matter what numbers you put up, the most important ones are in the won-lost column.

Ken Griffey, Jr., professional baseball player

These records are only borrowed, precious aspects of the sport, temporarily in one's keeping.

Sebastian Coe, champion runner

There's no such thing as a "presumed" record. It's either a record or it's not.

Seymour Siwoff, statistician, Elias Sports Bureau

We never try to put ceilings on anyone. Years ago certain records were unattainable, but it happens. In any given situation in any given time, anything can happen.

Sue Humphrey, track and field coach

Whenever that goal comes, it will be special, but I want it to be in a winning cause.

Mia Hamm, soccer player, on scoring the goal that would make her the world's highest-scoring soccer player

You couldn't play on my Amazing Mets without having held some kind of record, like one fella held the world's international all-time record for a pitcher getting hit on the ankles.

Casey Stengel, Hall of Fame baseball manager

Marciano couldn't carry my jockstrap.

Larry Holmes, champion professional boxer, after he lost his title, when he was questioned about falling one victory short of equaling Rocky Marciano's record for consecutive undefeated title defenses

Recruiting

Recruiting is like shaving. Do it every day or you will look like a bum.

Anonymous

I was promised money, credit cards, apartments, come home on weekends when I wanted to. Everybody was promising something. It was just who was promising me the most.

Derric Evans, high school football player

Just once I'd like to see a picture of one of these guys with the caption "He's a dog" underneath it. "Ate up $8,000 worth of groceries in four years and can't play worth a lick."

Abe Lemons, Texas University basketball coach

I have the job I want. I am not looking for a job. What I'm looking for is a tall player that can play.

Mike Jarvis, college basketball coach

I'm looking for guys you toss meat to and they'll go wild.

*Harold Ballard,
National Hockey League executive*

Religion

A rooster crows only when he sees the light. Put him in the dark and he'll never crow. I have seen the light and I am crowing.

*Muhammad Ali, champion boxer,
on finding the Muslim religion*

God gets you to the plate, but once you're there you're on your own.

Ted Williams, Hall of Fame baseball player

Fate? Synchonistic destinies? I prefer to think it was a guiding hand, the One who looks after fools, drunks, and sailors in distress.

Tristan Jones, sailor and writer

I find that prayers work best when you have big players.

*Knute Rockne, Hall of Fame
college football coach*

I never pray on a golf course. Actually, the Lord answers my prayers everywhere except on the course.

Lee Trevino, champion golfer

It's easy to see golf not as a game at all but as some whey-faced, nineteenth-century Presbyterian minister's fever dream of exorcism achieved through ritual and self-mortification.

Bruce McCall, writer

I understand that yesterday the daily double windows were kept open longer than usual and when they closed there were still lines waiting and 150 people were turned away. If any of those people are here this morning, we will cheerfully accept those bets, in the collection basket.

Priest at St. Peter's Parish, Saratoga

The biggest fallacy is people's perceptions of Christianity and their belief that you can't be a Christian and still be competitive . . . When you read the Bible, you'll find many places where it definitely says you don't have to live your life without being competitive.

*Dan Reeves, professional football
player and coach*

There are 108 beads in a rosary and 108 stitches in a baseball. When I found that out, I gave Jesus a chance.

> *Susan Sarandon, as Annie Savoy, in*
> Bull Durham

When I come back, I want to be re-incarnated as a dolphin—or as an F-16.

> *Bo Jackson, professional baseball and football player, speaking on reincarnation*

Responsibility

Never shirk responsibility.

> *Althea Gibson, profession tennis champion*

Reputation

If one's reputation is a possession, then of all of my possessions, my reputation means the most to me.

> *Arthur Ashe,* Days of Grace

Retirement

When an athlete doesn't—or can't—envision the end, it comes as a shock.

> *Pat Riley, professional basketball player and coach, commenting on the end of his own playing days*

Each is the last to learn from fate
That his story is finished—and out of date.

> *Grantland Rice, sportswriter*

For the big horse, it's all fun now.

> *Red Smith, sportswriter, regarding the retirement of champion thoroughbred Secretariat, who was already scheduled to stud*

He's all through as a racehorse; we expect him to be fine as a stallion.

> *Dr. Larry Bramlage, veterinarian, referring to the career-ending injury to failed Triple Crown hopeful Charismatic*

Hey, I'm not dropping off the face of the earth, you know.

> *John Shimooka, surfer*

I'd like to play long enough so that when I'm finished, I won't have to go out and dig ditches or punch time clocks.

> *Bobby Hull, Hall of Fame hockey player*

If a player, any player, feels he doesn't want to play, there's nothing a coach can do.

> *Bob Brett, tennis coach*

I feel like I just got rid of a 2,000-pound load.

> *John Elway, professional football player, after telling owner Pat Bowlen he was going to retire*

If the graceful exit were easy, it would have been executed more often by great athletes.

> *Richard Hoffer, sportswriter*

If you don't want me, I'll retire.

> *Ted Williams, Hall of Fame baseball player, to management*

I guess that time has come to stop thinking about what comes next and start acting on it. It's hard to look in the mirror and say it, but at twenty-eight I'm a lot closer to the end than I am to the beginning.

> *Pam Shriver, professional tennis player*

I'm also going to spend a little time just sitting on the grass and looking at the sky. I think I'm going to like that.

> *Julie Krone, jockey*

I'm definitely glad it's over, but I think I'm satisfied as I am because I went out on top. The seven gold medals count, of course, but what is more important to me is that I did the best I could, and when I finished I was on top.

Mark Spitz, Olympic gold medal swimmer

I miss football so much—heck, I even miss the interceptions.

Archie Manning, professional football player and broadcaster

I'm not Joe DiMaggio anymore.

Joe DiMaggio, Hall of Fame baseball player

I went back to my room and cried for hours. I swam my last race. That was it.

Ambrose "Rowdy" Gaines IV, Olympic champion swimmer, during one of his several "retirements"

No shooting man wants to be aware of when he shot that final shell, but when he does, let it be in the gun he loves most, at the bird he loves most.

George Bird Evans, hunter, outdoorsman, and writer

Sometimes you go to funerals and sometimes you go to weddings. And to me, this is a party.

Wayne Gretzky, Hall of Fame hockey player, at his retirement press conference

There will come a day when some of these fellows draw that pension money years from now and they will probably have completely forgotten how they earned it. They got it because a lot of guys stuck out their necks.

Tim McCarver, professional baseball player and broadcaster

This guy looks really interested.

Wayne Gretzky, Hall of Fame hockey player, referring to his son during the announcement of his retirement. His son was practically asleep.

This has been an incredible love for me. To even think about walking away from it, that's very painful.

Jerry West, Hall of Fame basketball player and basketball executive

Today, I consider myself the luckiest man in the world.

Lou Gehrig, New York Yankees, Hall of Famer, as he retired

I been all over the world. I fought maybe three, four hundred fights and everyone of them was a pleasure. If I just had me a little change in my pocket I'd get along fine.

Sam Langford, professional boxer

I could upset everything—tell 'em I'm making a comeback.

Stan Musial, Hall of Fame baseball player moments before his retirement ceremony

I was concerned that normal life would be a letdown after the excitement of football life, but I have found that there is a lot to life beyond football. I get excited about going to announce big games as I did in one, but I also am excited going to act in a segment of my series.

Merlin Olsen, professional football player, broadcaster, actor

So many great days, so much excitement. Then all of a sudden when most guys are just hitting their peak in business, you're through.

Sam Huff, Hall of Fame professional football player

The drum beats for everyone. It's important for every pro athlete to realize that. No matter who you are, there's going to come a time your career is over and you'd better be ready for it.

Doug Williams, professional football player; first African-American quarterback to win a Super Bowl; Super Bowl MVP

This will be my last decathlon. You can't keep this up forever.

Bob Mathias, gold medalist decathlon competitor, politician, and actor, after winning his second decathlon in as many Olympics, at 21 years old

Well, boys, better take a good look around you, because most of us won't be here next year.

George Metkovich, professional baseball player, played during the last year of the war, to his then teammates before the "real" major leaguers came back from World War II

We walked through the parking lot. Neither of us said anything. We thought the world had ended.

Anne Ryun, wife of Jim Ryun, track athlete

What would I do if I retired? Go into the middle of town, where nobody knows me and nobody talks about horses?

Woody Stephens, trainer

When it ceased to be fun, she had the good sense to know when to leave.

Jerry Izenberg, sportswriter, about Julie Krone, jockey

When you stop playing the game, it's like dying.

Tim Green, National Football League player

Yesterday I drove by the track at San Jose State, where I did a lot of training. I looked out the window at the rest of those guys and I felt sorry for them. And right then, I knew I'd made the right decision to quit when I did.

Bruce Jenner, gold medalist decathlon competitor

You know how I realized when I was through with football? It was during the Cincinnati game. I didn't want to hurt anybody.

Chip Oliver, professional football player

Rice, Grantland

(b. Nov. 1, 1880; d. July 13, 1954) *Sportswriter; coined "The Four Horsemen," Notre Dame backfield and Red Grange as "The Galloping Ghost"*

Nothing can be said of him that he didn't say better of someone else.

Red Smith, sportswriter

Rickey, Branch

(b. Dec. 20, 1881; d. Dec. 9, 1965) *Baseball general manager; instituted farm system in Major League Baseball; first GM to integrate Major League Baseball by calling up Jackie Robinson*

A hypocritical preacher.

Judge Kenesaw Mountain Landis, baseball commissioner, speaking about Branch Rickey

Branch Rickey, who supposedly is the finest scout in baseball history, chose Robinson with wisdom, that borders on clairvoyance, to right a single wrong.

Roger Kahn, writer

Next to Abraham Lincoln, the biggest white benefactor of the Negro has been Branch Rickey.

Grantland Rice, sportswriter

Riley, Pat

(b. May 20, 1945) *National Basketball Association player; NBA coach; won four out of six appearances in the NBA finals; all-time NBA playoff wins*

He vowed a crown, but he wanted a throne.

Mark Kriegel, sportswriter

Ten years ago, Pat carried the bags of West and Goodrich. In 1982, he's the coach of the West. The way he's going, in ten years he'll probably be the president of the United States.

Bill Fitch, professional basketball coach

Paramount Communications had not given us a basketball coach but some sort of a Warren Beatty facsimile.

Mark Kriegel, sportswriter

Rivalries

Gentlemen, you are about to play football for Yale. Never again in your lives will you do anything so important.

Tad Jones, college football coach

Damn, Alzado, another draw.

Art Shell, Hall of Fame football player, to Lyle Alzado, an opposing lineman, who battled each other regularly for many years

Defeat-less Army and victory-less Navy, crashing head-on, slugged it out toe to toe,

march for march, touchdown for touchdown, and point for point in a 21-to-21 tie that left their categories undisturbed and 102,581 spectators limp with excitement.

Jesse Abramson, sportswriter

Here were two teams that had made a career of failure and had enjoyed staggering success at it. One had lost four games, the other three. Neither had beaten anyone of importance.

Red Smith, sportswriter, referring to the 1947 Yale–Harvard game

I always had only male friends in the tennis world. The rivalry among women tennis players is overwhelming.

Steffi Graff, professional tennis player

I know there is a lot of animosity between the two teams. You have to be aggressive, but show poise too. You have to know when to back off.

Latrell Sprewell, professional basketball player

I would rather beat the Bruins than the Russians.

Ted Newland, college water polo coach

The Army–Navy game, dear reader, is a joke. An awful anachronism. As out of touch with the times as a plodding brontosaurus.

Jim Hawkins, sportswriter, The Awful Anachronism

The New York of the Giants, Dodgers and Yankees was an annual re-evocation of the War between the States. The Yankees were the North, if you could conceive a North grinding along with wealth and weight without the excuse of Lincoln. The Giants and Dodgers were the Confederacy, often undermanned and underequipped and running then because it could not hit.

Murray Kempton, Back at the Polo Grounds

Rizzuto, Phil

(b. Sept. 25, 1918) *Hall of Fame baseball player; longtime Yankee broadcaster*

Come on, admit it. You loved Phil. Come on, because he was always there, and because *you* knew who was on deck, a better recipe for red sauce and a quicker route to the bridge.

Bill Scheft, writer

Robinson, Jackie

(b. Jan. 31, 1919; d. Oct. 24, 1972) *Hall of Fame baseball player; first African American in the major leagues; Rookie of the Year (1947); league MVP; won one World Series*

He could have done anything he set out to do. It didn't have to be baseball. He was articulate and sharp—and when he started to speak out, easy to dislike. But he taught me a lot more than I ever taught him.

Pee Wee Reese, professional baseball player

There are certain people in American sports who are now valid figures in the nation's history books. Jackie Robinson is one.

Howard Cosell, broadcaster

Rockne, Knute

(b. Mar. 4, 1888; d. Mar. 31, 1931) *Hall of Fame college football coach; won three national championships; highest-winning percentage of all time (.881)*

Whenever Rock opened his kisser, the throng became as silent as a tomb.

Harry Grayson, sportswriter

Rocker, John

(b. Oct. 17, 1974) *Professional baseball player, controversial relief pitcher of the Atlanta Braves, who made racist statements in his interview with* Sports Illustrated

No one is defending Rocker's statements, although the Ku Klux Klan has yet to weigh in.

Stan Savran, sportswriter

We've got Hispanics in this band, Italians in this band, people who are Polish and Russian. We're all immigrants, all foreigners—quote unquote—and this is our way of saying his comments were not acceptable.

Jay Jay French, guitarist and cofounder of heavy metal rock band Twisted Sister, who asked that the Atlanta Braves no longer play one of their songs each time Rocker made an entrance

Imagine having to take the 7 train to [Shea Stadium] looking like you're [in] Beirut next to some kid with purple hair, next to some queer with AIDS, right next to some dude who got out of jail for the fourth time, right next to some 20-year-old mom with four kids. It's depressing.

John Rocker, controversial baseball player, from an interview with Sports Illustrated

The biggest thing I don't like about New York are the foreigners. You can walk an entire block in Times Square and not hear anybody speaking English. Asians and Koreans and Vietnamese and Indians and Russians and Spanish people and everything up there. How the hell did they get in this country?

John Rocker, controversial baseball player, from an interview with Sports Illustrated

Rodman, Dennis

(b. May 13, 1961) *Controversial All-Star professional basketball player, has won five National Basketball Association championships; two-time Defensive Player of the Year; changes hair color often*

And even if the birth certificate isn't lying, Dennis Rodman has absolutely nothing in common with the blankness, tumbleweeds and football loons of Texas, who tend to associate drag with cigarettes and hot rods.

Jay Mariotti, sportswriter

In the real world, people have to show up on time, listen to the boss, take care of their kids and try to be a decent role model. Anyone who hires Rodman on Rodman's terms is an insult to people who pay their hard-earned money to buy tickets.

Terry Pluto, sportswriter and best-selling writer

Role Models

The ability to run and dunk or to hit 40 homers or rush for 1,000 yards doesn't make you God Almighty. And secondly, they shouldn't look up to someone they can't be . . . They should be looking up to their parents.

Charles Barkley, professional basketball player

Mr. Rickey, I'm no pioneer, I'm just a ballplayer.

Roy Campanella, professional baseball player, to Branch Rickey, when discussing if he would be the first African-American baseball player in the major leagues

Professional athletes should not be role models. Hell, I know drug dealers who can dunk. Can drug dealers be role models?

Charles Barkley, professional basketball player

Some athletes today do not believe they should be considered role models, but I believe you don't really have a choice if you are a "celebrity," so I try to set the best example I can.

Shannon Miller, Olympic gold medalist gymnast

The problem I have with the idea of being a role model is that I like to skate . . . And just because I won a medal doing what I love to do, why should that make me a role model? I don't belong on a pedestal, not for winning a medal.

Rudy Galindo, champion figure skater

You become a role model whether you like it or not. People admire your talent and they see your character. I don't think of it as a burden; it is very satisfying to set a good example.

Hakeem Olajuwon, professional basketball player

Rookies

Being a rookie . . . meant you had to carry the rock. The rookie rock was a big, flat rock that was kept at a hotel in Switzerland, where the guys often stay in between races . . . The only way to get rid of it was to ski Kitzbuhel.

Mike Wilson, writer

He doesn't look like a rookie to me. He's a good kid and he knows how to put his foot on the gas.

Jimmy Vasser, automobile racer, about teammate Juan Montoya

In games he'll test the newcomers with an extra shove, a needless elbow, a protruding hip. To Russell all rookies on trial have the same name: "Boy!"

Fred Katz, sportswriter

The refs won't even call rookies by their names.

Jason Williams, professional basketball player

Where the hell do you suppose they dredge up these rookies from?

Terry Barr, professional football player,
referring to George Plimpton, writer,
who was posing as a rookie

Roosevelt, Theodore

(b. Oct. 27, 1858; d. Jan. 6, 1919) *President of the United States; Nobel Peace Prize winner; proponent of "the active life"; naturalist, author, sportsman*

He came down hard on market hunters or anyone who killed for sport. Virtually all the game he killed ended up in the pot, to be eaten around the campfire. He was one of America's first conservationists, and he is still her greatest, because of what he was able to do through the Boone & Crockett Club and as president of the United States.

Stephen E. Ambrose, historian

The charm about this ranch man as author is that he is every inch a gentleman-sportsman.

the British Spectator, *reviewing* Trips of a Ranchman

The overwhelming impression left after reading *Trips of a Ranchman* is that of love for, and identity with, all living things.

Edmund Morris, writer

Rose, Pete

(b. Apr. 14, 1941) *Professional baseball player; all-time record for most hits (4,256); won three World Series; League MVP; known as "Charlie Hustle"; banned for life from baseball by Baseball Commissioner A. Bartlett Giamatti for betting on baseball*

Just so nothing improper would take place, I had him sign balls in my office for each player. I put each ball in the player's locker the day after Pete was gone.

Bruce Keiter, owner, minor league
baseball team, who was questioned
by Major League Baseball for possibly
violating the ban on Pete Rose

Rothstein, Arnold

(b. Jan. 17, 1882; d. Nov. 6, 1928) *Sportsman; big-time gambler; person responsible for fixing the 1919 World Series; was the prototype for F. Scott Fitzgerald's character Meyer Wolfsheim in* The Great Gatsby, *"the man who fixed the World's Series back in 1919."*

Arnold Rothstein is a man who waits in doorways . . . a mouse waiting in the doorway for his cheese.

William J. Fallon, lawyer for Abe Atell, former
champion boxer, and associate of Arnold
Rothstein. Atell was a go-between for Rothstein
in the Black Sox scandal.

He had a deep love for the racetrack and a deeper loathing for the stock market.

Grantland Rice, sportswriter

Rowing

Always remember, there's more to life than rowing—but not much.

Donald Beer, Olympic medal-winning oarsman

Coxing is like sitting in a racing car with electric probes stuck to your ego.

Devin Mahony, coxswain

Down this narrow stretch we . . . race, graceful engines of pain, sinews and bones straining in the most powerful fluid of motions—the unison swing of the oars propelling the shells along until one of us overpowered the other, reaching the finish line first, proving once and for all which crew was the best.

Devin Mahony, coxswain

Form is for gymnastics and figure skating and diving, not rowing . . . Rowing is about winning. If you win, then everyone says your form is good anyway.

Tiff Wood, Olympic oarsman

It was in its way a very macho world. The egos were immense—they had to be for so demanding a sport. Men of lesser will and ambition simply did not stay around.

David Halberstam, writer

The noblest of sports. In rowing, everyone is part of the effort.

Anita DeFrantz, Olympic silver medalist oarswoman

The sophomores are good, but they haven't learned the humility of crew yet.

John Biglow, Olympic oarsman

Rugby

Both chess player and rugby player operate under stringent demands for speed of decision.

Jim Greenwood, rugby coach and writer

Breaking the line and setting up the outside or setting someone up for a try, I always find that an awesome feeling when I can break the defense line and really put someone away and see them score a try, it really gets me up and focused on the game.

Pita Alatini, New Zealand rugby player

From personal experience I can tell you there is nothing more frightening than to see eight All Blacks bearing down on you with malice aforethought.

Don Rutherford, professional rugby player

I could write a whole book on scrums and most of it would be junk.

Derek Robinson, journalist

If they do their job at scrum and lineout, get around the field and form the core of the rucks and mauls and push and work, they are fine players. If from time to time they can run with the ball and even score—that's a bonus. But we aren't interested in the bonus if it's at the expense of the rest.

Wilson Whineray, professional rugby player, referring to his front five

In rugby, there's active ignorance, passive ignorance, and cock-eyed ignorance.

Derek Robinson, journalist

In the amateur past, touring was regarded as a welcome break from the daily grind of normal work, however, for professional players, these visits are now strictly busmen's holidays.

Neil Robertson, sportswriter

It's no use criticizing our tackling. Tell us how to catch them first, then we'll tackle them all right.

Graham Wiliams, professional rugby player

More players have nervous breakdowns trying to understand the off-side law, than get kicked to death by green canaries.

Derek Robinson, journalist

The knowledge that others are relying on you and that you are relying on them is the very essence of the game of rugby.

J. J. Stewart, professional rugby coach and writer

The only thing I know about rugby is that there is more than one way to play it.

Neil McPhail, professional rugby coach

The blood-bin ruling was introduced because of obvious health concerns but the whole situation needs to be tightened up in the wake of serious abuses of the system such as this. The only way to do so would be to have an independent medical adviser on the touchline to ensure that there are sufficient grounds for a blood replacement, otherwise, we may as well go the whole hog and introduce rolling substitutes.

Neil Robertson, sportswriter

The way I want to play it, I want to be a No. 8 that gets the forward pack going forward. I want to be able to make yards for the team and be able to cut guys in half on defense.

Ron Cribb, New Zealand soccer player

There are times in your career when you get frustrated or you get disappointed, and things like that. I suppose that's when I did sit down and ask why I did want to play rugby. I just wanted to get out and enjoy it, and try and think about the results later. Just get out and enjoy your rugby! There's no difference between now and when I was a kid, I still enjoy the game and like getting out there with all my mates and having a lot of fun.

Todd Blackadder, New Zealand rugby player

What absurdity is this? You don't mean to say that those fifty or sixty boys, many of them quite small, are going to play that huge mass opposite.

Thomas Hughes, novelist, in Tom Brown's School Days

Your opponent may get you—but he must never get the ball.

Jim Greenwood, rugby coach and writer

Rules

Cheating is as much a part of the game as scorecards and hot dogs.

Billy Martin, professional baseball player and manager

Football has one glaring weakness. The game is built largely on constant rule breaking such as holding, off-side, backs illegally in motion, pass interference and other factors that play a big if illegal part in the results.

Grantland Rice, sportswriter

I am disgusted by any player who feels he doesn't have to play by the rules. The game is violent in nature, but if we accept players trying to hurt one another it will become something ugly and dangerous.

Merlin Olsen, professional football player

I believe in rules. Sure I do. If there weren't any rules, how could you break them?

Leo Durocher, professional baseball player and manager

One of the things unique about sailing is that it's one of the few sports where rules are enforced by the competitors themselves. We don't have referees out there calling the shots, or players trying to get away with anything they can. We have a system where conscience still counts and the way you play counts as much as the final outcome.

David Dallenbaugh, yachtsman

[The Raiders] are responsible for many rules changes. There's the no-clothesline rule. The no-spearing rule. The no-hitting out of bounds rule. No fumbling in the last two minutes of the game. No throwing helmets. The no stikum rule . . . So you see, we're not all that bad.

Ted Hendricks, professional football player

The rules of sport are founded upon fair play.

Hugh E. Keogh, sportswriter

Running

A lot of people run a race to see who's fastest. I run a race to see who has the most guts.

Steve Prefontaine, Olympic medalist track and field competitor and champion runner

Certainly the personal aspect of long-distance running, where success rests with the individual rather than the team, is similar to boxing. Perhaps the violence of boxing, directed at another individual, is sublimated in running, becoming a different kind of aggression. Both sports definitely require coming to terms with personal suffering in pursuit of success.

Don Kardong, runner and writer

Don't let anybody kid you. Runners make runners. Coaches like to take all the credit, but day after day, the upper classmen show the younger fellows how to run, how to train, how to take care of themselves.

James Francis "Jumbo" Elliott, champion track coach

Everyone knows about the bear. He's that invisible animal that waits for you about a hundred yards from the finish line. He jumps on your back and starts clawing and scratching and he seems so heavy that you want to stop running so that he'll get off and leave you alone.

Bruce Jenner, Olympic gold medalist decathlon competitor

Great running is an art so intensely personal, no two men do it quite alike. When a cat makes a beautiful run, it's poetry and jazz . . . Great runners are works of God.

Jim Brown, Hall of Fame football player

I always cringe inside when people say running comes naturally to me, that training is an uplifting joy. That's not why I race well. I'm competitive.

Eamon Coghlan, champion runner

I became a runner because it suited my personality. It suited me as an individualist.

Bill Rodgers, champion marathoner

I could run very fast. After all, in Alabama, all we kids had to do was run, so we ran.

Jesse Owens, Olympic gold medalist, track and field

If you have ever been around a runner who has just broken a barrier—say suddenly being able to run a 10-, 9-, 8-, or 7-minute mile—then you understand the magic.

Jeff Galloway, runner and writer

I have a good time. I let my mind go blank.

Jim Ryun, track athlete, about running

I was filled with relief that I hadn't been chewed over by the pack in the third lap. From then on I was just running for the tape.

Sebastian Coe, champion runner

I like it, the way I live, but I can't explain the satisfaction to people who do not run. . . . Once you know international racing, you can't just ease off a bit. It has to be one or the other, as hard as you can, or just for fun.

Grete Waitz, champion marathoner

I love to buy running shoes. I don't mean that I just enjoy the process of trying on new shoes. I mean I love buying running shoes.

John Bingham, runner and writer

I love testing myself more than I feared being beaten, and front running is the ultimate test. You need a total, irrevocable commitment to see the race through to the end or it cannot justify your effort.

Ron Clarke, champion runner

I run. I am a runner. I am an athlete.

Joan Benoit Samuelson, marathoner

It is not necessary for me that you are running. But if you don't run, I'm sure you'll be sorry for it later on.

Husband of Fanny Blankers-Koen, Olympic gold medalist in track and field, when she asked her husband if they could leave the 1948 London Olympics to see their children, including their six-month old daughter. She won four gold medals at those games.

It's something in me, deep down, that makes me different in a race.

Eammon Coghlan, champion runner

I've been running a lot of open races against Kenyans and they like to blow it out hard in the beginning . . . It's a little scary doing that because you can just die out there doing that.

Mike Mykytok, champion runner

I've learned that it's what you do with your miles, rather than how many you've run.

Rod DeHaven, runner

I like people to make people stop and say "I've never seen anyone run like that before!" It's more than just a race, it's style. It's doing something better than anyone else.

Steve Prefontaine, Olympic medalist track and field competitor and champion runner

I was born to run. I simply love to run. It's almost like the faster I go, the easier it becomes.

Mary Decker Slaney, champion runner

I was not very talented. My basic speed was low. Only with will power was I able to reach this world-best standard in long-distance running.

Emil Zatopek, Olympic gold medalist runner

I was now running for the tape, the mental agony of knowing I had hit my limit, of not knowing what was happening behind me. I was not to know they were fading, too. The anxiety over the last 20 meters was unbearable, it showed in my face as I crossed the line.

Sebastian Coe, champion runner

Jogging is what people do when they're so out of shape they can't do anything else. Running is what athletes do in training.

attributed by A. J. Poulin,
comedian and writer, to his girlfriend

Me thinks that the moment my legs begin to move, my thoughts begin to flow.

Henry David Thoreau, writer and philosopher

My thoughts before a big race are usually pretty simple. I tell myself: Get out of the blocks, run your race, stay relaxed. If you run your race, you'll win.

Carl Lewis, Olympic gold medalist track and
field competitor

Nobody running at full speed has either a head or a body.

William Butler Yeats, poet

Of all athletic forms running is perhaps the most taxing and the most exciting; that is, when carried to the extreme.

Alfred Shrubb, champion runner

Pain, like time, is a backdrop to running.

Sally Pont, writer and runner

People seem to think that running is much easier than it is. So I tell them that it's harder than they think, and that it'll take longer than they want it to take.

Dr. John Peters, cardiologist and runner

Running is a way of life for me, just like brushing my teeth. If I don't run for a few days, I feel as if something's been stolen from me.

John A. Kelly, champion marathoner

Running is for me. There's no coach telling me what to do. It's up to me whether or not to run each day.

Kerri Strug, Olympic gold medal–winning
gymnast

Running is my meditation, mind flush, cosmic telephone, mood elevator, and spiritual communion.

Lorraine Moller, Olympic bronze medalist
marathoner

Running is the greatest metaphor for life because you get out of it what you put into it.

Oprah Winfrey, actress and talk show host

Running well is a matter of having the patience to persevere when you are tired and not expecting instant results. The only secret is that it is consistent, often monotonous, boring, hard work. And it's tiring.

Robert de Castella, runner and writer

Set aside a time solely for running. Running is more fun if you don't have to rush through it.

Jim Fixx, runner

Start slowly and taper off fast.

slogan of the Dolphin Running Club,
San Francisco

That journalistic cliché "The Mile of the Century" has been applied to scores of races, each with claims to excellence, and it is an absorbing, if futile occupation to argue the merits of this mile and that as being the most sublime athletic event of the twentieth century.

Peter Lovesey, writer

There is no finish line.

Nike ad

The camera's eye
Does not lie,
But it cannot show
The life within,
The life of a runner.

W. H. Auden, poet

The custom of greeting every runner who passes, just because he or she happens to run, has become obsolete.

Joe Henderson, runner and writer, mourning the lack of civility in the sport

The difference between a jogger and a runner is an entry blank.

George Sheehan, runner and writer

The social aspects of running are not to be underestimated.

Bill Rodgers, champion marathoner

The difference between walking and running isn't speed or biomechanics. It's determination.

Amby Burfoot, runner, writer, and editor

There can be nothing superior to cross-country running for either pleasure or health. The sport itself is ideal, whether a race be contested in fine or muddy weather.

Alfred Shrubb, champion runner

There is an itch in runners.

Arnold Hano, sportswriter

Track is a hobby, but it is a life too.

Jim Ryun, track athlete

Whatever moves the other runners made, I knew I could respond . . . I felt like if I had to, I could fly.

Grete Waitz, champion marathoner

When testing the limits of your potential, racing can be harder mentally than physically. After all, your body is in pretty substantial distress, and your mind's main task seems to be to figure out how to better the situation as soon as possible.

Bill Rodgers, champion marathoner

Where you finish doesn't matter. The tragedy is when you have to walk in.

Dr. George Sheehan, runner

With victory in hand, running at maximum effort becomes very difficult. Without some company in the difficult miles, the body's mission becomes lonely and dark.

Frank Shorter, champion runner

You may run that fast again, but then again, you may not.

Ron Hill, champion runner, to Frank Shorter, champion marathoner

Ruth, Babe

(b. Feb. 5, 1895; d. Aug. 16, 1948) *Hall of Fame baseball player; second all-time home run record with 714 (that record stood for many years); prodigious home run hitter, who hit 54 or more runs four times in his career; two-time 20-game winner; may have single-handedly saved baseball after Black Sox scandal; known for the larger-than-life aspects of his athletic feats, as well of his personality and his appetites; Baby Ruth candy bar was allegedly named after him*

Born? Hell, Babe Ruth wasn't born. He fell from a tree.

Joe Dugan, professional baseball player

I know, but I had a better year.

Reply when a club official objected that the salary he was demanding was greater than the U.S. president's.

In his time, George Herman Ruth was a holy sinner. He was a man of measureless lust, selfishness, and appetites, but he was also a man undyingly faithful, in a manner, to both his public and his game.

> *Roger Kahn, sportswriter*

Ruth must have admired records because he created so many of them.

> *Red Smith, sportswriter*

I swing big, with everything I've got. I hit big or I miss big. I like to live as big as I can.

> *Babe Ruth, Hall of Fame baseball player*

That last one sounded kind of high to me.

> *Babe Ruth, questioning the umpire*
> *about three fast pitches that*
> *he had not seen*

The day I can use him in the outfield and take advantage of his bat every day—well, they'll have to build the parks bigger, just for Ruth.

> *Ed Barrow, professional baseball coach*
> *and Red Sox manager*

Ryan, Buddy

(b. Feb. 6, 1934) *Professional football coach; defensive guru was defensive coordinator for two Super Bowl champion teams (1969, 1986); head coach known for aggressive teams*

Buddy Ryan is a Neanderthal and he attracts Neanderthal players. Neanderthals can win certain kinds of wars, but they lose some they should win if you can find a way to make them make enough choices.

> *Bill Parcells, professional football coach*

S

Sacks

Rushing the passer is grueling work. It requires a great outlay of speed, strength, energy, and determination. A man must drive himself if he is going to break through on every pass play.

Stanley Woodward, sportswriter

Sacking the quarterback is why I'm here. It's the only glamour there is on the defensive line. Everything else is pretty dull.

*Cedrick Hardman, professional
football player and actor*

Sailing

A long voyage refreshes rather than tires me. Every healthy person ought to try it and see how it tones the skin and sharpens the sense.

*Philip S. Weld, champion solo yachtsman and
writer, winner of the OSTAR solo race from
England to the United States*

Although we go afloat for independence and solitude, we now and then crave talk with other people. Sometimes we're lucky enough to come across friends . . . but more often we strike up conversations with strangers who may own similar boats or be anchored close by. This has always been the way among seafarers.

Anthony Bailey, writer

A man in jail has more room, better food, and commonly better company.

*Samuel Johnson, writer,
referring to sailing voyages*

Anyone can hold the helm when the sea is calm.

Publius Syrus, writer, first century B.C.

Circumstance, not choice, places one in the middle of . . . a maelstrom. . . . Therefore when it happens, there can be no recriminations, no regrets. One must respond the best one can to the test, and only enjoy the rare opportunity— the privilege, in fact—that brings vessel, gear, and crew close to an outer limit of strength, resourcefulness, and endurance.

*attributed to Roger Vaughn "Fingers," sailor and
racer, after the 1979 Fastnet Race*

For hours I slice up my grand fish . . . Finally I slice these into sticks which I hang on strings to dry, like dozens of fat fingers, delicious fat fingers. I write in my log that this is a strange prison in which I am slowly starved but occasionally thrown a 20-lb. filet mignon.

Steve Callahan, sailor, lost 76 days at sea after his sloop sank in a race

Here was a sport in which enlarging experience could offset diminishing vigor. I found out, eighteen years later, that a 4,000-mile race at sixty-four tired me out less than a 3,000-mile race at fifty-six because I'd become wiser in choice of boat and gear and in the husbanding of my energies.

Philip S. Weld, champion solo yachtsmen

I am the closest to having dreadlocks as I will ever be. A week without shampoo, three days without brushing my hair, and salt water is all it takes.

Renee Mehel, sailor, in her journal during the Whitbread Around-the-World race

I turned my face eastward, and there, apparently at the end of the bowsprit, was the smiling first moon rising out of the sea . . . "Good evening, sir," I cried. "I am glad to see you." Many a long talk since then I have had with the man in the moon; he had my confidence on the voyage.

Joshua Slocum, first modern sailor to sail around the world alone

I was aware that no other vessel has sailed in this manner around the globe, but would have been loath to say another could not do it . . . I was greatly amused, therefore, by the flat assertions of an expert that it could not be done.

Joshua Slocum, first modern sailor to sail around the world alone

Frankly I would rather have my name on their trophies than on their membership list.

John B. Kilroy, yacht sailing skipper, when asked why he had not joined the New York Yacht Club

If you just did go to the 7-Eleven, then why the hell did you come back?

Deborah Scaling Kiley, sailor and writer, to a deranged sailing teammate after they had been lost at sea in a raft for weeks

In sailing there is a term called *lift,* which is both technical and poetic at once. It describes the moment of acceleration in a sailboat, the moment when the sails harden against the wind and the boat begins to slide forward faster and faster until you can feel what William Buckley meant by the title of his sailing book, *Airborne.* How something moving so slowly, about the pace of a moderate jogger, can impart something so exhilarating at this moment, is probably unanswerable.

Tony Chamberlin, sportswriter

Life at sea is fearfully demanding, and that is why its measured joys are so distinctive. But these pleasures—the obliging winds, the beneficent sky, the sweetly composed set of sail, the fleet speed—are building blocks for the supreme pleasure of camaraderie. I have always thought it impossible, and if possible abominable, to harbor it all to oneself.

William F. Buckley, writer, editor, yachtsman

The challenge of sailing 1,000 miles is something I've got to do. It's been a dream for some time.

Hans Meijer, sailor

Obstacles are obscured by the dark. Massive ships become skeletons of running lights floating through the night on an invisible horizon. Everything disappears in the dark. . . .

Dawn Riley, champion yachtswoman

One of the greatest moments in the history of mankind must have been when man first discovered that he could move in water either by swimming himself or by riding along on a log.

Jay Evans, Olympic kayaker and outdoorsman

People go sailing for different reasons. Some just seek peace and quiet, an escape from life's everyday sound and fury. Some sail for the challenge, physical and mental, of battling with the elements. Others cannot be enticed onto the water unless there is someone else out there to race against.

Mike Fletcher, sailor and journalist

Sailing a boat on a full-out plane is the essence of sensuality. The harder the wind blows, the steeper the seas, the faster the boat goes in its mad, futile attempt to become airborne, the closer it brings the crew to delirium, an edge that is unmistakably orgasmic.

Roger Vaughn, yachtsman and writer

Sailing is a wonderful and unique thing, and the sensation of being noiselessly and smoothly propelled without the cost of fuel is one of the most satisfactory pleasures known, but when you add to the fact that the sailboat itself is one of the most interesting things which God has let man make, well, then you get a combination which is almost too sacred.

L. Francis Herrshoff, sailor and writer

Sailboat racing is the thing I like to do most in my life and I get a great deal of personal pleasure out of it.

Dennis Conner, businessman and champion yachtsman

Take with a grain of salt anything told to you by anyone who claimed he or she was an expert celestial navigator, at least on yachts. On such unstable platforms as such small craft underway, celestial navigation, using a sextant, was never any easy task, and neither was the result often accurate.

Tristan Jones, sailor and writer

The man at the wheel was said to feel
 contempt for the wildest blow,
but it often appeared when the gale had
 cleared
that he'd been in his bunk below.

John Masefield, poet

To be able to face it all and come through it is exhilarating. Sailing in rough weather is what the sport is all about.

Ted Turner, yachtsman and baseball owner

The bottom line is, every job on the boat has its own specific requirements. If you look at both men and women, you have a perfect combination—power, agility, finesse and knowledge. Together, on a team, they can become very efficient.

Dawn Riley, champion yachtswoman

There are no old, bold sailors.

Tim Hebden, sailor and captain

The winning sailor consistently does everything just a little bit better than the competition. He anticipates windshifts more accurately than the rest of the fleet, plays his 'ith more finesse, handles his boat more effectively, knows his competition better, and has a sounder practice routine. His racing edge is a composite advantage, built from all the different phases of sailboat racing.

Ted Turner, champion yachtsmen and baseball owner

They that go down to the Sea in Ships, that do business in great waters, these see the works of the Lord, and His wonders in the deep.

Psalm 107

This crew has already mutinied once. Be careful.

Barry McKay to Dawn Riley, champion yachtswoman, about a boat she was taking over in midrace

When you look toward shore from miles out, you see what appears to be the skyline of a built-up city. But as you get closer, it is really ocean swells coming together, and the waves break right up into the air.

Michael Worrell, sailor

With these winds alone, and with the bounding seas which follow fast, the modern clipper, without auxiliary power, has accomplished a greater distance in a day than any seas steamer has ever been known to reach.

Matthew Fontaine Maury, oceanographer, who mapped wind patterns in 1853

Salaries

People always tell me to my face that I'm overpaid, but they're always drunk.

Brett Hull, National Hockey League player

Salary Cap

I think a lot of the NBA teams use the salary cap as an excuse. When a team wants to do something, it always seems able to do it.

Dennis Rodman, professional basketball player

Scalpers

I could sell drugs for a living because I'm a hustler. But why sell drugs and go to prison when I can sell tickets and make money?

Cleveland Chris, scalper

You get called a lot of things out here, a lot of cracks about your heritage and all that, but I just tell 'em, "Hey, buddy, I got the tickets and you don't."

Keylon, a scalper at Tennessee Vols games, as told to Tim Layden

Scoreboard Watching

You know you've come a long way when you look at the out-of-town scoreboards and there are no scores.

Wayne Gretzky, Hall of Fame hockey player, on looking at the scoreboard in the finals

Scoring

An average of twenty points in basketball is comparable to baseball's criterion for outstanding pitchers, whose immortality seems to be predicated on their winning twenty games a year.

John McFee, writer

There is no better tonic for an injured hockey player than scoring a goal.

Bobby Hull, Hall of Fame hockey player

This year we plan to run and shoot. Next year we hope to run and score.

Billy Tubbs, college basketball coach

Was Wayne Gretzky sick?

Larry Robinson, professional hockey player, upon the announcement he had won the National Hockey League Player of the Week Award

We had a game out in Denver and, oh, my God, Les Savage took 30 three–point shots . . . Not only was the other . . . team trying to block his shot, we were blocking it so we could touch the ball.

Steve Chubin, professional basketball player

When I was 12. The next year I got down to a plus three.

Jack Nicklaus, champion professional golfer, when asked after hip-replacement surgery when was the last time he had a handicap

The ball goes through the net, the team gets two points. A player hardly ever scores by himself.

Ervin "Magic" Johnson, Hall of Fame professional basketball player

Scouting

At the Asian games I saw more major league scouts than Asian scouts.

Acey Kohrogi, baseball executive

Half the time the scouts have their heads down making notes and don't even see which way the ball is hit.

Tom Greenwade, legendary professional baseball scout

Season (the)

Face it, people, this is the Black Hole on the sports calendar. The endless, meaningless hockey season trickles on, drawing slightly more attention than the endless, meaningless NBA season.

Jack Todd, sportswriter, referring to the time between the Super Bowl and baseball's spring training

The sports department usually goes into deep-sleep mode after the Super Bowl until pitchers and catchers report to their camps in Florida and Arizona. The minihibernation is disturbed only by the midseason plodding of the NBA and NHL, still months from their interminable playoffs.

Bill Conlin, sportswriter

In this season, I played on five continents, made 129 airplane trips, slept in 71 different beds and traveled 165,000 miles.

Arthur Ashe, Hall of Fame tennis champion and writer, from one Wimbledon to the next in 1975

Professional tennis has no real season, no linear progression from start to finish. Instead, the tour is cyclical and it leads to a condition rather than a destination.

Michael Mewshaw, writer

There isn't a single professional sports season now that doesn't go on at least a month too long. Baseball starts in football weather, and football in baseball weather, and basketball overlaps them both.

James Reston, writer

There's only one difference between a game in May and a game in September. You lose in September, there's less time to get it back.

Roberto Clemente, Hall of Fame baseball player

Second Place

I didn't come here to finish second. Rivalries are probably good for hype, and good for the sport. But nobody remembers who finishes second.

Pat Day, jockey

In this country, when you finish second, no one knows your name.

Frank McGuire, basketball coach

In this country, you either finish first or last, there is no second place.

Buddy Werner, writer

I was choked with tears . . . Was that it, the return for all the years of frenzied study, self-mastery, struggle, unyielding self-sacrifice? A silver disk on a colored ribbon?

Yuri Vlasov, Olympic weightlifter

When she didn't hug me on the podium, it was honest. She was just upset. And I can relate to that.

Katarina Witt, Olympic gold medalist figure skater, about Debbie Thomas, silver medalist

Secretariat

(foaled 1971; d. 1989) *Triple Crown winner— 1973; first since Citation in 1948; set track record at Belmont with 31-length Belmont Stakes win in a time of 2:24; took first 16 times; second three times; third once (finished fourth once—first race)*

He hasn't run, he hasn't worked, and he hasn't won, so he doesn't know why he's in the winner's circle.

Penny Cherney, owner of Secretariat, during his final farewell tour

I thought I was going to win, and win big. Then I see this thing coming up on the outside of me and it just went, whoosh. I couldn't believe it.

Laffit Pincay, Jr., jockey, about Secretariat, while he was aboard Sham in the Kentucky Derby

90% of the farm's visitors, even among clients who come to do business involving other horses, ask about Secretariat and want to have one look at the horse they can still remember seeing win the Belmont Stakes by 31 lengths.

Steve Crist, sportswriter

Sex

Fifty percent of life in the NBA is sex. The other fifty percent is money.

Dennis Rodman, professional basketball player

Going to bed with a woman never hurt a ballplayer. It's staying up all night looking for them that does you in.

Casey Stengel, baseball manager

I believe that skiing and sex have a special affinity.

Jean-Claude Killy, Olympic gold medalist skier

It has often occurred to me that sport, like sex, is an activity that should either be performed or watched—but not written about.

Paul Gardner, sportswriter

The other night someone asked Dr. Ruth what she thought about sex and sports. She said it was fine to make love the night before a game, because it releases tension. But you shouldn't do it with someone new, someone you've just met, because then you might stay up all night and end up exhausted!

Bob Gansler, professional soccer coach

There are a lot of weird relationships on the tour. A girl gets lonely or in the mood, and she meets a man and goes with him. But she can't be sure it's love. It may be the situation, the isolation of the circuit.

Andrea Temesvari, professional tennis player

The satisfaction of running downhill and the satisfaction of making love to someone I really care about are probably pretty similar . . . A lot of it is instinct. But to explain the physical sensations of downhill is really, you know, how do you explain sex to a virgin?

Shanny Shanholtzer, downhiller, U.S. ski team

Sheehan, George

(b. Nov. 11, 1918; d. Oct. 27, 1993) *Marathon runner; promoter; philosopher; best-selling author of* Running & Being

George's mind always outran us. More than anyone, he widened running's moral purpose, which was not to live longer but to live better, to have more energy and self-worth and clarify for all the more important things to do in life than run.

Robert Lipsyte, writer

The "guru" and "philosopher king" of running.

William Jefferson Clinton, president of the United States

Shoemaker, Willie

(b. Aug. 31, 1931) *Professional jockey; all-time wins record of 8,833; five-time Belmont Stakes winner; won Kentucky Derby four times and the Preakness twice*

He had such good hands. He was so easy on them, but they ran for the devil like him anyway. As small as he was, he could still make a big horse do whatever he pleased.

Charlie Whittingham, thoroughbred horse trainer

Ice water runs through his veins. He is never excited or bothered.

Eddie Arcaro, jockey

Shooting

And I left my gun
Forever standing in the hall.

Archibald Routledge, poet

I myself am not, and never will be, more than an ordinary shot.

Theodore Roosevelt, president of the United States, conservationist and outdoorsman

I've dreamed elaborate dreams about shooting, but that I would someday own a Purdey was not one of them. I had shot my Fox for thirty-four years, and while no love affair lasts that long without a crisis, after the restocking job we were closer than ever and I had intended to continue shooting it as long as the two of us lasted.

George Bird Evans, hunter, outdoorsman, and writer

Shooting friendships—probably residual from tribal hunting—are at their best when sharing the failures as well as the successes.

George Bird Evans, hunter,
outdoorsman, and writer

Some games Chinaglia took more shots than the entire opposing team.

Gerald Eskenazi, sportswriter, referring to
Giorgio Chinaglia, professional soccer player

Some of the three-pointers I took were bad shots . . . I was just trying to do too much. Instead of helping us, I was hurting us.

Allen Iverson, professional basketball player

The fascination of shooting as a sport depends almost wholly on whether you are at the right or wrong end of a gun.

P.G. Wodehouse, writer

We're shooting 100 percent—60 percent from the field and 40 percent from the free-throw line.

Norm Stewart, college basketball coach

Shor, Toots

(b. May 6, 1903; d. Jan. 23, 1977) *Restaurateur; saloon keeper; sportsman; raconteur; well-known friend of athletes, sportsmen, and entertainers*

Celebrating 40 years of Toots Shor is like celebrating a broken hip.

Red Smith, sportswriter

When I was a busher in Milwaukee, he was just as obnoxious to me as when I had world champions. He's a foul-weather friend, which is the worst kind.

Bill Veeck, baseball owner and racetrack operator

Showboating

I barely raise my arms when I score. I don't want people mad at me for making them look stupid. I don't want them looking for me.

Brett Hull, professional hockey player

Sifford, Charles

(b. June 2, 1922) *First African American to play on the PGA tour 1960; first African American to win a tour event; turned pro 1948; won two tour events (1967, 1969); won the 1975 PGA Seniors Championship*

I have always had a great deal of admiration for Charlie Sifford . . . he has made himself a symbol that has inspired young black golfers in this country and the world—past, present and future. Probably more than any other single individual, Charlie paved the way and made life in professional golf so much easier for others of his race who have followed and will follow him.

Arnold Palmer, champion professional golfer

The pain and suffering and sacrifice experienced by Mr. Sifford in being a lonely pioneer for black golfers on the PGA Tour will never be forgotten.

Tiger Woods, champion professional golfer

When any black man is making his mark in a sport or profession, black people are aware of it. Charlie stands out. He was . . . a hero to blacks.

Willie McCovey, professional baseball player

Simpson, O. J.

(b. July 9, 1947) *Hall of Fame football player; Heisman Trophy winner 1968; first to rush for more than 2,000 yards in a season; broadcaster; actor; accused of murdering his ex-wife, Nicole Simpson, and her friend Ron Goldman in 1994; acquitted in a criminal trial; lost civil suit*

The best of Jimmy Brown and Gale Sayers all rolled into one.
Art Hunter, professional football player

Skating

As soon as it's a woman's body, it's over. When they have lovely little figures like the girl on the street, they're probably too heavy. The older you get trying to do children's athletics, the thinner you must be.
Evy Scotvold, Olympic figure skating coach

Choreography is something very personal, and every individual skater should have some little trademark that separates him or her from the others.
Carlo Fassi, Olympic figure skating coach

Even now, people come up and say, "You should have won," and I'm like, "Come on, what competition were you watching?"
Debbie Thomas, Olympic silver medal figure skater

Good grief! What have we wrought the world? Oh my!
Dick Button, two-time Olympic gold medal figure skater and broadcaster, about Tara Lipinski, Olympic gold medalist

How do you expect to be taken seriously as a sport if you keep on having public relations blunders like this?
Jere Longman, sportswriter, to U.S. skating officials, they announced that Michael Weiss's

controversial quadruple toe loop was being withdrawn from the record books

I always felt a special connection with my audience. It's a bond I share with them that makes performing the thing I love the most.
Scott Hamilton, Olympic gold medal figure skater, broadcaster

I always say to them, "You never see a fat ballerina at the ballet."
Alex McGowan, Olympic figure skating coach

I have seen some Officers of the British Army, at Boston, and some of the Army at Cambridge, skait [sic] with perfect Elegence.
John Adams, president of the United States and patriot, in a letter to his son in 1780

I love to skate, skate, skate.
Rudy Galindo, champion figure skater

In my grief, I feared I had lost myself. To find myself again I did the only thing I could think of, the thing I knew best, the thing I'd been trained to do since I was four years old. I skated.
Ekaterina Gordeeva, champion pairs skater, referring to the death of her partner and husband, Sergei Grinkov

In skating, the thing that wins you the medal is your Long Program . . . You practice it until it is all you think throughout the day and then you dream of it all night. You practice until everything comes together naturally as breathing, and you hope you get it right when it counts.
Peggy Fleming, Olympic gold medalist, figure skating, broadcaster

I've never seen a little girl so determined to skate, with the ability to do it with so much sparkle and verve.

Oscar Holte, figure skating coach, about Sonja Henie

Jump every jump like it's the last in your life.

Alexi Mishin, legendary Russian figure skating coach

Kerrigan and Baiul staged a battle at the 1994 Olympic Games that defined the two central aspects of skating. Kerrigan's magnificent athleticism was matched against Baiul's timeless artistry . . . it was not political.

Christine Brennan, writer

Long before Tonya Harding and her associates crash-landed into the sport, women gunned for other women in practice sessions. They trashed their rivals—gossiping about nose jobs and stage mothers and bank accounts—for as long as there have been rivals to trash.

Christine Brennan, writer

Next thing you know, she'll make me kill someone on the ice.

Sergei Grinkov, Olympic gold medal–winning pairs skater, about his coach, who wanted him to "act" more on the ice

On the ice, my father was like a thoroughbred. I'm more like a train. I chug.

Brett Hull, professional hockey player, speaking of his father, Bobby Hull, Hall of Fame hockey player

Picking a winner in figure skating is more like choosing a sorority sister than crowning a sports champion.

Christine Brennan, writer

Seven minutes on the ice. Give or take a few seconds that's all a figure skater gets at the Olympic Games. After ten or fifteen years of training, after giving up school and families and any semblance of normalcy, it's all over in seven minutes.

Christine Brennan, writer

She went out there and flopped around like a dying walrus.

Evy Scotvold, Olympic figure skating coach

Skating is a sport and a form of artistic expression.

Carlo Fassi, Olympic figure skating coach

Skating was about flying, about feeling the wind in their faces, about interpreting beautiful music, about skimming across the frictionless ice below their feet.

Christine Brennan, writer

Skating was the only thing I did that really gave me confidence.

Tonya Harding, world champion skater, bizarre sports personality

The anonymity of our sport in the off-Olympic years virtually guarantees that Olympic experiences are all we have to deal with.

Dan Jansen, Olympic gold medal speed skater

The one thing I want to be able to do after it's all over is say, "That was my best." It's better to lose that way than to win with something less than that. But it's fun to win, isn't it?

Tenley Albright, Olympic gold medalist, figure skating

The skater must develop the ability to interpret the music with feeling. This will make the difference between a great champion and a mediocre skater.

> *Carlo Fassi, Olympic figure skating coach*

This is the corniest thing I've ever done.

> *Nancy Kerrigan, Olympic silver medal figure skater, during a parade in her honor at Disney World, for which she was a spokesperson*

This sport is so unforgiving. Finish second and all of a sudden you're a has-been.

> *Jurina Ribbens, ABC Sports, referring to international ice-skating competitions*

Two years ago people would say, "Gee, she really jumps." Now, people don't mention her jumps and spins anymore. They say, "That was gorgeous, that was beautiful."

> *Frank Carroll, figure skating coach, about Michelle Kwan*

Where first in my life, it being a great frost, did see people sliding with their skeetes [*sic*], which is a very pretty art.

> *Samuel Pepys, writer*

Why me? Why me?

> *Nancy Kerrigan, Olympic silver medal figure skater, after having her knee hit with a tire iron by friends of competitor Tonya Harding*

You can either skate to . . . music or you can express it.

> *Katerina Witt, Olympic gold medalist, figure skating*

You seduce with your fingers. Your body's worth twenty kopecks, but your fingers are worth gold.

> *Galina Zmievskaia, figure skating coach*

Skiing

Downhill is fast, sexy, perilous. Downhill racers go like hell from the top of the mountain to the bottom, sometimes at eighty miles an hour, frequently out of control.

> *Mike Wilson, writer*

Every time I launch myself off 120-meter ramp . . . I don't feel like I'm moving. I can't hear anything. I'm just flying.

> *Lindsey Van, ski jump champion*

I am going to kick your ass.

> *A. J. Kitt, champion downhiller, speaking to the mountains at Kitzbuhel*

I am often asked, was there not one special moment when I decided to be a ski racer. No, it was more that a series of experiences throughout my early life cast the mold for me. Ski racing had to become my world.

> *Jean-Claude Killy, Olympic gold medalist skier*

I'm standing in the slalom gates and I'm thinking of my classmates and some of them I know make twelve hundred dollars a month already and what am I doing here?

> *Spider Sabich, Olympic and professional skier, contemplating turning pro*

In a sport full of daredevils and smart-asses, Tomba was the most outrageous character. Off the snow, he was a notorious egomaniac and lecher . . . Even so, he was a genius on the hill, arguably the most powerful technical racer who ever lived.

> *Mike Wilson, writer*

It is unbecoming for a cardinal to ski *badly*.

> *Pope John Paul II, asked if he thought as a cardinal he should be skiing*

Just say no to slalom.

Tim LaMarche, coach, U.S. ski team

Of all the myriad dangers inherent in a journey by ski and dogsled across a frozen ocean, perhaps the most worrisome is the possibility of falling through the ice. During spring—the only period when this journey is feasible—the frozen surface of the sea is constantly shifting, cracking, opening up, and refreezing.

David Nolan, outdoor journalist

Racing is an art form . . . I'm not there to hear the crowd yelling or to achieve glory or to earn money. I'm there to ski a perfect race.

Jean-Claude Killy, Olympic gold medalist skier

Real expert skiing has been called "classic skiing." It's functional, not faddish.

Lito Tejaela-Flores, champion skier and instructor

Skiing combines outdoor fun with knocking down trees with your face.

Dave Barry, writer and humorist

Ski racing is unique. It is a dangerous, lonely sport, where each individual is racing against the clock and himself. It is a technical sport that demands precision and split-second reactions that are developed over years of training and constant practice; a ski racer can lose his timing after three weeks of being off his skis.

Peter Miller, writer

Ski wild and loose; ski over your head a bit.

Dick Duckworth, skiing coach, U.S. ski team

Speed hangs like an opium cloud over the start corral at a downhill.

Paul Hochman, writer

Summer vacations? Bah, humbug!

Herb Gordon, outdoorsman, skier, and writer

Telemark skiing was counter-cultural. It was a response to the alpine scene.

Paul Parker, telemark (or free heel) skier

That's all I've gotten this year—a bronze medal from an airline.

Steve Porino, downhiller, U.S. ski team

The American racer has never felt at home in Europe. There is a psychological barrier to crack, for he is competing in the opposition's front parlor. For some reason many Americans develop an inferiority complex when they cross the Atlantic.

Peter Miller, writer

The international race circuit is not all glamour and excitement. You might think this is what it's like for racers traveling from one glamorous resort to another. But ski racing for much of the time is hard work and drudgery.

Billy Kidd, Olympic silver medalist downhiller

The real fathers of the sport were not the men who made a few halfhearted experiments with skis and then abandoned the fickle boards in despair, but those who first proved by solid achievement the wonderful possibilities of the ski.

Arnold Lynn, telemark (or open heel) skier

There's nothing like flying down a mountain so fast that the run literally opens up before your eyes. I love to rock'n'roll right out of the gate.

Picabo Street, Olympic medalist skier

There was something very appealing about these American skiers. They wear Levi's and sleep in trucks and eat hamburgers, but they show up on the slopes with the best equipment they can buy. They'll join the ski patrol or wash dishes or do anything around a ski area that will keep them alive and let them go skiing because that is what they love to do.

Jean-Claude Killy, Olympic gold medalist skier

To me, skiing has always been more than just running gates. I wanted to do more on the snow than simply go fast.

Jean-Claude Killy, Olympic gold medalist skier

The mountain is skiing me, I'm not skiing the mountain.

Jeff Olsen, downhiller, U.S. ski team

We do everything to extremes. We work hard, we play hard, we train hard, and we ski hard.

Jeff Olsen, downhiller, U.S. ski team

When reduced to its basic elements, snow is piddling, uncomplicated stuff: water, dust, and air.

Peter Oliver, skier and writer

You haven't truly felt your heart ballooning in your throat until you've flown over a knife-edged mountain ridge in a helicopter . . . Imagine standing atop the world's tallest building and looking down to discern that the floor is gone. That's what it's like.

Peter Oliver, skier and writer

You need guts to run downhill and not everyone has it.

Karl Schranz, champion downhiller

Skill

Producing while making it look easy was the epitome of skill.

Spike Lee, writer, actor, director, basketball fan

Slumps

Hey, I went 0-for-24 once. And I turned out OK, didn't I?

Yogi Berra, Hall of Fame baseball player and manager

I never got down. I remained positive. I was swinging the bat well. It was bad luck here or there.

Nomar Garciaparra, professional baseball player, who broke out of a homerless slump with a three home run, 10 RBI night

The hardest part of any slump is looking up at the scoreboard and seeing your stats in huge numbers.

Jason Giambi, professional baseball player

Most slumps are like the common cold. They last two weeks no matter what you do.

Terry Kennedy, professional baseball player

Sneakers

Is it the shoes, Money? Is it the shoes?

Spike Lee, alias Mars Blackmon, to Michael Jordan, about the new Air Jordans

There is something about a new pair of sneakers that makes a boy feel he can run faster and jump higher.

Spike Lee, writer, actor, director

Snowboarding

Cliff jumps look spontaneous in videos and in movies. That's because all you usually see is the edited version of the film. You rarely get to see all the scouting and planning . . . or the terrifying crashes.

> *Matt Goodwill, champion snowboarder*

Just concentrate on being the board.

> *Master Fwap, Buddhist monk*

Last night's storm has blanketed the mountain in knee deep powder. Snow boarder's nirvana.

> *Jeff Bennett, snowboarder*

Skiing was too social for me; it lacked the pure intensity and grace of standing atop of a four-and-a-half-foot long fiberglass board while plummeting straight down mountains of snow.

> *Dr. Fredrick Lenz, snowboarder*

When you're riding fast on a flat base you're in *no-man's-land*—a place where either edge can take control without warning.

> *David Sher, snowboarding champion*

Snider, Duke

(b. Sep. 26, 1926) *Hall of Fame baseball player; known as "The Duke of Flatbush"; hit forty or more home runs five seasons consecutively; played in six World Series, won two*

A King of Kings, the Lord my God, the Duke himself.

> *Philip Roth, writer*

Soccer

Am I so round with you as you with me
That like a football you spurn thus?
You spurn me here and you spurn me hither;
If I last in this service you must case me in leather.

> *William Shakespeare,* Comedy of Errors

Chinaglia is one of those players who must have the ball. But when Pele is on your team you do not get the ball so often.

> *Gerald Eskenazi, sportswriter, about Giorgio Chinaglia and Pelé playing for the New York Cosmos*

Concerning football playing, I protest to you it may rather be called a friendly kind of fighting, than recreation. For, does not everyone lie in wait for his adversary, though it be on hard stones, in ditch or dale, or whatsoever place it may be he cares not, as long as it has him down.

> *Unknown, translated from Old English*

England has never exactly been an El Dorado for soccer players.

> *Paul Gardner, sportswriter*

Fifty million Brazilians await your victory!

> *Mayor of Rio de Janeiro, to the Brazilian national soccer team, which later lost to Uruguay*

Football is a suitable game for girls, but it is hardly suitable for delicate boys.

> *Oscar Wilde, humorist*

Football is my work, my life. I didn't cry because of second place, but because the referee had not the right to blow that penalty against us.

> *Diego Maradona, professional soccer player*

Football, it seemed to me, is not really played for the pleasure of kicking a ball about, but is a species of fighting.

George Orwell, writer

Football reflects the nationality, it mirrors the nation. Without football, we Brazilians do not exist—just as one would not conceive of Spain without the bullfight.

Betty Milan, writer

For as sundry complaints are made that several persons have received hurt by boys and young men playing football in the streets. . . .

notice posted by Boston town authorities in 1657

Gentlemen, if the Czechs play fair, we'll play fair. That's the most important thing. But if they want to play dirty, then we Italians must play dirtier.

Benito Mussolini, dictator

Good pay, good lodging, and a decent burial.

job listing in the United States for soccer referees in South America

I can teach things to players, things only I can do.

Diego Maradona, professional soccer player

I don't know how it can be done, General, but Italy must win the World Cup.

Benito Mussolini, dictator, to General Giorgio Vaccaro, president of the Italian Olympic Committee

If you're attacking, you don't get as tired as when you're chasing.

Kyle Rote, Jr., professional soccer player

I have been an avid football fan ever since my youth in Furth, a soccer-mad city in southern Germany. My father despaired of a son who preferred to stand for two hours—there were very few seats—watching a football game rather than go to the opera or visit a museum.

Henry Kissinger, secretary of state and author

In Latin America the border between soccer and politics is vague. There is a long list of governments that have fallen or been overthrown after the defeat of the national team.

Luis Suarez, journalist

It is an exciting experience to see young boys and even grown men . . . responding to the beauties of soccer.

Pelé, professional soccer player

It's a game of athleticism, a game of power and competition and strength. Anybody who thinks football is just a game of deftness of touch without those other things *wouldn't win.*

Bobby Robson, professional soccer manager

On the field, when you beat a player, you've always got to be looking for the next option.

Mia Hamm, champion soccer player

Other countries have their history. Uruguay has its football.

Ondino Viera, professional soccer manager

Soccer is not about justice. It's a drama—and criminally wrong decisions against you are part and parcel of that.

Pete Davies, writer

Soccer sells products all over the world. All this is due to my work.

Joao Havelange, Federation of International Football Associations executive, who brought in big-name sponsors and called them official partners and marketing sponsors

Some people say soccer's a matter of life or death, but it isn't. It's much more important than that.

> *Bill Shankly, professional soccer*
> *player and manager*

The Argentine team was not cowardly. It was not the penalty that caused our defeat . . . You can say that Argentina did not perform well, but do not say that it was afraid, because that would be slanderous.

> *El Grafico, Argentine magazine,*
> *about the World Cup loss to Uruguay*

"The Black Diamond" took his foot out of his shoe and kicked the ball with all his might to tie the game.

> *Diego Lucero, journalist, describing*
> *Leonidas Da Silva's famous*
> *"Stocking Goal," Brazil 6, Poland 5*

The culmination of a work of art. The most beautiful goal ever scored.

> *Andres Cantor, broadcaster, about Diego*
> *Maradona's second goal against England*
> *in 1986, generally considered as one of*
> *the all-time great goals*

The goal was scored a little bit by the hand of God, another bit by the head of Maradona.

> *Diego Maradona, professional soccer player,*
> *questioned after an illegal goal was*
> *allowed to stand*

The military right wing can be assured of at least five more years of peaceful rule.

> *Luis Suarez, journalist, referring to a Brazilian*
> *team that had won the World Cup*

The problem was a misunderstanding between our forwards and their defenders.

Their defenders weren't standing where our forwards had told them to.

> *Franz Beckenbauer, professional soccer*
> *player and manager*

The roots of our Soccer Tribe lie deep in our primeval past.

> *Desmond Morris, writer*

This is why I love soccer. Soccer is all about mistakes. I thought about my friendships on this team and I thought about the crowd.

> *Brandi Christain, soccer player, U.S. women's*
> *World Cup, referring to a miscue where she*
> *accidentally put the ball in her own net,*
> *but helped the team to overcome the*
> *mistake and win*

Today was just not a football match between two countries. This was one of the best matches ever played in my life.

> *Juergen Klinnsman, professional soccer player,*
> *after the West Germans beat the Netherlands*
> *2-1 in 1990 to win the World Cup*

To say these men paid their shillings to watch twenty-two hirelings kick a ball is merely to say that a violin is wood and catgut, that *Hamlet* is so much paper and ink.

> *J. B. Priestley, writer*

To the aesthete it is an art form, an athletic ballet. To the spiritually inclined it is a religion.

> *Paul Gardner, sportswriter*

Soccer is already the major sport of the rest of the world; it only remains for America to join the fray.

> *Rick Telander, sportswriter*

Soccer is like traditional jazz in that the players know the tune that is to be played, know there are an infinite number of varieties as to how to strike a note or chord—or a play.

Gordon Bradley and Clive Toye, writers

Unfortunately women's soccer still doesn't even have a chance in Brazil. The best woman player in Brazil will never be as popular as the worst male player, and the main reason is that women have been idolized as delicate objects of desire, incapable of playing a physical-contact, body-to-body sport.

Armondo Nogueira, broadcaster

Whenever the ball flew toward our goal and a score seemed inevitable, Jesus reached his foot out and cleared the ball.

Jornal dos Sports, Rio de Janeiro sports newspaper (one of the largest newspapers in South America), referring to a game between Brazil and England

While football has changed remarkably in terms of pace, competitiveness and anxiety for reward, it is still controlled on the field, where it matters most, from the ranks of the clerks and shopkeepers and foremen.

Arthur Hopcraft, writer, referring to the main occupation of referees

While soccer may have other hallowed matches—Barcelona–Real Madrid, Boca Juniors–River Plate in Buenos Aires, Roma–Lazio in Rome, Flamengo–Fluminese in Rio—none come close to matching Celtic–Rangers for a purity of hatred that involves politics, class and, above all, religion.

Grant Wahl, sportswriter

Women can now be doctors, lawyers, politicians—and even soccer players.

Mia Hamm, champion soccer player

You can tell the world, soccer has finally come to America.

Pelé (Edson Arantes do Nascimento), champion soccer player

Your mission is part of the confrontation between Iraq and the Forces of Evil embodied by the U.S. and its allies.

Al-Qadissiya, Iraqi newspaper, to the Iraqi national soccer team

Chelsea lose two-nil to Portsmouth, and you want to go home and bury an axe in your face.

M. John Harrison, novelist

Football is played at a series of levels, from Premiere League to where it's barely worth wearing a kit or marking out pitches. What separates serious professionals from those they leave behind—to scatter their dreams across council playing fields up and down the country—is not so much talent as a crucial difference in temperament.

Tim Pears, novelist

I set myself one goal when I started as national coach. That was winning the European championship. I failed, I have to take the consequences, and it's time now for a new coach.

Frank Rijkaard, coach of the Dutch national soccer team, resigning after the Dutch lost to the Italians in a shoot out 2-1, in the Euro 2000

It's a white world, soccer: the board members, the journalists, the referees. When I am in a stadium, I always look around the stands, and I hardly see black faces in them.

Humberto Tan, professional soccer player

These bouts of lunch-time football made going to work something to look forward to rather than dread. After playing, especially is the weather was fine, we were reluctant to return to the warehouse, and sat against the graffiti-mottled wall, the sun dazzling our eyes, gulping down water and chewing mouthfuls of bread and tomato, the minutes ticking by until, begrudgingly, like troops returning to the front, we tramped back . . . to work.

Geoff Dyer, writer

The spirit of soccer is no longer containable in the allotted ninety minutes.

Rob Hughes, sportswriter, after the Euro 2000 semifinals and final were all decided in overtime or shoot outs

The zigzags suddenly disappeared to reveal a cannonball of a football player burst out of a huddle of adversaries, to kick a blur of a football into a perfect arc that went between the outstretched arms of a vaulting goalkeeper and into the top right-hand corner of the net. And I couldn't help it. It rose up in a warm and intoxicating wave from my deepest inner recesses without my willing or understanding it.

Maureen Freely, columnist and novelist

Playing soccer is more fun than sitting around talking about soccer.

Vincenzo Sarno, 12-year-old Italian soccer prodigy on the set of CBS's Early Show

Speed
Act quickly, but never in a hurry.

John Wooden, champion college basketball coach

I never had the speed I used to have but I get the job done.

Tommy Heinrich, professional baseball player

The art of self-defense—100 yards in 10 seconds.

Hugh E. Keogh, sportswriter

The race isn't to the swift, but that is where to look.

Hugh E. Keogh, sportswriter

Speed makes him seven feet tall.

Eddie Robinson, college football coach, to George Young, football executive, about David Meggett, professional football player, after Young had commented that Meggett looked too small to play professional football

Team speed, team speed. Just give me some big c********* who can hit the ball out of the park.

Earl Weaver, professional baseball manager

Spending
There was nobody in the ballpark. And as soon as Mr. Piazza showed up, things picked up. You've got to put a nickel in to get a nickel out.

Nelson Doubleday, baseball owner, referring to Mike Piazza, professional baseball player

They need the money, baseball executives said . . . Those dreadful players have held them up so much that they must recoup their losses any way they can.

George Vecsey, sportswriter

Sports

A little over a century ago athletics was almost wholly a professional sport; some schoolboys and undergraduates competed as amateurs, while amateur oarsmen or gymnasts sporadically arranged diverting afternoons on the track.

Peter Lovesey, writer

A man described as a "sportsman" is generally a bookmaker who takes an actress to nightclubs.

Jimmy Cannon, sportswriter

Athletic competition clearly defines the unique power of our attitude.

Bart Starr, Hall of Fame football player

Athletics are all I care for. I sleep them, eat them, talk them, and I try my level best to do them as they should be done. You must feel that way.

Babe Didrickson Zaharias, champion golfer and Olympian track and field competitor

At three, four, five and even six years the childish nature will require sports; now is the time to get rid of self-will in him, punishing him, but not so as to disgrace him.

Plato, philosopher

Baseball is what we were. Football is what we have become.

Mary McGrory, journalist

Beyond the undeniable romance and sweet sentimentalities of fishing and wing shooting, beyond the elegance of fly rods and rising trout, the aesthetics of fine guns and noble gun dogs, beyond the esteemed history and venerable traditions of Sport, with a capital S, lies something that our spouses, especially if they themselves are non-hunters and non-fishpersons, have suspected all along: we're just great big kids.

Jim Fergus, outdoorsman, writer, and author

Every sport pretends to a literature, but people don't believe it of any other sport but their own.

Alistair Cooke, writer and historian

Football is easy if you're crazy as hell. Baseball is easy if you've got patience. They'd be easier for me if I was a little crazier—and a little more patient.

Bo Jackson, professional baseball and football player

Forget love and Esperanto: The only two international gauges are music and sports.

Steve Rushin, sportswriter

Games are the last resort of those who do not know how to idle.

Robert Lynd, writer

Games lubricate the body and the mind.

Benjamin Franklin, U.S. patriot and inventor

I am delighted to view any sport that may be safely engaged in.

Charles Dickens, novelist

I believe sport is a natural, wholesome, enjoyable form of human expression comparable to the arts.

Dr. Roger Bannister, champion runner and first man to run a mile in less than four minutes

If all the year were playing holidays,
To sport would be as tedious as to work.

William Shakespeare, playwright and poet

If you can keep your head when all about
   you
   Are losing theirs and blaming you;
If you can fill the unforgiving minute
   With sixty-seconds worth of distant run,
Yours is the earth and everything that's in it,
   And—which is more—you'll be a man,
   my son.

Rudyard Kipling, writer and poet

In defending athletics I would not for one moment be understood as excusing that perversion of athletics that would make it the end of life instead of merely a means in life.

Theodore Roosevelt, president of the United States, conservationist, and outdoorsman

In those days, a sportsman meant a rich man with a passion for hunting, fishing, and horse racing, a man who would shoot at the best lodges in the nation and fish distant waters for giant billfish, but who rarely knew about baseball, which was essentially a blue-collar sport.

David Halberstam, writer

I owe sport a great deal. Not only has it enabled me to earn a comfortable living; it helped me to grow up.

Grantland Rice, sportswriter

It is in games that men discover their paradise.

Robert Lynd, writer

I turn to the front pages of my newspaper to read about men's failures. I turn to the sports pages to read about their triumphs.

attributed to Oliver Wendell Holmes, U.S. Supreme Court justice, and to Tonto Coleman, executive of the Southeastern Conference

Literature and sports are not mutually exclusive, though at times one may despair of finding their common ground.

Garth Baptista, writer, publisher, and runner

Looking back, it would be *impossible* to overstate the impact of sports in my life.

Spike Lee, writer, actor, director

Observing team sports, teams of adult men, one sees how men are children in the most felicitous sense of the word.

Joyce Carol Oates, writer

Play is where life lives.

George Sheehan, runner and writer

Sports are too much with us. Late and soon, sitting and watching—mostly watching on television—we lay waste our powers of identification and enthusiasm and, in time, attention as more and more closing rallies and crucial putts and late field goals and final playoffs and sudden deaths and world records and world championships unreel themselves ceaselessly before our half-lidded eyes.

Roger Angell, writer

Sports and games have always been an inherent part of man's physical involvement in life. Play, properly perceived, is an essential element in life.

Barry C. Pelton, writer

Serious sports has nothing to do with fair play. It is bound up with hatred, jealousy, boastfulness, disregard of all rules and sadistic pleasure in witnessing violence: in other words it is war minus the shooting.

George Orwell, writer

Sports cut across racial, language, cultural, and national boundaries. It is what countries should use to compete instead of war.
Hakeem Olajuwon, professional basketball player

Sports gives us all the ability to test ourselves mentally, physically and emotionally in a way that no other aspect of life can.
Dan O'Brien, Olympic gold medalist decathlon competitor

Sport is a powerful tool that our society needs to understand better and utilize better.
Anita DeFrantz, Olympic silver medalist oarswoman

Sport is a right of the people.
Fidel Castro, president of Cuba

Sports do not build character. They reveal it.
Heywood Broun, writer

Sports has expanded the boundaries of bad behavior and violence.
Robert Lipsyte, writer

Sports is a lot of damn nonsense.
Harry S. Truman, president of the United States

Sports is human life in microcosm.
Howard Cosell, broadcaster

Sports is the toy department of human life.
Howard Cosell, broadcaster

The art of activity.
Sir Francis Bacon, artist

The essence of sports is that while you're doing it, nothing else matters, but after you stop, there is a place, generally not very important, where you would put it.
Dr. Roger Bannister, champion runner and first man to run a mile in less than four minutes

The lead-in drive, the fresh new feel of underfoot gravel going against the iron muscles of my legs.
Allan Sillitoe, writer and runner

The literature of athletics is rich in histories and technical manuals, but the historian of athletics is overwhelmed and embarrassed by the sheer mass of material on each branch of the sport.
Peter Lovesey, writer

There is no doubt that basic weekendmanship should contain some reference to Important Person Play.
Stephen Potter, writer

The rich soup that is the environment of the fan of team sports, with its franchises and divisions, its superstars and their agents, is very different from the sporting world occupied by the solitary angler on a woodland stream.
Thomas McGuane, writer

The sixties were a time for grunts or screams . . . The sports that fitted those times were football, hockey and mugging.
Bill Veeck, baseball owner and racetrack operator

The world of sports provides that first early test where a man meets obstacles and dangers and pressures. It is where a man begins to excel.
Arnold Hano, sportswriter

Those who seek to compete in sports do so because they have a specific need to be met. Somewhere there is a hole that needs to be filled; their involvement is a race, a game or match gives them an arena in which to seek their goal.

Scott Tinely, champion triathlete

We do not want our children to become a generation of spectators. Rather, we want each of them to become participants in the vigorous life.

John Fitzgerald Kennedy, president of the United States

When you're ten, eleven, and twelve, the most important lesson you can have in sports is to have fun.

Grant Hill, professional basketball player

Which game do I like better? I like baseball better in the spring. I like football better in the fall.

Bo Jackson, professional baseball and football player

Sportsmanship

Be strong in body, clean in mind, lofty in ideals.

Dr. James Naismith, inventor of basketball

Brutality and foul play should receive the same summary punishment given to a man who cheats at cards.

Theodore Roosevelt, president of the United States

For when the Great Scorer comes
   To write against your name,
He marks—not that you won or lost—
   But how you played the game.

Grantland Rice, sportswriter

Friendships born on the field of athletic strife are the real gold of competition. Awards become corroded, friends gather no dust.

Jesse Owens, Olympic champion, track and field

Good sportsmanship and reasonable standards of conduct are important.

Ted Turner, champion yachtsman and baseball owner

If you want to know the truth, I never liked the . . . players I butted helmets with. Not even when the game had ended.

Dick Butkus, National Football League Hall of Famer

In the ring, it was always for money; if you don't take him out, he'll take you out. But outside the ring I was always nice to everybody; it costs you nothing.

Jack Dempsey, world champion boxer

It's better to be a good person than to be good-looking or a good tennis player. Being a good person is for always.

Gabriella Sabatini, champion professional tennis player

It's how you get there, the work you do, the players you work with, how you live your life and help others to live theirs. Winning . . . winning isn't really that important to me.

Ted Newland, college water polo coach

I would like to be thought of as an athlete who enjoyed the sport, rather than any controversy he could create surrounding the sport. I would like people to feel I had done something to enhance not only myself, but the game itself.

John Havlicek, professional basketball player

One man practicing sportsmanship is better than a hundred teaching it.

Knute Rockne, college football coach

Sportsmanship should be the very mortar of an athlete but never an entity in itself for conscious display.

Grantland Rice, sportswriter

Take me to him. I want to shake his hand.

Jack Dempsey, champion boxer, temporarily blinded after being badly beaten by Gene Tunney

The tradition of professional baseball always has been free of chivalry. The rule is: "Do anything you can get away with."

Heywood Broun, sportswriter

Well, Ralph, it certainly is a pleasure to meet you. Now, my name is Cy Young. And these fellas over here are Zack Wheat and Ty Cobb.

Cy Young, Hall of Fame baseball player, to Ralph Terry, who unwittingly introduced himself as a major leaguer to three old men in the stands

What is really happening in American sports is that sportsmanship and fun and fair play have disappeared in favor of violence and winning and selfishness.

Maury Allen, sportswriter

You can't overestimate the importance of a high level of sportsmanship, because of the intensity and closeness of the players on the court. During a match you're at such a pace and your reaction time becomes so instinctive in your movement—if you do not maintain this high degree of sportsmanship, this character of the game, it just isn't going to be recognizable.

Charles Ufford, champion squash player

You just shake your head and tip your cap.

Ken Griffey, Jr., professional baseball player, remarking on watching opposing player Nomar Garciaparra hit three homers (two of which were grand slams) and chalk up 10 RBIs in one nine-inning game

Sportswriters

A dark day for sportswriters around the country indeed.

Tim Mowry, sled racer and sportswriter, about Brian Patrick O'Donoghue, a political writer, who finished ahead of the former in the Alaska Sled Race

All newspaper writers have heard that the stuff they compose today has an excellent chance of being used to wrap tomorrow's mackerel.

Ira Berkow, sportswriter

A writer sick—good, I hope they gave the son-of-a-bitch rat poison.

Lou Gehrig, Hall of Fame baseball player

The bias against sportswriting remains large, and any good sportswriter is usually dismissed as the world's tallest midget.

Frank Deford, sportswriter

Considering that most sportswriters I know are drunks, speed freaks, adulterers, hopeless chain smokers, or bad harmonizers (often all five if it's somebody I really want to hang out with), I find it amusing every spring when many of them turn lyrical as they sit down at their typing machines. Baseball does it.

Dan Jenkins, writer and best-selling author

Do you want to know the weirdest thing about being a sportswriter other than, of course, the requirement that you spend much of your time talking to naked men? The other weird thing is that you don't get to be a fan.

Mike Littwin, sportswriter

Give 'em your own story, 'cause if you don't, they're just gonna go ahead and make up their own, and what good'll that do ya?
Casey Stengel, Hall of Fame baseball player and manager, to Whitey Herzog, professional baseball player, executive, and manager

Good to meet you. A writer, huh? What paper you with, Ernie?
Yogi Berra, Hall of Fame baseball player and manager, to Ernest Hemingway, to whom he'd been introduced as an "important writer"

Go up and write a column and a side bar.
Woody Paige, sportswriter, to a woman who said she would do anything for $100

He knew the stars of the baseball team, and he was full of the inside dope, even if he did not always write it. He was also the source of tickets for big games, something of which senior editors were always aware.
David Halberstam, writer, referring to sportswriters in the 1940s

He treats fans with contempt and sportswriters even worse.
Murray Chass, sportswriter, on Graig Nettles, professional baseball player

Hey, you a nice fella. You a sportswriter?
Muhammad Ali, world champion boxer, to Tom Seaver, Hall of Fame baseball player, at dinner one night in New York

I can buy anyone of these sons-of-bitches for a five-dollar steak.
George Weiss, baseball executive

If I ever need a brain transplant, I want one from a sportswriter, because I'll know it's never been used.
Joe Paterno, college football coach

If I had my life to live over again, I'd have ended up a sportswriter.
Richard M. Nixon, president of the United States

If sports writing teaches you anything, and there is much truth to it as well as plenty of lies, it is that for your life to be worth anything you must sooner or later face the possibility of terrible, searing regret. Though you must also manage to avoid it or your life will be ruined.
Richard Ford, writer, from his novel
The Sportswriter

If you can't write the truth, you shouldn't write.
Jackie Robinson, Hall of Fame baseball player, to Dick Young, sportswriter

If you want someone to talk, talk, talk, you've come to the right person.
Thomas "Hollywood" Henderson, professional football player, to a sportswriter

I had a migraine the whole year. There weren't a lot of safe harbors. Your fellow staffers resented you, the players thought you were from Mars, and the wives hated you.
Lesley Visser, sportswriter and broadcaster, on being a pioneering female sports reporter

I never had any soaring ambition to be a sportswriter, per se. I wanted to be a newspaperman, and I came to realize I didn't really care which side of the paper I worked on.

Red Smith, sportswriter

I remember that last night in Yankee Stadium when Joe Louis knocked out Billy Conn in the eighth round of a fight that had been tautly dull, the way the slow hours are for reporters sitting on a stoop and waiting for a man to die.

Jimmy Cannon, sportswriter

It's amazing you still got jobs when you can't even write a sentence in English.

Toots Shor, restaurateur, to a group of sportswriters

It is the sportswriters' mission to bring the news from the field; they have more in common with war correspondents than they do with any other kind of writers.

Thomas McGuane, writer

It was like watching a friend of yours being run over by a trolley car, watching it coming and knowing what would happen but looking at it quietly, the curiosity dominating the horror and compelling you to be attentively silent. Maybe it was sudden but it was there all the time, the knockout inevitable and sure. It was there all the time like the rain in the night.

Jimmy Canon, sportswriter

I've just been a reporter.

A. J. McClane, outdoorsman and writer

I was not filled with social purpose. I didn't want to see sports as a "microcosm of real life." I wasn't zeroing in on myths to debunk or muck to rake. I just wanted to get out there and see what was going on and write better stories about it than anyone else.

Robert Lipsyte, writer

Long before I was allowed to eat fish with bones, could go all night without peeing in my bed, or understood *Gilligan's Island* wasn't real, I loved baseball. It's the reason I am a sportswriter.

Jennifer Briggs, sportswriter

Look, Mr. Knight, suppose I wrote three stinkers. I wouldn't have the rest of the week to recover.

Red Smith, sportswriter, to John S. Knight, publisher, refusing the offer to write three columns a week instead of six

Men of letters have always gravitated to sports. Witness yourselves.

A. Bartlet Giamatti, Major League Baseball commissioner, replying to a question as to why a learned man like himself would want to be commissioner of Major League Baseball, to a group of sportswriters

My readers never learned how to write, so I was entirely without contributions, and therefore hard up for material.

Ring Lardner, writer

Never look down at your notepad, or a player might think you're snagging a glimpse of his crotch.

Jennifer Briggs, sportswriter, recounting some of the wisdom passed on to her when she was a rookie sportswriter

Nothing on earth is more depressing than an old baseball writer.

Ring Lardner, writer

Nudity rarely bothered me, but I prefer never to see Nolan Ryan in anything but Ranger white or blue jeans. I have no idea why, except that Nolan Ryan and my daddy are my heroes, and I have no need of seeing either one of their white heinies.

Jennifer Briggs, sportswriter

On days when we're too tired to hunt or fish, play golf or go girl watching, we lie back in an easy chair with a scratch pad on our laps, doze, and stare at the ceiling. Occasionally we scribble down a few words for which our editors pay us incredible sums, and when our wives or children disturb our daydreams we run them the hell out and tell them we are working.

Ted Trueblood, outdoorsman,
editor, and writer

The only damn thing you have in your hand is a beer. You haven't written down a word I've said.

Lee Trevino, champion golfer, to a drunken
sportswriter who badgered him

Probably a professor of English.

Jimmy Cannon, sportswriter, after being told that
fellow sportswriter Gene Ward's house had been
burned down, due to arson

Shit-stirrers.

Roger Maris, professional baseball player

Somebody once wrote—another wise guy—that the only dumber thing than a grown-up playing a little kid's game is a grown-up writing about a grown-ups playing a little kid's games. Maybe there's truth in that. All I know is for twenty years I could never imagine doing anything else.

Mike Littwin, sportswriter

The British athletics press has this lazy, imperious attitude towards athletes. We run our guts out on the track, and if we've pleased them enough, we get a demand to attend the press box interview room, like a royal command. But if we don't say what they expect us to say, or we offend their sense of patriotism, then we're branded as arrogant.

Steve Ovett, champion runner

The so-called Golden Age of Sports, the twenties and early thirties, was really the Golden Age of Sportswriting. The Glories of the Babe, the Manassa Mauler, the Four Horsemen, were tunes composed on portable typewriters by gifted, ambitious, often cynical men who set customs and standards of sports journalism that are being dealt with to this day. . . .

Robert Lipsyte, writer

The most difficult aspect of dealing with sportswriters is their assumption of moral superiority. They insist on advising everyone.

Glenn Seaburg, University of Southern
California chancellor

The sportswriter whose horizons are no wider than the outfield fences is a bad sportswriter.

Red Smith, sportswriter

Sportswriting is assumed to be second-rate, and, therefore, if any sportswriting is not second-rate, then, ergo, it must not be sportswriting.

Frank DeFord, sportswriter

They'll tell they want a story about one thing and they'll get the quotes they want. But the story comes out a whole different way. They put your accurate quotes in there, but they change the context.

Maury Wills, professional baseball player, broadcaster, and manager

When they ask you a question, answer it and just keep going. That way they can't ask you another one.

Casey Stengel, Hall of Fame baseball player and manager

Why do I have to talk to these guys who make six thousand dollars a year when I make forty thousand dollars a year?

Yogi Berra, Hall of Fame baseball player, coach, and manager

You guys wouldn't like it if you had a box score on yourselves every day.

Casey Stengel, Hall of Fame baseball player and manager

You guys write this and say this about players, and criticize us, but half the time your information is wrong, and you're hypocrites, too. You guys drive drunk, do drugs, cheat on your wives. But you don't write about that.

Michael Irvin, professional football player

You wouldn't know a three step drop if it grew teeth, jumped up, and bit you in the ass!

Bill Parcells, professional football coach, to a sportswriter

Spouses

Ballplayer's wives live with some uncertainty now. Every time the plane comes back and all the wives go to meet it, some one says, "Oh my God, what if he isn't on the plane."

Margarita Valle, wife of Cuban national baseball player, about husbands defecting to the United States to play baseball

Bill James is a solitary genius in Westchester, Kansas. Well, not entirely solitary. He has, he says, a wife to neglect.

George Will, writer and baseball owner

I'm afraid for them, certainly. It's hard on any woman in a racing family. There's nothing we can do but wait and hope for the best.

Mrs. Elizabeth Petty, wife of Lee Petty and mother of Richard Petty

It's not a game. It's a lifestyle.

Beverlee Schnellenberger, wife of Howard Schnellenberger, college and professional football coach

Look at his eyes real good. There's a lot of sincerity and sweetness in those eyes. I don't know what I would have done without him.

Babe Didrickson Zaharias, professional golfer

That's the trouble. You can't get in the ring with them.

Norma Graziano, wife of Rocky Graziano, world champion boxer

When I played, wives caused as many problems among the players as anything else. They caused more trouble than the media ever could.

Maury Wills, professional baseball player, broadcaster, and manager

Spring Training

Spring training? They don't pay you for spring training!

Rickey Henderson, professional baseball player, when asked about his poor performance in spring training

The way to make coaches think you're in shape in the spring is to get a tan.

Whitey Ford, Hall of Fame baseball player

Squash

Jonathan Power is talented, eccentric, mouthy and wild. He could be the sporting world's next big-time rebel. Too bad he plays squash.

Bruce Grierson, writer

When most people think of squash—if they think of it at all—it's as a pastime enjoyed by toffee-nosed Ivy League seniors, captains of industry, TV psychiatrists. Or just dorks who spend the summers of their youth bouncing balls off the garage and never outgrew the fascination.

Bruce Grierson, writer

I encountered a series of mental hazards: a weakness for exotic, low-percentage shots; a vulnerability to distraction; a lack of patience in developing a point; a fondness for whaling away at ground strokes. I was in sum much more of a hot hitter than I was a cool thinker on the court.

Austin Francis, champion squash player

If you think squash is a competitive activity, try flower arrangement.

Alan Bennett, writer

I love this game. I played when I was a lad and rediscovered it at 41 when there was not enough time for golf and no sensible rationale for returning to rugby.

Sir Michael Edwardes, chairman
British Leyland PLC

It's hard to run around your backhand in squash.

Cal MacCracken, champion
squash player

Just play one point at a time. Forget everything else; just think about that one point. If you win that point, you move on to the next.

Roland Oddy, champion squash player

Played well, the international game of squash is more physically punishing than tennis and requires far more racquet skill than racquetball. It has all the bending and leaping of top-level badminton, the most aerobically taxing of all racquet sports.

Eliot Barry, sportswriter

Squash is a sport in which one's game constantly grows and evolves while utilizing all of the characteristics and abilities of the individual player. It's a game that can be likened to chess and boxing but has a three-dimensional element to it. It taxes the mind, body and character.

Victor Niederhoffer, champion squash player

Squash is my life.

Jahangir Khan, champion professional
squash player

The fitter player usually wins.

Eliot Barry, sportswriter

The game is getting tougher and rougher. With more money coming in, more incentive, more young guys are playing. The concept of the game as a gentleman's game . . . that's changing.

Sharif Khan, champion professional
squash player

When I first went on the squash courts, I couldn't believe how dangerous it was. I thought I was going to lose my head. . . .
Goldie Edwards, champion squash player and badminton player

Winning squash involves good decision making.
John O. Truby and John O. Truby, Jr., champion squash players

You can sum up the game of squash in one phrase. Move your legs fast and your racket slow.
George Cummings, legendary squash coach

Stadiums (and Arenas)
Ebbets Field was where one learned to duck a punch and get along with a lot of different people.
Tony LoBianco, actor

If you build it, he will come.
W. P. Kinsella, novelist, from Shoeless Joe

I've built the greatest tribute man ever paid to athlete's foot!
Jack Kent Cooke, owner, referring to the Los Angeles Forum

Some ballyard!
Babe Ruth, Hall of Fame baseball player, about Yankee Stadium

The Philadelphia Spectrum . . . has a basic griminess to it that is both inescapable and, in a strange way, charming.
John Feinstein, writer

There is no better place to play basketball than the Boston Garden. When you first walk onto the parquet floor, the moment is frozen in time. You're at the Garden, the place where championships were won.
Bill Walton, college and professional basketball player and broadcaster

The stadium . . . has only limited parking for those foolhardy motorists who enter the traffic caused by 200,000 spectators.
Janet Lever, sociologist, referring to Maracana, the world's largest stadium, in Brazil, which holds 220,000 at capacity

Stanley Cup
Every player who is sitting here who lifted up the Cup the first time will tell you the same thing. There's no feeling like lifting up that Stanley Cup.
Wayne Gretzky, Hall of Fame hockey player

The moment we won it, I felt awesome; it was thrilling, but it didn't give me as much joy as spending time with my daughter. We found the Stanley Cup didn't change our lives.
Steve Yzerman, professional hockey player

Statistics
Baseball fans love numbers. They love to swirl them around their mouths like Bordeaux wine.
Pat Conroy, writer

Do you want the statistics or the facts?
Mark Twain, writer

Every time I hear a ballplayer tell me, "Statistics are for losers," or the other maxim: "The only statistic that matters is win or lose," I wonder why everyone crowds around the bulletin board when the league stats are posted.

John Thorn, writer

The box score, being modestly arcane, is a matter of intense indifference, if not irritation, to the non-fan. To the baseball bitten, it is not only informative, pictorial, and gossipy but lovely in aesthetic structure. It represents happenstance and physical flight exactly translated into figures and history.

Roger Angell, writer

I gotta tell you I lost my scorecard and I'm trying to read McCarver's, but he's got the worst penmanship I've ever seen.

Richie Ashburn, broadcaster, during a baseball broadcast with Tim McCarver

Statistics always remind me of the fellow who drowned in a river whose average depth was only three feet.

Woody Hayes, Hall of Fame college football coach

Up to five goals is journalism. After that, it become statistics.

attributed by Pete Davies to a French journalist, at a match won by Sweden over Cuba, 8-0

What do you want, a higher average for me personally or value to the team? Every day, every at-bat, I do what's good for the team, I move runners around, and I knock runners in. But if you want batting average I'll give it to you next year.

Tommy Heinrich, professional baseball player, negotiating with management

When I was six, my father gave me a bright red scorebook that opened my heart to the game of baseball . . . Night after night he taught me the odd collection of symbols, numbers, and letters that enable a baseball lover to record every action of the game.

Doris Kearns Goodwin, writer and historian

You could look it up.

Casey Stegel, Hall of Fame baseball player and manager

You watch them all year and you say they aren't contributing that much to the team. Then they show you a lot of impressive statistics. They put you to sleep with statistics that don't win games.

Branch Rickey, baseball executive

If you really want to enjoy the game and understand it, you've got to score it.

Warner Fuselle, broadcaster, about scoring a baseball game

No other American sport has anything that genuinely approximates the scorecard—that single piece of paper, simple enough for a child—that preserves the game both chronologically and in toto with almost no significant loss of detail.

Thomas Boswell, sportswriter, on scoring a baseball game

Writing their names in a scorecard made them real to me; recording their exploits made them heroes.

Pat Edelson, sportswriter, on scoring a baseball game

Stealing (bases)

All of you guys, when you get into the locker room I want you to check your lockers. He stole everything out there he wanted today so he might have stole your jockstraps as well.

Casey Stengel, Hall of Fame baseball player and manager, to his team, the New York Yankees, after Jackie Robinson had stolen two bases in an exhibition game

I think that aggressive is an individual thing. You take a lot of pounding, you have to want to be a base stealer, you have to want to be the one to go out there and take that pounding. It's individual, it's not required.

Rickey Henderson, professional baseball player

Steeplechase

The horses treat the timber with the greatest respect and know clearly from experience that one mistake will be too many . . . The fences do not "give" an inch.

Dick Francis, champion jockey and novelist

There is no real equivalent in the United States to our Grand National, but the Maryland Hunt Cup is the most important social event in steeplechasing all year.

Dick Francis, champion jockey and novelist

Steroids

I knew it was all over for me. Every system in my body was shot, my testicles had shrunk to the size of peanuts. It was only a question of which organ was going to explode on me first.

Steve Michalik, world champion bodybuilder

Stickball

Nowadays, the automobiles, parked bumper to bumper, stifle the city boys' development, but in the late 1930s cars were a luxury and parking spaces were plentiful. If a man threatened to park in our stickball field—the distance between three manhole covers—we would say, "Would you mind moving down the street, Mister?" There was a kid named Lefty . . . who could ask that question with exactly the right balance between threat and appeal.

Dick Miles, U.S. tabletop tennis champion

Strikeouts

You mean I traveled 2,500 miles just to do this?

Mickey Mantle, Hall of Fame baseball player, after striking out in his one time at bat in an All-Star Game

Strikes (labor)

I look back on what I did as a contribution. I look back on what I did and realized that I derived a personal gain, too. I receive a pension from Major League Baseball.

Curt Flood, professional baseball player, and first to file for free agency

the game, and when it's there, I'm
.. if the players and owners want to ruin
it for themselves, let them do it.
*Fred Klein, New York Knicks fan, referring to
the 1998–1999 National Basketball
Association strike*

Buck Williams does it all: takes the kids to
school, washes the dishes.
headline from the New York Times *during
the 1998–1999 National Basketball
Association strike*

Success

At a certain level, success is determined by
mental factors, by dedication and motivation,
and these things can't be faked. You either
really care, or you don't. You're either happy
or your not.
*Arnold Schwarzenegger, champion
bodybuilder and actor*

I envied those who in success clung to a
measure of peace and tranquillity—I was
always too restless and life was a constant battle against boredom.
Sir Edmund Hillary, mountain climber

Ingenuity, plus courage, plus work, equals
miracles.
Bob Richards, pole vaulter

It's harder to stay on top than it is to get there.
*Don Shula, Hall of Fame professional
football coach*

It's important to set goals and work hard—
no matter how many people tell you it's useless or that you won't succeed. Without
determination, your dreams of a better life
won't come true.
*Jackie Joyner-Kersee, Olympic gold
medalist track and field competitor*

I watched the first Ali–Frazier fight in prison.
And I promoted the third one.
Don King, boxing promoter

I've had enormous success, but you have to
find your own happiness and peace. You can't
find it in other things and other people. I'm
still searching.
Chris Evert, champion tennis player

Success and failure cannot always be
judged . . . All a man can do is walk straight
and upright and believe that if behind him
things don't look so good, around the corner
they must be eye-popping wonderful.
Chuck Knox, professional football coach

Success is like surfing; you're doing what you
can to stay on the board, but you really aren't
in control of anything.
Kirk Shelmerdine, car racing crew chief

Success is not the result of spontaneous com-
bustion. You must set yourself on fire.
Fred Shero, professional hockey coach

Success is the result of the application of sci-
entific methods of training to the development of natural talents or skill, which we all
possess in some degree or another.
Walter Goodall George, champion runner

Sweat plus sacrifice equals success.
Charles O. Finley, Major League Baseball owner

That's really the biggest price you pay. Time
and privacy are luxuries that money can't
buy me now. In the back of my mind I
thought I could handle things becoming this
big, but I didn't really envision this whole
trip.
Billie Jean King, champion tennis player

The difference between a successful person and others is not a lack of strength, not a lack of knowledge, but rather a lack of will.

Vince Lombardi, professional football player and coach

The pole is slippery from top to bottom. I ought to know. I've been up and down it a few times.

Charlie Whittingham, thoroughbred horse trainer

To succeed in anything at all one should go understandingly about his work and be prepared for every emergency.

Joshua Slocum, sailor, first modern sailor to sail around the world alone

Whatever your goal in life, be proud of every day that you are able to work in that direction.

Chris Evert, champion tennis player

When we look at it, we look at him as still a great player but when he looks at himself, he looks at the time when he was totally dominating the game.

Jaromir Jagr, professional hockey player, about Wayne Gretzky

Willie Mays was my boyhood hero, but not because he was a great baseball player. Because he had a big house.

O.J. Simpson, Hall of Fame football player

You build a successful life a day at a time.

Lou Holtz, professional and college football coach

You can win and still not succeed, still not achieve what you should. And you can lose without really failing at all.

Bobby Knight, basketball coach

Super Bowl

It means $7,500 bucks, which in the whole scheme of life doesn't mean very much. In the final analysis, we're all going to wake up in the morning and be who we are and go where we go.

Alan Page, professional football player and state supreme court justice

Superstars

After scoring touchdowns and dancing in the end zone, after a stadium full of cheering fans had finally gone home, I was still empty inside.

Dion Sanders, professional baseball and football player

Anyone who thinks it's glamorous ought to go out and get the hell beat out of him like I do every Sunday, and then he'll see how glamorous it is.

Alex Karras, Hall of Fame football player

Fans wanted to rip his jersey right off of him. He wasn't a basketball player, he was a rock star.

Orlando Woolridge, professional basketball player, about Michael Jordan

He sits on the bench as if he were a teenager forced to attend an opera.

Bill Libby, sportswriter, referring to Hot Rod Hundley, professional basketball player

Hey, you're somebody too, right?

A fan, while asking Joe DiMaggio for his autograph, to Ernest Hemingway, who was with the sports star. Hemingway replied, "Yeah, I'm his doctor."

I Can't Wait Until Tomorrow 'Cause I Get Better Looking Every Day
> Joe Namath, Hall of Fame football player, the title of his autobiography written with Dick Schaap

If you accept the modern philosophy that there must be a ruthless and selfish motivation to succeed in sport then it could be justly claimed that Tenzing and I were the closest approximations we had on our expedition to the climbing Prima Donnas of today.
> *Sir Edmund Hillary, mountain climber*

In Seattle, they'll tell you Ken Griffey Jr. demands constant attention. He needs to be appreciated, loved, respected, stroked and sweet-talked. If that's the case, he has come to the right place.
> *Bill Koch, sportswriter*

It's incredibly tough on a rookie making $5 million to $7 million. Most of them are coming from families who have never had that type of money, and they can't go ask a successful uncle, "What would you do?"
> *Doc Rivers, National Basketball Association player*

I was never caught up in being a "superstar" because, for me, basketball is all about winning. It has never interested me who got the job done as long as it got done, even if it's not me.
> *Ervin "Magic" Johnson, Hall of Fame basketball player*

It wasn't unusual for me to run by the bench during a game and yell at Coach Wooden as I moved up court, "Get me some rebounders in here." I wanted to win. I was a bit overbearing at times.
> *Bill Walton, college and professional basketball player and broadcaster*

I used to say "I want to be like Mike," but now that I've had a taste of it, I think I'll pass.
> *Cynthia Cooper, Women's National Basketball Association player*

I want you to go out there; I want you to shine up my car. I'm gonna put on a show tonight, and I'm gonna have somebody ridin' home with me.
> *Attributed to Marvin Barnes by Steve Jones, professional basketball players. Barnes was supposed to have said this to the ball boys as he came into the sports complex.*

I wonder how many kids have made it in life—I mean really got to the top—because some son of a bitch made fun of their daddy?
> *A. J. Foyt, champion race car driver*

So famous is the bald pate that it is shaved by contractual agreement with Bic razors. And a particular shiver must have gone through is cranium as he got his customary prematch peck from Laurent Blanc. The defender had said that this would be his international farewell and—whatever the state of play in his on-off romance with Linda Evangelista—Barthez must find it hard to imagine being kissed by another man.
> *Jon Brodkin, sportswriter, about the famous French goalie Fabien Barthez*

The plan for my life had worked, I had it all—fame, money, cars, NFL stardom. The thinking had always been that everything I went through was going to be worth it if I ever made it this far. But when I finally got there, you know what I thought? I thought: "It wasn't worth it."
> *Kerry Collins, professional football player*

The players are richer, the arenas are nicer and the telecasts are better, but the financial and ideological divide has grown.

Harvey Araton, sportswriter

There's not one guy who is bigger than the game.

Wayne Gretzky, Hall of Fame hockey player

This team, it all flows from me. I've got to keep it going. I'm the straw that stirs the drink.

Reggie Jackson, Hall of Fame baseball player

The Kobe Bryants, the Michael Finleys, the Kevin Garnetts and the Shaquille O'Neals are Internet savvy with many of them owning their own websites. . . . Talk all you want about tattoos and corn rows, the real substance of this new group of players will come with their ability to market themselves digitally.

George Willis, sportswriter

This 30-year-old with the backwards hat, 398 homers, the center-field play of Willie Mays and the pizzazz of Tiger Woods has moved from the back of the stage to the center of the proscenium. And we the audience now get to watch him in the bright lights.

Rick Telander, sportswriter, referring to Ken Griffey, All-Star professional baseball player

Throw Me the Damn Ball!
Keyshawn Johnson, professional football player, the title of the controversial receiver's autobiography

When Sinatra settled onto a stool and took a mike, all the other singers sat down and shut

up. When Mark McGwire takes BP, even the strongest of the bombardiers put down their lumber and watch. And when Tiger Woods plunges a tee into a manicured greensward, coils and cocks—well, this is how you know it is a moment for the ages: Michael Jordan gets goose bumps.

Bill Lyon, sportswriter

Who's Bruce Springsteen?

Larry Bird, Hall of Fame player and coach

You know, they all want me to continue being the great mountain climber, in good condition and pursuing great adventures; yet they also want me to be sitting in their offices, cutting films or writing articles and books.

Reinhold Messner, mountain climber

Superstition

I am not a very superstitious person. I don't go in for rabbit feet or garlic cloves or lucky pennies or any of that. To me, luck is work, preparation, ability, attitude, confidence, skill.

Dennis Conner, businessman and champion yachtsman

Surfing

All right, so the waves are shitty, so why don't we just settle this thing with an arm wrestling match.

Keith Malloy, surfer, to competitors at the Body Glove Surfbout XII at Lowers

Alone on a board, speeding over a wave at fifteen or twenty miles an hour, the surfer experiences an ecstatic communication with natural forces, a delicious isolation, and total freedom from the anxieties and mundane cares of the workaday world.

Peter L. Dixon, surfer and writer

As I paddled I thought, "If I blow this I'll probably drown and no one will know." I only looked over my shoulder once, just to make sure it wasn't going to explode on my head, then it picked me up and sucked me into its vortex, and suddenly I'm flying down the face . . . It sucked me up into it about three times, totally in control of my destiny, then it just blew me apart and spat me out into the channel.

Jeff Hakman, surfer

Backdoor is my dream wave. I mean, I know a lot of magazines have talked about me and my surfer at Backdoor. I truly feel I could close my eyes and surf that place.

Dane Kealoha, surfer

Because of my knee, I had to avoid the lip for almost two years. In retrospect, that was the best thing ever for my surfing, because I learned how to use the entire wave and concentrate on carving.

Garth Dickenson, surfer

Even though it was a strictly female contest, the beach was filled with little boy groupies dying to meet one of the competitors. It was nice to see the roles reversed.

Daize Shane, surfer

Focus on your surfing. Too many kids nowadays are focusing on how many sponsors they have and what they're getting. I think they forgot about the main thing, which is surfing.

Conan Hayes, surfer

For the longboard contingent on the North Shore, winter means many different things. For the younger generation, it's a hurdle representing a time to deal with the fears that keep them up at night, haunt them on the playground, or disrupt their doodling waves on homework assignments. For those who've cleared this barrier, winter offers a chance to prove themselves further, and to demonstrate that they have what it takes to assume a place in the big-league lineup.

Jimmy Barros, writer and surfer

His ability to change his body shape in the deepest of barrels is masterful.

Wayne Lynch, surfer, referring to
Chris Ward, surfer

I did win more money than Kelly Slater last year, so I guess that says something about the state of women's surfing. Even though the sponsorship side of the sport is where the real money is, and the men's side still dominates the competitive arena . . . There are more companies out there today focusing on women's needs, which means there's a lot more opportunities for the girls who are marketable.

Layne Beachley, champion surfer

If I set my goal on being world champion, I'll go all out, but right now I'm going on trips because it's more fun.

Chris Ward, surfer, referring to being a writer in the meantime

If you asked him when he was twelve what he wanted to be, he would always say world champ. He doesn't say that now because he's getting closer to the real thing.

David Pu'u, surfer, about
Bobby Martinez, surfer

I get to travel so much and surf with all the really good guys—it's humbling.

Saxon Boucher, surfer

I grew up in California during the pre-Curren era. And for that reason all of my early surf heroes were Australian . . . untouchable idols living, or so I thought, in a dreamworld full of clearwater right pointbreaks and topless girls on the beach.

Chris Mauro, writer and surfer

I learned more in a few weeks in Hawaii than all the time I'd been surfing on the East Coast.

Dick Catri, champion surfer

I like single fins because they force you to concentrate on your style. They slow you down a bit, but I like that coming from a longboard.

Joel Tudor, surfer

I love the adrenaline of surfing, enjoy what I do, and have a common bond with other surfers of all ages in that we love to surf.

Herbie Fletcher, surfer

I'm always looking for something new day to day, whether it's surfing or just life in general. Style isn't always something you see on the cover of a magazine; sometimes it's a picture you paint in your head.

Kanoe Uemura, surfer

I take my children surfing every chance I have when I am home, and like all parents, I would like to be reassured that the water they are surfing in, or on any coast, is safe.

Brian Bilbray, U.S. representative, who sponsored HR 999 Beach Bill proposing clean water statutes and penalties

It's ten feet and SMOKING. None of this tiny Backdoor crap; full-on Pipeline, belching rage and fury . . . somehow this has become a huge pivotal moment.

Nick Carroll, writer and surfer

It was sometime in my second summer that one of these Prussian blue dream walls swept in out of Santa Monica Bay and caught everybody off guard except for me, and as the section between First Point and Second pitched over, cutting short some hotdogger's slide, I stroked down the face and felt the inertial transference and hitched onto that sweet gravitational slide.

Drew Kampion, writer and surfer

Kelly Slater, the greatest surfer of all time . . . First, he's in complete domination of the Bonzai Pipeline . . . Next, he has the continual desire to prove he's better than you.

Steve Zeldin, writer and surfer

Like an unwelcome houseguest who won't go away, La Niña's ball-numbing waters are expected to stick around till the end of July, affecting both swells and temperatures this summer.

Blair Mathieson, writer and surfer

Mate, me fire's rekindled, I just spent three months in Hawaii and I've never felt better. Whatever you do, don't ever turn your back on surfing. That was the biggest mistake of my life.

Wayne Lynch, champion surfer, after giving up surfing for many years

More than any other top pro since Mitch Thornson, Pipe master Jake Peterson is the embodiment of all the dust, flies, hazardous sealife and ass-kicking conditions that make up the rugged West Australian coastline.

Steve Barilotti, writer and surfer

Style is the result of confidence in your ability and your equipment, it shows in the water.

Duane De Soto, surfer

Thirty years ago, the shortboard revolution spread like the Melissa virus through the surf world. Almost overnight, surfers cut a few feet off of their lumbering 10' 0"s with the hope of surfing like one of those power-turning Aussies.

Chris Mauro, writer and surfer

To me, a bodyboard is something you'd use to slide a dead body into a bag.

Tim Mowery, inventor, created what he insists on calling "Boogie Boards"

Very early in his rise through the amateur ranks, Taj eclipsed most juniors in Australian surfing history as the "chosen one."

Derek Hynd, writer and surfer

Watermen just know the surf and pass it on.

Rabbit Kekai, surfer

We've all had that feeling. We've all paddled out and felt the ocean draw away all our fears and cares, and felt some primitive child spirit rise back to the surface of our beings, some animal beautiful infancy, something most people stop feeling somewhere around the age of twelve and never feel again their whole godforsaken legitimized lives.

Nick Carroll, writer and surfer

When I get depressed I go surf, come in and I'm refreshed.

Rabbit Kekai, surfer

While Cape Canaveral is world famous for its procession of high-flying astronauts, only the surfing population is aware of the astronomical number of champions and incredibly gifted riders launched from this tiny corner of the planet over the last 35 years.

Peter Interland, writer and surfer

While studying Buddhism, I learned to appreciate surfing for what it really is. It's totally humbling. I might get a 10-second tube and do the best cutback in the world, but without the ocean and the earth, I'm just an idiot.

Garth Dickenson, surfer

You need to surf more.

Todd Chesser, surfer, to his mother, Jeanine Chesser, on days when she was uptight

Yup, Briley's back. Put that on the cover with exclamation points.

Shawn Briley, surfer, after taking a year off, to Surfer *magazine, which actually followed his suggestion*

Sweat

Sweat is the cologne of accomplishment.

Heywood Hale Broun, sportswriter

Swimming

Apart from the Olympics, a swimmer finds it difficult to achieve any fame at all.

Daniel F. Chambliss, swimming coach and writer

A swimmer knows that magical blend of water and being and moment not once but every time he slips through the membrane from air to liquid—his skin wet and cool, his mind and body suspended, the water pressing against his palms and churning as his feet rise and fall.

Harvey S. Wiener, writer and swimmer

Everyone bad raps the big program, but swimming in the same lane with a world record holder or a world champion made it so much easier for them to accept that they could be like that.

Michael Schubert, U.S. Olympic swimming coach

My training was constant. I would start in the summer, just swimming, maybe going 2,000 yards, then continually building up so that by the end of September I would enter a schedule that was pretty substantial. At that point I was doing 10,000 yards in one workout, which took between two and two-and-a-half hours.

Mark Spitz, Olympic gold medal swimmer

Now I will you to be a bold swimmer. . . .

Walt Whitman, poet

Swimming is essential. It should be as basic to a child's education as learning the ABCs.

Mark Spitz, Olympic gold medal swimmer

There is a complex citizenship to the natural world we are part of when we swim. We have no special human powers, no superior dis-

pensation, then. In its mystery, its profound and changeable reverberations in both the memory and the mind, swimming is a decathlon all by itself.

The New York Times

This is swimming, not turns.

Mark Spitz, Olympic gold medal swimmer, remarking on the difference between indoor- and outdoor-length pools

Which is the ideal sport, the one that's least distressful physically, that uses all the most important muscles vigorously and without strain, and that is just all-around best for you? Swimming is the best exercise.

Harvey S. Weiner, writer

Racing . . . is an exercise in self-discovery. My final time interests me less than the broader revelation of how well my training has prepared me to race on this particular day.

Terry Laughlin, swimmer and swimming coach, editor, and writer

Stroke mechanics play the largest single role in creating a satisfying swimming career.

Mark Schubert, swimming coach and writer

Swimming is the closest thing on this earth to the perfect sport.

Jane Katz, Olympic synchronized swimmer and writer

T

Table Tennis

If you say ping-pong a few times with your eyes closed, you will realize how appropriately, poetically and musically the name describes the game. You can almost hear ping-pong being played.

Ding Shu De, Zhu Qing Zuo,
Chinese national Ping-Pong players

There was a table tennis parlor in the neighborhood, Manhattan's Upper West Side, and I passed it every day when returning from school. One day I courageously entered and saw that my idea of the game—to outlast your opponent in a monotonous duel of close-to-the-table pings and pongs—was completely wrong. Here, grown men and boys my own age played the game with drives and long-range retrieves and made it really look like a sport.

Dick Miles, U.S. table tennis champion

Once giggling young ladies and un-athletic youths tentatively patted a little white ball across the net in a parlor game called Ping-Pong. Today, superfit athletes, coached and trained to a peak, their bodies subjected to special diets and intensive exercises, blast the ball towards opponents at speeds of over 100 m.p.h. and with such violence that the ball has been known to disintegrate.

Chester Barnes, champion table tennis player

Talent

Character will only take you so far. You've got to have talent.

Karl Malone, professional basketball player

Talent is more than hitting the ball and moving well. I'm sick of hearing about guys who had the greatest strokes in the world, could have been champions if they'd felt like it. Feeling like it, even when you don't feel like it—that's talent.

Nikki Pilic, professional tennis player and
German Davis Cup captain

What did it mean for Aaron or Matthews to hit their .350 or their forty homers? Anybody with ability can play in the big leagues.

To last as long as I did with the skills I had, with the numbers I produced, was a triumph of the human spirit.

Bob Uecker, professional baseball player and broadcaster

You wonder why teams lose? That's a perfect example, if they can't recognize talent like that.

Fran Tarkington, professional football player, about Amad Rashad, who had been passed up in the draft by three losing franchises

Talk Radio

Talk radio, Philly style. Flak jacket required.

Mike Freeman, New York Times writer, on toughness of Philadelphia fans on local professional athletes

Tanking

I've got to get out of here tomorrow. I've got a flight booked, so I'm tanking and getting out of here.

Alex Antonitsch, professional tennis player, to Glenn Laydendecker, professional tennis player

Tanking—giving up, quitting, just going through the motions—when playing a tournament is a rotten thing to do.

John Feinstein, writer

Team

Ask not what your teammates can do for you.
Ask what you can do for your teammates.

Ervin "Magic" Johnson, Hall of Fame basketball player

A team is as skittish as a herd of animals—like gazelles—and a wrong word or decision can rile them up so they never can really be set straight again.

George Plimpton, writer

I don't like it when everyone wants to interview me and no one pays attention to my teammates. Without them, I'd be nothing. This is a team game, and I'm just one of the guys on the team.

Bill Walton, Hall of Fame basketball player

I don't plan on having any of these guys as friends when I'm finished here.

Bill Laimbeer, professional basketball player, about his teammates as well as his opponents

If I had my druthers, I'd rather have five guys in double figures than two guys averaging 20.

Jim O'Brien, college basketball coach

Individual commitment to a group effort, gentlemen, that's what makes a team work, a company work, a society work, a civilization work.

Vince Lombardi, Hall of Fame football coach

I wanted to lead this crew gently, by example, until this group of twelve women . . . could come together and become a team. After the meeting, I realized we don't have the luxury of waiting for this to happen.

Dawn Riley, yachtswoman

Once a player becomes bigger than the team, you no longer have a team.

Red Auerbach, Hall of Fame basketball coach and executive

Playing time is a problem now. Guys are bitching about their minutes, and if we don't get it straightened out, we can forget about winning anything.

Larry Bird, Hall of Fame basketball player and coach

Teamwork is the essence of life.

Pat Riley, professional basketball player and coach

The more we play unselfishly, the more everybody gets involved, the better the flow of the game.

Allan Houston, professional basketball player

The only guys I care about are the other 24 guys on my team.

Ken Griffey, Jr., professional baseball player

The secret of winning football games is working more as a team, less as individuals. I play not my eleven best, but my best eleven.

Knute Rockne, college football coach

There's the business side and there's the team. Once the season starts, I just want to win. And I don't care about hurting people's feelings if that's what it takes.

Michael Strahan, National Football League player

There's nothing worse than a sorry, pitiful, whining teammate. . . .

Charles Barkley, professional basketball player

The way a team plays determines its success. You may have the greatest bunch of stars in the world, but if they don't play together, the club won't be worth a dime.

Babe Ruth, Hall of Fame baseball player

They're dedicated, talented, and easy t[o get] along with. This team had no problem[s] that had a lot to do with our success.

Andy Petree, crew chief

To make any basket happen, somebody played good defense, somebody boxed out, somebody got the rebound, somebody hustled down the floor, somebody set the pick, somebody got open, somebody passed the ball, and somebody hit the shot. That's a lot of somebodies, but a lot of somebodies equals a team.

Ervin "Magic" Johnson, Hall of Fame professional basketball player

We're a good team, but maybe there are different kinds of good teams. Like good teams, okay teams and teams that screw up. We were okay there for a while. And then we seemed screwed up.

Fred Dryer, professional football player and actor

We were like the strings of a guitar. Each one was different, but we sounded pretty good together.

Willie Worsley, college basketball player

We were too young as a team to understand the tensions of a pennant race. Each days was an adventure. We weren't expected to win.

Ed Kranepool, professional baseball player, referring to the 1969 Miracle Mets

When I can't win and my teammate does, that's good for my team. That's good for me. I truly believe that.

Jimmy Vasser, automobile racer

Working hard individually is what builds a team collectively.

Karch Kiraly, professional volleyball player

Technique

All rods can catch fish; their success depends on that hand that uses them.

Charles Ritz, A Fly Fisher's Life

I don't know, I never think about it. Instinct, I guess.

Evonne Goolagong, champion tennis player, when asked about her technique

I never had technique.

Al Oerter, gold medal–winning track and field star

They have a pretty basic offense. No fancy blocking. Technique at its best.

Erik Howard, professional football player

Tee Time

English clubs are very exclusive . . . You can't get a starting time on Sunday unless you've been knighted.

Bob Hope, comedian

Television

His philosophy is that the networks are just renters. At the end of four years of a contract it's his product again, whereas they can walk away.

Gregg Winnick, television executive, talking about National Basketball Association commissioner David Stern

In baseball, the production toys are many: Bat Track, which measures bat speed; super–slo-mo cameras; CatcherCam and MaskCam; triple-split screens; instant replays; pitch-by-pitch sequences; Hit Zones; radar guns, plus managers, outfield walls, bullpens and bases are all wired for sound.

Richard Sandomir, writer

One team scores, ten guys party for the camera. Big 300-pounders shaking their ass. What the hell does that have to do with football?

Jim Brown, Hall of Fame football player

Roone Arledge, as anyone at ABC will tell you, was born in a manger.

attributed by Sports Illustrated *to an unidentified executive at ABC*

Sometimes, whether you're in the sixth grade or the eighth grade, you're going to make some shots to win the ball game and miss some shots to lose the ball game. Mine just happen to be on national TV.

Kobe Bryant, professional basketball player

Television's overpowering financial leverage must not obscure what I believe to be its greatest importance: its capacity to accelerate change.

James Michener, writer

We think TV exposure is so important to our program and so important to this university that we will schedule ourselves to fit the medium. I'll play at midnight if that's what TV wants.

Paul "Bear" Bryant, Hall of Fame college football coach

Tennis

A perfect combination of violent action taking place in an atmosphere of total tranquillity.

Billie Jean King, professional tennis player

Because she was so unlike any other tennis player in the world, no one ever said that this goddess "played tennis."

Larry Engleman, writer, about Suzanne Lenglen, champion tennis player

I am the best tennis player who cannot play tennis.

Ian Tiriac, professional tennis coach

I guess I was the first Englishman to bring the American attitude to the game of lawn tennis.

Fred Perry, professional tennis champion

In a racquets game, you are like a boxer. You attack and exploit another man's weakness. And a five-set singles match would be like going fifteen rounds.

Stan Hart, writer

It's one-on-one out there, man. There ain't no hiding. I can't pass the ball.

Pete Sampras, professional tennis champion

It seems to me that a primary attraction of the sport is the opportunity it gives to release aggression physically without being arrested for felonious assault.

Nat Hentoff, writer

On clay, you can't just kill the ball, because it's going to come back over and over.

Martina Hingis, professional tennis player

Physically, mentally and tennistically it's coming together.

Martina Hingis, professional tennis player

Tennis is structured, with lots of rules and regulations, but within those confines you can be very artistic, creative and aggressive.

With a racket in your hand, you can be whoever you really are.

Jason Cox, professional tennis player

The game of tennis and the atmosphere around it seem to narrow the intellect of the average good player and reduce his horizon. He tends to become petty and cantankerous.

Bob Considine, sportswriter

For a tennis player the only thing worse than playing in the U.S. Open, is not playing in the U.S. Open.

John Feinstein, writer

Tennis, anyone?

Anonymous

Tennis is my art.

Billie Jean King, champion tennis player

Tennis players start out so bloody young. Twenty-four is approximately the age that most football and baseball players *reach* the pros.

Frank Deford, sportswriter

The dictatorship of the players is deadly dangerous to the sport. The players get tremendous money without 100 percent effort.

Peter Kovarchik, tennis promoter

The list of girls who traded their adolescence for trophies haunts women's tennis.

Linda Robertson, writer

The primary object in match tennis is to break up the other man's game.

Bill Tilden, champion professional tennis player

That's when you know they're in trouble, when they start steering the ball.

Dennis Van Der Meer, professional tennis coach

The life we lead in tennis is most unlike that in any other sport. Tennis knows no season now, and is spectacularly international. I don't really live anywhere.

Arthur Ashe, Hall of Fame tennis
champion and writer

There is no doubt in my mind that tennis is *The Ring* [the opera]. As soon as they discover the gold the end was inevitable. Great and godlike as all these players are, the sport will have to be destroyed—before it will ever become sane. Ever since the game's been professional, there's been nothing but chaos.

Ted Tinling, tennis player and umpire

We are merely the stars' tennis balls, struck and bandied which way please them.

John Webster, English playwright

When you can hit a serve 120 mph on the line, there's not much you can do. This was just an old-fashioned street mugging.

Andre Agassi, professional tennis champion,
after losing in the finals at the U.S. Open
to Pete Sampras

With some noble exceptions among the three genders attracted to top flight tennis— male, female, and neuter—the game seems to draw the oddest characters in sports.

Bob Considine, sportswriter

World-class tennis players are tribal creatures, who regardless of national origin, share the same mores, totems and taboos.

Michael Mewshaw, writer

You're going to win the majority of points on your first serve, but you're only as good as your second serve.

Pete Sampras, champion professional
tennis player

Thorpe, Jim

(b. May 28, 1888; d. May 28, 1953)
Olympic pentathlon and decathlon gold medalist (1912); professional baseball player; professional football player; All-American college football player; considered by many as the world's greatest athlete

Jim Thorpe defeated Brown thirty-two to nothing—all by himself. Runs of fifty and sixty yards were nothing . . . the Indian was a tornado.

Michael Thompson, college football referee

Sir, you are the greatest athlete in the world.
King Gustav of Sweden, at the 1912 Olympic
Games, during the medal ceremony

We could have won if it hadn't have been for Thorpe. He's the best I've ever seen.

Dwight D. Eisenhower, U.S. president,
commander of Allied Forces in Europe during
World War II, and college football player,
when undefeated Army played the Canton
Bulldogs and lost 27–6

Ticket Prices

The cheapest way to see the playoffs is to drive to Indianapolis.

John Tierney, writer, advice to fans in the New
York Times, *referring to the disparity between*
playoff ticket prices between the New York Knicks
and the Indiana Pacers

The only crimes being committed out here are the ticket prices.

Bronx borough president Fernando Ferrer in
response to George Steinbrenner's charges that the
neighborhood surrounding the stadium was
crime-ridden

Tie(s)

A tie is like kissing your sister.

Paul "Bear" Bryant, Alabama
University football coach

Tilden, Bill

(b. Feb. 10, 1893; d. May 28, 1953) *Hall of Fame tennis champion; won U.S. Open seven times; won Wimbledon three times*

Bill Tilden was a stickler for the rules. He knew them inside out, sideways, what could be done, what could not be done. If you tried to bend the rules a little bit, he jumped you quick.

Fred Perry, professional tennis champion

Bill was stand-offish and show-offish. Proud, sensitive, he craved affection and respect from mature people—just as any man, but received it from few.

Grantland Rice, sportswriter

He's quite something. He's not afraid of work.

Ty Cobb, Hall of Fame baseball player

When he came out and started trotting down the stairs, it was the laird taking possession of his empire. Even if you were going to beat him, you knew you were only a subject.

Jean Borotra, champion tennis player

Who *is* this fruit?

Ty Cobb, Hall of Fame baseball player, upon meeting Tilden for the first time

Toughness

If me and King Kong went into an alley, only one of us would come out, and it wouldn't be the monkey.

Lyle Alzado, National Football League player

I saw him get hit with a beer bottle right across the forehead, and he just wiped it off. That's all I'm going to say. He just kind of blinked and said, "You shouldn't have done that."

Jack Patera, professional football player, speaking about Buzz Guy, professional football player

I'm not mean, just aggressive.

Harvey Martin, professional football player

To me being tough includes going into the corners without phoning ahead to see who's there.

Ted Lindsay, professional hockey player

They're so tough that when they finish sacking the quarterback they go after his family in the stands.

Tim Wrightman, on Chicago Bears' defensive unit

We're not tough enough.

Pete Babcock, National Basketball Association team executive, on his team's reputation for being soft

When the going gets tough, the tough get going.

Theodore Roosevelt, president of the United States, conservationist, and sportsman

Yes, I had a reputation for being tough. You had to be when you were Italian.

Gene Sarazen, champion professional golfer

Track and Field

Almost anyone can run or jump, but few can make a sport of it.

Kathleen McElroy, sportswriter and editor

As long as I'm here, I might as well throw.
Al Oerter, Olympic champion discus thrower, at the 1956 Melbourne Olympics

By breaking the world record every few days, those two Limeys are making a mockery of the mile race, which has traditionally been the core and kernel of any track meet.
Red Smith, sportswriter, referring to Sebastian Coe and Steve Ovett, world record–setting milers

In the next 50 years to 100 years, you'll see tremendous things in the 100 meters, tremendous times. The era started is going to continue and it's going to be great.
Gail Devers, Olympic track and field competitor

Leading is the best way to stay out of trouble.
Mary Decker Slaney, world champion runner

The decathlon is the most social of track events and promotes a strong sense of camaraderie among contestants. There is a lot of time to visit during and between events, much of which is used in helping other participants. Athletes will give and take advice, analyze each other's technique, assist each other in locating and checking take-off points, and even use each other's equipment.
Frank Zarnowski, writer

The strength events—such as the discus throw, hammer throw and shot put—are by and large won on the practice fields.
Al Oerter, Olympic champion discus thrower

The time you won your town the race
We chaired you through the market-place;
Man and boy stood cheering by,
And home we brought you shoulder-high.
A. E. Housman, poet

They weren't going to have a party without me.
Maurice Greene, track and field competitor, after setting a new world record in the 200-meter

Track and field has little in common with major American sports like football and basketball. But on the high school level, there is at least one similarity. If you are very good, you'll get recruited.
Carl Lewis, Olympic gold medalist track and field competitor

Track and field is not ice-skating. It is not necessary to smile and make a wonderful impression on the judges.
Emil Zatopek, Olympic gold medalist runner

We're the only professional sport that is not officially recognized as a professional sport. Track and field are where tennis was 20 years ago. It's time for the rules of the sport to catch up with reality.
David Greifinger, lawyer for Carl Lewis, gold medalist track and field competitor

Trades

I knew ballplayers got traded like horses, but I can't tell you how it felt when they traded me. I was only nineteen, but I made up my mind then it wouldn't ever happen again.
Curt Flood, professional baseball player and the first to file a lawsuit against Major League Baseball that eventually won players free agent rights

In the most lopsided transaction since the island of Manhattan was purchased for $24 worth of beads, Junior jilted Seattle and forced the Mariners to hand him over to the

Cincinnati Reds . . . It was more an extortion than it was a transaction, and if ever a deal screamed that it is not in the best interests of baseball, this one does.

> *Bill Lyon, sportswriter*

I've still got stuff in storage in Philly that I was going to move to Cleveland. I have stuff in storage in Cleveland that I was ready to put in the new place. Now I have no house, and my things—who knows where they are?

> *Jerry Spradlin, professional baseball player,*
> *who was traded twice in six months*

I didn't want you. I wouldn't trade 100 Bob Ueckers for one Gary Kolb.

> *Branch Rickey, baseball executive, to*
> *Bob Uecker, baseball player and announcer,*
> *after Uecker introduced himself to Rickey*
> *upon arriving at St. Louis against*
> *Rickey's wishes*

The Cowboys got nothing more than a handful of Minnesota smoke.

> *Randy Galloway, sportswriter, commenting on*
> *the trade of Herschel Walker to the Minnesota*
> *Vikings for eight players, many of whom went on*
> *to help Dallas win three more Super Bowls*

There were a great many people who thought the cards had made a great mistake, trading two ballplayers for one Uecker. As the season wore on Uecker proved that they were indeed correct.

> *Mark Stillwell, president of the Bob Uecker*
> *Fanclub, from the club newsletter*

Me for Tittle? You mean, just me?

> *Lou Cordileone, offensive lineman,*
> *asking about being traded for Hall of*
> *Fame quarterback Y. A. Tittle*

Smart managing is dumb. The three-run homer you trade for in the winter will always beat brains.

> *Earl Weaver, professional baseball manager*

The Spurs traded me to the Chicago Bulls for center Will Perdue, a guy with no game. Straight up for Will Perdue, bro. That's how much San Antonio wanted to get rid of me.

> *Dennis Rodman, professional basketball player*

You play bad and you hear you might get traded; you play good and you hear you might get traded.

> *Jack Youngblood, professional football player*

Trainers

Celebrity trainers who look as if they've walked out of the opera more than a smelly barn have become the marketing rage.

> *Harvey Araton, sportswriter, about horse trainers*

He couldn't train a vulture to eat.

> *Kelso Sturgeon,* Guide to Sports Betting, *in*
> *response when asked about a*
> *professional sports trainer.*

I was taught when I was a little boy that if you never lie, cheat or steal you'll be all right. But it's tough when you're a horse trainer not to steal a little here or there.

> *Charlie Whittingham, thoroughbred horse trainer*

The gift that God gave me is racehorses.

> *Diane Crump, trainer*

They all get beat if you run them often enough.

> *Oft-repeated saying in horse racing, attributed by*
> *William Murray, writer*

Trainers are the college basketball and football coaches of thoroughbred racing. They represent The Program. The Program, the continuum, as the horses pass in and out of prominence every few years.

Harvey Araton, sportswriter, about thoroughbred horse trainers

Trainers spend all their time looking for one thing . . . They're looking for *the* horse.

Brendan Boyd, sportswriter

We were compulsive buyers. I still am. You walk a good looking saddle pony by me and I'll want to buy it.

D. Wayne Lukas, thoroughbred horse trainer

When we saw that, everybody patted the trainer on the back.

Chuck Finley, professional baseball player, about seeing Mo Vaughn back in the lineup, coming back from a sprained ankle

You always have to have that big horse, that superstar to get noticed. To remind people we're still out here. And winning.

D. Wayne Lukas, thoroughbred horse trainer

Training

If I had practiced more, trained harder, taken the game more seriously, maybe even put on a big act, like it was a religion to me, I might have done better. But maybe not. You know, sometimes it's a matter of the club you land with.

Hot Rod Hundley, professional basketball player

If you train hard, you'll not only be hard, you'll be hard to beat.

Herschel Walker, professional football player

I never let my social life interfere with my athletic training. I set my standards early so that I would never get wrapped up in that manner.

Mark Spitz, Olympic gold medal swimmer

It is not a matter of how much you train, but how you train.

Rick Niles, triathlon coach

I took for granted that I had to be in good physical shape to win. I ran, cycled, lifted weights, practiced yoga, did everything the . . . trainers said was necessary.

Jean-Claude Killy, Olympic gold medalist skier

Never ask your body to do something it hasn't already done in training—and you'll have confidence that you can actually do it.

Alberto Salazar, champion marathoner

Nothing like the feel of the trail in your hair to make you want to train harder.

John Bass, mountain climber, about falling and getting banged up

The day I don't want to train in the off season, the day I don't want to work as hard as I possibly can, that's the day I'll quit.

Karl Malone, professional basketball player

The five S's of sports training are: stamina, speed, strength, skill, and spirit; but the greatest of these is spirit.

Ken Doherty, track coach

You've got to train.

Cyrille Guimard, cycling coach

Training Camp

The first thing you learn is never to learn their names until the last cut is made. 'Cause you feel bad when they get cut.

Eddie LeBaron, professional football player

Trash Talking

An old-fashioned ass-kicking.

Ervin "Magic" Johnson, Hall of Fame basketball player, about losing in the finals to the Chicago Bulls

Block that, Bitch!

Michael Jordan, professional basketball player, to John Salley, professional basketball player, who was defending against Jordan

Get up and fight, sucker! Get up and fight!

Muhammad Ali, world champion boxer, to Sonny Liston, world champion boxer, after knocking Liston out for the heavyweight crown

He did something stupid, and that's what he does best.

George Foreman, champion boxer, broadcaster, and pitchman, talking about Prince Nassem Hemed's victory over Paul Ingle

He'll have to grow a hell of a lot to get as big as his mouth.

John Nerud, thoroughbred horse trainer and owner, about a competitor

He missed me all night, at the plate and on the mound. That tells you how stupid he is. He's obviously frustrated—that's his problem.

Todd Stottlemyre, professional baseball player, about Charlie Hayes, with whom he started a fight in the middle of a Giants/Dimondback games

I don't like him. Nobody likes him because he's a———. I'm sick of people like that. Who is he, Sandy Koufax? He's a .500 pitcher, that's all. If he has a problem with me, we can get it settled. I told him I'd knock him out.

Charlie Hayes, professional baseball player, about Todd Stottlemeyre

I don't need to be practicing, I'm leading this tournament. You guys go on and practice, because you're behind.

Lee Trevino, champion golfer, to fellow competitors after a good first round

If you can't hit, you can't run, and can't throw, then you've got to holler at them.

Solly Hemus, professional baseball player and manager

I just gave him a look, and Steve Javie, the ref, told me to stop looking.

Marcus Camby, professional basketball player, about eyeballing Alonzo Mourning during a hotly contested New York Knicks–Miami Heat playoff game

I've been called a racist, a drunk and a quitter. Other than that, I'm fine.

Kerry Collins, professional football player

I will crush you like a grape.

Mark Tuinei, professional football player, the phrase he most liked to tell opposing linemen

Jesse, thanks for the directions.

Mark Tuinei, professional football player, who retorted to friend Jesse Sapulo that the road to the Super Bowl went through Candlestick, after the Cowboys beat the 49ers in the playoffs

One's a liar and the other's convicted.
Billy Martin, professional baseball player and manager, about Reggie Jackson and George Steinbrenner, respectively

The Knicks are going to win the East, more than likely, unless they get upset, 'cause they're playing against the Little Sisters of the Poor.
Charles Barkley, professional basketball player

Who's guarding me? Nobody's guarding me. You're supposed to be guarding me?
Larry Bird, to Dennis Rodman, both professional basketball player

This is what you're lookin' for.
Johnny Sample, National Football League player, to an opposing receiver after intercepting the ball and tapping him on the head with it.

You're next, big mouth.
Sonny Liston, world champion, to Muhammad Ali from inside the ring after beating Floyd Patterson a second time

Triple Crown

It's one of those things that is not on my resume. I'd love to have it. The chance comes along so seldom.
D. Wayne Lukas, thoroughbred horse trainer

Now I won't have to worry about a Triple Crown.
Bob Baffert, trainer, after not winning the Kentucky Derby for the first time in three years

We're at a cross roads in racing. Tracks are changing ownership and the business is searching for answers. A Triple Crown winner would be an enormous thing for racing.
D. Wayne Lukas, thoroughbred horse trainer

Trust

The foundation of getting people to do what you want them to do is built on a relationship based on trust. That is the critical element, the glue that holds everything together.
Marty Shottenhimer, professional football coach

U

Ultra-Marathon

Every year, two or three dozen elite ultra-marathoners come to Badwater, and every year Badwater beats them down.

David Ferrell, sportswriter

For a thin slice of society—zealots who live to train, who measure themselves by their mental toughness—the ultra-marathon is the constant test of human character. No other event in sport, except possibly a prize fight, is as punishing, as demanding of the mind and body.

David Ferrell, sportswriter

Umpires

As an umpire, when you make a call, you're alone.

Bernice Gera, umpire, first female umpire

F——— the safety of the umpires. I've got fifty thousand people out there who want to see baseball!

Bill Veeck, baseball owner and racetrack operator, to the umpires in their locker room, when thousands of rowdy fans had taken the field during a promotional day, and refused to yield for the second game. The game was eventually canceled.

I cursed him out in Spanish, and he threw me out in English.

Lou Pinella, professional baseball player and manager, referring to Armando Rodriquez, umpire, after being thrown out of a game

I don't recall.

Bobby Thompson, professional baseball player, when asked if he remembered who the umpire was when he hit the famous Home Run Heard Round the World

I normally shudder when I think I've really kicked one. I can't sleep that night and I don't feel good until I get back on the field the next day. My early years in umpiring, I might go back to the umpires' room and cry a little after missing a crucial call.

Durwood Merrill, umpire

It's wonderful to be here, to be able to hear the baseball against the bat, ball against the glove, and to be able to boo the umpire.

Douglas MacArthur, U.S. general, commander of Pacific theater in World War II, at a baseball game

I umpired more than two thousand games during my career. I was called every name in the book and then some. I was sworn at in two languages, blackballed by my own peers, ridiculed by fans, and abused by ball players and managers in five different countries.

Pam Postema, female umpire

Lately . . . we've been hearing that the umpires are trying to take over the game and that they're too arrogant and that some of them think they are bigger than baseball. It seems some umpires don't want to argue anymore. They just want to toss you out of the game.

Ken Griffey, Jr., baseball player

Players being more concerned about the next day's umpire than the next day's starting pitcher; there's something wrong there.

Sandy Alderson, league official

That guy has definitely done some wrestling. Only wrestlers know how to do that particular series of actions. It was basically a double leg takedown . . . it was a good three-point move.

Dan Gable, Olympic champion wrestler, on Cuban umpire Cesar Valdez's takedown of an anti-Castro protester during a game between the Baltimore Orioles and the Cuban national team

Today, conscious of the great unseen audience, they play every decision out like the balcony scene from *Romeo and Juliet*. On a strike they gesticulate, they brandish a fist aloft, they spin almost as if shot through the heart, they bellow all four parts of the quartet from *Rigoletto*. On a pitch that misses the plate, they stiffen with loathing, ostentatiously avert the gaze, and render a boot from *Gotterdammerung*.

Red Smith, sportswriter

When you think about it, you've probably spent more time with umpires than you spent with your wife.

Richie Ashburn, broadcaster to Tim McCarver, broadcaster and former baseball catcher

You argue with an umpire because there's nothing else you can do about it.

Leo Durocher, professional baseball player and manager

You're not even supposed to be watching!

Lou Pinella, professional baseball player and manager, to Durwood Merrill, umpire, after Merrill overruled a home run call because he cited fan interference. Merrill was correct, replays showed later

You're out, and you're ugly, too.

Durwood Merrill, umpire

Uniforms

Baseball outfits went through their gaudy period during the disco '70's, when the White Sox looked like softball players and the Athletics looked like "Saturday Night Fever" personified.

George Vecsey, sportswriter

I don't know. I'm not in shape yet.

Yogi Berra, Hall of Fame baseball player and coach, when asked during spring training what his cap size was

Instead of looking like an American flag, I look like a taco.

Steve Garvey, professional baseball player, referring to his new Padres uniform versus his previous Dodgers uniform

I wear a sombrero, silk neckerchief, fringed buckskin shirt, sealskin chaparajos or riding-trousers, and alligator-hide boots, and with my pearl-hilted revolver and beautifully finished Winchester rifle, I feel I can face anything.

Theodore Roosevelt, president of the United States, conservationist, and outdoorsman

Unions

They have no sense of history whatsoever.

Curt Flood, professional baseball player, first to file for free agency

Unknowns

At least I didn't swing and miss.

Mike Stone, rookie golfer, at the 1999 U.S. Open, referring to his first tee shot

You don't know me, I was just a ham-and-egger.

Lew Perez, club fighter

V

Veterans

Walt, you don't have to run the forties . . . If those rookies ever find out how slow you are and you've been playing six years, they'll think it's a snap to make this team.

Tom Landry, professional football head coach and player, to Walt Garrison, professional football player

Victory

I tried to get away from things tonight by going over to gamble at the Playboy Club, and who should I meet at the blackjack table but Joe Frazier. Frazier had no idea who I was. Other black athletes don't even know me, although the tennis boom has made me much more visible outside the tennis world.

Arthur Ashe, Hall of Fame tennis champion and writer

Everyone has the will to win, but few have the will to prepare to win.

Bobby Knight, basketball coach

Forget about style; worry about results.

Bobby Orr, Hall of Fame hockey player

How vainly men themselves amaze
To win the palm, the oak, or bays.

Andrew Marvell, poet

I am a winner each and everytime I go into the ring.

George Foreman, champion boxer

I don't think we can win every game—just the next one.

Lou Holtz, college and professional football coach

If you believe in yourself and have dedication and pride—and never quit, you'll be a winner. The price of victory is high—but so are the rewards.

Paul "Bear" Bryant, Hall of Fame college football coach

That's the big difference between victory and defeat for us. After a victory we want to be together . . . When we lose, everyone goes off in his own direction.

Rick Casares, professional football player

The more difficult a victory, the greater the happiness is in winning.

Pelé, soccer player

The price for victory is hard work.

Knute Rockne, college football coach

There is a pleasant taste to victory, and soon I was thinking, why not try for a bigger cup, a longer trip, a more important victory?

Jean-Claude Killy, Olympic gold medalist skier

Victory is not necessarily a gold medal.

Gale Tanger, Olympic figure skating judge, referring to Nancy Kerrigan's winning the silver medal after being attacked by friends of rival skater Tonya Harding

Violence

Despite all the moaning and gnashing of teeth over violence in the NFL over the past few years, I can safely say that anyone who didn't watch us play hasn't seen true violence in sports. In a way, I kind of miss it.

Art "Fatso" Donovan, Hall of Fame football player

I ain't ever liked violence.

Sugar Ray Robinson, champion boxer

I kept thinking about all the guys kneeled down before the game to say the Lord's Prayer. When they were done everyone leaped up, put on their helmets and charged out of the locker room screaming, "Let's kill the bastards."

Rick Sortun, professional football player

Knocking down an offensive lineman and breaking his head open is something that I enjoy.

Alex Karras, Hall of Fame football player

The only time I am really violent is on the football field. I'm going to catch him and knock his block off. It's as simple as that.

Alex Karras, Hall of Fame football player

Volleyball

Beach volleyball is a little like marriage—a doomed one. I don't think there's ever been a team that didn't break up at one point or another. It's inevitable.

Karch Kiraly, professional volleyball player

Between the pass and the attack, the setter is in control.

Doug Beal, volleyball coach and writer

In an ace-to-error ratio, how many mistakes are you willing to give up to score points by the ace? The ace is the easiest way to score. One contact of the ball and you have a point.

Mike Herbert, volleyball coach

The rule is a simple one: If you want to win the Association of Volleyball Professionals' Miller Lite U.S. Championships, you have to go through Karch Kiraly and Adam Johnson. That rule was enforced on Sunday.

Los Angeles Times

The setter has to be the most consistent player on the court, day in and day out.

Lorne Sawula, volleyball coach

Volleyball is among the purest of team sports. It is virtually impossible for one player to dominate the game as a great running back in football or a tremendous shooter in basketball.

Doug Beal, volleyball coach and writer

When a ball was dug up and put up for one of them, a point was almost automatic.

Karch Kiraly, professional volleyball player, about Steve Timmons and Pat Powers

W

Walton, Izaak

(b. Aug. 9, 1593; d. Dec. 15, 1683) *Biographer; fisherman; author of* The Compleat Angler *(1653) which is one of the most frequently reprinted books in the English language according to the* Encyclopaedia Britannica

It is said that many an unlucky urchin is induced to run away from his family and betake himself to a seafaring life, from reading the history of Robinson Crusoe; and I suspect that, in like manner, many of those worthy gentlemen who are given to haunt the sides of pastoral streams with angle rods in hand, may trace the origin of their passion to the seductive pages of honest Izaak Walton.

Washington Irving, writer

Water

Above all to be taken into account were some years of schooling, where I studied with diligence Neputune's laws, and these laws I tried to obey when I sailed over seas; it was worth the while.

Joshua Slocum, first modern sailor to sail around the world alone

A healthy respect of the sea is a must for all sailors, regardless of experience.

Bob Bond, sailor, instructor, and writer

A man who is not afraid of the sea, will soon be drowned, he said, for he will be going out on a day he shouldn't. But we do be afraid of the sea, and we do only be drowned now and again.

John Millington Synge, writer and playwright, from The Aran Islands

A river is like a piece of music. The score is basically the same every time, but everyone who plays it will play it a little differently, and no matter how many times you play it yourself, you'll play it a little differently each time.

Robert Kimber, outdoorsman and writer

But what is the test of a river? Who shall say? "The power to drown a man," replies the river darkly.

R. D. Blackmore, outdoorsman and writer

Each sea is different and because the North Sea is prone to bad weather, it is one of the biggest graveyards in the world.

John Beattie, sailor

I am haunted by waters.

Norman Maclean, writer

If there is magic on this planet, it lies in water.

Loren Eiseley, scientist, naturalist, and writer

If the Southern Ocean represents the consummate challenge for any long-distance sailor, then the Vendee Globe is the pinnacle—one man, one boat against the elements.

Pete Goss, champion solo sailor and writer, commenting on the Vendee Globe race, an around-the-world solo boat race

I had to keep guessing at the channel. I had to discern, mostly by inspiration, the signs of hidden banks; I watched for sunken stones . . . When you have to attend to things of that sort, to the mere incidents of the surface, the reality—the reality, I tell you—fades. The inner truth is hidden—luckily, luckily.

Joseph Conrad, writer, in his novella Heart of Darkness

It has something to do with the infiniteness of water, its vastness; it doesn't inhibit vision.

Stuart Williamson, yachtsman

It was a storm precisely like this one that saved England from the Spanish Armada. Whenever you sail in the English Channel, you've got to be prepared for the return of that storm.

Ted Turner, yachtsman and baseball owner, referring to the storm that struck the 1979 Fastnet Race

It's no worse than the Indianapolis 500 race. The danger is part of it. We were racing all the time.

Dennis Conner, yachtsman

Man marks the earth with ruin; his control stops at the shore.

Lord Byron, poet

Mid-September is not the ideal time to make a passage west through the Straits of Dover and down the English Channel. It's a boisterous stretch of water at the best of times, but during the equinoctial gales it is a 22-carat sod.

Tristan Jones, sailor and writer

Rivers are a constant lure to the adventurous instinct in mankind.

Henry David Thoreau, writer and philosopher

The fact that a man can drown while fishing is obvious . . . the very first lesson every young angler must learn are the techniques of water safety.

A. J. McClane, outdoorsman and writer

The people I respect are the ones who quit the race. The competitive urge can be a very unbalancing thing, and we are all guilty in a way of not respecting the sea enough.

Tom McLoughlin, sailor, participant in the 1979 Fastnet Race

The sea drives truth into a man like salt.

Hilaire Belloc, writer

The sea is a great leveler, and quickly humbles the big-headed sailor.

Alex Rose, yachtsman

The Southern Ocean is teaching us its lessons; respect the sea because I can snap you up like a twig if I want to; never think you are special or too important, because I can be arbitrary and unfair and I don't care who gets in my path of destruction.

Dawn Riley, yachtswoman

There is enough water in the world for all of us.

Annette Kellerman, swimmer and women's rights activist

To face the elements, is to be sure, no light matter when the sea is in its grandest mood. You must know the seas, and know that you know it, and not forget that it was made to be sailed over.

Joshua Slocum, first modern sailor to sail around the world alone

Very few people will actually travel an entire water trail, but the very fact of a water trail's existence is a siren for at least a few days' travel.

Tamsin Venn, kayaker and publisher of Atlantic Coastal Kayaker

Water is the blood of the Earth, and flows through its muscles and veins.

Kuan Tzu, philosopher

Water on the move is nimble as well as subtle. It is apparently made of an infinite series of layers that seem to slip over each other with very little friction. Running water is a truly dynamic medium.

Jay Evans, Olympic kayaker and outdoorsman

Water Polo

If we wanted to win, we had to be in that pool.

John Vargas, coach, U.S. national water polo team

They're different from swimmers. They don't see the world as a concrete prison, a place to swim lap after lap in pain. They like having their heads out of the water, having a good time.

Ted Newland, college water polo coach

Weakness

He doesn't cook very well.

Michael Chang, professional tennis champion, when asked to describe Pete Sampras's weakness

If there's a weakness, you want to exploit that weakness.

Michael Peca, professional hockey player

Weather

A storm never blows in when the action is slow.

Randy Voorhees, fisherman and writer

Depressions are born, reach maturity, and then decline and die. They travel in their youth and stagnate in their retirement; some are feeble from birth and never make a mark on the world, while others attain a vigor which makes them remembered with as much awe as a hurricane.

Ingrid Holford, weather specialist

Did you see it snow again in Scottsdale? That's God's way of telling the Diamondbacks it will snow in hell before they win.

Charlie Hayes, professional baseball player

Don't worry, it's not really raining. This is just Houston humidity.

Walter Bloxsom, chairman of the Pin Oak equestrian event

I couldn't care less about Greenland. I'm here for the golf.

William Starrett II, lawyer and avid golfer, who went to Greenland to golf at the World Ice Golf Championship

I have friends who claim the month of February offers us New Englanders, especially those of us who like to fish and hunt, nothing but memories and hopes. Savor the past, they recommend, or dream of the future. Try to ignore the miserable present.

William G. Tapply, outdoorsman and writer

I know I got loaded last night, but how did I wind up at Squaw Valley?

Jimmy Demaret, champion golfer, on waking up in Pebble Beach to find snow on the ground

Someone call the big man. Tell him to turn the heat on!

Percy Ellsworth, professional football player, referring to cold weather before a game in December

We joked that God's an Irishman because he brought us the weather we left at home.

John Morrin, runner, joking about bad weather at the Penn Relays

We're sorry. Too much snow. Too much indecision.

Bill Veeck, baseball owner and racetrack operator, a sign he had posted outside a racetrack in Massachusetts, because the city wouldn't help him open in a snowstorm.

Whether we could stick it out was not so much a question as whether the storm would allow us to stick it out.

Frank Smythe, mountain climber

Weightlifting

For years, coaches would not allow athletes to lift weights because it made them look muscle-bound. Now weight training is a main part of almost any team's training program.

Lou Ferrigno, champion bodybuilder, professional football player, and actor

Lifting a barbell ain't like eating no watermelon.

Toad, U.S. Olympic weightlifter

Since the earliest days of the human race, physical strength above the ordinary has been admired, envied, and striven for by the majority of men.

D. P. Willoughby, writer

Yuri Vlasov was enormously hardworking, but he underestimated the value of technique and failed to make the most of his potential. Leonid Zhabotinskii was exactly the opposite . . . My advantage over both of them is that I know exactly where I am going, I have a will to win, and I have the ability to keep up an incomparably more intensive training program.

Vasilii Alekseev, Olympic gold medalist weightlifter

Williams, Ted

(b. Aug. 30, 1918) *Hall of Fame baseball player; called the "Splendid Splinter"; won the batting Triple Crown twice (1942 and 1947); last player to bat .400 for a whole season; missed five years of his career as pilot in the air force in World War II and the Korean War; considered one of the great pure hitters in baseball history; also a world-class fisherman*

He's the best fisherman there is—the best. No doubt about it. How many people have ever been the absolute best there is at *two* things?

Bobby Knight, champion college basketball coach

He was sometimes unbearable, but he was never dull.

Ed Linn, sportswriter

Like a feather caught in a vortex, Williams ran around the square of bases at the center of our beseeching screaming. He ran as he always ran out home runs—hurriedly, unsmiling, head down, as if our praise were a storm of rain to get out of.

George Plimpton, editor and best-selling author

Winning

A dream I had worked for so hard had come true, and everything has turned red. Everything around me is going in slow motion. I have proved my point, and my blood is literally exploding in my head.

Jean-Claude Killy, Olympic gold medalist skier

A winner never quits and a quitter never wins.

Knute Rockne, college football coach

Because I wanted to win the game!

Roger Maris, professional baseball player, responding to a question about why he bunted in a run instead of swinging for a homer

He can't hit, he can't run, he can't field, he can't throw, but if there's a way to beat the other team, he'll find it.

Branch Rickey, baseball executive, speaking about Ed Stanky, professional baseball player

How much do you really want to win when you have as much money, attention, and fame as Shaquille O'Neal does?

Dennis Rodman, professional basketball player

I believe there is winning and misery and even when we win I'm miserable.

Pat Riley, champion professional basketball coach

I don't feel like dancing.

Tom Warner, triathlete, after winning the 1979 Ironman

I don't see any point in playing the game if you don't win.

Babe Didrikson Zaharias, champion golfer and Olympic track and field competitor

I don't think it's possible to be too intent on winning.

Woody Hayes, college football coach

In playing or managing, the game of ball is only fun for me when I'm out in front and winning. I don't give a hill of beans for the rest of the game.

John J. McGraw, Hall of Fame baseball player and manager

It's nice to be favored, but it doesn't put you in the winner's circle.

Nick Zito, thoroughbred horse trainer

I've won at every level, except college and pro.

Shaquille O'Neal, professional basketball player

I want to win now. Who cares about 2001? The world could blow up in two years. We could all be dead by then.

Jason Kendall, professional baseball player

That's why I took the extra lap. I wanted to wipe away the tears.

Jeff Gordon, champion race car driver,
explaining why he took two victory
laps at the 1994 Brickyard 400

The game could have gone either way. It came down to the women on this team having to win.

Tony DiCicco, soccer coach, U.S. women's
World Cup team

There's only a little margin between winning and losing. A lot of luck is involved. It's hard to get too excited when you know that you could have lost as easily as you won.

Doug Atkins, professional football player

People always try to jump on you when you're not winning. They try to rattle you . . . but that's part of the game. That's what makes it fun.

Jimmy Vasser, automobile racer

Wanting to win has zero to do with money. You can't buy your way into something that's worthwhile, and the only thing worthwhile out of here is trying to be the best team for one year.

Jeff Van Gundy, professional basketball coach

We can't win at home. We can't win on the road. As general manager, I just can't figure out where else to play.

Pat Williams, Orlando Magic general manager,
on his team's 7-27 record

We didn't come up here to ruin their season. We came up here to win. We'll let them ruin their season on their own.

Keyshawn Johnson, professional
football player

When you have a particularly good game, the community opens up to you—the key to the city and all that. The downfall is that they close up to you. It's all predicated on what you did on Sunday.

Jerome Bettis, National Football League player

Winning is an attitude.

John Chaney, college basketball coach

Winning is like shaving. You do it every day, or you end up looking like a bum.

Jack Kemp, professional football player
and U.S. congressman

Winning isn't everything. It's the only thing.

Vince Lombardi, National Football
League Hall of Fame coach

Winning is the only thing there is. Anything below first is losing.

A. J. Kitt, world champion skier

Winning tends to heal uneasiness and promote job security.

Selena Roberts, sportswriter

Winners are different. They're a different breed of cat.

Byron Nelson, champion golfer

You know, the house, the car, the money, the fame . . . I'd give it all away in a second to be cancer free.

Lance Armstrong, champion cyclist, winner
of the Tour de France, cancer survivor

You win on Sunday, but you can't expect them to roll over for you next week. You've got to go out there next week and prove you're a winner again.

Sam Huff, Hall of Fame football player

Women

Every city in the league has a group of women who hang around the arenas and know where the players go after the games. They're pros, and a lot of them are sexy as hell.

Dennis Rodman, professional basketball player

I got all that out of my system before I got married. Now, every town I go to, women come chasing after me, calling my room, sending me notes, but I don't pay them any attention. I wouldn't want any woman who chases after me, and I stopped chasing after them once I taught my wife how to fire my pistol.

Bo Jackson, professional baseball and football player

I frequently make my own clothes. And if it interests you, I'm a pretty good cook.

Babe Didrikson Zaharias, Olympian and champion golfer, responding to a jest by Grantland Rice, "How is your sewing?"

Everything a woman does has an emotional level. Paying attention to my emotional side without surrendering to it is one of the toughest parts of playing professional sports.

Gabrielle Reece, professional volleyball player

From the bedroom my wife calls. I grumble intelligibly and she calls again, winsomely. I grumble again and continue my work: I steel-wool the male ferrule of my Thomas and whistle into its mate.

Nick Lyons, outdoorsman, writer, and publisher

Let's face it, women are more interesting than football.

Roy Blount, Jr., wruter and humorist

Men are in danger of thinking everything is winning while women think winning is nothing.

Mariah Burton Nelson, professional basketball player

Mother, when I get a telephone call from a beautiful girl like Miss Margaret Foot, I must leave at once—remember, Mother, never let a pitch hang.

Tiny Tim, musician, sports fan

Real groupies present all kinds of dangers. First, a real groupie will travel around between guys and even different sports teams, bringing with her various sorts of abominable "luggage," or diseases, which she is more than happy to share. Second, for the married scoundrels, a groupie is like a live hand grenade without the pin.

Tim Gree, professional football player, broadcaster, and writer

The only way of preventing civilized men from kicking and beating their wives is to organize games in which they can kick and beat balls.

George Bernard Shaw, writer

We play big matches on tour these days. When more of the public realizes we're no carnival act, they'll be bigger.

Babe Didrikson Zaharias, Olympian and champion golfer

When I hear those foxes squealing, I get all jiggly inside. It makes me feel like I can do anything I want to on the court.

Walt "Clyde" Frazier, Hall of Fame basketball player and broadcaster

When we won the league championship, all the married guys on the club had to thank their wives for putting up with all the stress and strain all season. I had to thank all the single broads in New York.

Joe Namath, Hall of Fame football player

Women are more capable of pushing through the pain.

Robyn Benincasa, extreme athlete, adventure racer

You will come home with me tonight.

Alberto Tomba, Olympic gold medalist skier, to many local women in Calgary

Women Athletes

Any trainer will tell you that if a girl has good hands she can handle a fractious horse far better than any man. Especially in those early morning hours. There is a relationship between a female and a horse that transcends anything that can possibly exist between a male and a horse.

Bill Veeck, baseball owner, racetrack operator

As an athlete, I believe I was popular as long as I was demure, appreciative, decorative, obedient, and winning.

Shirley Strickland De La Hunty, Olympic track gold medalist

As a jockey she went where no female—and a hell of a lot of males before her—had ever gone. She is the only woman to ride a winner in a Triple Crown race. She fought for her mounts in a time when most trainers couldn't deal with the idea of turning over a thoroughbred meal ticket to a lady jockey.

Jerry Izenberg, sportswriter, about Julie Krone, jockey

Few athletes in any Olympic sport—and certainly none so young—face the unique pressure young female gymnasts and figure skaters do. They must instill an entire childhood of training into one perfect performance, and they must do it on the largest stage in the world.

Joan Ryan, journalist and writer

Fishing gear for woman isn't what it used to be. It used to be there wasn't any.

Laurie Morrow, sportswoman and writer

Girls of all colors, sizes, shapes, gritty kids bonding through hard, clean competition.

John Edgar Wideman, writer

I have never felt—I have a hard time even saying the word—*unfeminine* while playing sports.

Jackie Joyner-Kersey, Olympic gold medalist track and field competitor

I'm not so sure we have changed the perspective of men, but I do think that women are saying to themselves, "If they can do it, why can't I?"

Dawn Riley, champion yachtswoman

I'm not sure that women know what they want to do with tennis. A lot of the girls, when they quit, they go back to school or try something else. The men don't.

Joan Pennello, Women's Tennis Association executive

I see elegance and beauty in every female athlete. I don't think being an athlete is unfeminine. I think of it as a kind of grace.

Jackie Joyner-Kersey, Olympic gold medalist track and field competitor

I wanted to be a major league umpire . . . Turns out I took more than anybody—just because I was a woman, a she instead of a he. In professional baseball, there is no worse crime.

Pam Postema, female umpire

I well remember wearing exotic hairstyles and Chanel No. 5 during my competitive days to reassure myself, as well as everyone else, that I was female.

Shirley Strickland De La Hunty,
Olympic track gold medalist

Men who find women athletes sexy are more apt to accept women in all of their dimensions. Athletic women sweat, blow snot from their noses, grunt and lose their tempers. That is sport.

Steve Marantz, sportswriter

My boyfriend's going to take your husband's job.

Attributed to a girlfriend of Stacey King,
professional basketball player, to Donna Grant,
wife of Horace Grant, professional
basketball player

People say PGA first, then LPGA, like a little behind. I don't like that. We're all professionals. Nothing different, many great players.

Se Ri Pak, professional golfer

She was the sort of woman who took off tight shoes which hurt and wiggled her toes, no matter where she was . . . the first athlete to make people confront the issues of femininity: how much muscle is too much? how much is unfeminine?

Adrianne Blue, writer, about
Babe Didrikson Zaharias

The most rewarding moments have been when little girls, 10 and 11 years old, would run up to me and say things like, "I played soccer with boys and I was the best goalkeeper out there." This has happened hundreds of times.

Julie Krone, jockey

The sooner little boys begin to realize that little girls are equal and that there will be many opportunities for a boy to be tested by a girl, the closer they will be to better mental health.

Sylvia Pressley, hearing officer, in her 1973
decision to integrate Little League

The story of women in sports is a personal story, because nothing is more personal than a woman's bone, sinew, sweat, and desire, and a political story, because nothing is more powerful than a woman's struggle to run free.

Mariah Burton Nelson, writer

There's still more pressure on men. If a girl doesn't make it on the tour, she can always get married and have her husband support her.

Marty Mulligan, sponsor representative

The women walk through the gates and see the men and say, "Why should he get more than me?" It's like a heavyweight and a middleweight in boxing. They might be on the same bill, but no matter how good the middleweight is, the heavyweight gets paid more.

John Curry, tennis grand slam executive

We run with women in road races all the time. It would have seemed strange to run without them.

John Benkert, runner, about competitive
running events

With the single exception of the improvement of legal status of women, their entrance into the realm of sports is the most cheering thing that has happened to them in this century just past.

Anne O'Hagen, writer, in 1901

Women athletes are no longer curiosities . . . no longer revolutionaries, pioneers or tokens . . . just another bunch of jocks.

Grace Lichtenstein, writer

Women in sports now receive equal recognition. But they still have to work twice as hard as men to be recognized.

Jackie Joyner-Kersey, Olympic gold medalist track and field

Women tennis players call themselves girls . . . If we go to a party or a function where we have to get all dressed up, we're women, but if we're at the tennis club wearing track suits, we're girls—except when we're bitches, of course.

Pam Shriver, champion professional tennis player

World's Fastest Woman is an Expert Cook

headline from the Daily Telegraph *(London) about Francina Blankers-Koen, Olympic track gold medalist*

Woods, Tiger

(b. Dec. 30, 1975) *Professional golfer; first African American and youngest golfer to win the U.S. Amateur in 1994 (also won 1995 and 1996); won Masters by record 18 under par (with a 13-stroke lead); won 1999 PGA; won nearly $10,000,000 in prize money on the PGA tour in 2000; possibly the most recognized active athlete in the world today*

Bottom line is that I am an American and proud of it.

Tiger Woods, professional golfer, youngest winner of the U.S. Open

He's got the heart of a lion. He may be the type of player that comes around once in a thousand years.

Tom Watson, champion professional golfer

World Cup

I never thought that the World Cup would be such a test of nerves.

Gustave Sebes, deputy of sports, Hungary, after the Hungarians won a wild final, complete with fights and injuries, beating Brazil 3-2

It was terrible. Everybody was sick about this . . . I had a feeling in my skin the robber was not Brazilian. He has no feeling for patriotism.

Pedro T. Natal, chairman of Kodak Brazil, after the country's retired World Cup Jules Rimet Trophy soccer statue was stolen. The robber was found dead, but the statue was not recovered. A replacement—a duplicate—now stands in its place.

It wasn't a very good final.

Franz Beckenbauer, professional soccer player and manager, after West Germany won the World Cup in a lackluster game against Argentina

The lines go from a base rising in a sphere and covering the world. From the body of the sculpture, two figures stand out—two athletes in a moving celebration of victory.

Silvio Gazzaniga, sculptor, who sculpted the new World Cup trophy

The World Cup is the world's grandest sporting event. Every four years, the best 24 teams in the world come together to celebrate this beautiful game with a spectacular tournament and cultural celebration that cannot be duplicated anywhere.

Pelé, professional soccer player

The World Cup was going on and people who maybe make $1 a day were using all their money to go into town to watch it. They'd been saving up for three years to go there.

Leslie Downer, journalist

You cannot run a bid on the cheap and people are naive if they think otherwise. We were the only campaign which had been open about what it has spent and there is no doubt that some people will say it is money down the drain. But if you look at it properly, £10 million is an amazingly modest investment compared to the rewards.

Alec McGivan, leader of England's 2006 World Cup campaign

World Series

I don't think you play this game for any other reason than to get to the World Series. I've thought about it since Little League, when you dream of hitting that home run in the ninth inning.

Ken Griffey, Jr., professional baseball player

Worry

Earl Monroe was the only man I would dream about. He gave me nightmares.

Walt "Clyde" Frazier, champion professional basketball player

Wrestling

As a kid, I remember Archie the Stomper mauling my dad in the ring. Then later, I'd see Archie the Stomper come to get his check, and hug my mom. I couldn't figure it out.

Brett Hart, second-generation professional wrestler

Give a good wrestler a microphone, push him out the door, ask him for ten minutes and you'll get ten great minutes. Who else can do that?

Michael Braverman, agent

I don't want to say that wrestling has taken over this country, but pretty soon I expect my accountant to be wearing a diaper and boots.

Mitch Albom, sportswriter and best-selling writer

I have very hard feelings towards the W.W.F. because they continued the show after Owen's death. It was very cold-blooded.

Brett Hart, second generation professional wrestler, whose brother Owen (also a professional wrestler) fell to his death during a bout

In wrestling you never see anybody get seriously hurt. When was the last time you heard of a wrestler who was out for the season with a knee injury?

Darryl Dawkins, professional basketball player

I saw *Shakespeare in Love,* how the Elizabethan actors and stagehands set up the stage and set. It sounds bizarre, but wrestling's much like that.

Bret Hart, second generation professional wrestler

293

The professional wrestling addiction that has afflicted segments of my family began in the early 1950s. First to drink at the early fountain of television fraud was a widow in her 60s, whose only flirtation with danger until then had been puffing a single Viceroy filter tip after each meal. She bristled at suggestions she was committing her emotions and several hours a week to a game phony as a three-dollar bill even in the days when TV reception was so poor it was difficult to tell.

Bill Conlin, sportswriter

This business is a lot like Hollywood in the 30s and 40s, when the studios had all the power.

Al Snow, professional wrestler

People told me I could get into wrestling and make millions. I did it for about 12, 13, 14 years. It was tough work, and I didn't make millions.

Brocko Nagurski, Hall of Fame football player and professional wrestler

Pro wrestlers are wondrous athletes, traditionally in better shape than baseball players and even most football players, and they work harder at entertaining us.

Robert Lipsyte, writer

When a guy comes into the ring, he's fair game. You've got to take him out.

Goldberg, champion professional wrestler

Yachting

Certainly America's Cup is the pinnacle of yachting and the Holy Grail of our sport.

Dennis Conner, businessman and champion yachtsman

I can't tell you why, but I wanted very much to do the race. I don't know whether it was vanity, escapism, the zest for competition, a hoped-for sense of independence, or what. Something deep within me said that I should throw all caution and common sense aside and try it.

Hal Roth, yachtsman, about the solo sailing race BOC Challenge

If young Joe and Jack ever lost a sailboat race, his rage was a caution; the only way to avoid it was to win.

William Manchester, writer, referring to Joseph Kennedy, Sr.'s, passion for victory and his attitude toward his sons Joseph Kennedy, Jr., and John Fitzgerald Kennedy, president of the United States

If we still value the qualities of daring, comradeship, and endurance in our national life we should cherish the sports which foster them with the risks they carry . . . they can never expel the danger from yachting and the conviction that it will be a sad and bad day when this seafaring people declines the challenge of the ocean.

The Daily Telegraph *(London)*

If you want to win in heavy weather, you've got to keep thinking. No matter if you're tired, wet, or even seasick, if you want to keep going, you've got to pull yourself together and use all your resources.

Theodore A. Jones, yachtsman

I hereby publicly retract anything and everything I have ever said about inland sailing.

Ted Turner, champion yachtsman, after hitting a storm during the 1970 Chicago–Mackinac race, after having made several derogatory comments about "lake sailing"

In a survival gale of Force 10 or over, perhaps gusting at hurricane strength, wind and sea become the masters. For skipper and crew it is then a battle to keep the yacht afloat.

K. Adlard Coles, yachtsman

I remember very clearly how astonished we all were during that first encounter with *Australia III* . . . We all looked at each other with insolent amazement, but no one dared utter a word even though we were all thinking the same thing . . . She turned faster than any boat I had ever seen.

Dennis Conner, businessman
and champion yachtsman

It only blew there for five hours. During Sydney-to-Hobart, it blew for two straight days.

Andrew Buckland, champion sailor, comparing
the tragic 1979 Fastnet race to the tragic 1998
Sydney-to-Hobart race, as he had sailed
competitively in both storm-racked races

Everyone gets to Hobart and comments on how they beat the Bass Strait. But deep inside they know the Strait allowed them to win.

Adrian von Friedberg, champion sailor,
about the Sydney-to-Hobart race

Fifteen men died, not in wartime, or on a hunt for whales, or in a typhoon on the South China Sea, but during a yacht race only seventy miles off the coast of England.

John Rousmaniere, yachtsman and writer,
about the 1979 Fastnet Race

Frankly, I knew *Freedom* was a better boat than *Courageous,* and I knew we were far more prepared than Ted and his crew. There was little doubt we'd kill them, but I certainly wasn't going to say that.

Dennis Conner, businessman
and champion yachtsman

Like Jupiter among the gods, *America* is first and there is no second.

Daniel Webster, author, about the ship for which
the America's Cup is named, after having beaten
all comers in races off Newport

Most expert seamen I know sail fast. They don't know any other way. To sail slowly or inefficiently is to be unseamanlike.

Theodore A. Jones, yachtsman

Newspapers crowing over the victory of the Stevens yacht, which has beaten everything in the British seas. Quite creditable to Yankee shipbuilding, certainly, but not worth the intolerable, vainglorious vaporings that make every newspaper I take up now so ridiculous. One would think yachtbuilding were the end of man's existence on earth.

George Templeton Strong, lawyer
and diarist, 1851

No matter how good the helmsman the most brilliant tactics will look ridiculous if your boat is not moving fast enough through the water.

John Oakley, yachtsmen

People who say that ocean racing is boring have never worked hard at it.

John Rousmaniere, yachtsman and writer

Perhaps as never before in 100 years of challenges had a series been fought so directly on the water, rather than having already been settled on the designer's board, towing tank or sail loft.

Bill Robinson, sportswriter, referring
to Intrepid's victory over Gretel II in
the America's Cup

Racing is meant to be difficult, yes. Dangerous, no. Life threatening, definitely not. I wouldn't go out there again if I lived to be a thousand years.

Larry Ellison, American industrialist and
champion sailor, after surviving the tragic 1998
Sydney-to-Hobart race

Stop surviving and race.

> *Bruce Kirby, yachtsman*

The captain was the cook, the navigator, the dishwasher, the sail changer, the radio operator, the plumber, and the bed-maker.

> *Hal Roth, yachtsman, referring to his solo trip around the world in the BOC Challenge*

There may have been some moaning at the bars by those who mourn the passing of the gentler age of big boat racing, but the cries of despair were unheard in the excitement along the Fremantle waterfront. Here was a real international competition, a really world-class event. Whatever exclusivity had still surrounded 12-meter racing at Newport had disappeared at Fremantle.

> *Walter Cronkite, journalist and sailor*

The tops of the waves were breaking and toppling over in the wind. We could imagine what they could do to a small boat. We continued racing, but it was survival conditions, really.

> *Gerry McGarry, yachtsman, referring to the 1979 Fastnet Race*

Those that built a single boat and sent a single crew to Australia never were seriously in the running, although they gave the big boys a scare now and again. Their expenditure of only seven, eight, or nine million dollars wasn't nearly enough. The "serious" syndicates with multiboat programs spent fifteen or twenty million, maybe even more, to make their bid.

> *Walter Cronkite, journalist and sailor*

When the mast was jammed into the trough we stopped like we hit a brick wall. Food exploded out of the refrigerator and flew into the navigation station. Cottage cheese became a lethal weapon.

> *John Tuttle, yachtsman*

Yachtsmen generally tend to over-complicate and surround their tuning problems with highly technical and confusing discussion that has no bearing on the immediate issue.

> *Mike Fletcher, sailor and journalist*

Yankees, New York

The residents of other cities who hate the Yankees really only hate New York.

> *Leonard Koppett, writer*

It is impossible for anyone who does not live in New York to know what it truly is to hate the Yankees.

> *Murray Kempton,* Back at the Polo Grounds

The Yankees are only interested in one thing, and I don't know what it is.

> *Luis Polonia, professional baseball player*

Youth

The key to success for any pro team is young players, unformed, eager, ready to learn, playing on legs not yet pounded and broken.

> *Peter Golenboch, sportswriter*

Z

Zone (the)

He's playing real, real, real good.

Ed Gray, professional basketball player, about Latrell Sprewell

I can tell you right now, I'm soooo on a different wavelength.

Tara Lipinski, after winning the U.S. Skating Championships

It is not merely mechanical, it is not only spiritual; it is something of both, on a different plane and a more remote one.

Arnold Palmer, champion professional golfer

I was rising above myself, doing things I had no right to be doing.

Bruce Jenner, Olympic gold medalist decathlon competitor

There comes that moment when I have lost myself and only the play finds me.

Brett Hull, professional hockey player

Bibliography

The titles listed below represent only a small portion of the number of volumes that were used in compiling this collection. It is also important to note that not all the books listed below were used for quotation, but were sometimes used as informational guides to primary sources. Also not listed are the countless newspapers, magazines, websites, television interviews, movies, and other media venues that gave me the opportunity to cull the many bits of wisdom I found over the last two years.

Abt, Samuel. *LeMond.* New York: Random House, 1990.

Allen, Kevin. *Crunch.* Chicago: Triumph Books, 1999.

Allen, Maury. *After the Miracle.* New York: Franklin Watts, 1989.

———. *Now Wait a Minute, Casey!* New York: Doubleday, 1975.

Allison, Stacy (with Peter Carlin). *Beyond the Limits.* New York: Little, Brown, 1993.

Andretti, Mario. *What's It Like Out There?.* Chicago: Regnery Publishing, 1970.

Angell, Roger. *The Summer Game.* New York: Viking Press, 1972.

———. *Late Innings.* New York: Simon & Schuster, 1982.

———. *Five Seasons.* New York: Simon & Schuster, 1977.

———. *Season Ticket.* Boston: Houghton Mifflin, 1988.

Ashe, Arthur, Jr. *A Hard Road to Glory 1619–1918.* New York: Warner Books, 1988.

———. *A Hard Road to Glory 1919–1945.* New York: Warner Books, 1988.

———. *A Hard Road to Glory Since 1946.* New York: Warner Books, 1988.

———. *Days of Grace.* New York: Knopf, 1993.

Asinov, Eliot. *Eight Men Out.* New York: Holt, Rhinehart & Winston, 1963.

Axthelm, Pete. *The City Game.* New York: Harper & Row, 1970.

Auerbach, Red (with Joe Fitzgerald). *On and Off the Court.* New York: Macmillan, 1988.

Babcock, Havilah. *The Best of Babcock.* New York: Holt, Rinehart and Winston, 1974.

Baily, Anthony. *The Coast of Summer.* New York: HarperCollins, 1994.

Barber, Red. *1947 When All Hell Broke Loose in Baseball.* Garden City: Doubleday, 1982.

Barnes, Chester. *Advanced Table Tennis Techniques.* New York: Arco, 1977.

Barzini, Luigi. *Peking to Paris.* Chicago: The Library Press, 1973.

Bergman, Ray. *Fishing with Ray Bergman.* New York: Knopf, 1970.

Berkow, Ira. *Pitchers Do Get Lonely.* New York: Atheneum, 1988.

Berra, Yogi (with Tom Horton). *Yogi: It Ain't Over . . .* New York: McGraw-Hill, 1989.

Bird, Larry. *Bird Watching.* New York: Warner Books, 2000.

———. *Drive.* New York: Doubleday, 1990.

Bissinger, H. G. *Friday Night Lights.* Boston: Addison-Wesley, 1990.

Boliteri, Nick and Schaap, Dick. *My Aces, My Faults.* New York: Avon Books, 1996.

Bradley, Bill. *Values of the Game.* New York: Artisan, 1999.

Brander, Michael. *The Roughshooter's Dog.* London: The Sportsman's Press, 1989.

Brennan, Christine. *Inside Edge.* New York: Scribner, 1996.

———. *The Edge of Glory.* New York: Scribner, 1998.

Brokhin, Yuri. *The Big Red Machine.* New York: Random House, 1978.

Brown, Jim (with Steve Delsohn). *Out of Bounds.* New York: Zebra Books, 1989.

Brown, Nigel. *Ice-Skating: A History.* New York: A.S. Barnes, 1959.

Boukareeve, Anatoli. *The Climb.* New York: St. Martin's Press, 1997.

Bouton, Jim. *Ball Four.* 20th Anniversary Edition. New York: Macmillan, 1990.

Burfoot, Amby. *The Complete Book of Running.* Emmaus, Penn.: Rodale, 1997.

Bursey, Kevin. *Icestars.* Chicago: Triumph, 1999.

Cannon, Jimmy (edited by Jack and Tom Cannon). *Nobody Asked Me, But . . .* New York: Holt, Rinehart & Winston, 1978.

Cantor, Andres. *Goooal!* New York: Fireside, 1996.

Capstick, Peter Hathaway. *Death in the Tall Grass.* New York: St. Martin's Press, 1977.

————. *Death in the Silent Places.* New York: St. Martin's Press, 1981.

Caras, Roger. *Death as a Way of Life.* Boston: Little Brown, 1970.

Casio, Chuck. *Soccer U.S.A.* Washington: Robert L. Bruce, 1975.

Casper, Billy. *My Million Dollar Shots.* New York: Grossett and Dunlap, 1971.

Charlton, James and Thompson, William. *Croquet.* New York: Scribner, 1977.

Coe, Sebastian. *Running Free.* New York: St. Martin's Press, 1981.

Connor, Dennis. *Comeback.* New York: St. Martin's Press, 1987.

Cooke, Alistair. *Fun and Games with Alistair Cooke.* New York: Arcade, 1994.

Cosell, Howard (with Mickey Herskowitz). *Cosell.* New York: Playboy Press, 1973.

Crist, Steven. *The Horse Traders.* New York: W. W. Norton, 1986.

Crowe, Phillip A. *Sporting Journals.* Barre, Mass.: Barre Publishers, 1966.

Dawidoff, Nicholas. *The Catcher Was a Spy.* New York: Pantheon, 1994.

Dawkins, Darryl (with George Wirt). *Chocolate Thunder.* Chicago: Contemporary Books, 1986.

De, Ding Shu, et al. *The Chinese Book of Table Tennis.* New York: Atheneum, 1981.

De Ford, Frank. *Big Bill Tilden.* New York: Simon & Schuster, 1976.

————. *The World's Tallest Midget.* Boston: Little Brown, 1987.

Dent, Jim. *The Junction Boys.* New York: St. Martin's Press, 2000.

Dickson, Paul. *The Joy of Keeping Score.* New York: Walker, 2000.

Didinger, Ray. *Game Plans for Success.* New York: Little Brown, 1995.

Dodson, James. *Final Rounds.* New York: Bantam, 1996.

Dugard, Martin. *Knockdown.* New York: Pocket Books, 1999.

Durocher, Leo (with Ed Lynn). *Nice Guys Finish Last.* New York: Simon & Schuster, 1975.

Elliott, James Francis. *Jumbo Elliott.* New York: St. Martin's Press, 1982.

Elman, Robert and Seybold, David. *Seasons of the Hunter.* New York: Knopf, 1985.

Englade, Ken. *Hot Blood.* New York: St. Martin's Press, 1996.

Eskenazi, Gerald. *Gang Green.* New York: Simon & Schuster, 1999.

Evans, George Bird. *The Upland Shooting Life.* New York: Knopf, 1971.

Fassi, Carlo. *Figure Skating with Carlo Fassi.* New York: Scribner, 1980.

Feinstein, John. *A Good Walk Spoiled.* New York: Little Brown, 1995.

————. *A March to Madness.* New York: Little Brown, 1998.

————. *A Season Inside.* New York: Villard Books, 1988.

————. *Forever's Team.* New York: Villard Books, 1989.

————. *Hard Courts.* New York: Villard Books, 1991.

————. *The Majors.* New York: Little Brown, 1999.

Fergus, Jim. *The Sporting Road*. New York: St. Martin's Press, 1999.

Fischler, Stan. *Cracked Ice*. Chicago: Masters Press, 1999.

Firestone, Roy (with Scott Ostler). *Up Close*. New York: Hyperion, 1993.

Fitzpatrick, Frank. *And the Walls Came Tumbling Down*. New York: Simon & Schuster, 1999.

Fleming, Peggy. *The Long Program*. New York: Pocket Books, 1999.

Foreman, George and Engle, Joel. *By George*. New York: Villard Books, 1995.

Foyt, A. J. (with William Neely). *A. J.* New York: Times Books, 1983.

Francis, Austin. *Smart Squash*. Philadelphia: J.B. Lippincott, 1977.

Francis, Dick. *The Sport of Queens*. New York: Harper & Row, 1969.

Freidman, Arthur. *The World of Sports Statistics*. New York: Atheneum, 1978.

Frey, Darcy. *The Last Shot*. New York: Houghton Mifflin, 1994.

Gallwey, W. Timothy. *Inner Skiing*. New York: Random House, 1977.

———. *Inner Tennis*. New York: Random House, 1976.

———. *The Inner Game of Golf*. New York: Random House, 1981.

Garagiola, Joe and Quigley, Martin. *Baseball Is a Funny Game*. Philadelphia: J.B. Lippincott, 1960.

Garvey, Cynthia. *The Secret Life of Cyndy Garvey*. New York: Doubleday, 1989.

George, Nelson. *Elevating the Game*. New York: HarperCollins, 1992.

Giamatti, A. Bartlett. *A Great and Glorious Game*. N.C.: Algonquin Books of Chapel Hill, 1998.

Gibson, Bob and Wheeler, Lonnie. *Stranger to the Game*. New York: Viking, 1994.

Glanville, Jerry. *Elvis Don't Like Football*. New York: Macmillan, 1991.

Golenbock, Peter. *American Zoom*. New York: Macmillan, 1993.

———. *Personal Fouls*. New York: Carroll & Graff, 1989.

Goodwin, Doris Kearns. *Wait Till Next Year*. New York: Simon & Schuster, 1997.

Goolagong, Evonne (with Bud Collins). *Evonne!* New York: E.P. Dutton, 1975.

Gordeeva, Ekaterina. *My Sergei*. New York: Warner Books, 1997.

Gordon, Herb. *Essential Skiing*. New York: Lyons & Burford, 1996.

Greene, Bob and Jordan, Michael. *Hang Time*. New York: Doubleday, 1992.

Green, Tim. *The Dark Side of the Game*. New York: Warner Books, 1996.

Greenlaw, Linda. *The Hungry Ocean*. New York: Hyperion, 1999.

Halberstam, David. *The Amateurs*. New York: William Morrow, 1985.

———. *The Breaks of the Game*. New York: Knopf, 1981.

———. *October '64*. New York: Villard Books, 1994.

————. *Summer of '49.* New York: Villard Books, 1990.

————. *For Keeps.* New York: Random House, 1999.

Hamilton, Scott. *Landing It.* New York: Kensington, 1999.

Hanks, Stephen. *The Game That Changed the World.* New York: Carol Publishing, 1989.

Harding, Anthony, ed. *The Race and Driver's Reader.* New York: Arco Publishing, 1972.

Hart, Stan. *Once a Champion.* New York: Dodd, Mead & Co., 1985.

Heisler, Mark. *The Lives of Riley.* New York: Macmillan, 1994.

Hemingway, Ernest. *The Dangerous Summer.* New York: Scribner, 1985.

————. *Death in the Afternoon.* New York: Scribner, 1936.

————. *Green Hills of Africa.* New York: Scribner, 1930.

Herne, Brian. *White Hunters.* New York: Henry Holt, 1999.

Hill, Graham (with Neil Ewart). *Graham.* New York: St. Martin's Press, 1977.

Hogaan, Marty and Turner, Ed. *Skills and Strategies for Winning Racquetball.* Chicago: Leisure Press, 1988.

Hollis, David W. *National to National.* New York: Howell Book House, 1992.

Hope, Bob. *Confessions of a Hooker.* New York: Doubleday, 1985.

Hornung, Paul. *Woody Hayes.* Champaign, Ill.: Sagamore Publishing, 1991.

Hovdey, Jay. *Whittingham.* Lexington, Ky.: The Blood-Horse Inc., 1993.

Hurt, Harry. *Chasing the Dream.* New York: Avon, 1997.

Izenberg, Jerry. *No Medals for Trying.* New York: Macmillan, 1988.

————. *The Jerry Izenberg Collection.* Dallas: Taylor Publishing, 1989.

Jackson, Phil and Delehanty, Hugh. *Sacred Hoops.* New York: Hyperion, 1995.

Jacobs, Barry. *Three Paths to Glory.* New York: Macmillan, 1993.

James, Bill. *The Politics of Glory.* New York: Macmillan, 1994.

Javorsky, Ben. *Hoop Dreams.* Atlanta: Turner Publishing, 1995.

Jenkins, Dan. *Fairways and Greens.* New York: Doubleday, 1994.

————. *Saturday's America.* New York: Little Brown, 1970.

————. *You Call It Sports, But I Say It's a Jungle Out There.* New York: Simon & Schuster, 1989.

Jenner, Bruce (and Phillip Fitch). *Decathlon Challenge.* New York: Prentice-Hall, 1977.

Jones, Tristan. *One Hand for Yourself, One Hand for the Ship.* New York: Macmillan, 1982.

————. *Yarns.* Boston: Sail Books, 1983.

Kahn, Roger. *The Games We Used to Play.* New York: Ticknor & Fields, 1992.

———. *The Boys of Summer.* New York: Harper & Row, 1972.

———. *A Flame of Pure Fire.* New York: Harcourt Brace, 1999.

Kardong, Don. *30 Phone Booths to Boston.* New York: Macmillan, 1985.

Karras, Alex (with Herb Gluck). *Even Big Guys Cry.* New York: Holt, Rinehart and Winston, 1977.

Katz, Jane. *Swimming for Total Fitness.* New York: Doubleday, 1992.

Kerasote, Ted. *Bloodties.* New York: Random House, 1993.

Killy, Jean-Claude. *Skiing . . . The Killy Way.* New York: Simon & Schuster, 1971.

——— (with Al Greenberg). *Comeback.* New York: Macmillan, 1974.

Kimble, Martha Lowder. *Robin Cousins.* Baltimore: Gateway Books, 1998.

King, Billie Jean (with Frank Deford). *Billie Jean.* New York: Viking Press, 1982.

King, Peter. *The Season After.* New York: Warner Books, 1989.

———. *Inside the Helmet.* New York: Warner Books, 1993.

Kislevitz, Gail Waesche. *First Marathons.* New York: Breakaway Books, 1998.

Klapisch, Bob and Harper, John. *The Worst Team That Money Could Buy.* New York: Random House, 1993.

Kleinbaum, Nancy H. *The Magnificent Seven.* New York: Bantam Books, 1996.

Kowalchik, Dagny. *The Complete Book of Running for Women.* New York: Pocket Books, 1999.

Krakauer, John. *Into Thin Air.* New York: Villard Books, 1997.

Krich, John. *El Beisbol.* New York: Atlantic Monthly Press, 1989.

Krone, Julie (with Nancy Ann Richardson). *Riding for My Life.* New York: Little, Brown, 1995.

Ladew, Harvey S. *Random Collections on Fox-hunting.* Monkton, Md.: Ladew Topiary Gardens Foundation.

Lane, Mills. *Let's Get It On.* New York: Crown, 1998.

Lardner, Ring. *You Know Me, Al.* New York: Collier, reprint 1991.

Laughlin, Terry and Delves, John. *Total Immerson.* New York: Fireside, 1996.

Lee, Spike. *Best Seat in the House.* New York: Crown, 1997.

Lever, Janet. *Soccer Madness.* Chicago: Univ. of Chicago Press, 1983.

Levine, David. *Life Above the Rim.* New York: Macmillan, 1989.

Lewis, Carl (with Jeffrey Marx). *Inside Track.* New York: Simon & Schuster, 1990.

Lewis, Fredrick (edited by Dick Johnson). *Young At Heart.* Waco, Tex.: WRS Publishing, 1992.

Lewis, Michael. *World Cup Soccer.* London: Moyer, Bell, 1994.

Libby, Bill. *Great American Race Drivers.* New York: Cowles Books, 1970.

——— (with Richard Petty). *King Richard.* New York: Doubleday & Co., 1977.

Lipsyte, Robert and Levine, Peter. *Idols of the Game.* Atlanta: Turner Publishing, 1995.

———. *Sports World.* New York: Quadrangle Books, 1975.

Louganis, Greg. *Breaking the Surface.* New York: Random House, 1995.

Luchiano, Ron and Fisher, David. *The Umpire Strikes Back.* New York: Bantam Books, 1982.

Lyons, Nick. *Fisherman's Bounty.* New York: Crown, 1970.

MacCambridge, Michael, et al. *Eson Sports Century.* New York: Hyperion, 2000.

Madden, John (with Dave Anderson). *Hey, Wait a Minute (I Wrote a Book).* New York: Villard Books, 1985.

——— (with Dave Anderson). *One Knee Equals Two Feet.* New York: Villard Books, 1986.

Mahony, Devin. *The Challenge.* Chicago: Contemporary Books, 1989.

Manley, Dexter. *Educating Dexter.* Nashville, Tenn.: Rutledge Hill Press, 1992.

Mantle, Mickey and Pepe, Phil. *My Favorite Summer 1956.* New York: Doubleday, 1991.

Maraniss, David. *When Pride Still Mattered.* New York: Simon & Schuster, 1999.

Mathias, Bob and Tassin, Myron. *Bob Mathias.* New York: St. Martin's Press, 1983.

McCullagh, James C. *Cycling.* New York: Dell, 1995.

McGuane, Thomas. *An Outside Chance.* New York: Farrar, Straus and Giroux, 1980.

McLaggan, Doug and Torbet, Laura. *Squash.* Garden City, N.Y.: Doubleday, 1978.

McManus, Patrick F. *They Shoot Canoes, Don't They?.* New York: Holt, Rhinehart and Winston, 1981.

McIntyre, Thomas. *Days Afield.* New York: E. P. Dutton, 1994.

McPhee, John. *A Sense of Where You Are.* New York: Farrar, Straus and Giroux, 1965.

Merrill, Durwood. *You're Out, And You're Ugly Too!* New York: St. Martin's Press, 1998.

Mewshaw, Michael. *Ladies of the Court.* New York: Crown, 1993.

Michener, James A. *Sports in America.* New York: Random House, 1976.

Millburn, Frank. *Polo.* New York: Knopf, 1994.

Miller, Peter. *The 30,000 Mile Ski-race.* New York: Dial Press, 1972.

Merrill, Christopher. *The Grass of Another Country.* New York: Henry Holt, 1993.

Miles, Dick. *The Game of Table Tennis.* Philadelphia: J. B. Lippincott, 1968.

Mitchell, John G. *The Hunt.* New York: Knopf, 1980.

Morris, Willie. *The Courting of Marcus Dupree.* New York: Doubleday, 1983.

Mosconi, Willie and Cohen, Steve. *Willie's Game.* New York: Macmillan, 1993.

Multi-Media Partners. *Grace & Glory.* Chicago: Triumph Books, 1996.

Murphy, Michael and White, Rhea A. *In the Zone.* New York: Penguin Books, 1995.

Murray, Jim. *Jim Murray.* New York: Macmillan, 1993.

Murray, William. *The Wrong Horse.* New York: Simon & Schuster, 1992.

Nicholson, T. R. *The Wild Roads.* New York: W. W. Norton, 1969.

Oates, Joyce Carol. *On Boxing.* New York: Viking Press, 1985.

Oates, Joyce Carol and Halpern, Daniel. *Reading the Fights.* New York: Henry Holt, 1988.

O'Connor, Jack. *The Big Game Rifle.* Long Beach, Calif.: Safari Press, 1952.

Olajuwon, Hakeem. *Living the Dream.* New York: Little Brown, 1996.

Oriard, Michael. *Reading Football.* Chapel Hill, N.C.: University of North Carolina Press, 1993.

Ortega y Gasset, José. *Meditations on Hunting.* New York: Charles Scribners, 1972.

Osius, Alison. *Second Ascent.* Chicago: Stackpole Books, 1991.

Pennick, Harvey (with Bud Shrake). *For All Those Who Love the Game.* New York: Simon & Schuster, 1995.

———. *Harvey Pennick's Little Red Book.* New York: Simon & Schuster, 1992.

Petty, Richard. *King Richard I.* New York: Macmillan, 1986.

Pitino, Rick (with Dick Weiss). *Full Court Pressure.* New York: Hyperion, 1992.

——— (with Bill Reynolds). *Born to Coach.* New York: NAL Books, 1988.

Plimpton, George. *Paper Lion.* New York: Harper & Row, 1966.

Reaske, Christopher R. *Crouquet.* New York: E. P. Dutton, 1988.

Reese, Paul and Henderson, Joe. *Ten Million Steps.* Waco, Tex.: WRS Publishing, 1993.

Reeves, Dan (with Dick Connor). *Dan Reeves.* Chicago: Bonus Books, 1988.

Rice, Grantland. *The Tumult and the Shouting.* New York: A. S. Barnes & Co., 1954.

Richardson, Donald Charles. *Crouquet*. New York: Harmony Books, 1988.

Riley, Pat. *The Winner Within*. New York: Putnam, 1993.

Ritter, Lawrence S. *The Glory of Their Times*. New York: William Morrow, 1984.

Robinson, Ray. *The Home Run Heard 'Round the World*. New York: HarperCollins, 1991.

Robyns, Gwen. *Wimbledon*. New York: Drake Publishers, Inc., 1974.

Rodman, Dennis (with Tim McKeown). *Bad As I Wanna Be*. New York: Delacourt Press, 1991.

Rogers, Bill (with Joe Concannon). *Marathoning*. New York: Simon & Schuster, 1980.

Roosevelt, Theodore. *Hunting Trips of a Ranchman & the Wilderness Hunter*. New York: Modern Library, 1996.

Roth, Hal. *Chasing the Rainbow*. New York: W.W. Norton, 1990.

Rousmaniere, John. *Fastnet, Force 10*. New York: W.W. Norton, 1980.

Rust, Art. *Art Rust's History of the Black Athlete*. Garden City, N.Y.: Doubleday, 1985.

————. *Get That Nigger Off the Field*. New York: Delacourt Press, 1976.

Ryan, Bob and Pluto, Terry. *Forty-eight Minutes*. New York: Macmillan, 1987.

Sampson, Curt. *The Masters*. New York: Villard Books, 1998.

Schulberg, Budd. *Sparring with Hemingway*. Chicago: Ivan R. Dee, 1995.

Schubert, Mark. *Competitive Swimming*. Lanham, Md.: Sports Illustrated Books, 1996.

Schwarzenegger, Arnold. *The New Encyclopedia of Modern Bodybuilding*. New York: Fireside, 1999.

Seidel, Michael. *Ted Williams*. Chicago: Contemporary Books, 1991.

Sheed, Wilfred. *Baseball and Lesser Sports*. New York: HarperCollins, 1991.

Sheehan, George. *Running and Being*. New York: Simon & Schuster, 1978.

————. *The Running Life*. New York: Simon & Schuster, 1980.

Silverman, Al. *The Best of Sport 1946–1971*. New York: Viking Press, 1971.

Simpson, Joe. *Touching the Void*. New York: Harper & Row, 1988.

Sisco, Peter, et al. *Ironman's Ultimate Bodybuilding Encyclopedia*. Chicago: Contemporary Books, 1999.

Siner, Harold. *Sports Classics*. New York: Coward-McCann, 1983.

Smith, Lissa. *Nike Is a Goddess*. New York: Atlantic Monthly Press, 1998.

Smith, Red. *The Red Smith Reader*. New York: Random House, 1982.

————. *To Absent Friends*. New York: Atheneum, 1982.

Smith, Robert. *A Social History of the Bicycle*. New York: American Heritage Press, 1972.

Smith, Sam. *The Jordan Rules.* New York: Pocket Books, 1994.

Spitz, Mark and LeMond, Alan. *The Mark Spitz Complete Book of Swimming.* New York: Thomas Y. Crowell, 1976.

Sports Illustrated. *Sports Illustrated Book of Badminton.* Philadelphia: J.B. Lippincott, 1967.

Stump, Al. *Cobb.* Chapel Hill, N.C.: Algonquin Books, 1994.

Sturgeon, Kelso. *Guide to Sports Betting.* New York: Harper and Row, 1974.

Sugar, Bert. *Hit the Sign and Win a Free Suit of Clothes from Harry Finklestein.* Chicago: Contemporary Books, 1978.

Suster, Gerald. *Champions of the Ring.* London: Robson Books, 1992.

Swan, James A. *In Defense of Hunting.* San Francisco: HarperSanFrancisco, 1995.

Tapply, William G. *Those Hours Spent Outdoors.* New York: Scribner's, 1988.

Tatum, Jack (with Bill Kushner). *They Call Me Assassin.* New York: Everest House, 1979.

Thorn, John. *The Armchair Quarterback.* New York: Scribner's, 1982.

Thorne, Gerard and Embleton, Phil. Ontario, Canada: MuscleMag International, 1997.

Torrez, Danielle Gagon (and Ken Lizotte). *High Inside.* New York: G.P. Putnam, 1983.

Trueblood, Ted. *The Ted Trueblood Hunting Treasury.* New York: David McKay Company, 1978.

Unsworth, Walt, ed. *Peaks, Passes and Glaciers.* Seattle: The Mountaineers, 1981.

Valerio, Anthony. *Bart.* San Diego: Harcourt, Brace, Jovanovich, 1991.

Walton, Izaak. *The Compleat Angler.* New York: Modern Library, 1996.

Wartman, William. *Playing Through.* New York: William Morrow, 1990.

Waterman, Jonathan. *In the Shadow of Denali.* New York: Delta Books, 1994.

Watson, J. N. P. *The Book of Foxhunting.* New York: Arco Publishing, 1976.

Weaver, Earl (with Berry Stainback). *It's What You Learn After You Know It All That Counts.* Garden City, N.Y.: Doubleday and Co., 1982.

Weider, Joe (with Joe Reynolds). *Joe Weider's Ultimate Bodybuilding.* Chicago: Contemporary Books, 1988.

Weld, Philip S. *Moxie.* New York: Little Brown, 1981.

Williams, Doug (with Bruce Hunter). *Quarterblack.* Chicago: Bonus Books, 1990.

Wills, Maury and Celizic, Mike. *On the Run.* New York: Carroll & Graf, 1991.

Whiting, Robert. *You Gotta Have Wa.* New York: Macmillan, 1989.

Whittingham, Richard. *The Meat Market.* New York: Macmillan, 1992.

Wideman, John Edgar. *Brothers and Keepers.* New York: Holt, Rinehart and Winston, 1984.

———. *Philadelphia Fire.* New York: Henry Holt, 1990.

Wiener, Harvey S. *Total Swimming.* New York: Simon & Schuster, 1980.

Willoughby, David P. *The Super Athletes.* New York: A.S. Barnes, 1970.

Wilson, Mike. *Right on the Edge of Crazy.* New York: Times Books, 1993.

Wiltse, David. *It Only Hurts When I Serve.* Norwalk, Conn.: A Tennis Magazine Book, 1980.

Wind, Herbert Warren. *The Realm of Sport.* New York: Simon & Schuster, 1966.

Wolf, Warner. *Let's Go to the Videotape.* New York: Warner Books, 2000.

Wulff, Joan. *Joan Wulff's Fly Fishing.* Harrisburg, Pa.: Stackpole Books, 1991.

Woog, Dan. *Jocks.* Los Angeles: Alyson Books, 1998.

Zafferano, George J. *Handball Basics.* New York: Sterling Publishing, 1977.

Index

Boldface page numbers denote main topics.